Kilvert's World of Wonders

Well might it be said that of all decades in our history a wise man would choose the 1850s to be young in.

Cyril Bibby, *T.H. Huxley, Scientist, Humanist and Educator*

The world does change so quick that one doesn't think of anything now as one used to do.

Anthony Trollope, *The Way We Live Now*

Kilvert's World of Wonders

Growing up in mid-Victorian England

John Toman

Ⓛ
The Lutterworth Press

The Lutterworth Press
P.O. Box 60
Cambridge
CB1 2NT
United Kingdom

www.lutterworth.com
publishing@lutterworth.com

ISBN: 978 0 7188 9301 9

British Library Cataloguing in Publication Data
A record is available from the British Library

First Published, 2013

Contents

Illustrations

Acknowledgements

In writing this book I have been greatly helped by the staff of the Bath Central Library, Battersea Library, Bodleian Library, Bristol Central Library, Bristol University Library, Friends Library, Gravesend Library, Hereford Cathedral Library, Lambeth Archives and Minet Library, New College Library (University of Edinburgh), Shakespeare Institute Library (Stratford-on-Avon), University of the West of England Library, Bath Record Office, Darlington Centre for Local Studies, Dorset History Centre, Swindon and Wiltshire History Centre.

Michael Richardson, librarian for the Special Collections of the University of Bristol Library, deserves my special thanks.

Rob Randall and Matt Williams of the Royal Bath Literary and Scientific Institution have patiently answered many queries and helped me find my way through the Institution's archives. Staff of Swansea Museum provided valuable help about locations in Gower. Staff of the Science Association provided useful information and materials.

I am also much in the debt of the following individuals: Dr Terry Rogers (archivist of Marlborough College), Emma Goodrum (archivist of Worcester College, Oxford), Mark Dickerson (Oxford University Museum of Natural History), Dr Kellyanne Ure (Texas Tech University), Dr Schulenberg (St Helena Institute), Malcolm and Ruth Ridge (Gower Society), Colin Dixon and Michael Sharp (Kilvert Society), and Richard Morris, editor of the *Dilwyn Journals*, for permission to quote from them.

I am most grateful to Dr Philip Dunham, Head of Geography Department, University of Coventry, and to Dr Martin Crossley Evans, University of Bristol, for offering to read and comment on *Kilvert's World of Wonders*.

I have valued once again the support of Adrian Brink at The Lutterworth Press and especially Emily Reacher, who brought a knowledge of and an enthusiasm for *Kilvert's Diary* to her rigorous, sensitive copy-editing.

Francis Kilvert

Introduction

There were various aspects of Evangelicalism. There was the religious aspect, concerned with the Evangelical's own beliefs and incorporating an emphasis on personal salvation, reliance on the Bible, missionary endeavour and an uncompromising Protestantism. There was the moral aspect, deriving from the desire to strive for piety and righteousness in private and public conduct. And there was the social aspect, the result of the Evangelical's impulse towards benevolent and philanthropic activity.

G.B.A.M. Finlayson, *The Seventh Earl of Shaftesbury*

As yet no-one has properly evaluated Kilvert's character.

Frederick Grice, *Francis Kilvert and his World*

This book is the third in a trilogy that offers a revaluation of Francis Kilvert both as a man and as a writer. The assertion by Grice quoted above, though it dates from 1981, continues to be true. Much can be understood about the driving forces behind Kilvert's character and behaviour from Finlayson's analysis of Evangelicalism quoted above. The picture of Kilvert's background which emerged in the first two books of the trilogy has been substantially expanded in the third. One important result of this expansion is that it is now possible to recognise the elements which encouraged him to develop a vision of moral and material progress as he grew up. This entails a fundamental shift in the accepted view of him in which he appears naïve, lacking in confidence, parochial in outlook, and most at home in the country cottage or the country vicarage. Now we are able to see him as a man of sophisticated outlook, confident in the values he inherited, in touch with metropolitan culture and the urgent issues of the time, eager to enquire and to be informed.

Kilvert's World of Wonders also represents a fundamental shift in viewpoint because its predecessors laid almost exclusive emphasis on the diarist as a recorder of country life. My second book, *Kilvert's Diary and Landscape*, was concerned chiefly with the countryside. My first, *Kilvert: The Homeless Heart*, focused on his relationships within the rural society of his Radnorshire and Wiltshire parishes. If anything it overstated his love of traditional society, presenting his diary as 'his hymn of love for old things' and as a desire to hold back change, although it also noted his 'ambivalent attitude to modernity'. Peter Conradi, in his recent evaluation of the diarist, made similar points: 'Kilvert has the tendency of all romantics to be tender towards the past'; like most romantics, he was also 'more equivocal' about the present. Conradi exemplified Kilvert's concern with the present by instancing his fascination with the electric telegraph and 'the new laughing gas used by his dentist'.[1] His ambivalence towards modern things has also been underlined by Karl Miller: 'Kilvert . . . could be intrigued by past times and old places. . . . What generally compels him, however, is what is going on in Clyro in the 1870s – his here and now'.[2] My new book concerns Kilvert's here and now.

The first two books of my trilogy were written when only a partial exploration of Kilvert's background and of his reading had been undertaken. Thus his family's endorsement of industrial and scientific achievement and the involvement of his uncle Francis in Bath's Literary and Philosophical Association (BLPA), which provided lectures on science, natural history, astronomy, archaeology, botany, geology and literature, were barely glimpsed. Furthermore, Kilvert's admiration for the scientist John Tyndall had not been examined at all. The influence on Kilvert of the highly intellectual, charismatic Victorian preacher Frederick Robertson had been discovered but his strong interest in science was not explored in relation to the diarist. The significance of the fact that the latter was familiar with Brooke's *Life of Robertson*, which is a detailed, far-ranging critique of the writers, ideas and issues of mid-Victorian life, was not fully appreciated. Although *Kilvert: The Homeless Heart* acknowledged that Kingsley was a major influence on the diarist, account was taken only of his social, political and religious ideas; *Kilvert's World of Wonders* focuses on Kingsley's approaches to natural history, geology, sanitary reform and evolution. One of the reasons for arguing that *Kilvert's Diary* should receive greater recognition is that it is an invaluable account of life in mid-Victorian Britain. In its documentation of the tensions between tradition and change, inertia and progress, rural and urban/industrial, it is an incomparably rich source.

Kilvert's World of Wonders begins with the generation of his grandparents, who were young in the last quarter of the eighteenth century when massive social changes associated with the Industrial

Revolution were beginning to make an impact. People felt the strain on society caused by staggering increases in population and the growth of towns. The population of Britain grew from 12.5m in 1811, to 14.5m in 1821, to 21m in 1851. In 1801, the country's 70 largest towns contained 23% of the population, but by 1851 the figure was 34%. However, most people continued to live in the country and in small semi-rural towns until the mid-nineteenth century.[3] While these changes brought their own problems, they also signalled an era of prosperity and power, of invention and discovery. Britain's foreign trade exceeded the combined total of that of France, Germany and Italy in 1870. In that year Kilvert began his diary, and it testifies to his pride in the country's booming trade as well as to other stirring national developments.

Asa Briggs's *The Age of Improvement* covers the years 1783 to 1867, the period (roughly) between the births of Kilvert's aunt Sophia (1789) and of his uncle Francis (1793) and the start of Kilvert's diary-keeping. The writings of his aunt and uncle illustrate clearly Briggs's observation that the period 1783 to 1867 cut into two contrasting centuries – 'the age of balance and the age of progress'. In the ensuing pages we shall see how Kilvert's aunt and uncle, in whose home he received most of his early education, struggled to make the adjustment from one age to the other, a difficult adjustment for them because, in addition to being born in the eighteenth century, they both had essentially eighteenth-century temperaments. 'Balance' was to a great extent what they stood for. Briggs chose his period because it was one of 'formative changes', when man was both 'fascinated and horrified by the "march" of events', divided over 'the merits of improvement'.[4]

Kilvert's World of Wonders is in many ways the story of the diarist's own class, which rose to political prominence as a result of the 1832 and 1867 Reform Bills. Bounded on one side by the traditional dominance of the aristocracy and on the other by the growing power of the working class, the middle class experienced competitiveness and insecurity, driven by the hope of rising socially and by the deep fear of sinking. Kilvert's family suffered bankruptcy and loss of fortune, and their sons had to make their way in the world. His family was strengthened, however, by its Evangelical faith, 'the highest virtue [of which] was self-improvement'.[5] The family benefited too from the fact that in the middle class there was 'a disproportionate number of Quakers, Unitarians, and dissenters with a strong moral sense, liberal political views, and independent outlook'.[6] The middle classes were often carriers of the very idea of improvement itself.[7] The Kilvert family emerges as a highly representative example of this ethos. Though humble and relatively obscure, it yet had significant contacts, either directly or through intermediaries, with many leaders in the fields of science, literature, politics, exploration and humanitarian causes.

Over the last twenty years I have come to recognise a Kilvert who is more complex, more interesting, and altogether more important than the received picture of him, which shows a man of deep feeling but shallow intellect. The characterisation of him in the *DNB* as 'the poet who needed his solitary walks to admire and wonder at the power and splendour of the world God had made' reinforced other judgements that pictured him as quiet and retiring almost because he lacked confidence in his intellectual powers. Thus the received view of him creates a paradox – that of a moderate, conventional, dull, unintellectual clergyman with an undeveloped taste in literature, fit only for such rural backwaters as Clyro and Langley Burrell, but who somehow managed to produce a vibrant, passionate, and perceptive work of literature.

Critics have emphasised the fact that Kilvert's reading was undiscriminating and haphazard, that he favoured undemanding contemporary novels while avoiding the classics of fiction, and that this marked him out as a man with little real interest in books and ideas. Since the condemnation of Kilvert's reading over the years has not been supported by any analysis of it, it inevitably led to the conclusion that it must have been desultory and un-serious. My book *The Books that Kilvert Read*, which examined some of his choices, found that 'his reading had purpose, organisation, and encompassed writers and ideas that were far from trivial.'[8] That survey sought an understanding of his reading in its cultural context because only then could it be a guide to Kilvert's character and intellect. The present study has the same aim. It sets out not only to lay bare the pattern of his reading, and the reasons why particular writers, books and ideas figure in it in a mutually reinforcing way, but also examines contemporary reading forms and practices. We need to acknowledge that, for example, in Victorian times there was a continual 'two-way relationship between "minor" and "major" writers, the 'recognised giants' rubbing shoulders with melodramatic and sensational novelists. Victorian readers looked to novels of all kinds to 'live out the issues of the day', a motive that was partly responsible for Kilvert's choice of books.[9] We shall see that he was always reading something, that he lived in a milieu constantly informed by books, and that he had a highly developed cultural awareness. The following pages provide an opportunity to engage with a Kilvert who is excellent company and who has an incomparably rich story to tell.

Prologue

'Some Great Change Must Take Place' [1]

> The 'facts' of improvement were so striking that they made
> men dream dreams: the word 'improvement' itself which
> now sounds sober, respectable and emotionally threadbare
> was capable then of stimulating daring flights of imagination.
>
> Asa Briggs, *The Age of Improvement*

> I should fear to tell the dreams which I have now beside
> the electric telegraph, and on the railways, and within the
> regions of the god-like inventors and makers of machinery.
> There is a time coming when the realities shall go beyond
> any dreams that have yet been told of these things.
>
> Alexander Somerville, *Autobiography of a Working Man*

One of the many fascinating aspects of *Kilvert's Diary* is its depiction
of a rural society which had hardly changed for hundreds of years
beginning to give way to modernity. A *Diary* entry for 25 January 1871
encapsulates something of the state of that society. Penny Readings were
then in vogue as a means by which the well-to-do middle class provided
a modicum of learning and entertainment for the rural poor. The Rev.
Daniell, Vicar of Kington Langley near Chippenham, had written to
Kilvert – in Latin and on one of the new-fangled postcards – asking
him to help at his Penny Reading. Daniell's caprice of communicating
to another clergyman in Latin demonstrated what real learning was.
Kilvert walked over to Kington Langley Vicarage to find only Mrs
Daniell there, who told him about 'the 5 Japanese pupils, all noble',
who were living with them. He was misinformed about their nobility.
Cobbing described them, the first in England to have lived outside the
capital, as 'five officers from Tosa [who] lived in Daniell's home and
received lessons in English'.[2] Kilvert also stated that one was 'of royal
blood', part of an official Japanese deputation which was studying the
Franco-Prussian War. This prince would have been Higashi Fushimi,
who merely visited the Langley Burrell students.[3] Various Japanese
students visited Britain in the nineteenth century, some in 1830 to see

railways, completely unknown in their country. Those who came to Britain in the 1860s marvelled at such wonders as gas lighting, electric telegraphs, and drills (such as seized Kilvert's attention – see chapter five) which could cut holes in steel plate.[4] The villagers of Kington Langley in 1871 would have regarded their Japanese visitors as even more exotic wonders. Even Kilvert was intrigued by what he heard of their 'perfect manners' and of the way they regarded Saturday nights as 'a solemn time'. The ever-shrinking world of the 1870s had brought in its steam-ships visitors from the farthest limits of the Far East to report, via the electric telegraph, on a European war. Their presence in rural Wiltshire would have been unthinkable thirty years before.

The Victorian country clergyman was almost invariably a teacher. Kilvert's teaching in school, which will be examined later, was a mixture of the traditional (the Catechism, Bible stories, annals of pious lives) and the modern (geographical exploration, missionary travels, scientific and technological discovery). To some extent therefore he was mediating change to his school pupils and to his congregation (he also used sermons to teach what was happening in the world at large). At times he marvelled at country people's ignorance as, for example on 29 February 1872: 'There is a general belief amongst the Clyro and Langley people that I cannot travel from Radnorshire to Wiltshire without going over the sea'. The census returns of Clyro and Langley show that the great majority of their inhabitants were born either in those parishes or in neighbouring villages and towns. Most would not have travelled much beyond them nor have any real grasp of the geography of their region. Perhaps in Kilvert's view the subject that his flocks were in most need of was geography, especially at a time when the world was shrinking due to the invention of steam-ships, newspapers, railways, and the electric telegraph. We shall see later that his imagination was stirred by these developments, and also that as a teacher he had a particular concern for geography.

The story of Kilvert and his family is a story about teachers and teaching, schools and schooling, and a nineteenth-century subculture in which education was an activity of paramount importance. The story is not primarily of formal lessons with textbooks, slates and chalks, and inky copybooks, though they have their place in it. It is rather the story of individuals learning values and attitudes from parents and siblings, places and people, personal and national heroes, Penny Readings, museums and zoos, books and magazines, religion, science, and nature. It is also about one kind of society learning, often painfully because the process of change was at times frighteningly rapid, to become a quite different kind of society. The diary which Kilvert kept from 1870 to 1879 recorded one phase of this monumental change. He was thirty when he began the diary, and enormous changes had already taken place since his birth in 1840. Many entries indicate his awareness that his was a society in ferment and that he saw himself as its historian, documenting the period in which the world became recognisably 'modern'.

When Kilvert was born on 3 December 1840 at Hardenhuish, on the edge of Chippenham (Wilts.), Victoria had been on the throne for three years. His father, Robert Kilvert, youngest son of a coachbuilder in Bath, became a clergyman. Kilvert's mother was Thermuthis Coleman, of a Quaker merchant family, which had lived for generations in the village of Kington St Michael near Chippenham, and which had intermarried with the Ashe family, gentry of neighbouring Langley Burrell. Francis Kilvert, the diarist, was educated first at his father's school at Hardenhuish Vicarage and later at his uncle Francis's Claverton Lodge school in Bath. Kilvert died from peritonitis in 1879, only weeks after his marriage, but it wasn't until 1937 that his nephew, Mr T. Perceval Smith, submitted his diaries (originally 27/8 notebooks but only 22 by this time as 6 had been destroyed) to the publisher Jonathan Cape. After Smith's death, the notebooks passed to his sister, Mrs Essex Hope.

The *Diary*'s first publication in three volumes, coming at a historically momentous time – between 1938 and 1940 – encouraged nostalgia for the peace and safety of the countryside. Its editor, William Plomer, told how their publication caught the mood of the time: 'Already the last decades of silence were passing . . . before the pandemonium set in, of motor traffic, radio, aircraft and bombs. In that doomed hush [Kilvert] lived and wrote.'[5] Of course, for Victorians the pandemonium had set in a good deal earlier, experienced by workers in factories, foundries, docks and shipyards, and dwellers in large towns and cities. Kingsley's eponymous hero, Alton Locke, spoke of having become inured in London to the 'ceaseless roar of the human sea'. In 1853, Matthew Arnold was complaining in *The Scholar-Gipsy* of 'this strange disease of modern life, / With its sick hurry. . . . ' We get little overt sense of this in Kilvert's diary, although he did express relief at escaping from London into the quiet of the country.

In the main it is country life that is Kilvert's subject. Plomer referred to the *Diary* as an 'intimate record of English country life in the last century'.[6] Brought up to love the countryside and nature, and with a sharp awareness that rural ways were becoming extinct, Kilvert consciously set out to document them before they were gone forever. V.S. Pritchett was right to see the diarist as a historian: 'He was very much aware of recording history, if only with a small "h".' And Pritchett believed that Kilvert was conscious of 'belonging to a society . . . and it was this sense that made Kilvert a historian'.[7] Because so much of the *Diary* deals with rural life, the idea has grown up that it records little or nothing else; but in the narrative there is an urban, industrial life whose encroachments Kilvert was keen to set down. Plomer may have omitted some urban and industrial references because they had little interest for him and, he assumed, his readers. However, many have survived and this study highlights them and scientific references in order to show that Kilvert's vision extended beyond the country parish. Ronald Blythe wrote of the *Diary*: 'It is, comparatively speaking, minutiae that fill it, the deepest, remotest, richest provincialism that speaks, yet the voice is neither quaint or old-maidish but young, direct and vital'.[8] The emphasis on the vigorous voice is accurate as is the emphasis on the provincialism's depth. However, Kilvert was not merely provincial: there was a metropolitan dimension to his character that has hitherto gone unnoticed.

The following words were written about another nineteenth-century diarist, but they fit Kilvert closely:

[His diary's] varied contents and its vivid and spontaneous style reveal a young man full of energy and with an interest in all that goes on around him. . . . He is quick to sympathise with human weakness, but equally quick to laugh at cant and humbug when he meets them. He takes a fresh and intelligent look at men and their affairs, but is sensitive to the beauty of the countryside and has a genuine concern for animal life. His pages provide a graphic account, enlivened by youthful good spirits, of what life was like . . . he was aware of the larger issues of the day, political, spiritual and intellectual. . . . One could hardly have a more observant, thoughtful and yet entertaining recorder of his times.[9]

The diarist being described here is Robert Barclay Fox of the famous Quaker family of Falmouth in Cornwall, which ran a shipping business. His generation directly preceded Kilvert's. He was born in September 1817 and his *Journal* extends from 1 January 1832 to October 1854.[10] He died prematurely at the age of 38, as Kilvert did. His father, Robert Were Fox (1789-1877), was a distinguished scientist and Fellow of the Royal Society.

One branch of the family produced several doctors, one of whom, Edward Long Fox (1761-1835), was well known by reputation to the Kilverts. Kilvert's aunt Emma, wife of the Rev. Edward Kilvert, younger brother to Kilvert's father, was a patient in Brislington House, a Bristol asylum founded in 1806 by Edward Long Fox. It was a progressive establishment, pioneering a humane treatment of the mentally ill known as 'Moral Therapy'. After Fox's death in 1835, the asylum was continued by his sons. Aunt Emma, who, Kilvert recorded on 5 October 1871, regarded it as 'a hell upon earth', was in the care of Dr Charles Fox.[11] The Fox family would also have been known to Kilvert because it was related to the leading families of the Quaker establishment and he, with a Quaker mother and aunt (Sophia), would have been informed about these families' humanitarian and scientific achievements. Furthermore, there was a Kilvert family link to the Fox family. Barclay's mother was Maria Barclay of Bury Hill, Dorking. Her sister, Anna, had married the Quaker businessman, Jacob Reynolds, whose sister Ann was the second wife of Thomas Woodruffe Smith, the guardian of Kilvert's aunt Sophia. A later chapter gives details of this last relationship.

Barclay was only fourteen when he found an exhibition of steam-engines 'particularly interesting'. In Dublin in August 1835 at the British Association for the Advancement of Science (BAAS) Meeting with his family, he was greatly impressed by the geology lecture of Professor Adam Sedgwick, about whom we will hear in connection with Kilvert. Fox was with his family viewing what he called 'the wonders of Birmingham' in 1837. He witnessed the launch of the new steamer, *British Queen*, '1836 tons, larger by 500 tons than any other on the ocean. It was a superb sight'. The next day he was at an anti-slavery meeting at Exeter Hall, the Evangelical centre in London. It was entirely typical of the Fox family that Barclay's eldest sister, Anna-Maria, set up in 1833 (when she was eighteen) the Falmouth Polytechnic, which stimulated and showcased scientific and technological developments in Cornwall. Following those developments nationally was one of Barclay's chief interests. He toured foundries and factories, and made frequent visits to London's Polytechnic Institution whose display of new inventions showed, he said, 'the progressive spirit of the age'. In Bristol in 1843 he visited the Coalbrookdale iron products warehouse and saw the *Great Britain*, Brunel's wonder ship, referred to by Barclay as 'the greatest experiment since creation'. After attending a lecture in London on phreno-mesmerism, he entertained his friends by recounting its 'wonders'. In 1840, the year Kilvert was born, Barclay marvelled that the rail journey from London to Bristol took only 4½ hours, adding: 'Certainly *steam* is the one great *Fact* of the present age. To be deprived of it would be like going back to barbarism' (his italics). He had expressed anxiety a few days earlier about whether religion ('call it superstition if you please') had been replaced by Utilitarianism; instead of churches, his society built railway stations.

In 1842, he took over the management of the family's Perran Foundry[12] after it suffered decline in the charge of its previous manager and partner, Benjamin Sampson. Kilvert showed marked interest in this establishment when staying in July 1870 with his friends William and Emma Hockin in Tullimaar, a house built by Sampson for himself near Falmouth. William had inherited the house from his mother Ann, Sampson's daughter. We may assume that Kilvert was told of this family connection to the Foxes. He referred three times in his *Cornish Diary* to the foundry chimneys that could be glimpsed from Tullimaar's windows. Fascination with Cornwall's industrial past and present permeates *Kilvert's Cornish Diary*; the Perran Foundry interest is not an isolated example. His Cornish tour is full of references to foundries and mines, to industrial processes and products. The reason for this is simple: he belonged to the same social group and was raised with the same outlook as Barclay Fox. He too was excited by new scientific and technological developments and exulted when their application resulted in increase of wealth and comforts. He shared Barclay's faith in 'the progressive spirit of the age' and his passion for philanthropic causes.

The origins of Kilvert's outlook derived partly from the circumstances that brought his paternal grandfather, Francis, along with representatives of other Shropshire families, to Bath in the late eighteenth century. In the annals of one of those families, the Falkners of Claverley, can be found motives for the migration. Originally yeoman farmers, the Falkners had a paper mill from the early eighteenth century, 'always maintaining an excellent position among the yeomen and gentle people of the neighbourhood', in the words of Anne Falkner.[13] It seems the paper mill could not provide for the younger Falkner sons, Francis and Robert, and the former went to Bath in 1778, becoming a partner in the wine business of Thomas Collett. The Colletts, a Quaker family, had been bakers, brewers, and clothiers in Somerset throughout the eighteenth century.[14] Francis became related to the Kilvert family in July 1780 when he married Catherine Parsons, elder sister to Anna, who married Francis Kilvert, the diarist's grandfather. This latter Francis could also see business opportunities in Bath, where he moved in November 1780 to set up as a coachbuilder. Anne Falkner underlined the slowness and inconvenience of coach travel when these newlyweds were struggling to keep contact with their families in Shropshire: 'coach journeys were a long and weary business', taking a whole day to get from Bath to Birmingham.[15] Robert Falkner migrated to Bath only in 1787, to enter into partnership with a Quaker corn factor and miller. Further insight into the values of both the Falkner and Parsons families can be gained from the comment made in a letter by Catherine Parsons' brother, William: 'I have always heard Mr Robert Falkner spoken of as a sober industrious and good man'. In another letter he approved Robert's Quaker partner: 'I have a great predilection for that sect'.[16] William also recommended 'a Counting House or Warehouse as a proper place' for young men after school. Desire to make something of themselves drove the young Falkner and Kilvert men to Bath to join its trading community. Sympathy for Evangelical religion may also have cemented friendship between the two families because when Francis Falkner died in 1797 he was buried in the crypt of St James's Church, Bath, 'a massive Simeonite trustee church', where he had also been a churchwarden.[17] Evangelicalism had begun to flourish in Bath at this time and Kilvert's grandfather may have embraced it after the city's building boom collapsed in 1793 with the failure of his coach building business and bankruptcy.[18]

Honest tradesmen could see the possibility of thriving in a society where wealth, fashion, and ostentation ruled. A regular influx of visitors seeking health cures and excitement came to Bath, whose population was growing rapidly at this time: 26,000 in 1793, 33,000 in 1801, and 38,000 in 1811. The Falkners and Kilverts were part of this influx and their businesses were calculated to serve the needs of the rich and fashionable. Rises in population and in house-building brought with them greater demand for coaches and coach services; those to London increased by 70%. The young Francis Kilvert with his modest workshop in Monmouth Street was thus part of a burgeoning national industry that was contributing to the accelerating pace of change of the Industrial Revolution. The iron he needed for his work was supplied by George Stothert, a Presbyterian from Scotland, whose ironmongery business in Bath was the outlet for products from the Coalbrookdale (Shropshire) works of the Quaker Abraham Darby.[19] Since Stothert had married a Parsons' grand-daughter, he was related to Francis Kilvert and the Falkner brothers. On 24 October 1871, Caroline Stothert introduced herself to the diarist as his cousin. She was the 35-year-old grand-daughter of George Stothert. Francis Falkner's son, Francis Henry, was a contemporary in 1800 at Bath Grammar School with two of Stothert's sons.

The Rev. Christopher Anstey, in *The New Bath Guide* (1776), contrasted Bristol, 'renowned for Commerce and Dirt', with Bath, 'a gay place' of pleasure and frivolity, a city of 'loungers'.[20] Other contemporary and later writers pictured Bath this way. When the Evangelical preacher, William Jay, began his pastorate in its Argyle Chapel in 1791, Bath was 'the resort of fashion and folly in the pursuit of pleasure'.[21] Elliott-Binns wrote: 'Life at Bath was intensely artificial. . . . Pleasure and diversion were the chief occupations' (he was referring to the late eighteenth century).[22] An anonymous writer observed in 1814: 'pleasure seems [Bath's] only business'.[23]

The change of address in 1787 of Francis Kilvert, coachbuilder, to Bath's Westgate Street is one indication of his relative prosperity. It took place during a boom period that lasted from 1785 to 1793. However, the crash of 1793 then occurred, partly because war with France depressed the demand for houses, and banks had made rash loans to speculative builders who were then unable to pay them back. Francis's business failed. He had served the rich and fashionable but in the slump they, by and large, 'lounged' on while he and others like him went under: he was declared bankrupt in 1794.[27] This disaster was compounded by the failure of the bank in which his and his mother's assets were lodged (it is believed a five-figure sum was involved). Francis's situation could hardly have been worse: in debt, in depressed times, with neither employment nor savings. Furthermore, his wife Anna was pregnant: Kilvert's uncle Francis was born on Good Friday 1793. Around 1799, the family moved to Widcombe, a relatively poor suburb of Bath.

Loss of fortune produced a crisis – economic and social – for the Kilvert family that was felt particularly after Francis died in 1817 and his sons approached adulthood. 'In 1818 . . . it became needful that all of us who were of an age to do so should set to work,' wrote Robert. Perhaps the worst element of Francis's position after the bankruptcy was that he had no place in society. His sons began to seek their place: William was to be a merchant (had he not died in 1818), John to be a doctor, Richard emigrated to Canada, and Francis, the eldest, who had become surrogate father to his siblings, had entered the Church while simultaneously teaching at Bath Grammar School.

For Francis Kilvert and his brother Robert, making their own way in the thrusting, competitive society of the early nineteenth century involved seeking patronage from local landowning families and from the élite of Bath by offering to tutor their sons. They were learning the importance of being gentlemen and of mixing with gentlemen. However, the range of occupations pursued by all the Kilvert sons indicated the ways in which society was changing. The Industrial Revolution brought with it not only wealth but a desire for improvement among a middle class increasingly aware of its worth and unique character. Its members included those dubbed by Briggs 'the new men', who were 'struggling against old oligarchies and enthusiastic in the cause of local "improvement". He noted the passing, between 1785 and 1800, of no less than 211 Local Improvement Acts that focused on street lighting, water-supply, the clearing of 'nuisances', and the providing of watchmen.[28] It is of some significance therefore that the disillusion of that failed coachbuilder, Francis Kilvert, did not make him completely idle: between 1805 and 1817 he was Widcombe's 'Collector of Lamp, Scavenger and Watch Rates', a lowly paid but useful Council job.[29]

Later chapters will show various members of the Kilvert family, including Kilvert himself, embracing municipal, industrial, and cultural movements that were gaining ground in the first quarter of the nineteenth century: local government reform, elementary education, popular literature, improved transport, 'rational' leisure pursuits, museums and, above all, popular science. Traditionalists, particularly those of the landed interest, regarded these developments with alarm. The Tory friend and patron of the Kilverts, Sir Robert Inglis, opposed the 1832 Reform Bill in the House of Commons because it represented 'a revolution that will overturn all the natural influence of rank and property'. With Shropshire forebears who were for generations yeoman and tenant farmers, the Kilvert family inevitably favoured traditional country ways. *Kilvert: The Homeless Heart* emphasised how much Kilvert was a defender of rank and property but it also pointed out that he naturally sided with the small man trying to raise himself by education and hard work. In addition, the Quaker and Evangelical elements in his background rejected aristocratic notions of rank and family pride. It should be remembered too that Kilvert's maternal forebears, the Quaker Colemans, were originally tradesmen.

Briggs, in his picture of the 'energetic initiative' of the emergent middle class, highlighted the provincial Literary and Philosophical Societies that began to appear in the late eighteenth century; the Manchester society, founded in 1781, was among the first. One of the founders of the Bath Philosophical Society, dating from December 1779, was William Matthews, the Quaker partner of Robert Falkner in their corn and seed business. We also find that Francis Henry Falkner (1782-1866), son of Robert's brother Francis, who came to Bath as a wine merchant, was a member of the Bath Philosophical Society in the 1820s. And finally, as a later chapter shows, the Society became the consuming interest of Kilvert's uncle Francis, eldest son of the coachbuilder. Clearly, the Bath Philosophical Society reflected and furthered the interests and aspirations of the social group to which these men belonged. We will see later how Kilvert's uncle Francis and the Society were pivotal in developing in Kilvert interests in natural history and science and technology.

It is important here to note the significance of 'Lit and Phil' Societies for the generation and the social group that included Kilvert's grandfather, the Falkners, and George Stothert. Their period – 1780s to the late 1820s – was one in which science became extremely popular. Its popularity was reflected in the Lit and Phils, which Briggs saw as a characteristic product of the period's 'new men'. Their motivation for founding these societies was, according to Inkster, a consequence of the social changes of the period, which witnessed 'the making of social class, a process which centred upon the economic and social evolution of the industrial provinces'. During this flux, when 'there was no longer *one* social world', individuals felt the absence of 'central . . . values, beliefs and norms' on which they could rely.[30] There emerged in industrial provincial England 'social groups who were essentially "marginal" to society because neither overtly of the capitalists and often decidedly not of the working masses'. Such men were drawn to Lit and Phils not simply from a desire to move up socially, though that was no doubt a factor, but chiefly because they sought to join others with similar interests in an organised group. It was a question of identity, Inkster believed: 'The institutions and groupings of science culture were utilised by the marginal man in first gaining then propounding his social identity'.[31] Lit and Phils were in effect Mutual Improvement Societies.

Cooter laid emphasis on the kind of knowledge with which this kind of man was identifying. The Lit and Phils pursued practical knowledge, 'independent of the knowledge's technical utility or validity'. Their endorsement of 'natural knowledge' challenged the 'unnatural' basis of traditional agrarian society, and sought to legitimate change from that society, in which position depended on land ownership and 'good' family, to one in which 'urban utilitarian and meritocratic values would predominate'. These new professionals 'by locating themselves in Lit and Phils . . . confirmed through the use of natural knowledge and the rhetoric of utility the legitimacy of bourgeois dominance'.[32] The Dillwyn family, with which uncle Francis Kilvert and Robert Kilvert ('the diarist's father) made significant contact in their role as teachers, provides examples of 'new men' for whom these values held overwhelming importance.

One of the elite Bath families whose sons Francis and Robert Kilvert were teaching in the early 1820s was that of Sir William Hotham. The family was Evangelical, and had traditionally supported Quakers.[33] Robert Kilvert recounted that in 1822 he was invited to accompany Sir William as his son's tutor on a tour through France and Switzerland. Illness prevented him from going and his friend Henry Moule replaced him. A short time later, Moule was approached again through the Evangelical network to act as tutor to a gentry family. The family was that of Lewis Weston Dillwyn (1778-1855), landowner and industrialist, whose home of Penllergare was on the edge of Swansea. His journal[34] contains few expressions of piety but his Evangelicalism is evident in strict Sabbath observance, family prayers, membership of a Bible Society, and friendship with the Evangelical Bowdler family of Bath. His 16 January 1823 journal entry reads: 'Received a letter from my Sisters enclosing a strong recommendation from the Revd. Mr Kilvert of Bath in favour of Mr Henry Moule as a Tutor for my Boys'. Dillwyn then offered Moule a temporary engagement and on 1 February 1823 Moule arrived.

It is not clear why uncle Francis Kilvert's recommendation of Moule should have come via Dillwyn's sisters, who are not identified (there were five). Perhaps they knew Sir William Hotham, who in turn knew that uncle Francis maintained a private school at his home. Dillwyn went to Bath on 9 February 1823 with his friend Sir Christopher Cole to obtain a first-hand account of Moule from Hotham, who was an intimate of Cole. Dillwyn did not actually meet Hotham: it was Cole who gave Moule 'an extraordinarily high character' (Dillwyn's words). If Kilvert's father had not begun at Oriel College, Oxford, in October 1822, he might have become tutor to Dillwyn's boys. However, Oriel College provided another contact in the web that brought like-minded families together at this time. Two of Robert's fellow students were from families friendly to Dillwyn's. One was Christopher Rice Mansel Talbot, landowner and industrialist, of Margam Castle and Penrice Castle; the other was Richard Calvert Jones, clergyman and pioneer photographer, of Veranda near Swansea, and friend of the great photographer Henry Fox Talbot. Either Christopher Talbot or Jones could have mentioned that Dillwyn needed a tutor to Robert Kilvert, who then recommended his friend Moule. In addition there was the fact that Christopher Talbot's stepfather was Sir Christopher Cole, who had married Talbot's mother, Lucy Fox-Strangeways.

Moule tutored Dillwyn's sons, John (born 1810) and Lewis (born 1814), from 1 February 1823 to 30 April 1824. Contact between Dillwyn and uncle Francis became even closer when, on 18 August 1824, the former called on the latter in Bath about a replacement for Moule, who had become curate in Melksham. By December 1827 John, having had a number of temporary tutors, had matriculated at Oriel, but Lewis became a boarder at uncle Francis's school at Darlington Street, Bath, on 10 December, where he was to remain for 3½ years – until the summer of 1831. The very large amount of trust signified by this arrangement is further indication that although the Dillwyn and Kilvert families were sharply divided in terms of income and status, they were one in values and outlook.

Dillwyn, before he became an M.P., devoted much of his time to his Cambrian Pottery business in Swansea, a town whose population and coal, iron, copper, and harbour industries were expanding rapidly in this period. Dillwyn maintained close contact with owners and managers of these enterprises and ensured that his children knew of them and respected them. On 2 August 1824 he took his son John to see a turning lathe in London and over the next few days both John and his sister Fanny had turning lessons. John, Fanny, and their mother were taken by Dillwyn to the first of a series of lectures on the steam-engine in September, followed by lectures on hydrostatics, hydraulics and pneumatics. Dillwyn introduced his children to all the wonders of the industrial age that was dawning. In August 1819 they saw the *Favourite*, the Margate steam-ship on the Thames. John and Lewis had regular trips on steam vessels plying between Newport and Bristol. Fanny was given a tour of Crawshay's ironworks on 20 September 1838. When in London all the Dillwyn children were taken frequently to Bullock's Museum, the British Museum, and the Polytechnic Institution.

Nothing epitomises more powerfully Dillwyn's admiration for technological energy and enterprise than his stance towards towns which lacked these features. He singled out Bath in particular for criticism. During a visit there on 15 December 1828 he referred to 'lounging about this idly busy place all day'. The town was 'busy' he acknowledged but only with pleasure and frivolity, not with productive work. He was repeating the criticisms made in the 1770s by the Rev. Anstey, who had characterised Bath as a city of 'Loungers'. Dillwyn's irritation surfaced on other Bath visits. Visiting his son Lewis at 'Mr Kilvert's' in early May 1829, he wrote that he did little but 'lounge about' and on 14 May he wrote again 'Did nothing but lounge about in Bath!' He used 'lounge' again in the 11 June entry, while on the 12th he wrote: 'Dawdled and lounged all day'. Spa towns whose ethos was idleness both offended and sapped his spirit. Cheltenham provoked a similar, even more revealing reaction: 'Dawdled away my time Cheltenham fashion' (12 September 1843).

Uncle Francis Kilvert, to whom Dillwyn had entrusted his son Lewis, lived in Bath but his household, like that of Kilvert's father, engendered work and usefulness. In a very real sense, Dillwyn and Francis had chosen each other because their values and attitudes coincided. The latter kept a record of men and women who had achieved great and good things, his Quaker wife (Kilvert's aunt Sophia) praised Quakers' 'patient industry' and 'toilsome acts of Christian charity',[35] Kilvert's Quaker mother had a horror of what she called 'Bathy people', meaning 'loungers'. Kilvert himself expressed contempt for 'the idle lounge' that was Bath's chief feature. Dillwyn and Francis also came together in their support for Lit and Phils. The former regularly visited the Bristol society and was President of Swansea's. When he wrote on 10 December 1827 'Spent the morning chiefly in introducing Lewis to Mr Kilvert', he added that he had also visited the Bath Literary and Scientific Institution, in which, as he knew, Francis played a central role. Furthermore, Dillwyn formed close friendships with John and Philip Duncan, Oxford academics, who also figured prominently in that body. One imagines that its activities were the subject of conversation on the many occasions when Dillwyn deposited and picked up young Lewis at the Bath school and dined and breakfasted as he did with its headmaster. Quaker links also cemented contact between Dillwyn and Francis because the former not only had the Quaker family connections,[36] which have been noted, but also knew Robert Were Fox. On 21 June 1847 Dillwyn recorded the visit to his home of 'the two daughters of my old friend Robert Were Fox' (i.e. Anna-Maria and Caroline).

The Fox and Dillwyn families had the same relish for their progressive society. We have already noted that Barclay Fox and Dillwyn made a point of seeing as many wonders of the time as they possibly could and supported the educational institutions that popularised them. Dillwyn, when he wasn't serving on Swansea committees concerned with paving, lighting, harbour and infirmary improvements, was working towards the founding of the Royal Institution of South Wales, which was thrown open to the public on 16 May 1842, when he noted: '5,000 people of all sorts attended, most orderly . . . very gratified'. A year before, he had attended a lecture at the Institution by a Mr Nichol[37] on phrenology. Initially cautious about railways – he voted in the Commons on 26 April 1836 in favour of a second reading of the Great Northern Rail Road Bill while considering it 'Humbug' – he quickly welcomed them.[38] He had complained in 1823 that a coach took eight hours to travel from Oxford to London. Bath to London took twelve hours. However, on 26 April 1844 he rejoiced that this latter journey took only five hours by rail. He wasn't going to miss seeing in April 1850 work on the new railway viaduct at Landore, near Swansea – Brunel's longest (1,760 feet) timber viaduct.

In addition to being a F.R.S., Dillwyn was a member of the Mineralogical Society (forerunner of the Geology Society), the BAAS, the British and Foreign School Society, and the Linnaean Society. He was also President of the Natural History Society: natural history, especially conchology, was his passion. The list of savants who frequently stayed in his home reads like a scientific who's who of the time: Sir Joseph Banks, Sir Humphrey Davy, Dr Daubeny (Oxford Professor of Chemistry), the astronomer John Herschel,

Charles Babbage (whose calculating engine was the forerunner of the computer), Charles Wheatstone (inventor of the electric telegraph), and a clutch of geologists: Dr Buckland, Dr Wollaston, Henry de la Beche, W.D. Conybeare, Gideon Mantell, and Roderick Murchison. Many of these men were also friends of the Foxes of Falmouth.

Given this background it was highly likely that the lives of John and Lewis Dillwyn would follow the pattern set by their father. In choosing Henry Moule as his sons' tutor, on the recommendation of uncle Francis Kilvert, Lewis senior was exposing them to a man who steadily pursued useful inventions.[39] When John Dillwyn Llewellyn[40] was twenty-two, his father engaged for him a private tutor to teach him engineering and not long afterwards John was experimenting with a boat powered by an electric motor. By 1837 he had become a F.R.S. like his father. It was in photography that he made a name for himself. He married Emma Talbot of Penrice Castle, daughter of Thomas Mansel Talbot and Lucy Fox-Strangeways. Lucy was the sister of Elisabeth, mother of the pioneer photographer Henry Fox Talbot. Following the announcement in 1839 of revolutionary photographic processes by Fox Talbot and Henri Daguerre, John began to experiment with the encouragement of the former, who knew John's father through botanic interests.[41] Fox Talbot spent some of his childhood at Penrice, home of the Welsh branch of his family. John's earliest daguerreotype dates from 1840. Fox Talbot's process, which he called the calotype, also known as the Talbotype, was superior to the daguerreotype because it produced a negative from which prints could be made. *The Pencil of Nature*, his collection of twenty-four calotypes accompanied by short texts, came out in instalments between June 1844 and April 1846. In it Fox Talbot characterised photography as a 'marvel'. It was 'The first commercially produced book to be illustrated with photographs'.[42] While it was appearing, he published *Sun Pictures in Scotland* (1845). Emily Kilvert, sister of the diarist, whose passion for pictures will be illustrated later, referred in an informed comment to 'Mr Talbot who invented the talbo-type which either preceded or succeeded the daguerreotype, in the early days of sun-pictures'.[43]

Photography was quickly recognised as a valuable adjunct to botany, the specialism of Lewis Dillwyn senior, because applied to the microscope it could produce marvellously detailed images of leaves and cross-sections of plants. The *Journal* of Lewis junior shows a man interested in all aspects of natural history. Since later chapters will examine Kilvert's knowledge of natural history, it is relevant here to note those aspects that excited young Lewis, especially since both spent a considerable time as pupils at uncle Francis's school where, as we shall see, natural history loomed large. Lewis was especially interested to record when flowers and shrubs bloomed in spring as Kilvert was, so that at times the diary of the one reads like that of the other. On 24 May 1838 Lewis noted 'Bog beans in flower'; on 1 June 1872 Kilvert wrote: 'I went to see if the bog beans were yet in flower'. Lewis was most like Kilvert in his love of birds.

A marked similarity between the two men exists in their concern with geology, the study of which was actively encouraged by uncle Francis. Lewis had a laboratory and in 1838, when he was twenty-three, he recorded putting lime and silica into a furnace to observe changes in their composition. He conducted several similar experiments, the purpose of which was the reproduction of the very hard rocks, such as granite, found in nature. On some occasions he tried melting granite itself and porphyry. He was guided in these experiments by the geologist Henry de la Beche, with whom he spent much time in 1838. There had been controversy for some time over the nature of granite. Some naturalists argued that granitic mountains had been laid down at the Creation, but geologists like Hutton refuted this idea, insisting that granite rocks could not be primary since they were composed of several elements. While on honeymoon in North Wales in 1838, Lewis and his wife Bessie (de la Beche's daughter) climbed Cader Idris. He was impressed by the forbidding appearance of its summit, the result largely of the fact that it was composed of 'a sort of slate' and of 'a kind of greenish granite'. We shall see that Kilvert, when he climbed this mountain in June 1871, was similarly preoccupied with the composition of its rocks.

Like his father, Lewis was routinely concerned with practical improvements to Swansea and regularly attended paving, lighting, harbour board and infirmary meetings. He was equally keen to record more exciting developments such as the expanding railway system. He recorded with satisfaction on 7 June 1841 that the journey from Bristol to Bath took only twenty minutes. On 9 July 1850 he went to see progress on Brunel's revolutionary bridge over the Wye at Chepstow, considered his best, and the prototype for his bridge over the Tamar on the Cornwall line. An even greater wonder was what he called 'the gorilla ape', which he saw on display at the British Museum on 12 April 1859. He backed the building of the Metropolitan underground railway, travelling on its first trip with carriages on 30 October 1862. Time for viewing wonders had to be found even on his honeymoon in 1838 in North Wales. He journeyed from there by train to Liverpool, 'whisked along at an almost incredible rate of

30 miles an hour,' he wrote. Not many honeymooners would tour copper works, iron furnaces, and slate quarries, but he and Bessie did. The *Journal* entry on the iron furnace visit was written by Bessie, who said the processes were 'interesting and beautiful' and that she wanted to stay longer. She accompanied Lewis to lectures on the nervous system, the brain, galvanism, artificial light, phrenology, and chemistry.[44] They went together to view factories in Chippenham that made pins and buttons and one in Manchester that made paper trays. Lewis was keen, as his father was, that others were able to share knowledge. On 19 September 1839 he chaired a meeting to found a Mechanics' Institute in Swansea.

The account that follows of the elements constituting Kilvert's outlook will show that it was substantially the same as that of the Dillwyns with regard to the improvements and wonders of the age. He too toured iron furnaces, factories and dockyards, enthused over railways, steam-ships, viaducts, lathes, balloons, microscopes, and the electric telegraph; he too took a deep interest in natural history, geology, astronomy, archaeology, and phrenology; he too was regularly to be found at museums, art galleries, and displays of scientific and technological experiments and products. His parents, like Lewis Dillwyn (junior) and his wife Bessie, ensured that their children visited the Great Exhibition in 1851. Kilvert, like the Dillwyns, was shaped by the culture of the Lit and Phils and, like them, gravitated towards the mercantile and professional middle class who led and supported them. He was brought up as the Dillwyns were to admire entrepreneurial spirit and achievement, especially among the ranks of Quakers. Such humanitarian causes as abolition of slavery, espoused notably by Quakers and Evangelicals, was a major factor in his background as it was in that of the Dillwyns. Like them, he was habitually to be found at sacred music concerts at London's Exeter Hall, which was opened in 1831 and enlarged later to accommodate 3,000 persons. Every May it was used for the anniversaries of most of the leading Evangelical societies. When Kilvert visited London it was often in May (e.g. 1872, 1873, 1875); the *Diary* does not record his attendance at Evangelical Meetings, though that is the sort of thing Plomer omitted. *Punch* mocked Exeter Hall in 1842 as a building 'dedicated to piety and virtue' and to the 'moral excellencies of hundreds of pilgrims who . . . congregate to talk and sing there'. Although the Dillwyn family showed Evangelical traits, their approach to natural history was not marked, as was that of the Kilverts, by a disposition to see the hand of God in all created things. Perhaps

View of the Railway across Chat Moss. Laying a stable trackbed across the
deep bog was a remarkable feat of engineering in its time.

the former took it for granted and declined to be explicit about it.
The frequent visits of Dillwyns to balls and theatres and their card-
playing suggest that their Evangelicalism was less strict than that
of the Kilverts. One feels that the latter would not have done what
Lewis Dillwyn (senior) did on Christmas Day 1822: he went to see
experiments at Vivians' Copperworks in Swansea in the company
of a clergyman and Sir Humphrey Davy.

It is difficult to be too precise about the impact that uncle
Francis Kilvert's teaching had on young Lewis Dillwyn. Inevitably,
one feels that the latter appreciated the large presence of natural
history in the school curriculum of the former. Two other facts
should be emphasised: the first is that Lewis was Francis's pupil
for 3½ years; the second is that Lewis took the trouble to revisit
his old teacher eight years after he left his school. We might note
too that Henry Moule, tutor to both Lewis and his brother John,
was invited to stay at the Dillwyn home on 6 November 1828 –
4½ years after his tutoring ended. These facts tend to confirm that
the Dillwyn boys acknowledged Francis Kilvert and Henry Moule
not only as inspiring tutors but also as embodiments of an ethos
complementary to their own.

Chapter 1

Piety, Progress and Print: Kilvert's Background

> Most Evangelicals believed that God gave man the printing press to reinforce the message of salvation through the Word, not to induce questioning or doubts.
>
> James Secord, *Victorian Sensation*

> There was now (1824) some chance that the steam-engine would accomplish for printing what it was accomplishing for navigation.
>
> Charles Knight, *Passages of a Working Life during Half a Century*

The case for recognising Kilvert as a highly intelligent man and a thoughtful, sophisticated, critical reader introduces the rest of this book, whose picture of a Victorian with an informed interest in many aspects of his society is the logical extension of it. His *Diary* entry for 31 August 1870 in many ways typifies him. It records his visit in the evening to Hay-on-Wye schoolroom to hear a 'Mr Bodiby' (actually 'Bodily'). The way in which Kilvert formulated the speaker's offering is significant: '[He] gave a very interesting address about what he himself had seen in St Helena'. The diarist had gone along to this meeting of the Society for the Propagation of the Gospel (SPG)[1] because he valued *first-hand accounts* of experiences, especially in foreign parts or in unusual circumstances. He was, of course, also interested in missionary work, support for which had been a feature of his family background. Kilvert's sister Emily told how 'Mama's Missionary Working Parties were great events in our quiet lives. . . . Mama used to send out 2 boxes a year to various parts of the Mission Field'.[2]

Henry James Bodily (born 1830) was a clergyman, Rector of St Matthew's parish, St Helena, from 1862 to 1867. He did some missionary work: 'In 1864 J H Bodily reported: "I go on Thursdays to teach [the Africans] and examine what Jacob Faithful has been doing with them".[3] St Helena was controlled by the East India Company from 1659 to 1834. By 1673, it had become a British Crown Colony, often referred to as 'the lost county of England'. Kilvert would have known some of its intriguing history. Apart from Napoleon's exile there (Kilvert's entry included details of that), a stone-built observatory had been established on a high ridge by Maskelyne, the Astronomer Royal, from which Edmund Halley observed the transit of Mercury and Venus in 1676. Darwin visited in 1836 on his way home in the *Beagle*.

'Bodiby', wrote Kilvert, 'spoke of the devastations of the white ants imported accidentally in some wood from –'.[4] The behaviour of these ants aroused Kilvert's curiosity: 'The white ants die on the higher grounds, but eat the woodwork of the houses in James Town. . . . ' His curiosity was aroused too by 'the rollers on the N coast of the island [which] are very destructive in February. . . . These great cylindrical waves are caused by some disturbance close to the Rock and do not come from a distance where the sea is quite smooth'. This concern with the operation and causes of natural phenomena appears also in these remarks: 'They have scarcely any earthquakes or thunderstorms. Lightning has been seen once, towards America. . . . Kilvert also noted the island's size and shape: 'St Helena is 10 miles, by 7, very hilly'. A number of other things stand out from this *Diary* entry. Firstly, it demonstrates Kilvert's lively interest in factual information. Secondly, its concern with detail is impressive. Thirdly, its reportage is exactly that which characterised the popular literature Kilvert read in his childhood, as will be seen. Fourthly, the interest shown in it is that of the naturalist or physical geographer. Subsequent chapters will show that Kilvert's account of his evening in the Hay schoolroom is a good reflection of his character and interests.

Bodily's address, covering the island's history, weather, topography, buildings and places of note indicates that, like Kilvert, he had 'wide interests. He also had similar social roots to those of the diarist. Bodily was the son of a London watchmaker and his school, Liverpool Collegiate, provided a curriculum of science, commerce, and religion for middle-class boys. It is of some significance that St John's College, Cambridge, figured in Bodily's background. St John's was a college where sons of middle-class commercial, industrial and professional (especially doctors, schoolmasters, public servants) families were 'more numerous in aggregate and proportionately'.[5] This was partly because of the number of sizarships, which enabled men from poor backgrounds to enjoy reduced fees. That exemplar of ministerial devotion to the Kilvert family, the Rev. Henry Moule, had been a student there (1817-21). St John's had importance for Kilvert also because he based his own parochial practice on *The Duties of the Parish Priest* by Professor J.J. Blunt, who was its Lady Margaret Professor of Divinity.

St John's had been largely responsible for the founding in 1816 of St Bees Theological College, where Bodily was a student from Easter 1852 to December 1854. Between school and college he had been a teacher. Theological colleges came into being not only to meet the Church's need for more clergy, but also to provide the training that Oxbridge failed to provide. (It is noteworthy that uncle Francis Kilvert was offered the principal's post at a theological college – Queen's College, Birmingham.)[6] St Bees' entrants came from professional, commercial, farming, teaching, and army families.[7] The leading figures in the history of the College had come from St John's. Bodily was just one of the many St Bees men who chose to serve in the mission field.

The interest Kilvert showed in Bodily's lecture was the product of his background. The kind of reading encouraged in Kilvert's family and its effect upon his personality and writing will be a theme of this chapter. The focus will be on his attitudes to education, nature, and science, areas which overlap. We begin by considering the influence of his earliest teachers, those who formed his basic outlook. He had many 'teachers', in both the formal and informal sense, in his life. All mothers are teachers but it seems that Mrs Kilvert set out to bring particular values and experiences to bear on her children. Raised by Quakers and taught by Moravians, both of whom valued education highly, it was inevitable that she too would have a high respect for it. The Quaker influence on Kilvert was broad and deep,[8] shaping what can be seen as his primary impulse to write: a desire to praise the beauty of God's world. In this his mother played a key role by introducing her family to *The Children's Year* by the Quaker writer, Mary Howitt, which asserted that the home would be happy 'if the young are induced to desire those lessons from Nature which Nature is so well able to teach'.[9] Born in 1799 at Coleford, Gloucestershire, Mary was of Quaker farming stock although her father, like many Quakers, was involved with the iron industry.[10] Mary's own childhood was coloured by his love of nature.

Mary's interest in the way children learn shows aptitude for teaching. She opened her autobiography thus: 'It has often been a subject of regret that so little is known of the workings of a child's mind during its earlier years'.[11] She clearly felt that she knew something of those workings because of her reiterated conviction that natural processes and natural objects should form a substantial element of early education, complementing and stimulating the development of child-nature. Children, she said, *felt* things keenly but 'reason and reflection come later'.[12] She recalled fondly one of her teachers, Mrs Parker, whom she loved as a child because she reinforced a habit, already part of Mary's home life (as one recognises it was of Kilvert's), of focusing on natural objects: 'She would take a little flower . . . and preach a sermon from it'.[13]

Another of Kilvert's teachers when he was very young was the Rev.

Legh Richmond (1772-1827),[14] whose *The Dairyman's Daughter* he recalled when visiting Yaverland, Isle of Wight, on 17 June 1874. He was only nine when he read it so presumably it was brought to his attention by his parents (it was 'one of Evangelicals' favourite books').[15] In the same collection of stories (*Annals of the Poor*) is another one, *The Young Cottager*, which teaches other lessons Kilvert never forgot. It noted that it was very 'gratifying . . . to an affectionate mind . . . to walk through the fields, and lead a little child by the hand, . . . and to improve the time by some instruction'. Natural objects were to be the basis of this 'useful instruction',[16] because 'Natural scenery, when viewed in a Christian mirror, frequently affords very beautiful illustrations of divine truths'.[17] Richmond explained that he taught classes of children in his garden, because 'the very flowers and leaves of the garden are emblems of higher things when grace teaches us to make them so'.[18] Later, we shall see Kilvert conducting Sunday School classes in his garden. When he left home to join the Claverton school of his uncle Francis at eleven, the theme of natural objects as the source of moral and spiritual values was continued.

Confirmation that uncle Francis had an image of the Christian poet as hero, largely in the person of Wordsworth, comes in the inscription he wrote in a copy of Adam Sedgwick's *Discourse* that he gave to Frederick Falkner on 16 February 1835. Frederick was a son of the Francis Falkner who had come to Bath in 1778 to set up a wine business.[19] The inscription reads: 'To Frederick Falkner the ardent admirer of Nature and the humble adorer of Nature's God, this book dictated by a kindred spirit and calculated to touch his inward sympathies'. (Cf. Anne Falkner's characterisation of Frederick: he was 'greatly interested in Natural Philosophy. In all that relates to the origin, analysis, and laws of all created things'.)[20] The wording of Francis's inscription tells us a lot about the man who chose it. The reference to 'Nature's God' is from Pope's *Essay on Man*; he wrote of looking through Nature, up to 'Nature's God'; 'kindred spirit' is from Gray's *Elegy*. Uncle Francis had effectively defined natural theology in the inscription he wrote in Sedgwick's *Discourse*. The Rev. Adam Sedgwick was a man of science, Professor of Geology at Cambridge, and his *Discourse* was 'an argument for the place of geology within natural theology'.[21]

The *Discourse* was a sermon delivered on 17 December 1832 in the Chapel of Trinity College, Cambridge and was addressed particularly to the young, which is partly why was important to uncle Francis as both clergyman and teacher. Sedgwick stated in it that he wanted to speak of the University as 'a place of sound learning and Christian education'. Its studies had three aspects: the laws of nature, ancient literature, and 'the study of ourselves' (i.e. ethics, metaphysics, moral and political philosophy). He particularly recommended the first of the three aspects because the laws of nature, 'by which God . . . governed the universe are surely subjects of lofty contemplation'. The study of natural phenomena induced devotion in that it led us to recognise 'the feebleness of our powers and we see at every step new cause for wonder'.[22] As both clergyman and scientist, he was quite easy about urging study of the 'higher sciences'; many gentlemen of science were then. It is too easy from the standpoint of the early twenty-first century to assume that Kilvert as a clergyman could have had neither interest in nor sympathy for science. The idea that religion was in conflict with science in the early nineteenth century results, in Rudwick's opinion, from failure to distinguish between natural and revealed theology.[23] The latter was the view that scripture and human history revealed God's design. Many gentlemen of science of the period found that their researches confirmed design in the natural world (i.e. natural theology). Kilvert's uncle Francis, though not a scientist, taught his pupils natural theology and followed Sedgwick, who sought to underpin revelation with science.[24] Claverton pupils also learned something of geology itself.

Other modern commentators have rejected a conflict between science and religion in the early nineteenth century. Morrell and Thackray, for example, noted that though it was quite impossible for early Victorian gentlemen 'to study nature without confronting nature's God', in the late 1820s and early 1830s the view prevailed that 'the book of nature and the book of God were in ultimate accord.'[25] Young had the same understanding: natural theology was able to claim up to the mid-1830s that each new discovery of science proved God's design in Nature. Science therefore supported religion.[26] 'The opposition of science and religion, often taken for granted in the twentieth century, is a social and intellectual construction,' Yanni stated, 'and not a fact of history.'[27]

As the son of a clergyman and a clergyman himself, Sedgwick allied himself with those natural scientists who resisted notions of evolution. 'From the 1790s onwards, the natural sciences became an increasingly significant part of the Establishment's response to unbelief.'[28] He considered that such branches of natural science as astronomy, geology, and anatomy were handmaidens to natural religion and 'teach us to see the finger of God in all things animate and inanimate.'[29] The crucial area of conflict between the natural theologians and the evolutionists was the question of natural laws and what they seemed to suggest about the meaning and purpose of the Earth. Sedgwick wrote to Darwin on 24 December 1859, regarding the latter's *The Origin of Species*: 'You do not deny causation. I call causation the will of God'. He was stating his belief that the laws of nature represented God's will, God's *design*: 'God acts by laws which we can study and comprehend'. Thus developments over time apparent in living forms were part of God's plan, they were natural laws which needed to be seen in the context of the 'final cause', i.e. the purpose of God's Creation. Sedgwick's letter to Darwin closes with these words: 'I humbly accept God's revelation of Himself both in His works and in His word'.[30]

In spring 1878, Kilvert was suffering from congestion of the lungs. The book he chose to read then was Charles Mackay's *Forty Years' Recollections of Life, Literature and Public Affairs from 1830 to 1870*. The choice makes particular sense in the context of this enquiry into the evolution of his attitudes to the burning questions of his day. Mackay's life (1814-1889) reflected self-improvement and dedication to work and usefulness. The *DNB* entry on him stated that 'he extolled the virtues of self-help, temperance, and "independence"' and that he believed that 'the working man could educate himself in the fine fruits of the human intellect and the wonders of God's universe as revealed by science'.[31] He himself was determined to 'climb up the slippery heights of ambition' to become a writer.[32] A volume of his poems caught the attention of John Black, editor of the Liberal *Morning Chronicle*; Dickens was on the staff when Mackay joined. This was the man whose life-story, a story of achievement and progress, Kilvert found comforting when he believed his own life was nearing its end. In the *Diary* entry recording his reading of *Forty Years' Recollections*, he wrote of his Bredwardine Vicarage: 'How long will it be "Home"? How long will it last?'

The *Vestiges of the Natural History of Creation* that Robert Chambers published (anonymously) in October 1844 was 'part of the emerging genre of "popular science" that aimed to diffuse known truths to the mass audience in useful knowledge tracts and newspapers'.[33] Although the knowledge he displayed in it was patchy, he was correct in demonstrating that fossils found in the geological record gave evidence of increasing complexity among living creatures. He wrote of 'those petrified remains of vegetables and animals which . . . tell so wondrous a tale of the past history of our globe'.[34] In 1844, when Mackay was assistant editor of the *Morning Chronicle*, he wrote of Chambers's *Vestiges*: 'it excited a great sensation at the time . . . highly praised by some, violently abused by others'.[35] It went through ten editions in as many years, and was read by a great cross-section of society.[36] Sedgwick became its fiercest opponent. Secord stated that it was 'as readable as a romance, based on the latest findings of science, . . . it suggested that the planets originated in a blazing Fire-mist . . . that humans had evolved from apes'.[37] Evolution had reached a turning-point in the early nineteenth century and that turning-point was readers' response to *Vestiges*. 'Evolutionary theories had become a common currency of conversation' in the wake of it.[38]

Several pieces of evidence confirm uncle Francis's firm belief in natural theology, one of the best of which is the poem composed by his wife Sophia about the Bath Literary and Philosophical Association (BLPA), of which her husband was the leading light:

They talked of Planets as they roll,
Of Nature's wise mysterious whole,
Of Him who cast this Orb in space,
And lent it to our fallen suffering Race.[39]

A later chapter traces the history of the BLPA and its influence on Kilvert. It is enough here to note the poem's reference to astronomy, to 'nature's mystery, to the wisdom of its Great Designer, and to Man as the target of its design. Kilvert had been brought up with natural theology, its principles and assumptions part of the very air he breathed. The Book of nature could be read as confirmation of man's special relationship with God, just as the Bible, God's other great book, could. The Bible was the revealed Word of God (a notion of particular importance to Evangelicals like Kilvert) and 'the mark of true revelation, [Paley] claimed, is miracle – some phenomenon not covered by ordinary laws of nature'.[40] Kilvert must have experienced some conflict over the issue of miracles and natural laws because, as is shown later, the scientist he greatly admired, John Tyndall, refuted miracles. It seems that Kilvert had accepted, much in the way his uncle Francis and Adam Sedgwick had, a compromise between the findings of science and continued reliance on the Bible. This involved recognising, *inter alia*, that the Earth was very much older than the traditional Christian viewpoint allowed, as proved by the existence in rock strata of remains of creatures which existed millions of years before, while at the same time managing to repose faith in the Bible as a divinely inspired account of God's relationship with Man, independent of Earth's earlier history.

All of these elements are given prominence in a book Kilvert read as a boy, a fact that makes it centrally important. The book was *Masterman Ready* by Frederick Marryat (1792-1848), known as Captain Marryat. The diarist indicated he knew it in his childhood from his entry: 'I went to see Mary Davies and took her dear old *Masterman Ready* to amuse herself with.'[41] Marryat must be included among Kilvert's early teachers. The book appeared in 1841, the first of a series of books for children produced by Marryat after he had retired from the sea, and it reflects the emphasis on factual information and scientific knowledge current in the 1830s. *Masterman Ready* blends didactic purpose with adventure and a strong moral tone, so it is easy to see why the Kilvert parents approved it for their son. Marryat's aim in his book was 'to enter more deeply into questions which may induce children to think or, by raising their curiosity, stimulate them to seek for information'.[42] Marryat was adopting the role of teacher.

The concern with actuality and practicality is one feature linking the book to *Robinson Crusoe*; another is that it deals with people stranded on a desert island. The core of *Masterman Ready* is the relationship between twelve-year-old William Seagrave and the sixty-four-year-old sailor Ready, who stays with the Seagrave family when their ship founders. He is not only a good moral example for William ('he had read his Bible over and over again'), but is that best kind of teacher who learns as he teaches: 'I have learnt something today, which every one will . . . if he will only ask questions'.[43] The narrative of Ready's life-story, told in sections, is the background to the development of William, who becomes Ready's companion and helper. As William meets a series of challenges, he gains strength, independence, and knowledge, partly through his continual posing of questions, in what amounts to a rite of passage.

The trope of continual, inevitable development and progress is a dominant one in Kilvert's reading, writing and thinking. It is there in the figure of Bodily – teacher and missionary – working to raise the natives from their primitive state to civilisation. It also permeates much of Marryat's fiction, of which Bodily showed some awareness. His African helper on St Helena was Jacob Faithful, named half-humorously perhaps by Bodily himself after the eponymous hero of Marryat's 1836 novel in which Jacob Faithful, son of a Thames lighterman, becomes an orphan and charity-boy, but is given an education by a kind schoolmaster. Jacob's description of himself may have suggested to Bodily a parallel with his African disciple: 'I was literally a *savage*, but still a kind and docile one'. Marryat enforces two 'lessons' at the end of the story. The first is that 'there is no such thing in this world as independence, unless in a *savage state*. In society, we are all mutually dependent upon each other . . . the more refined the society may be – the more civilised its parts – the greater is the mutual dependence'. The second lesson is 'the advantage of a *good education* and *good principle*'.[44] These lessons are reiterated in *Masterman Ready*. Ready is a tower of strength in that story, particularly for his practical skills. He teaches William how to make fire, using a glass from a telescope and some touch paper, the process of 'trail-blazing'

– the marking of trees so they can retrace their steps when exploring the island – and the making of salt by evaporation or boiling of sea water. Even Mrs Seagrave, though a lady ('not a fine one', she pointed out), is determined to be 'useful'.[45] The story of the Seagraves and Masterman Ready on their desert island illustrates the values of the Kilvert family – work, self-help, self-education, usefulness, and faith. The story reflects what Stott referred to as 'the culture of purposeful energy and earnest moralism known by the convenient shorthand of "Victorianism".'[46]

Marryat assumed that children were curious about natural phenomena. Thus, early in his story there is a focus on clouds sometimes seen rolling over the top of Table Mountain 'in a very curious manner'. Mr Seagrave explained to William that coral is 'raised by the work of little insects not bigger than a pin's head . . . is not this wonderful?' Such wonders are used to advance natural theology. As he tells William that the sea anemone is really an animal and not a plant, he adds 'Creation is very wonderful'. The idea of God as the Great Designer is launched at the beginning of the book by Mr Seagrave: 'the Almighty, in His wisdom, has so arranged it that no animal shall be multiplied to excess' (instanced as an example of 'natural law'). God's particular care of Man is seen in the way he is often the beneficiary of natural laws: '[God] has so fashioned the world, that from natural causes . . . effects are produced which are beneficial to mankind'. As examples of the 'fixed laws [by which] everything is governed', Mr Seagrave cited the seasons, tides, and animal instincts. All nature followed the same 'unvarying laws'.[47]

Kilvert saw no reason to comment explicitly on the laws of nature because they were an accepted element in his faith. The understanding that the regularity of seasons, of stars' movements, and of weather conditions were signs of divine design is implicit in many observations of such phenomena in the *Diary*. Kilvert had a particular pleasure in moonlight which can be seen in these examples: 'one of the magnificent sights of the world, the crescent moon setting'; 'the full moon shining in all its brilliance was setting upon the hill beyond the church steeple'; 'To be alone out of doors on a still soft clear moonlit night is to me one of the greatest pleasures that this world can give'. The night's 'wonderful beauty' in this passage is linked, as it is in the last quotation, to his church.[48] One theme of these passages is of course the moon's beauty, and beauty too was one of 'nature's laws, as he saw it. When he thanked God in his diary for making the world so beautiful, as he frequently did, he was tacitly accepting that beauty was a central part of God's design. Similarly, he was expressing satisfaction in the notion of an ordered nature when, after an unseasonal fall of snow on 13 April 1876, with everything seeming so wintry, the birds were nevertheless 'singing undaunted'; Kilvert added, 'Surely the birds must have great faith'.[49] He was pointing out that while design in nature gave evidence of God, faith too was needed.

In the *Diary* excerpts above, we can clearly detect the influence of Marryat's book. Kilvert's feeling of reverence as he contemplated the moon's movements corresponds to William Seagrave's comment: 'I never do look up on a starry night without feeling inclined to pray'. In *The Settlers in Canada*, another Marryat novel known to Kilvert, Malachi Bone testified to finding God's design in the night sky: 'the moon and the stars, as I watch, make me think of him'.[50] William Seagrave advanced the case for natural religion with respect to atheists: 'I'm sure a mere examination of the works of God ought to make them good Christians'. His father replied, however, that that argument was misconceived because although 'an examination of His works may make them good and devout men', it would not make them Christians. Faith also in the unseen was needed in order to bring men to salvation. 'There is little merit in acknowledging what is evident to our senses', he pointed out. Similarly, Kilvert was complimenting the birds for their faith by disregarding the evidence of their senses when they sang as though it was spring in spite of the snow.

That Kilvert's understanding of natural theology was intelligent and sophisticated becomes very clear from the *Diary* entry in which he commented scathingly on a book borrowed from another clergyman, who was, significantly, an accomplished amateur astronomer. He was the Rev. Thomas Webb (1806-1885), another of Kilvert's teachers, as will appear. Kilvert wrote: 'Reading Edmund Jones' curious book which I brought from Hardwick Vicarage last night, an account of Aberystruth Parish, Monmouthshire.[51] A ludicrous naïve simplicity about his reflections and conclusions'. According to Harris, Jones had 'a native curiosity for knowing about things' and was largely self-taught, with no 'formal training in the natural sciences'.[52] The preface of his book indicates one aspect of the 'naïve simplicity' that irritated Kilvert. Jones noted that though all Creation confirmed the existence of God, some parts provided more convincing demonstration of it. Mountains and valleys did, for example, and Aberystruth had mountains and valleys. To this somewhat dubious claim that the Creator had a special interest in the parish, Jones added that Aberystruth exemplified the way the 'agencies of God' were remarkably evident 'upon the land and its inhabitants . . . the like whereof cannot be showed out of any other Parish in the Kingdom'.

Jones attributed the formation of local mountain and valleys to 'the Flood, Earthquakes and Excessive Rain', the causes of which 'must be the sins of the World both Original and Actual'. Mountains and valleys were to him proof of God's existence and he refuted Descartes's view that they were formed by 'a Fortuitous concourse of Atoms'. (It will be shown later that Kilvert was preoccupied with the agency by which valleys were formed among mountains.) God's design was seen too in 'the exceeding useful Coal Mineral, most properly placed for the use of the parish'. These claims, in particular, Kilvert found ridiculous: '[Jones] thinks Providence took particular pains in making his parish one of the most wonderful in the world'. Kilvert rejected the idea that Aberystruth was in any sense a wonder. He had assimilated the natural theology of the 1820s and 1830s, in which 'the preoccupation with coal . . . reflects the providentialism of the day'.[53] (Professor Buckland was one of its leading spokesmen.)[54] However, Jones's viewpoint of natural theology (informed by revealed theology) was to Kilvert both too extreme and too simplistic, and conflicted with his geological understanding.

Webb's loan of Jones's book to Kilvert was typical. His influence on the diarist was considerable and centred on two fundamental, linked elements which they had in common: their Evangelical religion and astronomy. The Kilvert family's interest in astronomy is evidenced by the fact that a copy of Webb's *Optics without Mathematics*, which refers throughout to 'God's wonderful works', was found amongst their books. Kilvert had been dead for four years when the book was published in 1883. Webb's *Celestial Objects for Common Telescopes* had appeared in 1859 when there was a growing market for books on science. Chapman called it 'a classic of serious amateur astronomy literature'.[55] Astronomy figured in the curriculum of Claverton Lodge school, according to Warde Fowler, who was a contemporary of Kilvert there. Fowler recalled that the comet of 1858 was used by uncle Francis to press home spiritual messages for the benefit of his charges. Francis also wrote poems about astronomy: one celebrated the astronomers Leverrier and Adams, while another, *To the Concord of Astronomers*, praised their piety and wisdom. Francis's wife Sophia, in her *Home Discipline*, placed astronomy at the head of her list of 'scientific amusements' to be shared in an upper-middle class family by 'all ages and both sexes'.[56] One of the treats in store for the Kilvert children at the London Polytechnic was the astronomy lectures of John Henry Pepper (1821-1900), described by Lightman as 'one of the most well-known popularisers of science in the second half of the nineteenth century'.[57] Kilvert's appetite for astronomy was already whetted when he met Webb.

Kilvert had known Webb since he first went to Clyro in 1865, and they had been brought together by their love of astronomy.[58] The diarist referred on 7 July 1870 to 'old times' at Hardwicke Vicarage (Webb's home near Clyro) when he had seen in the observatory 'the light of the Great Meteor'.[59] He recorded several other visits there to observe astronomical and other natural phenomena. Webb was, like Lewis Weston Dillwyn, interested in everything. He went to see a working steam-engine in 1826, and was greatly excited by the Deptford Tunnel under the Thames on 26 May 1828. In May and early June 1830, he attended Buckland's lectures on geology in Oxford. He visited the London Polytechnic to see scientific experiments. His notebooks contain entries on alloys, photography, geology, electric light, the over-heating of railway-waggon axles, and galvanic batteries. His 23 April 1831 diary entry, addressed to the woman he married in 1843, shows his stance towards nature: 'may I never entertain any feelings of wonder and pleasure, not even at [God's] works, that I cannot share with thee'.[60]

The notion of Creation as a singular demonstration of God's benevolence was central to Mary Howitt's upbringing, which was marked by a high degree of freedom according to Quaker principles. The aim was to preserve children in 'unsullied innocence. . . . A singular exhibition this of the natural . . . growth of a young . . . intellect'.[61] As a young woman, she went on country walks and learned from God, 'the great Botanist, simple, natural tastes'. She raised her own two younger children on these same principles. Their education was, she said, 'very simple and true to Nature'.[62] Her daughters Mary and Meggy 'often talked about the minds and hearts of everybody being like gardens'.[63] This analogy between human growth and plant growth presupposes that the essential nature of both is innocent.

Belief in the innocence of the child was central to Romanticism and largely stemmed from the writings of Rousseau (1712-1778). The classic Romantic attitudes were all characteristic of him: belief in the essential goodness of Man, the individual, intuition and feeling (as opposed to intellect), the imagination, and nature. All of these ideas were part of Kilvert's background and became part of his outlook. His mother's Quakerism endorsed the idea of child innocence. However, there were conflicting elements in Kilvert's background on this issue (the many paradoxes in his nature reflect these conflicts). His mother's Moravian theology and his father's Calvinist theology placed heavy emphasis on original sin. The *Diary* entries which show Kilvert heartily approving of the whipping of children confirm the extent to which he had assimilated this doctrine.[64] Corporal punishment was used at his father's Hardenhuish school and his uncle Francis's Claverton Lodge school; he was a pupil at both.[65] Conflict between primal innocence and original sin surfaced in Kilvert's own teaching, as chapter nine relates. In spite of these authoritarian influences, Kilvert's personality and writing are coloured more by the outlook of the Romantic poets, by the image of Rousseau's *Émile*, the delicate plant, the child of nature. Not only was this the message of *The Children's Year* but also of the books by William Howitt that Kilvert knew. All natural forms have beauty 'as they are contemplated in love', William wrote. Through knowledge of 'the quality of all plants, minerals and physical substances' we could, he said, 'see into the life of things'. The moral heart of the nation depended on 'simple Christianity, love of nature' and a literature which reflected both.[66]

As Kilvert was growing up in the 1840s there was a huge increase in the volume of published material because of technical improvements in printing which made magazines and books much cheaper. This increase was especially marked after 1850, by which time he was ten. 'The number of serial publications (magazines, reviews and newspapers) in England and Wales grew from 129 in 1801 to 4,819 in 1900'.[67] Most of this new material was aimed at the working class, many of whom were eager for knowledge and self-improvement. At the time, science was increasingly seen as in conflict with religious faith, but many Christians sought to show that they were complementary. The period saw the emergence of cheap, popular printed material as a means of bringing understanding of science to the people. William Howitt was fired by the challenge, becoming an editor and part-owner of the *People's Journal* which, he said, was 'to teach and enlighten the working classes'.[68] He and Mary Howitt founded their own magazine, *Howitt's Journal*, the first issue appearing on 1 January 1847.[69] Its informative articles were permeated by a Christian spirit, but there was not enough in it to entertain and it ran for only eighteen months.

Boyd Hilton emphasised that it has often been assumed that Evangelicals were hostile to science in the first half of the nineteenth century, 'but this is only true of extremists . . . and supporters of the *Record*'.[70] It was Evangelicals in particular who were concerned with the publishing explosion, especially regarding public knowledge of science, as Fyfe noted: 'Evangelicals undoubtedly took an interest, even an active involvement, in the sciences'. To study the sciences was not a way to faith, but it was something that people with faith should engage with. In mid-Victorian England, Evangelicals did not see science in itself as a danger to faith; they were concerned that scientific discovery should be presented within a Christian framework. Disturbed by the overtly secular, if not actually atheistical, tone of much popular reading material they therefore set about producing 'alternative works of Christian popular science'.[71]

One of the main adopters of the new approach to popular publishing was the Religious Tract Society (RTS), founded in 1799. Kilvert was a firm believer in the RTS and in the importance of tracts. Like all Evangelicals, he was convinced of the value of print as a means of spreading the Word. 'Evangelicals believed that the grace of God could, and did, descend to the individual man and woman through the printed page.'[72] This helps to explain both why a study of Kilvert's reading is important, and why his distribution of books to children was a vital part of his teaching. He was in the habit of leaving tracts (sometimes several at a time) at parishioners' cottages.[73] He intended his poem, *Honest Work*, which he had printed on cards, to function as a tract. There is ample evidence to show that he was familiar with and approved of the RTS approach to the education of the poor. As we have seen, he knew Legh Richmond's *Annals of the Poor* stories; these were published by the RTS. Kilvert would also have known the RTS from his mother's missionary working parties because it produced tracts to be distributed overseas. The pious stories – Hesba Stretton's *Jessica's First Prayer* and *Alone in London* – which he regularly gave out to children, were RTS publications. And finally he was familiar, probably from being brought up with it, with the RTS's magazine, *Sunday at Home*.[74] This steady involvement with the RTS over many years means that he would be bound to have known from his childhood its publication *The Leisure Hour*, subtitled *A Family Journal of Instruction and Recreation*, launched in January 1852, price one penny.[75] Its first title, *Friend of the People*, indicated that it was in the same tradition of publishing as *Howitt's Journal*. Its later title referred to the campaign to reduce the working hours of the labouring classes (the campaign's supporters insisted that 'every man should have a leisure hour').[76] RTS members were middle-class evangelicals and *The Leisure Hour* was aimed at them as well as at the working class. The RTS 'promoted *The Leisure Hour* as the ideal blend of mental and religious improvement . . . it was the Society's response to the threat of the popular press'.[77]

The content of *The Leisure Hour* was a mixture of biography, geography, history, natural science and fiction. The RTS argued that Christians had a duty to study natural history, history and geography 'to better understand the world and God's relation to it'.[78] Its *Leisure Hour* epitomised the spirit of early Victorian periodicals as defined by Secord: 'the reader is led by an earnest companion or guide . . . moving in and out of a crowd of phenomena', so that narrator and reader appear to be exploring the world of nature together.[79] The magazine gave direct expression to the idea of the compatibility of religion and science. It reported, for example, on the meeting of the British Association for the Advancement of Science (BAAS) at Cheltenham on 6 August 1856. Parts of the inaugural address by its president, Dr Daubeny, Professor of Chemistry and Botany at the University of Oxford, were quoted: 'the contemplation of the works of the Creator [and of His laws] was in itself an act of praise and adoration'. The article then quoted, 'for the consideration of those . . . who consider revelation and science antagonistic', words by 'Mr Close', who gave the vote of thanks to Dr Daubeny. 'Mr Close' was the Rev. Francis Close (1797-1882), perpetual curate of Cheltenham parish church.

Educated at Merchant Taylor's School and at St John's College, Cambridge, Close favoured extreme Evangelicalism and its paper, the *Record*. He had a particular interest in education. Not only was he one of the founders of Cheltenham Ladies' College, but he built a dozen infant and junior schools. Before the British Association scientists and their audience, Close took the opportunity to assert that 'there was no connection between science and infidelity, between knowledge and irreligion'. The reporter of these proceedings was excited to record that 'the pump room was lighted up most brilliantly, for the first time since its erection, with gas. The electric light was introduced over the principal front of the building'.[80] It was as though the most brilliant wonders of science were being deliberately deployed to illustrate the brilliance of the learned scientists and the glory, scientific and religious, of the cause that brought them together. A highly patriotic tone informed the *Leisure Hour* article 'The dawn of science in England', which contrasted the England two hundred years before when 'there hung round the popular mind long-set mists of ignorance and superstition'. Among the fruits of science were 'the wonder-working wire' (presumably the electric telegraph) and 'the mighty feats of steam . . . bright examples for all lovers of their country'.[81]

In the period when the fruits of science were being recommended to the general public, Kilvert was a full-time pupil (1851-1858) at his uncle Francis's Claverton Lodge school All his siblings came under its influence. Emily Kilvert recorded that the Kilvert children sometimes stayed there in the winter and that their uncle shaped their outlook: 'How we loved and revered him'. She also revealed that he supported the new popular journalism, facilitated by the age's developing print technology, that was such an important factor in her family. At Claverton Lodge, 'There was a large cupboard with shelves in the dining-room,' Emily remembered. 'In this abode many magazines we used to be allowed to read, and among them were copies of the "Penny Post".' The presence of *Penny Post* issues at Claverton Lodge raises questions about the complexity of the issue of religious belief in

Victorian times. It has become a truism of Kilvert studies that uncle Francis was, in the words of Williams and Grice, 'a reasonably High Church Anglican'.[82] The *Penny Post* magazines that Emily discovered as a cache of treasure seem to confirm this view because the publication was produced by upper-class Tractarians for working-class readers. She understood this as is clear from her comment that the *Penny Post* was 'my first acquaintance with High Church literature!'[83] It first appeared in 1851 when she was nine. Her uncle cannot, however, have believed the magazine would subvert the Evangelical faith in which she had been raised; it was accessible to her, her siblings, and (presumably) the Claverton Lodge pupils. Furthermore, Boyd Hilton noted that Evangelicals and Tractarians could sound very much the same in terms of their doctrines.[84]

Emily referred to uncle Francis as 'High Church' and to his taking the *Guardian* newspaper in contrast to her father, an Evangelical who favoured the *Record*, known for reflecting extreme Evangelical opinion. The logic of her comment is that the *Guardian* was a High Church paper, whereas it too was an Evangelical one, though of moderate views. Hylson-Smith characterised it in terms of its 'majority Evangelical approach'[85] while Elisabeth Jay said of it: 'It reflected the views of the Evangelical clergy, being aimed at a readership . . . less affluent, more conservative, and above all pietistically rather than politically-minded' than the *Christian Observer* (the organ of the wealthy, metropolitan, Clapham Sect of Evangelicals).[86] To Emily, used to the ethos of the *Record*, uncle Francis could have appeared as High Church. Other evidence confirms, however, that he was of Evangelical persuasion. Falkner, for example, referred him and his friend, the Rev. Harvey Marriott (whom we shall meet later) as 'Evangelical clergy'.[87]

The fact that a clergyman of Evangelical leanings not only had Tractarian magazines in his house, but encouraged their use by the children of his even more Evangelical brother, needs further explanation. The *Penny Post* appeared when such leaders of the Tractarian or Oxford Movement as Keble and Newman were attempting to spread their ideals to the working classes. The first two volumes of the magazine have been studied by Dr Kellyanne Ure and the account of it that follows is deeply indebted to her.[88] It aimed at a dual readership – while appearing to address working-class concerns it also appealed to an upper-class audience. It was published in London by John Henry Parker, who published Tractarian literature, including *The Christian Year*, the volume of poems by Keble. (Poems by Tractarian leaders were acceptable in the Kilvert home: Mrs Kilvert bought for her diarist son, as a birthday gift on 3 December 1875, *Lyra Apostolica*, a book of devotional verse by Hurrell Froude, Keble, Newman, and Isaac Williams. Kilvert also showed a knowledge of *The Christian Year*.)[89] Ure emphasised another goal the *Penny Post* shared with scores of others addressed to the working class: the provision of wholesome material to counteract the sensational features and radical politics of cheap journals. A later chapter will show that this was a cause to which Kilvert's aunt Sophia, a powerful presence at Claverton Lodge, was devoted. The *Penny Post*, a force bolstering society's traditional values in the face of change, would have been welcome there. Country clergymen bought multiple copies of it for distribution to parishioners and this is perhaps why Emily found an abundant supply in the cupboard.

In its mix of fiction, natural history, biography, topography, and science and technology, the *Penny Post* resembled *The Leisure Hour* (the latter may have been found with the former among the 'many magazines' in the dining-room cupboard). Evidently Emily enjoyed the *Penny Post* – 'too delightful for words' was her judgement on it. Part of its appeal to her would have been its stories and (from 1854) its illustrations. A common theme in stories is the relationship of a working-class parishioner with his clergyman (cf. the close relationship Kilvert forged with John Jefferies, John Hatherell, and 'the Old Soldier'). The intelligence of working men is seen as limited but capable of being improved through education. Class-based stereotypes are common. Work is presented not only as a working-class duty, but partaking of the nature of a sacrament.[90] Articles were designed to be 'practical and expository', in accordance with the opening piece, 'The Old Year and the New', in the 1862 bound volume.[91] It looked back over 1862 in order to 'assess our progress . . . in the history of the nation'. The nation was prosperous and all classes happy and content. Although magnificent buildings appeared everywhere, they were unaccompanied by new churches. Progress was being made in the Colonies but it was insignificant when compared with the 'vast territory' the nation ruled. However, the increase in clergy and missionaries continued. Satisfaction was expressed at the growth in reading, at increase in lending libraries, reading-rooms, and book-hawkers, 'by whose means books of high moral and religious tendency are sold'.

The Leisure Hour's emphasis on technological achievement was repeated in the *Penny Post*. Kilvert and his siblings were raised on a vision of (particularly British) history, science, and industrial progress, as Emily Kilvert recorded: 'The volumes of "Old England" were a never-failing source of pleasure'.[92] She was referring to the work by Charles Knight, first published in 1844, the full title of which is *Old England: A Pictorial Museum of Regal, Ecclesiastical, Municipal, Baronial and Popular Antiquities*.[93] It was in two volumes, each containing four books, with three chapters in each book, and it surveyed English history from before the Norman Conquest to the present. As soon as one opens it, it is immediately apparent that Kilvert has passed this way. In Knight's description of Stonehenge we find a phrase echoed in Kilvert's account of his visit there. Knight said that the 'real character' of the monument was that it represented 'the Chorea Gigantum – the Choir of Giants'. Kilvert likened the stones to 'ancient giants' who formed 'a true "Chorea Gigantum"'.[94] The marks of Kilvert's footprints are visible too at many of the other locations in the journey through *Old England*. It is not hard to see why the Kilvert children would have enjoyed Knight's volume, though even for Victorian children brought up to be 'serious', it still represents a formidable read. However, its 800 double-columned pages of small print, packed with factual information, are relieved by a number of stylistic features. Accounts of places, people and periods are liberally furnished with literary quotations and actual words spoken by historical personages. There is a wealth of anecdote and informal, personal details. Another reason for its appeal is that there are over 2,500 steel engravings so that every other turn of a page brings more pictures; in addition, there are 40 pages of 'illuminated engravings' – full-page colour pictures. Colour printing was sufficient of a wonder for it to be the most popular of the printing attractions at the Great Exhibition of 1851.

A fervent believer in the power of the printed word was Charles Knight (1791-1873). He was of lower-class origins, the son and apprentice of a printer. Ambitious to be a journalist and publisher, he began a journal, *Knight's Quarterly Magazine*, in the 1820s. The venture failed after six issues but his determination to be involved in the education of the people is signalled by his becoming the superintendent of the publications of Lord Brougham's SDUK. He still yearned to be his own publisher and in 1832 and 1833 started *The Penny Magazine* and *The Penny Cyclopedia*.[95] Altick paid tribute to Knight as a man: '[he was] an attractive person, energetic, idealistic, resilient . . . and thoroughly in love with life'; and to his cultural significance: 'he wished simply to make the printed page the agent of peace, justice and pleasure. . . . Among the pioneers of cheap books in the first half of the nineteenth century, Knight was held in perhaps highest respect'.[96]

The slight but steady favouring of Protestantism in *Old England* would have made it more acceptable in the Kilvert household.[97] Protestantism holds that the individual thinks for himself, pursues his own salvation and moral, spiritual, educational improvement, which naturally implies the improvement of society. It led naturally therefore to Knight's *Old England* and its vision of 'Discovery and Invention' – the title of chapter one of Book VIII, which examines 'The Progress of Society for the Last Hundred Years'. This chapter told its readers that 'we live in a world of wonders' and contrasted eighteenth-century people with the nineteenth-century: 'We have no longer the same modes of life, the same habits of thought and sympathy, and the same bigoted adherence to old and established customs which characterised them'. Modern society was 'more efficient in the arts of living . . . because of the increase in various branches of industry that sustain life. . . . Science, arts, manufactures, inventions and discovery, have all made prodigious strides'. Knight then glanced at the key inventions that had facilitated progress towards 'complete civilisation'. Foremost was the steam-engine, the 'vital principle of our machinery and manufactures'. Next came the railways, which had resulted in 'a general diffusion of . . . information and knowledge' and contributed to the sweeping away of 'old prejudices'.[98]

All kinds of inventions excited and intrigued Kilvert. At one point a carriage of his train had been derailed but, by what he called the 'marvellous implement' of a screw jack, it was lifted back onto the line. His interest in the electric telegraph was even greater and will be dealt with more fully later, but Knight's singling it out as one of the new age's key inventions was probably the start of Kilvert's joy in it. Knight expected his readers to be excited by it, as he himself was: 'Of all the advantages derived from the knowledge of the subtle electric medium, there is none will bear any comparison with the Electric Telegraph'. He also pointed readers to the invention of gas which 'not only lights our streets, dwellings, theatres, churches and workshops, but melts our precious metals, warms our apartments, and cooks our food'. Inevitably, the steam-printing machine – the invention that symbolised the entire revolution in popular publishing and represented both Knight's career and his cause – was appropriately underlined. This machine had produced 'a complete revolution' in the bookselling and publishing trade, he stated.[99]

Marryat's *Masterman Ready* was a seminal influence on Kilvert in much the same way that the way Knight's *Old England* was and for much the same reasons. It offered, as did much of the reading material with which the young Kilvert was surrounded, a combination of instruction and amusement. The novel's concerns and themes will continually surface in chapters that follow. One of its themes – that God provides for Man's needs even in a wilderness – is a corollary of the idea that the universe itself was fashioned by the Great Designer for Man's benefit. Knight and Marryat come together in their exaltation of Man's efforts to tame the wildernesses of the earth via what the former called 'the arts of living that sustain life'.[100] Mr Seagrave embodies this force in his roles as farmer, botanist, and teacher. However, the main embodiment of it is Ready himself, as Mr Seagrave acknowledges after the latter's death: 'What do we not owe to that good man? . . . He provided for our wants, added to our comforts, instructed us how to make best use of our means, was our adviser and . . . protector. . . . What an example of Christian fortitude and humility'.[101] He was in fact the personification of progress, of civilisation. Kilvert never forgot the old sailor chosen to be his role model when he was at his most impressionable. There was perhaps no teacher in his life, apart from uncle Francis, who provided a better example.[102] Marryat's novels, it seems, held meaning for Bodily; certainly they would because of their Evangelical values and explorer/missionary ethos – which is why they held meaning for Kilvert. He and Masterman Ready, Oak and Bodily were all dedicated to usefulness, progress, and enlightenment.

Chapter 2

Nature's Classroom

I knew [our cock] always crowed at midnight and I had the
curiosity to get out of bed and look at my watch to see if he
was true to the time.

Kilvert's Diary

I had climbed up to the water-butt for the purpose of fishing
out of the dirty fluid some of the great larvae and kicking
monsters which made up a large item in my list of wonders.

Charles Kingsley, *Alton Locke*

In the *Leisure Hour*'s science coverage, natural history featured
more than later discoveries in chemistry, physiology, and electro-
magnetism.[1] Sometimes explicitly religious pieces appeared but the
task of its writers was to link their subject matter to Christianity
and this involved adopting a pervasive 'Christian tone.'[2] The article,
'Curiosities of Sound' (12 November 1857) provides a good example
of how this was managed. The writer stated that his purpose was 'to
note down some of the curiosities of sound occurring within our own
experience, or received on testimony which we can trust', emphases
which typify the empirical and rational standpoint of *The Leisure
Hour*. He continued:

> While meditating on the government of God in the material
> world we have sometimes wondered whether it lie within
> his plan that each sense in turn is to be aided and perfected
> by science; and whether, in some future age, when the eye
> shall have mastered all the wonders of minute and far-off
> creation, the ear shall be taught to discover sounds of which
> now it can form no notion.

The Kilvert children could hardly have escaped natural history because
all classes of society were influenced by it from the 1820s to the 1860s.
Barber called it 'a national obsession' and said that its germ lay 'in the
mood and taste of the times'. The reasons for it were that it was not studied
at school so people came to it fresh, it was 'useful' as science was, and

the kind of 'rational amusement' (i.e. one with educational/moral value) which Victorians pursued avidly. It was seen to develop important qualities of mind and character, a wholesome filler of leisure time. It also fitted in with 'the contemporary mania for forming collections'. Mothers, in particular, were encouraged to interest their children in it for the very good reason that it was *religious*: 'Natural theology made the study of natural history . . . almost a pious duty'.[3] Natural history was considered especially suitable for children and the working class.[4]

Mary Howitt
author of *The Children's Year*

The account given by Emily Kilvert of the Kilvert children's upbringing gives the clearest possible indication of sensibilities nurtured by interest in natural objects. In this, the influence of both Kilvert parents (and, as will be argued later, of the children's uncle Francis) was decisive. It has already been noted that Mrs Kilvert introduced her family to Mary Howitt's *The Children's Year*, in which nature is seen as the great educator. The book was probably a present from Mrs Kilvert to her daughter Emily and its influence on her was enormous. 'I was always very fond of living creatures of all kinds,' Emily wrote, 'especially frogs and toads. I shall never forget my first sight of a frog's leg under the magnifying glass shown us children . . . ' (the reference to the magnifying glass shows that scientific study was encouraged from the beginning). She had been encouraged to focus on the 'curiosities' represented by natural objects. This was true of the toads and newts which lived at the bottom of the space in which the cellar window of the Hardenhuish school-room was placed. The newts had, she said, 'beautiful orange and black spotted stomachs which were my great admiration'.[5] The viewpoint here is that which characterises so many *Leisure Hour* articles: scientific observation combined with a sense of wonder.

The *Leisure Hour* article quoted earlier looked towards the time when the microscope and the telescope would allow the human eye to perceive 'minute' and 'far-off' wonders. Science's role in this amazing increase in human potential, fulfilling a divine plan, far from undermining our sense of wonder, actually enhanced it. Holmes has explained in detail how the idea of 'a permanent, instinctive, deep-seated antagonism between Romantic poetry and science' was formed on 'one signal occasion'. At a dinner party in December 1817, attended by Wordsworth, Lamb and Keats, was the painter Benjamin Haydon, whose large partly-finished painting *Christ's entry into Jerusalem*, was being celebrated. Conversation, increasingly lively and drunken, concentrated on the theme of Reason versus the Imagination. The painting portrayed Newton as the representative of analytical science. Keats observed that Newton had 'destroyed all the poetry of the rainbow, by reducing it to a prism'. He was referring to the scientist's experiment of passing a ray of sunlight through a prism, separating it into its different colours, and proving that white light was a mixture of them all. That this was not an exercise in disenchantment is forcefully underlined by Holmes:

> In fact the point of the experiment was that when the separated rainbow colours were *individually* passed through a second prism, they did *not* revert to white sunlight, but remained true colours. . . . The rainbow was *not* a mere scientific trick of the glass prism. It genuinely and beautifully existed in nature, through the natural prism of raindrops, although paradoxically it took a human eye to see it, and every human eye saw it differently. . . . Newton had actually *increased* the potential 'poetry of the rainbow' . . .

Keats, who had had two years of medical training by the time of the 1817 dinner, was likely to have known the details of Newton's experiment but, in that company, was disposed to be provocative. Holmes also emphasised that if Coleridge or Shelley, who were fired by science, had been at the dinner, the conversation would have 'taken a rather different tack'.[6]

Holmes did acknowledge that Keats had attacked the 'demystifying' aspects of science in his *Lamia* (1820), where he wrote:

> Do not all charms fly
> At the mere touch of cold philosophy?
> There was an awful rainbow once in heaven:
> We know her woof, her texture; . . . Philosophy will clip an
> Angel's wings,
> Conquer all mysteries by rule and line,
> . . . Unweave a rainbow.

The eminent historian of science, Richard Dawkins, has made the challenge of Keats's last line the theme of his book *Unweaving the Rainbow*, which argues in favour of 'good poetic science'. To him, scientists and poets come together in their celebration of wonder:

The feeling of awed wonder that science can give us is one of the highest experiences of which the human psyche is capable. It is a deep aesthetic passion to rank with the finest that music and poetry can deliver. . . . Science is, or ought to be, the inspiration for great poetry.[7]

Dawkins rejected Keats's assertion that 'cold philosophy' destroyed nature's wonders, insisting that 'Mysteries do not lose their poetry when solved. Quite the contrary; the solution often turns out more beautiful than the puzzle'.[8]

Emily Kilvert's response to natural objects – personal, passionate, aesthetic – is typical of the natural history books of the period, which set out to arouse *wonder*: '"Wonder and Curiosity" – two words that set the tone for Victorian natural history'.[9] Lorraine Daston, in her article *Curiosity in Early Modern Science*, explored the incidence in this period of the words 'curiosity' and 'wonder'. She set out 'to analyze the emotional restructuring of early modern curiosity, and to show how this new-style curiosity shaped both the objects and subjects of early modern science'. She found that 'the word "curious" at once betokened a state of mind; a quality of things; and a kind of person; a sensibility of curiosity . . . united all three usages'.[10] Kilvert had this sensibility. Furthermore, the idea of probing objects to learn their hidden qualities, which was a feature of this sensibility, is frequently found in his poems. For example, he recommended, in *A Pageant*, that the person of 'humble soul shall find/ A world of wonder on his vision rise' provided he had a 'holy mind' able to see that 'old things are new, and common things [are] dear' (chapter one noted that Charles Knight urged his readers to recognise that 'we live in a world of wonders').

This notion of treasures deeply hidden is significant. In the eighteenth century, curiosity was excited by the rare, extravagant and precious, and collections of such objects were housed in the 'cabinets of curiosities' of wealthy men.[11] Increasingly, curiosity focused on 'the hidden secrets of nature bespeaking the privilege of knowledge'. Daston noted that, in the transition from 'cabinets of curiosities' to serious study, it was never clear which natural objects merited scientific investigation; but the idea of their giving access to nature's 'secrets' was strong. Objects could give insight into nature's *causes*. 'Wonder, aroused by the ignorance of causes, engaged the curiosity of the puzzled observer, and was thus the fountainhead of science'.[12] Let O'Connor's be the final word in this brief examination of the notion of 'curiosity' that Kilvert inherited: '"curiosity" [was] a word which, in the early nineteenth century, implied a much greater emotional and intellectual investment than it does today'.[13]

Emily Kilvert's mother's youngest sister Sarah had emigrated to
Canada and was the source of more 'curiosities' (referred to as such
by Emily) entering the lives of the Kilvert children. Emily told of such
'curiosities' sent from Canada as a round flat cake made of maple
sugar and 'a squashed mosquito carefully folded up in a bit of foreign
newspaper'. She also remembered in a nearby field 'a curious pond
with a kind of tidal wave in it at certain times of the day'.[14] Annual
picnics were a feature of the lives of Emily and her siblings, in company
with the pupils of their father's school, and these too were the means
of teaching and learning. Castle Combe was a favourite location and
Emily recalled the 'large anthills [with] very large and fierce black
ants'.[15] Sometimes the summer picnics were to Slaughterford or the
grounds of Bowood, where the Kilvert family had permission to
walk.[16] An autumn excursion yielded a collection of 'little grey and
black caterpillars' as well as blackberries. Summer holidays took them
to Sidmouth, Dawlish, Teignmouth, and Clevedon. The children made
a collection of pebbles 'picked up on Clevedon beach'.

Particularly revealing of Emily's attitude towards the beauties of
nature is the way she preserved 'skeins of silkworm's silk' in a copy
of Henry Kirke White's poems, a present to her from a Hardenhuish
school pupil; it was, she noted, 'a beautiful copy full of steel
engravings'.[17] Though she claimed she never read it, the choice of
it by a pupil is a guide to the interests and values encouraged at the
school. One of the tutors employed there was a Mr Wyncoll and she
remembered him: 'I still have a set of flower cards he gave me; they
were yellow with a perforated border and the names of the flowers
on each card in his beautiful handwriting'.[18] The tutor's gift is also a
true reflection of the ethos of Hardenhuish school. Emily's account of
life there evokes a childhood in which observation of natural objects
was a planned element. These included ponies, dogs, cats, rabbits, and
birds kept at Hardenhuish. As she noted, the Kilvert children had few
toys; the curiosities and delights provided by nature were the preferred
substitute. Play and recreation were thus merged with learning, which
was the message enshrined in *The Leisure Hour's* subtitle: 'A Family
Journal of Instruction and Recreation'.

Many of the Howitts' books fulfilled the same purposes as *The
Leisure Hour* and their own short-lived *Howitt's Journal*. In addition
to instruction, information, and entertainment, they contained poetry,
imaginative stories, and natural theology. Most of these elements are to
be found in Emily Kilvert's account of her Hardenhuish childhood. The
account given by Mary Howitt in *The Children's Year* of the activities
that occupied her children parallels Emily's in so many ways that it is

not over-fanciful to imagine her parents, but especially her mother, applying its messages in a general way to her upbringing and that of her siblings. Mary Howitt's children's year began on 8 January 1845 and her book was published in 1847. Thus during the early childhood of Kilvert (born 1840) and of his sister Emily (born 1842), *The Children's Year* would have been a quite recent publication. The first keynote struck by its author is the importance of actual experience (the quality that made Bodily's St Helena lecture satisfying): 'everything in the book is true'. Though the Howitts' childhood home was on the edge of London, they owned a piece of land at the bottom of their garden with meadows beyond so that, Mary emphasised, 'it was quite a country prospect'. It is as though, as a country-loving Victorian, she sought to reassure herself that the great spreading metropolis had not yet engulfed her home. The younger Howitt children were Meggy and Herbert, the older ones Alfred and Mary. Early in the book, we are told that 'Meggy liked natural history of all kinds' and she is presented very much as a child of nature like Emily Kilvert.

   On winter evenings, when rambles among 'nature's curiosities' were impossible, the Howitt children, like the Kilvert children, had books to extend their experience and to whet their appetites for real exploration.[19] Coincidentally, but importantly, the Howitts, like the Kilverts, had relatives in North America. Mary Howitt's younger sister Emma had emigrated to Ohio and Mary wrote a book, *Our Cousins in Ohio*, based on Emma's experiences. Similarities of outlook with regard to education, the natural world, science, and the proper progressive and religious goals of human life, may be seen between the Howitt family and the family of Charles Darwin in the reading material they favoured. Darwin's grandfather, Erasmus, endorsed Rousseau's approach to education with its emphasis on learning about and through nature, and on personal experience instead of second-hand learning. Darwin was brought up by his elder sisters, who were great admirers of Pestalozzi, in whose work learning through observation and experience were central principles. Darwin's insistence on industriousness as a prime virtue to hold up before the young was fostered partly by the interest he took in emigration and life in the colonies. Accordingly, he bought a copy of Mary Howitt's *Our Cousins in Ohio* for his children. It was 'another life' to talk about with them.[20] The Howitt parents used Captain Marryat's *The Settlers in Canada* (1844) for the same purposes: it was a means of setting their children thinking about how they would cope with the challenges and privations of frontier life.[21] At this time *Masterman Ready* was also being read to the Howitt children and it became their favourite.

   As a resource for her children, Mrs Kilvert not only had *The Settlers in Canada* which, though fictional, was based on Marryat's own sojourn around the Great Lakes 1837-1839, but also the actual experiences in letters from her sister Sarah, who had married Herbert Griffith, 'one of the many sons of Dr Griffith of Elm Rectory'.[22] The couple were in Canada between the mid-1840s and mid-1850s.[23] The Kilvert family viewed Sarah's emigration through the prism of Marryat's account, as emerges in Emily Kilvert's reference to her aunt as 'a Settler in Canada'. Sarah's husband had his way to make in the world and was caught up in 'the great tide of emigration [that] flowed westward' from 1830, as Susanna Moodie put it in her *Roughing it in the Bush* (1852). Emily knew Moodie's book, referring to some 'pretty verses' in it. Moodie, née Strickland (1803-1885), was British born, with strong Anglican roots though she attended a Congregational chapel. *Roughing it* was highly controversial because of its attacks on newspapers which advertised rich prospects in Canada while concealing the hardships and on 'dealers in wild lands' for exploiting public credulity. Canada became, she wrote, 'the great land-mark for the rich in hope and poor in purse. . . . A Canada mania pervaded the middle ranks of British society'.[24]

Emigration to Canada had continuing significance for the Kilvert family. Richard Kilvert, one of Kilvert's uncles, had emigrated there in the early 1820s. Kilvert referred also to 'my first cousin', Francis Edwin Kilvert who, he was proud to recall, had become by December 1878 'Mayor and Member for Hamilton'.[25] The Kilverts were in a perpetual state of anxiety about the prospects of aunt Sarah and her family in the wilds of Canada: 'There was much rejoicing when the emigrants returned to England', Emily wrote. Mrs Kilvert sent boxes of useful things to her sister to ease her spartan life.[26] Sarah's family, like the Campbell family of Marryat's story (published just as Sarah arrived in Canada), were facing 'a great and undeveloped continent'[27] with all its dangers and hardships. Mr Campbell is a doctor ('of course, he was brought up to a profession') and is left a large fortune, but loses it and his country estate when another claimant appears. The parallel with the Kilvert family is strong because it lost its business and its funds in a Bath bank. Robert Kilvert told how, after his father's death, 'it became needful that all of us who were of an age to do so should set to work' (Richard Kilvert left for Canada at this time).[28] Similarly, when the Campbell loss of fortune comes, Mrs Campbell tells her husband that their children 'must work. Employment is happiness'. Alfred, one of the Campbell sons, proposes they move to Canada where land was cheap. The drawbacks were, he said, 'hard labour, occasional privation, a log-hut, severe winter, isolation . . . dangers of wild beasts and savages'.[29]

That this is to be a story about education is clear at the outset. The

Campbell family is assessed on its capacity to learn in the face of the challenges ahead: '[the family] was now about to leave civilisation – to isolate themselves in the Canadian woods – to trust to their own resources'. New skills must be acquired, prompting Henry, the eldest son, to observe that his Oxford education was 'not likely to be useful'. Felling trees was not part of that education.[30] Mrs Campbell sums it up: 'We must not here put the value upon a finished education which we used to do . . . the most important knowledge is to learn to gain our livelihoods'. Mr Campbell stresses that their success will depend on having 'a lively faith'. Their faith is strongly Evangelical as becomes clear when the parents console themselves about their son Percival, who was lost in a snowstorm, He had died 'before he had lived to be corrupted by the world'.[31]

Kilvert showed his relish for placing this kind of literature before the young by making presents of books by R.M. Ballantyne (1825-1894). He gave *The Young Fur Traders* (1856), set in Canada, and *The Gorilla Hunters* (1861) to the sons of one of his friends. The theme of self-help and self-improvement is reiterated in both. In *The Gorilla Hunters* we are told that 'Trials, when endured in the proper spirit, improve our moral nature'.[32] Paul Turner drew attention to the educational aims of Ballantyne's books, noting how the preface of his *The Coral Island* (1858) promised 'valuable information, much pleasure, great profit and unbounded amusement'. The information, Turner observed, was 'mostly about natural history, geology and anthropology',[33] the staple diet of *The Leisure Hour*. That this was a deliberate policy among children's writers of the period was acknowledged in a *Quarterly Review* article of 1860: 'At present so many ingenious devices have been discovered for insinuating moral or scientific truths into story-books . . . a conversation of some children with their papa is too often only the prelude to a conversation on chemistry'.[34]

The moral lessons of *The Children's Year*, often drawn from natural theology, are invariably overt. We are told that God is 'the Great Head Gardener; He clothes the lily in all its beauty, and cares for the poor little sparrows. . . . This was a little lesson. Meggy understood every word of it, and endeavoured to profit by it'. She is told by her sister Mary that 'by care and attention her own nature might be like a beautiful garden'. Each season in the book brings fresh opportunities for discovery. In spring, when Mary Howitt's children 'spent many hours each day in the garden', they studied rooks: 'they often stood and watched them for a long time together, and they saw how they went on'. Meggy studied the many sparrows which nested in the ivy on the back of her house. The focus of Herbert's attention during the summer were the bees that nested in an old wall. 'He stood for an hour at a time to watch them and learned many things *by his own observation*'. What he was learning was the interdependence of 'mason bees who worked very industriously. . . . ' He also 'studied with great interest a colony of ants'. In addition 'he was very glad to have a live bird in his hand: to see its beak, its eyes, its breast, its little legs – to know really what it was like'.[35] The last emphasis indicates the seriousness of the learning involved.

If the focus predominantly on Meggy in *The Children's Year* helped Emily Kilvert to feel the book was written specially for her, Kilvert may well have believed that William Howitt's *The Boy's Country Book* (1839) was peculiarly his own. 'Country knowledge,' wrote William, 'is the peculiar property of all boys – knowledge of all sorts of sports, mischief, climbing, rabbit-keeping, birds'-nesting, fishing. . . . '[36] His book encompassed a wide variety of other kinds of knowledge, with a steady emphasis on, and a deep respect for, practical tasks: he and his friends 'haunted the joiner's shop' and the blacksmith's forge.[37] His long description of the coal pits of the district have all the concerns and the emphases found in *Leisure Hour* articles. The words 'curiosity' and 'wonder' recur frequently in Howitt's account of childhood experiences, as they do in *The Children's Year*'s account of those of his children.[38] This interest in practical details is combined with a respect for the men who are masters of the practical and dangerous tasks of coal-mining. A theme of the whole Howitt passage is exaltation of Britain's industrial progress: 'Steam-engines of stupendous power are there continually at work, bringing up to the surface the coals that supply not only that part of the kingdom, but the vast city of London . . . and many other lands'. Howitt even singled out as 'the most beautiful and wonderful sight of all' the arrangement by which wagons ran to the end of a railway line where they were lowered to the decks of waiting ships to discharge their coal.[39]

The Boy's Country Book is permeated, like Knight's *Old England*, by a pride in England and its people as an industrious, capable, manufacturing race. There was an old man in Howitt's village, too old to be employed, but 'ever and anon, manufacturing' all the practical things (nut-crackers, mouse-traps) that people needed.[40] A 'retired iron master, Christopher Bancks', was admired by Kilvert's father for being just such 'an ingenious mechanist', who used to make 'all sorts of contrivances for home use', for example 'a pair of tin overshoes, to keep his feet dry'.[41] Ingenuity was the message of countless articles in *The Leisure Hour*. It was implicit too in the busy, practical world of the Dillwyns of Swansea. An important part of that message was the need for *energy* and determination. When Kilvert contrasted on 23

October 1872 the industrial city of Bristol with Bath and exulted in the former's 'life, movement and work . . . instead of the idle lounge', he was endorsing Howitt's outlook. He was also echoing John Britton's forthright statement about the two cities:

they are singularly dissimilar in all their characteristics . . . as if belonging to different nations, and different races of people. Bath seems to be adapted for, and accepted by, the gay and the idle, the old and the invalid, . . . it has nothing of sea-port, or factory, or trade in its whole area.[42]

Kilvert's *Honest Work* poem celebrated, *inter alia*, Man's capacity to produce useful things, improvements, progress.

The review above of the themes of Howitt's *The Boy's Country Book* and of the part it played in shaping Kilvert's upbringing and outlook can usefully culminate in examining that book's central statements on nature and natural history. It is important to underline that they were of a piece – love of the one led to love of the other, and ultimately to love of science (and, of course, all reflected love of God). Howitt noted that children who lived in the country had the chance of acquiring 'a great and familiar knowledge of [Nature]'. He continued:

There is no part of natural history, whether it be botany, entomology or the pursuit of birds or other creatures, but has this one great advantage – it leads you into every part of the country at its most agreeable seasons; and opens your eyes and your hearts to what is going on in its more secret recesses. You are led away into green valleys, through woods and heaths, up into the mountains; and everywhere the charms of nature sink deep and imperceptibly into your soul.[43]

If these words appeared in a preface to *Kilvert's Diary* they would be entirely in keeping with the rest of his writing and this is true even about the reference to 'natural history'; a corollary of the picture presented of the diarist here is that we should regard him as a naturalist, as well as an imaginative writer. His naturalist bent manifests itself in his interest in and feel for the whole range of natural things, and in his close observation and precise description of them. Darwin borrowed William Howitt's *The Boy's Country Book* from the London Library to read to his daughter Annie, partly because it encouraged these activities.[44]

The Kilvert children had learned to love archaeology from their antiquarian uncle Francis, who had dubbed John Britton in a poem as the father of British archaeology.[45] The poem's theme is that no matter what fame or wealth a man's career has brought, he is always happy to return to his humble beginnings. Typically, *The Leisure Hour* featured an article on Britton for his was the classic 'rags-to-riches' story of hard work, suffering, self-help, and eventual triumph: 'The history of Britton's career is, in many respects, remarkable and instructive'. He lacked real genius, special talents, and was 'utterly without patronage or favour . . . yet he raised himself from a menial position to a respectable rank in society'. His father was a poor man and John had only a rudimentary education, but always loved reading and managed to buy, when twelve years old, the *Life of Peter the Great, Robinson Crusoe*, and *Pilgrim's Progress*. They provided him with 'a new world in which his imagination loved to wander'. At sixteen, he was employed by a tavern-keeper in London and spent years in 'a dreary cellar' looking after barrels and bottles. He escaped from the wine-cellar and obtained better-paid and more congenial employment, which gave him more leisure to read. A friend offered him the chance to work on a projected volume, *The Beauties of Wiltshire*, recording its buildings, history, topography, but the work proceeded slowly. Britton in the meantime worked on a new topographical work, *The Beauties of England and Wales*, originally planned as six volumes in 1800, which grew to twenty-five volumes.[46]

The *Leisure Hour* article, in its reference to the three books bought by the 12-year-old Britton, included these details of the circumstances: 'He attended a sale by auction at the "Great House", where the effects of the Squire, who had ruined himself at a gambling house in London, were being sold off'. This was how the boy came by the books that changed his life. These were details beloved of the Religious Tract Society writers who penned the *Leisure Hour* articles: rich landowner, corrupted by idleness and profligacy, forced to sell priceless treasures of knowledge, utilitarian and spiritual, that became the means by which a poor country boy raised himself. Britton told how he acquired the books in the sale of the goods of Squire White 'who had wasted his property in London gaiety and gambling'.[47] At his death, all his estates were put in the hands of trustees, one of whom was Henry Britton, father of John, who owned a shop in Kington St Michael. Britton highlighted his father's industriousness against a background of villagers 'undisciplined, illiterate, and deprived of good example, apart from Mr Coleman, who has been too quiet to interfere'.[48] This 'Mr Coleman' was Kilvert's maternal great-grandfather, whose family had lived for centuries in Kington St Michael. That Britton's ambition was driven by the same vision of social progress that drove the Kilvert family is evident in his contrast of 'man in a state of semi-barbarism, and man enlightened by art, science, and refinement'. It comes as no surprise, therefore, that he regarded Charles Knight as his 'much-esteemed friend', the author of 'many literary works of national utility and influence'.[49]

Thus Britton had significance for the Kilverts on several counts. He came from the same parish as their Coleman ancestors; he was an antiquary and topographer; he stood for individual and social progress; and he saw Charles Knight as his ally. We cannot be sure whether the Kilvert family knew, from the *Leisure Hour* article or other sources, the origin of the books that set the young Britton on the path to learning and fame but it is a story that would have had great resonance for them, marking him out as a local hero and of special interest to Evangelicals. Britton's influence, as both an archaeologist and antiquarian and as a moral exemplar, was channelled through uncle Francis and Robert Kilvert to all the Kilvert children. Kilvert's father recalled how a room in his grandmother's house in Widcombe, Bath, 'inaugurated [his] taste for archaeological literature', because it was there that he had access to 'the earlier numbers of Britton's *Beauties of England and Wales*'.[50] Britton's volumes were a source of Kilvert's knowledge of the countryside.[51]

Mary Howitt's *The Children's Year* also fed Emily Kilvert's interest in topography. The title of chapter 31 of the book – 'How the children make an excursion into the country and what they saw' – is fully representative of the writer's stance towards natural history, topography, and antiquities. The chapter focuses on visits to Hastings and the adjacent coast, which provided experiences pictured as key moments in the children's learning. A review of the cruelties of the Middle Ages is used to encourage the children to have faith in the idea of moral progress: 'Herbert and Meggy for the first time began to rejoice in the belief that the world is mending. People would not dare to do such things in England now'.[52] The idea of moral (and industrial and scientific) progress was a favourite one of the Howitts; the title of their own journal was *Howitt's Journal of Literature and Popular Progress*. It is also a steady theme of *The Leisure Hour*.

A very strong imaginative dimension permeates the passage in which Herbert experiences what it is like being a scientist discovering a new species. 'Was it a fish or a land animal? It had such a quantity of legs ... it might be a duck-bill platypus'. This latter idea is discarded. Then perhaps, Herbert suggested, 'it was quite a new kind of creature which nobody had ever seen before'. He is not cast down when an old man tells him it is a sea-mouse because this provokes him into a new idea: he had heard in Germany stories of sea-cats and he fancies 'the sea-cat lying in wait for the funny little sea-mouse. It was quite a poetical idea, and *was very interesting to him*'.[53] Herbert's imagination was seeing other connections, other possibilities, making sense of new experiences: it was the method of all true learning. Dawkins emphasised its importance in scientific study:

Science at its best should leave room for poetry. It should note helpful analogies and metaphors that stimulate the imagination, conjure in the mind images and allusions that go beyond the needs of straightforward understanding.[54]

Again, it is both relevant and illuminating to make a comparison with Charles Darwin, who 'remembered his pleasure as a ten-year-old child "walking along the beach . . . and seeing the gulls and cormorants wending their way home". He was surprised to realise how early in his life he had first experienced "such poetic pleasures, felt so keenly in after years"'. In this passage, Randal Keynes underlined the links that Darwin had seen Wordsworth making between poetry and science in his Preface to the *Lyrical Ballads* (it is one of the arguments in this book's analysis of the elements which influenced Kilvert's understanding that he too had assimilated the poet's arguments in that Preface).[55] Wordsworth's words about the pleasure of imagination are worth quoting: 'the Poet, prompted by this feeling of pleasure . . . converses with general nature, with affections akin to those which . . . the Man of science has raised up in himself. The knowledge both of the Poet and of the Man of science is pleasure'. The pleasurable imaginative connections which Herbert made between one facet of his experience and another is a perfect illustration of the process of knowing shared by poet and scientist.

Darwin's experience of nature as a child and as a scientist has similarities to that of Kilvert. The two men are united in their reverence of Wordsworth. It has already been suggested that the poet's writings, mediated through uncle Francis of Claverton Lodge, were a formative influence on the diarist. *Kilvert's Diary and Landscape* has shown that Kilvert's knowledge of Wordsworth was both detailed and profound. Nothing is more illustrative of the accord between diarist and poet than their attitude to memory, particularly memories of natural phenomena that had special importance. Such memories Wordsworth called 'spots of time', moments of 'renovating virtue, whence . . . our minds are nourished and . . . repaired'.[56] They became part of one's consciousness, of one's identity. Levine, in his revaluation of Darwin, identified 'spots of time' with 'moods of enchantment . . . moments that, while they can be relatively rare in one's life, fill it with meaning and value'.[57] Appalled by the idea that Darwin had banished mystery and magic from the natural world by remorseless analysis and rationalisation, Levine argued that Darwin's writing, informed as it is by 'intense love of nature', actually opens up hidden *wonders*: 'For Darwin, the project of establishing the theory of evolution by natural selection was not so much the affirmation of a mindless and Godless world, as the revelation that we walk in the midst of wonders'.[58]

In his notion of 'enchantment', Levine was influenced by Jane Bennett,[59] who wrote: 'To be enchanted is to be is to be struck and shaken by the extraordinary that lives amid the familiar and the everyday'.[60] *Kilvert's Diary* is full of entries in which he records moments when he was shaken by extraordinary experiences among the ordinary and, as discussed earlier, formulated a philosophy built on them. A notable example is the sight he had of the Black Mountains whose snow-capped tops were caught in a burst of sunshine: 'I could have cried with the excitement of the overwhelming spectacle . . . it seemed to me as if I might never see such a sight again'.[61] His experience corresponds precisely to that which Bennett called 'enchanted': 'The mood I'm calling enchanted involves . . . a surprising encounter' that contains 'the pleasurable feeling of being charmed by the novel and as yet unprocessed encounter'.[62] It is a striking fact that Kilvert habitually and consciously expressed his most powerful experiences of nature in terms of 'enchantment'. At Restormel Castle in Cornwall, for example, he enjoyed its weird, sombre atmosphere, adding: 'Happily we were uninterrupted and the *spell* was unbroken, and the *charm* remains, and will remain'.[63] Other entries reiterate the 'enchantment' idea: 'Above the young larch plantation the fairy valley opened suddenly like enchantment. . . . '; 'I came down through the fold into the enchanted dingle'; 'Sweet Glasbury . . . a bright enchantment over all. . . . '[64] His most explicit statement of enchantment as a response to natural scenery is the entry referring to his first visit to Aberedw, where the Wye is overlooked by strange rock bastions: 'every step was through an enchanted land . . . there was a glamour and enchantment'. When he stated of this experience 'I was discovering a new country', he did not simply mean it was a country (i.e. of the Wye Valley) new to him, though it was, but that its special beauty was apprehended as a transcendental moment, a moment when he was inducted into an inner, *hidden* world of magic and intensity.[65]

In *The Children's Year*, Kilvert had met with passages in which Mary Howitt conveyed moments of enchantment. One particular passage from Mary Howitt's book stands out. The children become aware during an outing of 'low sweet music, which, if it had been moonlight, [they] might have fancied it a revel of the fairies'. The music came from a flock of sheep on a hillside, each of which wore a little bell, 'which sent forth the most musical cadence, low and liquid'. Meggy likened the effect to '*the music [that] was heard through a magnifying glass*'. Captivated, the children sit there listening 'for a long time'.[66] Meggy's phrase about the music's effect epitomises the idea that scientific discovery or learning is often accompanied by imaginative insight and imaginative pleasure. Levine made this idea an important factor in revaluing Darwin: a close reading of his writing 'can put us in touch with the possibility of the blending of reason and feeling . . . and with the wonders of the ordinary movements of nature'. Darwin's writing, in Levine's view, 'infuses the world with value' and 'combines fact and value', rationality and imagination.[67]

The shaping influence of *The Children's Year* on the Kilvert children can be better understood by seeing it in relation to other contemporary natural history publications for the young. Arabella Buckley was born in Brighton in 1840, the same year as Kilvert. She was hired by the geologist Sir Charles Lyell as his secretary in 1864, a post she held until 1875, enabling her to mix with leading scientists and have exposure to scientific ideas of the time. Her first publication, *A Short History of Natural Science* (1876) won Darwin's praise. She collected one set of her popularising lectures into *The Fairy-Land of Science* (1879). In the first lecture she staked her claim to science as a 'fairy-land': 'most of you probably look upon science as a bundle of dry facts, while fairy-land is beautiful, and full of poetry and imagination. But . . . science is full of beautiful pictures, of real poetry, and of wonder-working fairies'.[68] She was expressing the view of natural history engendered in the Kilvert children, the best moments of which were characterised in terms of enchantment. Throughout her book, Buckley equated natural phenomena with 'fairies', 'more wonderful, more magical' than those found in fairy tales, and her aim was to open people's eyes to 'these forces or fairies', to induce them to ask 'How all this is done?' Her conception was, as Kilvert's was, essentially Wordsworthian. Imagination was basic to it, as was the retention by adults of 'that childish clearness of vision, which enables us through the temporal things which are seen, to realise those eternal truths which are unseen'.[69]

Buckley's approach to science has further relevance to Kilvert's. She was a child of the vicarage, as he was, and like him was influenced by natural theology. Scientific curiosity had as its long-term aim, she declared, understanding that 'The forces of nature . . . are one and all the voice of the Great Creator'. Her object in teaching science to the young was the same as that of Kilvert's mother and his uncle Francis: 'even the little child who lives with nature . . . must rise in some sense or other through nature up to nature's God'.[70] In treating aspects of science other than botany, Buckley was unusual among women writers. Her guide as a populariser of science was Professor John Tyndall, to whom she referred several times.[71] He was also Kilvert's guide, as will be shown later. Buckley's 'fairy forces' of nature (e.g. heat, electricity, gravity) were accessible to children through observation – they must 'open their eyes'.

It is unlikely that Kilvert knew Buckley's book because it appeared in 1879, the year he died, but he might have known of her lectures that began in 1876 and of her first book (also 1876). His childhood experience may have included the publications of Mrs Gatty (1807 – 1873) because they mirrored closely both the values and the publishing environment in which he and his siblings were raised. Mrs Gatty was another daughter of the vicarage and had married the clergyman and antiquary, Alfred Gatty. 'Margaret Gatty's *Parables from Nature* would soon be in every nursery', Thwaite wrote in her biography of Tennyson's wife, who was a close friend of Mrs Gatty. She was referring to the mid-1850s.[72] Mrs Gatty conceived a passion for marine biology, especially seaweeds, and embarked on a writing career that embraced fairy stories, moral tales, and books of natural history. Her *Aunt Judy's Tales* (1859) and *Domestic Pictures and Tales* (1865) reflect the same world as Mrs Howitt's *The Children's Year*. Mrs Gatty brought out *Parables from Nature* in five series between 1855 and 1871. The *Parable*, 'The Light of Truth', is fully representative of the book's natural theology stance: 'The laws of Nature, which are the acted will of God, work together . . . for a good end. And it is given to us, both as a privilege and a pleasure to search them out . . . whilst we admire the wonders of the great Creator'.[73] In all the *Parables* is found the steady emphasis on the value of applying reason to nature's problems and mysteries that characterises *The Children's Year* and *The Fairy-Land of Science*.

The popularity of Mrs Gatty's book led her publisher, George Bell, to launch *Aunt Judy's Magazine* with her as editor. Its mix of stories, poems, natural history, and miscellaneous articles made it the equivalent of *The Playmate*, a book given to Emily Kilvert by her godmother, Mrs Hare. This was such a favourite that Emily said it was 'nearly worn out with reading'.[74] The book – its full title was *The Playmate: a pleasant companion for spare hours* (1847) – was by Joseph Cundall, who was also its publisher. Like *Aunt Judy's Magazine*, it was a monthly, though its run lasted only one year. Cundall had a varied career in publishing. He ran a children's lending library in 1848 and published stories, heroic tales, history and religious books for children. In 1852 he was one of the founder members of the Photographic Society of London and throughout the 1850s produced books of photographs.[75] Pictures were very important to Emily Kilvert, as they were to Cundall. He promised readers 'pictures such as a playmate has seldom offered you before'. Those in *The Playmate* were supplied by the Dalziel brothers, George (1815-1902) and Edward (1817-1905), who were in demand by several publishers.[76] *The Playmate* opens with this address to the reader: 'Let us take a quiet stroll along the meadows. . . . And I will unfold the wondrous marvels that are found in faerie land . . . and the greater marvels that are discovered in the wide domains of Nature'.[77] *The Playmate* featured a series of articles entitled 'The Natural History of Birds', a series of 'Historical Sketches', an article on cats, and 'Thoughts of the Little Star-Gazer' by the Rev. C.H.H. Buckley.

Kilvert too had a fond memory of a book from his childhood: 'Went to [Clyro] Vicarage . . . and got for myself my old favourite the "Settlers at Home".'[78] He was referring to a story by Harriet Martineau (1802-1876), one in a series called *The Playfellow* (1841) that had been requested, funded, and published by Charles Knight. *The Settlers at Home* concerns the Linacres, a family of Dutch Protestants who have settled at the time of the Civil War in the Isle of Axholme, Lincolnshire. Originally a swamp, it had been drained to support farms. The children of the family live close to nature, participating in their parents' commercial activities. Mr Linacre supplied local farmers with manure made of ground-up gypsum,[79] while his wife sold water from a mineral spring to sick people. The need to seek 'honest maintenance' is urged on the Linacre children who, though young, 'were not too young to have a great deal to do'. All their activities give the story the feel of the outdoor adventure stories, by such writers as Captain Marryat and R.M. Ballantyne, which Kilvert enjoyed. The authentic detail of those writers is a characteristic of Martineau's *Playfellow* stories.

As a result of the flooding of the Isle, Martineau's characters are isolated from civilisation amid nature, as those of Marryat and Ballantyne are. This gives the story topographical interest, reinforced by a lengthy passage near the end which connects with the culture of curiosity and observation that was so important in Kilvert's upbringing. The words 'curiosity' and 'wonder' recur frequently in the tale. The Linacre children hear that a 'gentleman of science', the Earl of Arundel, often visited the area to find 'curiosities', and his castle is said to be full of 'wonderful things'. The children have to find a suitable place to bury their infant brother George and they discover that their chosen place is 'already a place of the dead'. Roger finds in the earth his own 'curiosity' – 'a mummy – a human body . . . buried for hundreds and thousands of years'. Another boy explains, in this focus on a natural phenomenon, the preserving power of peat water.[80] A later chapter will show that Kilvert had an interest in ancient relics which could have had its origin in such stories. An additional aspect worth noting about *The Settlers at Home* is that Kilvert's knowledge of it was an example of Charles Knight's influence on his childhood reading.

It was the view of natural history contained in *The Children's Year*, *The Playmate*, and *The Settlers at Home* that informed Kilvert's attitudes to children, those who were his parishioners and those he taught. The influence on him of the great Swiss educationist Pestalozzi (1746-1827) will be examined in more detail later. At present, the link between Rousseau's and Pestalozzi's view of child-nature will simply be noted. Pestalozzi was born in Zurich, famous then for embracing Enlightenment philosophy, including Rousseau's *Émile*. Pestalozzi too was 'a pioneer in the study of child-nature',[81] and in his educational philosophy, as in Rousseau's, the idea of nature is central: 'I wish to entrust [education] to the eternal powers of nature herself', he wrote.[82] This involved, as it did for Mary Howitt, seeing the infant mind as a plant to be nurtured: 'The fundamental principle of Pestalozzi's method of education [is] the analogy between the moral/intellectual development of man and the physical development of the plant'.[83]

There was another writer, apart from Mary Howitt, on whom Mrs Kilvert founded her child-rearing methods – Grace Aguilar (1816-1847), whose *Home Influence* and *A Mother's Recompense* were remembered 'very well' by Kilvert's sister Emily because their mother read these novels to her children on 'weekday evenings'.[84] Mary Howitt and Grace Aguilar were close friends, a further example of the links that existed between so many of Kilvert's 'teachers'. Furthermore, in the 1840s she lived in Brighton, the home of Kilvert's aunt Sarah and of his mentor, the Rev. Frederick Robertson. The preface to her *Home Influence* states that the author intended to illustrate 'the spirit of true piety, especially as it concerned parents and children'.[85] Aguilar was keen to see 'tales read for recreation and enjoyment' utilised in the education of young children to promote piety.[86] Fostering human sympathy, or 'true feeling' as Aguilar called it, was the novel's theme, and again the source is nature. Kilvert's aunt Sophia had also insisted that 'God's *bounteous goodness*, in the natural creation all around us, is our proper theme to our children'.[87]

It is likely that Kilvert's uncle Francis, himself a teacher, had felt he must introduce his nephew to such a significant educationist as Maria Edgeworth (1768-1849). There were local connections between them: Maria's father, Richard Lovell Edgeworth (1744-1817), was born in Bath and she herself stayed with the third Lord Lansdowne at his Bowood home near Calne. The fact that he was descended from Irish peers (the Fitzmaurices of Kerry) was one reason for their friendship.[88] Maria's father Richard, engineer and educationist, was a representative of the Nonconformist educational tradition that advocated utilitarian learning. After a youthful enthusiasm for Rousseau's *Émile*, he turned to the modern syllabus of the chemist (and Unitarian), Joseph Priestley (1773-1804), as part of his study of education that culminated in the writing of his *Practical Education* (1798), a work in which Maria collaborated.[89] She had charge of the education of her many siblings and experimented with teaching techniques. Staying in Clifton with her sister, she told how they were 'running upon the Downs and hunting fossils'.[90] Her own interest in science is seen in her enthusiasm for 'Mr Davy' (Sir Humphrey Davy, 1778-1829, chemist and philosopher), who had made 'discoveries of some importance in science', especially 'wonders that will be performed by certain gases'.[91] This awareness of the way in which science was changing the world was shared by Kilvert, as will be seen. It is important to note that, in addition to Rousseau, Pestalozzi had played a part in the evolution of her educational ideas. While staying in Switzerland, she visited his school at Yverdon: 'he recognised me and I him', she wrote, so they had met before this.[92] Pestalozzi is 'the link between Rousseau and the Edgeworths', noted Russell.[93]

At the start of the nineteenth century Maria Edgeworth was the most successful and highly praised novelist in the country. We know that Kilvert had his own copy of one of her story collections – *The Parent's Assistant* (1796). The book may have appeared in the Kilvert children's library on the recommendation of their godmother, Mrs Hare, who loved it – 'a perfect treasure [which] I read and re-read' – when she was young. Kilvert lent his copy to a Clyro girl, Mary Collett, eldest daughter of Samuel Collett of Cabalva Mill. She went to Whitney-on-Wye school and proudly showed Kilvert her school prizes. He underlined on 12 March 1870 that 'she is a very good girl very fond of reading and going to school and devours books'. Perhaps he thought she might become a teacher herself and that *The Parent's Assistant* might be a catalyst. Maria's basic premise in the stories, which were intended to be used in children's education (hence its title), was that they should be enjoyable – a novel approach then. Augustus Hare referred to the stories' 'simplest language . . . wonderful understanding of children'.[94]

In her preface, Maria emphasised the importance of early impressions in the shaping of children's character. The stories are notably realistic ('in real life children inevitably see vice,' she wrote, 'and should not be shocked by its portrayal in stories'). Moral dilemmas are presented dramatically though with excessive moralising.[95] Self-improvement is a steady theme, and in some explicit comments are made on women's role in society.[96] In *The Bracelets* we have the classic Edgeworthian heroine: 'well-educated but gentle, modest, domestic'.[97] And what kind of heroine did Mary Collett become? Alas, not a teacher but – a barmaid! She is listed as such in the 1881 Census, living at New Bridge Street, London, in a hostel for Spiers and Pond employees.[98] Kilvert's loan of *The Parent's Assistant* to Mary was as much the action of a teacher as that of a clergyman, although for him the roles were closely linked. When he handed out books to children they were intended to guide development as well as to entertain. Of course they were highly moral but not overtly devotional.[99] The confidence Kilvert had in his literary judgement is seen in the fact that Maria Edgeworth's books were extremely suspect to some because they lacked religion: 'The omission of religious education brought down on her novels . . . the hostility of the growing forces of Evangelicalism'.[100] She was an orthodox Christian but not greatly pious.

This last point is important because it means she represented for Kilvert something other than piety: she stood for the Enlightenment, reason applied to social and individual ills (though feeling also mattered to her). Importantly too, she was the pre-eminent woman writer, concerned with the cause of women, among the many women writers Kilvert read. The fact that she was Irish also had meaning for him because of his interest in ethnic and racial issues (note his concern with colonial matters, Welsh/English differences, and the nature of Cornish Celts).[101] Irishness linked Maria Edgeworth to Annie Keary (1825-1875), whose novel *Castle Daly* he was enjoying on 30 December 1874. The story is about English and Irish approaches to governing Ireland and therefore owes something to Edgeworth's *Castle Rackrent*.[102] *Castle Daly* has a rich, complex plot, vivid characters, natural dialogue, subtle insights into feelings, and satisfying themes of friendship, loyalty, politics, and love. It is particularly penetrating in its analysis of the limitations and opportunities in the lives of women. *Castle Daly*, like Aguilar's novels, is about the education of a young girl.[103] Annie Keary was a teacher of her siblings as Maria Edgeworth was. She also became governess to three motherless children in the period 1848 to 1854, bringing to their attention 'whatever new thing she learned of insect, bird or flower', and 'She delighted especially in natural history, and in telling stories of its wonders'. She was always interested in the 'child-sphere' inside and outside the home.[104] A great admirer of Charles Kingsley, she enjoyed his 'wonderfully bold' opinions.[105]

Enthusiasm for Kingsley's progressive views reflects Annie's background. She was related to the mercantile, clerical, professional group of middle-class Chippenham people to which the Kilverts belonged, and whose outlook was substantially the same as that of the Fox and Dillwyn families and of those who founded and supported Lit and Phils.[106] Her brother was Alfred Keary, partner in the firm of solicitors Keary, Stokes and Goldney. Annie's and Alfred's father, William Keary, originally from Galway, was

Annie Keary

rector of Bilton near Wetherby, moving later to take up a living in Hull. The Rev. Frederick Robertson, who lived for a time in nearby Beverley, knew the Kearys because he was offered the post of curate to William Keary in Hull.[107] *Kilvert's Diary and Landscape* establishes the fact that Kilvert had close knowledge of Robertson's writings and of his national fame as a preacher. It must be assumed that Kilvert knew of the Robertson/Keary connection and that it increased his respect for the Kearys, whom he and his mother regularly met (for example on 25 May and 30 December 1874). Annie Keary, like Robertson, favoured

the Broad Church School [which] seemed . . . to lift mankind out of the darkness into the light, to give free scope to human sympathies, whose every impulse the young had been taught to condemn by the ascetic evangelical teaching of the past.[108]

In this account of influences shaping Kilvert's outlook and writing, Nonconformity has particular importance because it favoured a modern education that took account of scientific developments and was geared towards vocational training. It was a model that increasingly challenged the traditional gentleman's liberal education, largely in Latin, Greek and mathematics, experienced by Kilvert, his father, and his uncle Francis. In this way, as in so many others, Kilvert was pulled in two different directions. In the group of mainly Shropshire businessmen (that included Kilvert's coachbuilder grandfather) who migrated to Bath in the late eighteenth century were both Quakers and Presbyterians, men proud of being tradesmen and craftsmen, and the kind of education they naturally endorsed was practical and utilitarian. Because the universities and most professions were closed to Quakers, trade and agriculture became their chief occupations.[109] The values of hard, useful work and honest trade were reinforced in Kilvert's mother through her Quaker background and her Moravian education. The motto of her East Tytherton Moravian school, founded by a Quaker, urged pupils to drive 'disorder, discord, idleness' from their behaviour and to strive for 'order' and 'business'. The school's main educational goal, apart from piety, was '*useful*' learning.[110] Furthermore, Moravian educational standards were famously high, with girls' education being accorded the same importance as boys' (this was true also of Quaker schools).[111] In her book *Home Discipline*, Kilvert's Quaker aunt Sophia, to whose influence he was subject as a boarder at her husband's school, had praised the Quakers' 'plain but sound practical education [that] fits them for any station in life'.[112] The sense of wonder that was the Christian's proper stance towards God's world was also an important common denominator of the technology and natural history which were that education's twin dimensions. Both of those dimensions could be sources of enchantment.

This chapter has underlined that for the Kilverts there was a close interdependence between their reading and their lives. This interdependence, which is traced in subsequent chapters, is exemplified most clearly by Marryat's books. The educational vision of the Kilverts was shaped by the experiences in the wild, remote places portrayed in *Masterman Ready* and *The Settlers in Canada*, which enabled one to draw nearer to God. Nature's classroom was the setting in which one learned the arts of living and of actual survival. These lessons also had relevance to the Kilverts' involvement in missionary work, the subject of a later chapter. Some of Kilvert's relatives – aunt Sarah, uncle Herbert, uncle Richard – had all been 'Settlers in Canada', and his sister Emily and her husband faced the rigours of Indian Army life. Although Marryat's settlers, the Campbells, like the Kilverts, valued what Alfred Campbell called 'refined habits and cultivated minds', they recognised too the need to be active and practical. We have been 'taught wisdom practically, by the events of a chequered life', Campbell concludes. Living fully in the world, experiencing all its aspects including harsh ones, seizing opportunities to improve it for the benefit of others, was the core of the Campbells' and the Kilverts' religion: 'As Christians, we are not to fly from the world', Mrs Campbell proclaims.[113]

Chapter 3
Kilvert the Naturalist

To turn the imagination not inwards, but outwards; to give
it a class of objects which may excite wonder, reverence, the
love of novelty and of discovery . . . this is one of the great
problems of education; and I believe from experience that the
study of natural history supplies in great part what we want.
Charles Kingsley*How to Study Natural History*,
lecture delivered at Reading in 1846

Collecting, microscopes, curiosity, wonder, and close vision –
these were the hallmarks of natural history. For the Victorian
naturalist, every fact, every detail inspired amazement.
Lynn Merrill, *The Romance of Victorian Natural History*

The passion for collecting . . . was very strong in me.
Charles Darwin, *Recollections of the Development of my Mind
and Character*. He was recalling himself at the age of eight.

The previous chapter suggested that it is fruitful to see Kilvert in the
role of naturalist, but is it accurate to do so? Was he among those
described by Barbara Gates as 'the numberless amateurs out in the
field . . . avidly collecting butterflies, marine animals, ferns and rocks,
and filing their discoveries away . . . in drawers and notebooks'?[1]
Certainly it was clergymen who, from the eighteenth century onwards,
were most to be found in their ranks because they had the time for
natural history, believed it to be good for their health, and a useful
means of keeping in touch with parishioners.[2] Such clergymen were
'well represented within the ranks of popularisers of science in the
second half of the nineteenth century'.[3] Books written by them, or by
lay people equally keen to advance natural theology, were welcomed in
the Kilvert household, as will be seen.

One historian of natural history in Britain has shown that its
beginnings were characteristically Evangelical, so that it was entirely
to be expected that those Kilvert men who were clergymen – Kilvert's

uncle Francis, Kilvert's father, and Kilvert himself – should make it part of their spirituality. Various strands of development in natural history from the eighteenth century continued into the nineteenth and they did so, according to Allen, because they were 'founded in a certain well-defined emotional-cum-religious attitude which . . . we may define as Evangelicalism'. A key feature of Evangelicalism was that 'the moral and the useful became, increasingly, intertwined: pursuits like geology could be justified . . . as a means of revering the earthly grandeurs of Creation', in other words as an expression of natural theology. And even when pursuits lacked obvious usefulness, like mountain climbing, moral content was attributed to them in their justification. The wonders and beauties of nature came to be seen as sacraments. As the influence of Romanticism faded by the 1830s, a new view of nature took over, which was often marked by sentimentalism. A whole series of books appeared, aimed primarily at the middle class, which combined natural history with sentimental verses (e.g. Mrs Hey's *Moral of Flowers*, Miss Twamley's *The Romance of Nature*, Joseph Marrin's *Butterflying with the Poets*).[4] Fatuous as this development may appear, to it 'we owe the massive strength of Victorian natural history. . . . The natural history that now emerged was in its whole essence an Evangelical creation'. Its value lay partly in the fact that it allowed for the discharge of powerful emotions that Evangelicalism regarded as taboo (a sensuous feel for beauty, a semi-pagan response to nature) which, having to achieve some release, appeared as sentimentalism.[5] O'Connor has defended works combining natural history with sentimental verses, rejecting Allen's dismissal of them as 'a debased substitute' for a real appreciation of nature. Publishing of any kind was rarely profitable in this period, O'Connor argued, and 'publishers needed to try every trick in the book to attract readers'. Furthermore, the appeal through sentimentality does not, O'Connor insisted, imply insincerity. Such works were 'multi-layered imaginative commodities . . . and they deserve sympathetic historical attention'.[6]

We are fortunate to have, in Edmund Gosse's *Father and Son* (1907), a 'case-history' documenting the impact of natural history on an Evangelical family around the time the Kilvert children were growing up. In the words of its editor, the book 'conveys a sense of the traumatic scientific and religious ferments of the mid-nineteenth century'.[7] Like the Kilverts, the Gosses were a middle-class and Evangelical family, though their Calvinism was much more extreme. 'No fiction of any kind, religious or secular, was admitted into the house', wrote Edmund.[8] The Kilvert parents were not so strict, although there is a parallel in that in both households the father's

Evangelicalism was more extreme than the son's. Edmund Gosse was born in 1849, only child of Philip Gosse, son of an engraver. Philip was keen on natural history as a boy, an interest encouraged by his aunt, who was herself a naturalist.

The books allowed to Edmund were 'a queer variety of natural history', travel books, some geography and astronomy, and 'much theology'. Significantly, he had access to Charles Knight's *The Penny Cyclopedia*, which was 'his daily, and for a long time almost [his] sole study'. Philip Gosse's *A Naturalist's Rambles on the Devonshire Coast* (1853) 'brought before the public the science of marine biology and was partly responsible for the sea-shore craze of the mid-Victorian period'.[9] The book resulted from nine months' residence on the Devon coasts in company with his wife and 'a little naturalist in petticoats' (his son Edmund), pursuing 'the study of the curious forms, and . . . curious instincts, of animated beings'. Gosse earnestly urged readers not to be found among the 'idle pleasure seekers' oblivious to the 'strange, beautiful, or wondrous objects' of the sea shore, to which his book could be a 'hand-book'.[10] In 1856, he was elected a Fellow of the Royal Society and 'was now the leading populariser of natural history in the country'.[11]

The specimen-hunting recorded by Mary Howitt in *The Children's Year* may be seen as a manifestation of this mid-century enthusiasm for natural history. The Kilvert family's summer holidays to seaside resorts in Somerset and Devon, noted in the last chapter, were coloured by Mary Howitt's descriptions of her children's experiences. Certainly Kilvert had a developed interest in marine flora and fauna, as we shall see when we examine his account of his Cornish holiday. One wonders whether the collection of pebbles picked up on Clevedon beach by the Kilvert children (mentioned by Emily Kilvert) gained in significance because William Howitt had recorded that a local schoolmistress had impressed him 'with the perception that there was wisdom in the formation of a common pebble'.[12] The pebble was often recommended in natural history books of the period as an object for the pious mind to contemplate. Charles Kingsley, who typified the clergyman-naturalist, urged that the young should be taught 'wonder in every insect, sublimity in every hedgerow, the records of past worlds in every pebble'.[13]

Kilvert's instinct for the striking and the unusual, discovered often in ordinary experience, was in essence his artistic vision, his talent as a writer, nurtured by a family ethos which, as has been shown, encouraged children to take an interest in both the natural world and the world of man-made inventions, and to find 'wonders' in them. His great ability to convey the physicality of objects and scenes, commented on by virtually all critics, stems partly from a relish for, and a sensitivity to, the qualities that make them different or 'curious'. He enjoyed visits to his 'philosopher' friend, Richard Meredith, because he usually heard him expound upon 'antiquities and curiosities'.[14] It is highly significant that he expressed the motive behind his diary-keeping in terms that connect with a background in which showing an interest in the wonders of creation appeared as a moral duty: 'because life appears to me such a *curious* and *wonderful* thing . . . some such record as this' was called for.[15] Kilvert was a collector of 'curious' things and his *Diary* is his collection – of experiences, places, characters, landscapes, memories, and natural objects.

Lynn Merrill's observation that *singularity* was 'the motive engine of Victorian natural history' provides further insight into the way Kilvert wrote. '"Singular" is,' she stated, 'a particularly felicitous word for natural history, since it suits the aims of the pursuit so well'. Its key meaning for natural history is 'unique, individual, one of a kind', and 'extraordinary, unusual ... rare, precious'. This quality is responsible in her view for the characteristic discourse of Victorian natural history: just as natural objects could be 'colourful, sensuous, visually complex, minutely detailed', so was the language used to describe them.[16] To the Victorian field naturalist, intent on detailed, accurate observing and recording, objects were particular, moving and exciting. The accounts given in *The Children's Year* of the adventures of the young naturalist Herbert exemplify perfectly the discourse Merrill had in mind – a blend of the factual and the imaginative.

The Kilvert family's penchant for curiosities and wonders is well illustrated by its visit to the Great Exhibition of 1851, which was at that time the greatest collection of them ever assembled. One clergyman stated in his sermon on the Exhibition: 'This repository of wonders may be regarded as a Beneficent Stimulus to Human Diligence and Industry'.[17] When Emily Kilvert described the family visit as 'a *wonderful* event in our childhood', there was literal force in her use of the word. She recalled that unique curiosity the Kohinoor diamond (in fact, her typically nine-year-old's memory of the 'great brass cage' that protected it).[18] Another curiosity she remembered was Queen Victoria herself, looking very cross on a gallery above. Our knowledge of the values informing the Kilvert family's outlook enables us to see why it should have made the Exhibition a prime target, just as it was for John Dillwyn and his family, who visited it in 1851 on 21 March, 6 and 23 June. It represented work, which the Kilverts respected. The Exhibition's motto, chosen by Prince Albert and redolent of natural theology, was 'The Earth is the Lord's and the fullness thereof'. It was also 'an outward and visible sign of how readily capitalism could conquer the globe'. In other words, it stood for the progress proclaimed in *Old England* and, as in Knight's portrayal, it chiefly meant British progress: 'It was fundamentally designed as a demonstration of British superiority to other nations', exporting its modernity and importing all the goods and curiosities of other nations, which were displayed in the 'emblematic hothouse' in Hyde Park.[19] The Crystal Palace, a structure of glass and iron, was designed by Joseph Paxton as a larger version of the conservatory he had built for the Duke of Devonshire.[20] The motives that brought the Kilvert family to the Exhibition along with six million other visitors between 1 May and 15 October 1851 can be gathered from Greenhalgh's summary of its significance. Exhibitions of this kind 'embodied the transformation of Victorians' existence and contributed to the shaping of the Victorian consciousness'; they were 'political propaganda', 'the first events committed to mass education', 'sale-rooms' for all kinds of manufactured goods, 'they celebrated religion [and] intellectual culture', and were the beginning of the 'mass-tourist industry'.[21]

The salient feature of the Exhibition was, in Briggs's view, 'an emphasis on power', epitomised by Nasmyth's steam-hammer, which apparently 'caught the imagination of visitors more than any other object'.[22] The Victorian, Henry Mayhew, a visitor to it on 26 May 1851, also found 'the machinery . . . the grand focus of attraction', with the power-looms 'the chief centres of curiosity'. He praised working people for their behaviour, showing no sign of the disorder widely predicted: 'The fact is, the Great Exhibition is to them more of a school than a show' because the working man had little 'book-learning', but such knowledge as constitutes the education of life – viz. the understanding of human motives, and the acquisition of power over natural forces'.[23] To the Kilvert family, the Exhibition was both a school and a show. Its lessons were those taught by the trade element in its background and by the writers they valued – the Howitts, Britton, Knight, Martineau, Marryat – whose works celebrated practical education, 'the arts of living', as well as the 'wonders' of the man-made and of nature.

The Kilvert tourists up in the capital from Wiltshire were intent on seeing other aspects of its intellectual culture. They went to the Zoological Gardens where the 'hippo was a recent acquisition having been brought over to England in 1850'.[24] Established by the founder of Singapore, Sir Stamford Raffles, the Gardens were based in Regent's Park and, like Kew Gardens, combined scientific work with popular entertainment. 'From its beginnings it had functioned explicitly both

View of the Crystal Palace, Hyde Park

as a symbol and an agent of national power'.[25] The hippo the Kilvert children saw was called Obaysch and was such a curiosity to the public that annual attendance rose from 168,895 to 360,402. Emily's memory of the creature was always coloured by her brother's response to it: 'When [the hippo] came dripping out of his tank, Frank (i.e. Kilvert) naively enquired where his bath towel was, at which the people standing nearby tittered a good deal'.[26] The Kilvert children were being entertained by Obaysch but their background ensured that they were also learning. Lightman explained the context in which visits to the Zoological Gardens and other London locations took place:

> The Victorians were fascinated by the strange new worlds that science opened to them. Exotic flora and fauna from across the empire poured into London daily, many later to be displayed in the British Museum (Natural History) or Kew Gardens to a public hungry for science. Visitors of every rank, at many sites, in many ways, defined knowledge, ordered nature, practised science.[27]

Emily Kilvert couldn't remember whether they were taken to the British Museum,[28] but she did remember going to the Hans Sloane Museum and 'having various curiosities pointed out'. She had many reasons, as had her family, for regarding Sloane (1660-1753) as a hero. He came from a relatively humble background that encouraged useful work.[29] Emily Kilvert and her siblings would have seen a vast range of objects at his Museum including plants and seeds, shells, parts of animals, fossils, insects, minerals, classical and oriental antiquities, paintings and drawings, coins, and machines. 'Sloane's Museum acquired the reputation of being the most desirable repository for . . . objects of scientific importance'.[30] After his death, his collection was bought by the government and became the British Museum.

Something of the serious purpose behind the Kilvert family's trip to London may be gleaned from the fact that its pattern of visits to the Exhibition, Zoological Gardens, and the Polytechnic Institution was mirrored by Charles Darwin's family in July 1851. Darwin 'took an intense interest in the exhibits at the Crystal Palace', though his children became bored. The next day they too went to see Obaysch and after that to the Polytechnic Institution in Regent Street.[31] This was 'an exhibition hall for popular science with working models, lectures, and a "gas microscope" projecting images of minute objects on to a large screen'. On its roof was the first studio where daguerreotype portraits were made. Maria Edgeworth had hers done there and wrote about the experience enthusiastically to a friend: 'It is a wonderful, mysterious operation'.[32] Emily Kilvert remembered the Polytechnic as 'one of the most delightful places . . . which was the wonder of all of us children'. Looking back sixty years later, she was still excited: 'Here we saw the great Electric Eel in its tank, the diving bell. . . . The great wheel spinning glass, of which the man at work gave us specimens to our great joy, and all the other marvels of the place'.[33] When looking forward to her visit, Emily would have remembered the *Children's Year* passage which told how the Institution was one of Alfred's 'favourite places' because of 'all the *wonders* of the place'. Alfred had sampled the 'diving-bell . . . the electrical machine . . . the magnified figures and the dissolving views'. He had also seen 'the glass-blower at work, and brought away spun glass'.[34] Emily was, it seems, thrilled to be experiencing exactly what Alfred experienced.

The glass 'specimens' were not the only things Emily collected on that exciting day: for the child brought up on *The Children's Year*, the 'collecting' of the London experiences would have been a special form of the natural history collecting encouraged by that book and by her background, in which 'religious and scientific knowing were neither separate nor separable categories'.[35] Collecting specimens expressed both kinds of knowing. The Victorian and Evangelical work ethic 'introduced a new note of fervour' into collecting specimens. A good collection was a sign of devotion, effort, reverence, achieved 'while gazing all the time "through Nature up to Nature's God"'. Collecting, in short, received religious sanction'.[36] Mary Howitt's account of her children's early education instilled both this mentality and the habit of collecting, particularly in relation to their experience of the seaside at Hastings, where their rented house was situated. Herbert was intent on finding 'treasure and wonders', and when the tide was out 'they found treasures at every step: there were shells, and sea-weed, and star-fish'. And such collecting had an inevitable outcome: having, like proper naturalists, arranged their 'treasures' on shelves in a cupboard, 'It was to them like a little marine museum'.[37] Producing and ordering a collection were significant activities of the period, as Endersby explained: 'The mid-Victorian natural history sciences were pre-eminently concerned with collecting and classifying, activities that some practitioners of the physical sciences regarded with disdain. As a result natural history tended to be held in low esteem',[38] and this was particularly the case with botany.

Mrs Emma Hockin, Kilvert's hostess during his Cornish holiday, exemplifies a number of themes relevant to this chapter, the most obvious of which is that she was in the tradition of Victorian women with a strong interest in botany. Kilvert's stay with her and her husband William at their home of Tullimaar from 19 July to 6 August 1870 could almost be described as a naturalists' field-trip, so full was it of excursions in which the collecting of specimens was a primary activity. Towns and historic buildings were sometimes the target of excursions, but no matter whether the objects targeted were man-made or natural, Kilvert's approach to them was that of the avid collector. Some places visited were on a list he had prepared beforehand, some were chosen by his hosts, who shared his 'collecting' mentality. On 1 January 1867, Emma married William Hockin, son of the rector of St Stithians, Cornwall. His maternal uncle, Benjamin Sampson, was an industrialist, supplying gunpowder for blasting to Cornish mines. It was he who built Tullimaar in 1830, as the Prologue noted.

One of Kilvert's excursions during his Cornish holiday was to Kynance Cove and his account of it includes the following passage: 'We gathered some seaweed off the rocks to take home for a weather gage [sic], and H knocked off the cliff a piece of serpentine rock for me to bring away as a remembrance of the place and a specimen of the rocks. He described it as having been "struck off by the hoof of the learned Erasmus".'[39] This last reference perplexed the Cornish Diary's editors, who set it aside as 'a baffling joke'. They had failed to find a link to the 'sixteenth-century humanist scholar', Erasmus. They were focusing on the wrong scholar – and here we came across again the 'iceberg' nature of Kilvert's Diary, one of those brief glimpses into the diarist's knowledge and experience, indicating larger elements below the surface. 'H' (Kilvert always designated Hockin thus) had meant Erasmus Darwin (1731-1802), grandfather of the author of The Origin of Species, and Kilvert had understood Hockin's allusion,[40] which means he knew something of this 'Erasmus'. Hockin's knowledge perhaps came from his maternal uncle's involvement with the Cornish mining industry; Hockin could have known that Erasmus Darwin had accompanied the entrepreneur Matthew Boulton (1728-1809) during his two months' stay in Cornwall on a geological expedition in 1780.[41] Hockin certainly knew that Erasmus Darwin was in the habit of chipping off any fragments of stone, or quartz, or spar he found interesting.[42] Kilvert recognised that Hockin had a knowledge of geology, one which matched his own.

Kilvert's enthusiasm for the serpentine rock at Kynance Cove may have been fired in part by Hockin's own. Kilvert wrote: 'I never saw anything like the wonderful colour of the serpentine rocks, rich, deep, warm, variegated, . . . veined with red, green and white, huge blocks of precious stone, marble on every side, an enchanted cave, the palace of the Nereids'.[43] The passage's combination of detailed, precise observation with a flight of fancy (it was another moment of enchantment) is frequently found in Mary Howitt's The Children's Year, and echoes the following passage from it that describes rocks at East Cliff near Eastbourne:

The angles of many of the blocks of stone are worn off . . . and this roundness [and the green sea-moss] give to them the fanciful appearance of huge heads covered with green wigs. Herbert and Meggy . . . recalled all the stories that they had ever heard of mermen and mermaids, sitting on rocks in the sea, combing their long green hair. Surely this must be a great company of sea gods and goddesses.[44]

The co-existence of detached scientific viewpoint with imagination was a marked character trait of Dr Erasmus Darwin. Educated at St John's College, Cambridge, he trained as a doctor but was interested in everything. He loved electrical experiments as a boy, and was one of the founder members of the Lunar Society[45] of Birmingham, leading figures of which were the entrepreneur Matthew Boulton, the engineer James Watt, the pottery king Josiah Wedgwood, the chemists James Kerr and Joseph Priestley, the geologist Whitehurst, and the inventor/educationist R.L. Edgeworth.[46] Most were Nonconformists. When Erasmus Darwin noticed fossilised shells in the walls of caves in Derbyshire, he became very excited at the idea that all species had developed from one original microscopic ancestor and on this idea he based his theory of evolution.

Erasmus Darwin's range of enquiry, imagination, and enthusiasm for knowledge were qualities shared by Kilvert, not in the same degree but basically of the same kind. It was these qualities that made him a writer, and the instrument that channelled and focused him was his pocket-book, which he always had with him. His stance towards experience, towards the 'collecting' of experience, is typified by the 3 May 1870 Diary entry: 'I stood by the window making notes of things in general in my pocket-book'. From the stockpile of 'things in general' there emerged the particular, finished elements that make up the Diary. The raw material, the 'specimens' that were initial impressions of things, people, places, experiences, were later sifted, classified, their essential features isolated and intensified through reflection and imagination.

It is Kilvert's Cornish Diary that provides the clearest evidence of Kilvert the naturalist, the collector, and this is so for a number of reasons. His holiday in Cornwall partook of the nature of a 'field-trip' because it was a unique area and one unknown to him. One of his first impressions of it was its industry: 'the most striking feature being the innumerable mine works of lead, tin, copper crowning the hills with their tall chimneys' and he noted ships in the river near Truro waiting for cargoes of tin and copper. From the home of his hosts, he could glimpse the Perran Foundry belonging to the Fox family. His preoccupation with Cornwall's mining industry appears in the numerous references to it. 'The red flames burst and roared from the tops of the tall mine chimneys' is one entry that shows that his imagination was aroused by the sights and sounds of industry. Another is this: 'We came to a mine called St Ives Consoles, and the works, rattling, clanking, clumping, at "stamping" and "streaming" tin'. And noticeably, even when visiting Tintagel, the centre of Cornwall's tradition of King Arthur legends and described very romantically by Kilvert, he felt moved to note: 'they have just begun mining for iron in this cliff'.[47] This is not a man who could find beauty, interest, things worth writing about only in the conventionally pretty and picturesque, but one whose imagination, like that of Erasmus Darwin, was fired by anything and everything.

Examination of his three-week stay with the Hockins confirms this impression. He had prepared for it by purchasing Bottrell's book on Cornwall,[48] which stimulated his interest in what he experienced. It was of course Cornwall's coast that was the centre of his attention. He rejoiced in the beauty of Mullion Cove: 'the deep blue sea rippling into the deep small cave shut in by the great dark cliffs, the fringe of white foam along the rocks . . . the streaks and patches of deep brilliant intense emerald green "playing" into blue'. He and his hosts were particularly drawn to rock pools: 'After luncheon we went down on the beach to look for sea-anemones among the rocks and pools at low water for Mrs H. We found a few red specimens and she found a green one'. Allen credited Philip Gosse with drawing the Victorian public's attention to sea-anemones, describing him as 'the loving painter and describer of sea-anemones and starfish'.[49] Barber wrote of sea-anemones: 'By 1858 [they] had become universal pets' and quoted the comment by G.H. Lewes (from his *Seaside Studies*): 'the lovely Sea-Anemone, now the ornament of countless drawing-rooms'.[50] Evidently, Kilvert knew the different kinds of weed of the sea-shore, noting at one place 'forests of seaweed and ore weed'.[51] Shells were one target of his collecting: 'We picked up a number of pretty shells on the beach, and I meant to have taken them home. . . . '[52]

The editors of the *Cornish Diary* commented: 'This notebook is full of allusions to the Victorian mania for collecting ferns, which prompted a whole collection of fern books. Emma Hockin was clearly a passionate collector'. 'In the decade from 1845 to 1855 [the public's tastes] moved successively from seaweeds to ferns to sea-anemones', Lynn Barber noted.[53] Kilvert too was both very passionate and very knowledgeable about ferns. When he was a teenager, in the mid-1850s, the fern craze was at its height. It exemplified 'a society in the grip of a powerful emotion, a "collective projection", rooted in some deeply buried psychological layer'.[54] Boyd wrote of it: 'Members of the cult were men and women for whom ferns were more than a fad or fashion.[55] Ferns aroused little interest before 1830 and the first book on them appeared in 1837.[56] Allen linked the craze to Evangelicalism: 'there was something about ferns uncannily in tune with the spirit of the age. They matched the new mood of sombreness: the Fern Craze opened as men's clothes, quite suddenly, turned black', some of its moral fervour deriving also from Romanticism and medievalism.[57] Women were encouraged to be collectors and experts. Kingsley was writing in 1855: 'Your daughters, perhaps, have been seized with the prevailing "Pteridomania", and are collecting and buying ferns, with Ward's cases wherein to keep them.[58] (Nathaniel Bagshawe Ward had invented a glass case for nurturing and displaying ferns; it was on show at the Great Exhibition.) The fern became a dominant motif in Victorian decoration on wallpaper, china, glass, tiles, and fabrics. The Victorian botanist Thomas Moore (1821-1887) said that ferns' attractiveness did not lie in their colour, 'sober green', but rather in their 'elegant forms and graceful habits.[59]

When Kilvert was holidaying in Cornwall, the craze was subsiding (by the end of the 1870s ferns were unfashionable), but he was in the very best region for specimens. Nona Bellairs's book, *Hardy Ferns: how I collected and cultivated them* (1865) asserted that the South-West was the best area for them, 'especially the dear Cornish land . . . [which] is a land of ferns.[60] It seems that Kilvert knew her book. Her attitude to ferns rested on pious foundations, as his did. 'The Book of Nature is the Book of God', she declared, and study of ferns would help to 'turn the child's heart to the love of the pure and beautiful instead of the vile and debasing.[61] Nona Bellairs (1824-1897) was the daughter of the Rev. Henry Bellairs (1790-1872), who became a legend for good works in his parish of Bedworth (Warwicks.) The targets of Mrs Hockin's fern hunting in Cornwall may have been suggested by Kilvert, guided by Bellairs. The latter recommended the rocks of St Michael's Mount for specimens of Asplenium Marinum and Asplenium Lanceolatum and that was where the former searched.[62] (Kilvert observed, just as Bellairs did, that he should like to see 'a great storm from St Michael's Mount'.) Naturally he was carried along in the wake of his hosts' enthusiasm for fern-collecting during his stay at Tullimaar, but he had his own interest independent of theirs. On 17 March 1870, before his Cornish holiday, he recorded: 'English maiden-hair fern was growing plentifully about the rocks and I brought away a plant'. In another entry (3 June 1876) he noted: 'Seeing some pretty ferns growing on the bank of a hedge. . . . I gathered them for Dora'. Dora, his youngest sister, born 1848, often shared natural history experiences with him.

Other of Kilvert's friends knew of his enthusiasm for plants (and for Wordsworth): '[Jane Dew] and Emily have just returned from the Lakes and have come back full of Wordsworth, Rydal and Grasmere and with a store of photographs, ferns and other plants connected with the poet'. The girls (daughters of Henry Dew, rector of Whitney-on-Wye) also knew that Kilvert was, as they were, among the army of *collectors*: 'They very generously gave me six photographs and Jane gave me some ferns she gathered at Dungeon Ghyll and a piece of Portugal laurel she picked up in Wordsworth's garden at Rydal Mount'.[63] A facet of Kilvert's collecting habit known to the Dew girls was his keeping of a scrap book. Alice was one of the youngest Dew sisters (born 1860) and she was pleased on 25 July 1871 to help to keep his scrap book up-to-date: 'Alice has been pasting my photograph scraps into my scrap book and illuminating their titles under them'.[64] Further illustrative of the linked cults of remembrance and collecting is the *Diary* entry for 4 May 1872, again involving the Dew girls: 'Jenny Dew has sent me two manuscript albums with a request that I will write in it "the lines you said to me under the trees" – (Newman's I think, signed J.H.N.) and "something of your own"'.[65] The emphases here indicate the role the cults had in stimulating and reflecting *sympathy* as a crucial element in Victorian personal relations.

Kilvert's naturalist self appears frequently in the *Diary* in entries which repeatedly exemplify curiosity and knowledge, knowledge and curiosity. He made explicit in the *Diary* entry for 27 May 1871 the way in which those twin elements complemented each other in his approach to wild flowers. He had met the Morrell children with their governess, Miss Sandell, one of those ladies who knew botany. Kilvert was impressed by the collection of wild flowers that the Morrell children had made, under her guidance:

> They had found the bog bean, the butterwort, milk-wort in four varieties, butterfly orchis, mouse ear, marsh valentine, marsh buttercup, hawkweed fumitory, yellow pimpernel, yellow potentilla. The children showed me what I never found out for myself or knew before, that the bog bean grows in the wern below Great Gwernfydden. And I have walked 14 miles for that flower, when it grew close by. Miss Sandell taught me more about these flowers in ten minutes than I have learnt from books in all my life.

Kilvert's tribute to Miss Sandell is significant in a number of ways. Firstly, he was acknowledging what a good teacher she was, partly because of her comprehensive knowledge, and partly because she had fired the children's enthusiasm. Secondly, he was revealing his own enthusiasm as a naturalist in his comment about the bog bean. Thirdly, he was revealing that some of his own knowledge came from years of reading botanical handbooks. Fourthly, he was acknowledging the limitations of botanical books – discovering and experiencing flowers for oneself was superior to theoretical knowledge.

We can identify a botanical handbook that figured in the Kilvert family library from which some of the diarist's knowledge must have come: Maund's *The Botanic Garden*, held in the collection of Kilvert memorabilia in the National Library of Wales. The book is volume one, published in 1825, of what was a thirteen-volume work and was left by Kilvert's mother to her daughter Emily.[66] The undated inscription in it reads: 'Thermuthis Kilvert, Langley Burrell Rectory'. Emily had inscribed her own name below with the date September 1889. It bears the name of a Chippenham bookseller so it might have been bought by Mrs Kilvert's parents who lived nearby (perhaps as a present for her).[67] It is not hard to see why the book found favour with the Kilverts when one knows what kind of a man Benjamin Maund (1790-1864) was. He was born at Tenbury, Worcestershire, the son of a farmer, and had some formal education, 'because of the knowledge of the Classics, as well as comprehensive reading and sound knowledge of literature' evident in his writings.[68] Maund was apprenticed to a printer in Ludlow from the age of sixteen and when he was twenty-three he bought a printer's business in Bromsgrove. He combined printing with the roles of stationer, bookseller, publisher, and chemist. A model and progressive citizen, he was a churchwarden, member of several parish committees, and 'prime mover in the building of a new town hall and cattle market'.[69] Another source noted that 'he did much to raise the town's intellectual tone'.[70]

Humphreys stated that 'Maund must have been a striking personality, with an intense love of nature, and a deeply religious character'.[71] Emphases in *The Botanic Garden*[72] show his natural theology. The preface to volume one (Mrs Kilvert's volume) stated that 'Man, by nature, inherits the love of flowers', though this 'divine excitement' was often suppressed by 'the busy scenes of life'.[73] The fullest statement of Maund's natural theology appears in the preface of another ambitious work of his: *The Botanist* (five volumes, 1836-1842):[74]

> To a mind impressed with the belief in the infinite wisdom and goodness of the Creator, Botany affords a perpetual course of the very highest description, of mental gratification, in the never-ending proofs it entails of an all-pervading intelligence.

The first volume of *The Botanist* appeared in 1836 and it is clear from Maund's wording in the above passage that he was intending to make a connection between his work and the recently launched *Bridgewater Treatises* 'on the Power, Wisdom and Goodness of God, as manifested in the Creation'. The 8th Earl Bridgewater commissioned a series of works, by the leading scientists of the day in the period 1830-1836, designed to show that science and religion complemented each other.

We have another insight into Kilvert as teacher and naturalist when we recall that one of the books he sent on 23 March 1872 as a present to Hugh Thomas, son of his Mitcham friend, was R.M. Ballantyne's *The Gorilla Hunters*. The book has two heroes: Ralph Rover,[75] a naturalist, and Peterkin Gay, a hunter, whose mission to West Africa epitomises Victorian attitudes to the natural world and to Empire. They have interdependent roles: Ralph wants to collect specimens, some of which Peterkin will shoot. The former states that he intends to take home specimens in the interests of science.[76] This is one of the ways in which the book justifies colonialism; trade and Christianity are the other justifications. The thousands of specimens of exotic flora and fauna flooding into Britain from all over the Empire signified an attempt to control nature.[77] The BAAS took the lead in the classification of specimens and was well known to the public, although it 'existed primarily to serve the interests of élite naturalists',[78] with many clergymen playing a key role in its founding. There were also county natural history societies, known as 'field clubs', that encouraged a social cross-section of local people to make trips into the countryside to collect specimens.

Kilvert's essentially ambivalent attitude to field clubs is seen in his shunning of his local club – the Woolhope Naturalists' Field Club of Herefordshire. One *Diary* entry records its imminent arrival in Hay-on-Wye in May 1871 to open up an ancient barrow. Kilvert wrote: 'I had intended to be present, but I did not go as I hate going about in herds and hated the idea of seeing the mountain desecrated by this particular herd'. Three days later, he went close to the barrow: 'Imagine my delight to find the place perfectly silent and solitary except for the sheep'.[79] This is Kilvert the solitary, spiritual man for whom nature was a thing of beauty and quietness, a vehicle for meditation, and the source of private memories and dreams. The formal collaborative, recording/classifying aspect of the naturalist's work did not appeal to him. Rational scientific enquiry seemed at odds with the spiritual dimension, the *mystery*, of nature. Nevertheless, such enquiry, conducted by others, excited him (this ambivalence is explored later vis à vis his admiration for the scientific work of John Tyndall).

Kilvert's younger brother Edward, nicknamed 'Perch', was a naturalist of the recording, classifying kind, as was evident when he came to stay in Clyro in June 1870 and the brothers embarked together on several outings which had the character of field trips. On 11 June we find Edward identifying some beetles, while Kilvert stood back and admired his knowledge: 'These beetles seemed to be old acquaintances of Perch who recognised them immediately as the wailing beetle or Necropherus sepultor'. (Kilvert himself never used Latin names for fauna and flora.) It was Edward too who 'found the curious circular nest of the ground bee' two days later. He was regularly to be found 'groping' in streams in the hunt for creatures, as on 17 June when he found a crayfish, 'which crawled about the table . . . like a fresh water clean brown lobster'. Kilvert had learned something from his brother: 'I did not know there were any crayfish in the brook'.[80]

Kilvert was brought up, as this chapter and the previous one have shown, to be a collector. The seminal volumes of his early reading – The Boy's Country Book, The Children's Year, Old England, The Beauties of England and Wales, The Leisure Hour and (Maund's) The Botanic Garden – all had a collecting ethos. The idea of 'collections', often actual museums, figured strongly in his background. Old England is characterised as a 'Pictorial Museum'. He must have had something like a museum at home or in his lodgings to house the shell, plant, and mineral specimens he collected.[81] The 'memorials' (locks of hair, bookmarks etc.) of child lovers in his desk's secret drawer were a kind of museum. The Great Exhibition, to which he was taken as a child, was an inspiring museum of Empire: a coming together of exotic wonders and wonders of everyday usefulness. His endless parochial journeying ('villaging' he called it) combined the naturalist's hunt for specimens of various kinds with a concern for parishioners' needs. His naturalist self was supported by his sisters Emily and Dora and by his brother Edward. In the environs of Clyro it was supported by the Dew sisters, Richard Meredith, and Thomas Webb (of whom more will be said later). And he always had his close friends, the Hockins.

The historian Lynn Merrill's analysis of the characteristic discourse of Victorian natural history contains various insights relevant to Kilvert's mode of writing. She showed that agricultural, historical, and topographical information was typically blended with folklore and anecdote – a marked feature of Kilvert's Diary. In addition, natural history writing of the period was 'intimately entwined' with travel writing; Kilvert's work shows this too. Merrill regarded the tone of G.H. Lewes's books – 'emotional, awed, subjective' – as typical of the genre. This subjective quality is important. Unlike scientists who sought to understand natural objects, naturalists were content to look at them simply for their beauty and complexity. Thus, 'the natural history that captivated . . . so many Victorians was a personal, evocative, aesthetic science'. All of this explains why the natural history parts of *Kilvert's Diary* read the way they do; its author was recording science of a kind but it was 'a science endowed with literary qualities'.[82] It also had the spiritual dimension that this chapter has traced, represented often by clergymen/naturalists such as Gilbert White, Kingsley, Philip Henslow (1796-1861), Buckland, and, notably, Kilvert's close friend, Thomas Webb, as well as by lay figures such as Maund. The involved nature of Kilvert's approach to natural history illustrates what this chapter has set out to show, that 'Natural History was part of a complex social practice; it was not a single set of ideas'.[83] According to Merrill, two motifs dominated Victorian natural history: the cabinet and the microscope. The former became 'one's own personal museum' and arranging its contents was 'a creative act'. It stood as 'a metaphor for personal consciousness of nature – consciousness of remembrance'.[84] Kilvert's pocket book had the same role in this process: it recorded memories because the best, most significant ones, became part of his own identity.

Chapter 4
Steamboats, Viaducts and Railways

My Father told me he had heard his grandmother say that she remembered the time in the middle of the eighteenth century when the only public conveyances were stage waggons. . . . The stage waggon that plied between Bath and Bristol spent a whole day on the journey.

Kilvert's Diary

The telegraph unleashed the greatest revolution in communications since the development of the printing press.

Tom Standage, *The Victorian Internet*

Today I sent my first postcards. . . . They are capital things, simple, useful and handy. A happy invention.

Kilvert's Diary

A railway train is a dusky piece of utilitarianism to look at and yet is not without poetry, particularly when in motion.

Barclay Fox's Journal, February 1843

This chapter seeks to show the way in which Kilvert's passion for, and varied experience of, railways, as well as other forms of communication, were interwoven with his family history, upbringing, friendships, values, religion, almost his entire outlook. The *Diary* entries above are indicative of the satisfaction he took in improved forms of communication. In the following discussion it should be remembered that his paternal grandfather had a coach building business and the wealth of his Quaker maternal grandfather had come from trade. Such men were inevitably fired by efficiency and new opportunities. 'Everywhere railways were welcomed as the very symbol of progress.'[1] Their benefits included reduced costs to farmers, enlarged markets for agricultural and industrial products, improved postal and telegraph services, cheaper coal and newspapers, reduced rural isolation,[2] and greater employment opportunities. By the time of Kilvert's birth (3

December 1840) 'railways had become the most important symbol of industrial, economic and financial power, the most characteristic vehicle for men's dreams of power, wealth and glory'.[3] The fact that Kilvert had yeoman farmers in his ancestry and celebrated country life in his writing has obscured the importance of trade and technology in both his background and writings. The blessings of technology were exalted in a poem by Charles Mackay, whose life-story Kilvert was reading when he thought his own life was ending:

No poetry in Railways! foolish thought
Of a dull brain . . . .
Blessings on Science, and her handmaid Steam!
They make Utopia only half a dream.[4]

Kilvert rejoiced in the beauty of landscape and, *at the same time*, in the promise of railways, as his hero Wordsworth had done. Even though, the poet said, railways may 'mar/ The loveliness of Nature', they should not prevent the mind from 'gaining that prophetic sense/ Of future change, that point of vision'.[5]

In his very early years, Kilvert would not have had this awareness of creating the future, which was to become very strong in Victorians, but it would have developed alongside the child's excitement at the new monsters of steam with their attributes of power and speed. One can imagine him, as he read *The Children's Year*, sharing in Meggy's joy as she 'skimmed along in the railway carriage' and saw from it 'all the new and wonderful things'. His excitement as each new line opened can also be easily imagined. He had just been born when the Great Western Railway line between London and Bristol was opened in 1841. Bradshaw's first Railway Guide was published in December that year, covering the 66 lines already open. Kilvert's childhood from then on was to be filled with news of the ever-expanding railway system. By 1841 there were 1,600 miles of track; by 1845 there were 2,400; by 1851 there were 6,890. As average speeds increased – 20mph in 1840, 26.1 in 1843, 37.2 in 1848 – so did the number of passengers – 25m in 1843 and 47.5m by the end of 1851.[6] In 1841, a railway line had come to Bath, the town in which Kilvert's family had taken root, and by the time he was five, railway mania was at its height.

Gentry folk had the opportunity to view railway works before lines opened. Catherine Stanley, wife of Edward Stanley, Bishop of Norwich, was writing on 19 December 1829 to her sister, Maria Hare, godmother to the Kilvert children, about visiting the railway at Prescot, near Liverpool. Her account shows a mind struggling to come to terms with a phenomenon which she knew would transform human consciousness. The 'wonderful locomotive engine flying past . . . comes with such novelty and force,' she wrote.

This thing is to convey carriages, people, goods, everything from Liverpool to Manchester, thirty miles *in an hour*. The effect of the velocity is that when you stand on the railroad and watch the machine coming, it seems not to *approach*, but to expand into size and distinctness like the image in a phantasmagoria[7] (her italics).

The next day she and her husband went into the mile-and-a-quarter long railway tunnel under Liverpool and saw wagons on which gentry carriages and horses could be transported 'as upon a fairy carpet for thirty miles'. Seeing lamps flash past her as she travelled at thirty miles an hour, she 'never felt so strange, so much in a state of magic, of enchantment, as if surrounded by new powers and capabilities'. Maria Hare replied to her sister on 22 December: 'Your account of seeing the railway takes my breath away, and puts my head into a perfect whirl. What will all this come to? Some great change must take place'.[8] Kilvert was born into this age of 'great change', although the change from carriages' ten miles an hour to railway engines' thirty miles an hour must have had most impact on his father, who recalled a thrill from the time before the 'great change': 'to get on the roof of the Star coach and go through the air on a fine September day behind four splendid greys at the rate of ten miles an hour was a pleasure such as I never enjoyed before'.[9]

Kilvert's father was a young man of 26 when passengers' accounts of first experiences of rail travel were appearing in newspapers, magazines, and letters. Fanny Kemble's account, in an 1830 letter to a friend, is a typical example. She had been privileged to take a train ride from Liverpool in a private party with George Stephenson himself, before the Liverpool-Manchester line was opened on 15 September 1830. Her sense of expanding horizons is caught in her opening observation that foolscap paper was needed to 'contain a railroad and my ecstasies'. The 'ecstasies' were provoked by a whole series of 'wonders', the first of which was a railway tunnel 2,200 yards long, 'the whole way under the town'. Charles Knight saw this tunnel being excavated in 1828 and was fascinated by it: 'Such a triumph of engineering was then a wonder. The locomotive was as yet little more than a dream'.[10] The locomotive itself, inevitably likened by Fanny Kimble to a horse, was 'a wonderful beast', whose 'reins, bit and bridle . . . is a small steel handle'. Another wonder was the sense of free movement: 'You can't imagine how strange it seemed to be journeying on thus, without any visible cause of progress other than the magical machine'. Across a valley, Stephenson 'had thrown a magnificent viaduct of nine arches, the middle one seventy feet high. It was lovely and wonderful beyond all words'. On the return journey they travelled at 35 miles an hour, another wonder: 'You cannot conceive what that sensation of cutting the air was . . . a sensation of flying . . . strange beyond description.'[11] Throughout his history, man had never travelled faster than a galloping horse.

Sophia Kilvert, although a Quaker and an advocate of scientific study, deplored the changes brought about by railways, chiefly their tendency to undermine people's sense of home. 'The love of movement and separation has infected every class,' she wrote, and 'This thirst for speed, and being carried away from home, . . . is a fearful feature of our national domestic history.' Her nature, like her background, was aristocratic, used to traditional communities in which families, rich and poor, had lived for centuries, in homes that had always been theirs. She insisted that she wasn't seeking to limit people's horizons but travel had to have the benefit of the community as its object. Railway travel was usually undertaken, she believed, for 'selfish motive'. She was glimpsing a democratic, urbanised future in which 'this disease of the day' (railway travel) was spreading 'downwards through the different gradations of society . . . converting the whole island into one city, surrounded by its immense suburbs!' The result would be alienation from our own homes. At bottom, Sophia was struggling to come to terms with the changes from an agricultural to an industrial society. When she wrote of rich and poor meeting together 'in their own domestic residences', it was part of her acknowledgement that her book 'spoke so much of the rural population'. Blank incomprehension marked her references to 'mere mechanics' (i.e. the industrial poor), who are 'so deeply involved in the peculiar habits, distresses, and vices attendant on ... their trades, that I feel at a loss to enter into *their* unnatural condition' (her italics). Her conclusion was that 'With all our improvements, we cannot boast that the human machine has the power and strength of former times.'[12]

Kilvert's outlook regarding technological and social progress can be illustrated further by examining in greater detail his contact with the Keary family, who were introduced in chapter three. Kilvert referred to meeting the Kearys socially on several occasions in the years 1871-5. The 1871 Chippenham Census records the solicitor Alfred John Keary, aged 38, his wife Lucy, aged 41, and daughter Pauline, aged 6, living at 12 High Street. Kilvert recorded in the *Diary* (NLW edition April-June 1870) that Pauline Keary came to the Kilvert home in Langley Burrell on 21 May to have tea with the children of his sister Emily. On 30 December 1874, Kilvert made this entry in his diary:

Mrs Keary and Miss Annie Keary, the authoress of the charming story 'Castle Daly' now coming out in *Macmillan*, came to luncheon with us today. I liked Miss Keary very much. She is a singularly pleasant woman with a very pleasant kindly face. We talked a good deal about 'Castle Daly'. . . . I told her how much I liked her story.

The entry in which he described his meeting with Annie is another vignette of the true Kilvert: sensitive towards other people, informed about books, enjoying literary exchanges, a regular reader of intellectual journals, and excited by ideas.

The 'Mrs Keary' who accompanied Annie to lunch at the Kilverts was the wife of the Chippenham solicitor and sister-in-law to Annie. She was born Lucy Mewburn. In their dealings with the Keary family the Kilverts must have learned something of Lucy's background, which not only had particular significance for them but was also permeated by the values that brought them together in the first place. Lucy's father was Francis Mewburn, born in 1785 at Bishop Middleham, twenty miles north of Darlington. After little formal education, he was articled to a Durham solicitor called Smales. He moved to Darlington in 1809 and married Smales's daughter Elizabeth in 1813. Lucy, one of their daughters, was born in 1830. The gravestone of Mewburn credits him with being the 'First Railway Solicitor' because he was central to the movement to establish railways in the north-east.

Knowing Lucy Mewburn gave Kilvert access to the dizzying moments of the railways' beginnings. As a boy he had read Knight's account of the way in which 'the success of the Stockton and Darlington Railway . . . aroused the emulation of the inhabitants of Manchester and Liverpool . . . '[13] A member of Darlington's Quaker community, Edward Pease (1767-1858), could see advantages both in terms of efficiency and economy in a railway carrying coal from pits in south-western Durham to the port of Stockton-on-Tees. He was the son of a wool merchant, and after years in the family business became excited by railways. In 1821 he founded, with a group of other businessmen, the Stockton and Darlington Railway Company. George Stephenson was then working as an engine wright at a local colliery and, hearing of Pease's interest in railways, he approached him. The two men instantly liked each other and Stephenson became engineer for the proposed new line. They had the same vision of railways' potential. In his *Lives of the Engineers*, Samuel Smiles wrote of Pease: 'He was a thoughtful and sagacious man, possessed of indomitable energy and perseverance', and he quoted a remark by one of Pease's friends: 'He was a man who could see a hundred years ahead.'[14]

Such a man inevitably saw wonders in railways which could usher in a time when, he said, 'it will be cheaper for a working man to travel

upon a railway than to walk on foot'. Francis Mewburn too was fond
of telling of the wonders of railways. On 11 June 1829, he astonished
an audience by prophesying that one day it would be possible to leave
Darlington by train in the morning, attend the opera in London in
the evening, and arrive back in Darlington for breakfast.[15] Although
Mewburn was not a Quaker,[16] the Quaker brothers Edward and Joseph
Pease[17] (1772-1846) recognised that he was the right man to back their
enterprise and accordingly he became solicitor to the Stockton and
Darlington Railway Company. The 13 May 1859 entry in the diary he
meticulously kept reads:

> This day is the 50th anniversary of my arrival in Darlington.
> What events have occurred in that period! What discoveries
> and improvements have been made in the arts and sciences
> – railways, telegraphs, penny post, Armstrong guns, and I
> know not what.[18]

It is a passage that might have been penned by Charles Knight –
or Kilvert. Mewburn became an expert in the new legal practices and
precedents connected with railways, working alongside the Peases and
George Stephenson, smoothing their path. He successfully lobbied
in Parliament to prevent the Duke of Cleveland from destroying
the Stockton and Darlington Railway. It seems certain that Kilvert's
Quaker mother would have admired both the man who became the
first Quaker M.P. (Joseph Pease) and the founding, when she was
seventeen (1825), of the Stockton and Darlington Railway, famous as
'the Quakers' Line'. (That enthusiastic admirer of railways, Barclay Fox,
married Jane Backhouse, niece of Joseph Pease.)[19]

Kilvert was a noticeably enthusiastic railway traveller. One *Diary*
entry (29 October 1874), an anecdote that might easily have been
found in *Old England*, shows his satisfaction at the progress railways
represented:

> William Pugh said the day the railway was opened to Brum
> as the first train was going up a bull took exception to it and
> came roaring down the line full charge to attack the train.
> However the train went on its way and sent the bull flying.
> The engine knocked him all to pieces. 'So much the worse
> for the Coo', as George Stephenson said.

The story's significance resides in a number of factors. Kilvert was
interested in a first-hand account of the coming of the railway age (he
also recounted the reaction of a farm labourer to 'the first train that ever
came down the Great Western Railway'). The two stories encapsulate
the idea of the traditional agricultural world being forced to give way
before the new industrial world. And finally, we have Kilvert's evident

satisfaction at George Stephenson's laconic comment and its lack of sympathy for the 'Coo'. Did Kilvert learn initially of the Pease brothers and of George Stephenson from Smiles's book? Knight's *Old England* referred briefly to the challenge of building the Liverpool-Manchester Railway over the Chat Moss bog but didn't refer to the engineer by name. Stephenson's famous remark about a cow coming off second-best in a confrontation with a locomotive, referred to by Kilvert, is recounted by Smiles. Kilvert could also have read the story in the *Leisure Hour* article (24 December 1857), 'George Stephenson', part II. The Bill for the railway went before a Commons committee in March 1825 and Stephenson was asked by one of its members whether a cow straying upon the line would not be 'a very awkward circumstance'. "'Yes,' Stephenson replied, "very awkward – *for the coo!*'"[20] In Kilvert's reference – 'So much the worse for the Coo' – he was paraphrasing the original, as has become the pattern over time. He was applying Stephenson's comment to the story told him by William Pugh (a 64-year-old Clyro farm labourer) about the cow which attacked an engine on the London-Birmingham line. The cow, like the Duke of Cleveland and the objectors to the Liverpool-Manchester railway, belonged with forces opposing progress.

There is a note of excitement and pleasure in Kilvert's many references to rail journeys as, for example, 'The lighted trains rushed up and down the line through the dark, following the fiery pillars of illuminated steam'.[21] Here the trains' progress is presented as not only beautiful but inexorable as they follow, because it is destiny, the 'vital principle' (Knight's phrase) of steam. Kilvert gave his *Diary* entry a particularly significant religious overtone. 'Fiery pillars' is a reference to the Biblical passage in which, after years of slavery in Egypt, the Israelites are released and set out for the Promised Land. 'And all the time God went before them, by day a pillar of cloud to guide them on their journey, by night a pillar of fire to give them light' (Exodus, 13.21, *New English Bible*). There could hardly be a more positive endorsement by a clergyman of industrial progress.

Kilvert took deep pleasure in railways' power, efficiency, and convenience. When he exulted in the thought that he could be 'rushed up from Bristol to Chippenham in 39 minutes' he was echoing Charles Knight, who wrote of being 'shot down' to Southampton from Waterloo Station, of being 'whirled through' eastern England to the North Sea.[22] The phrasing here is significant in its suggestion that Victorian railway passengers felt themselves to be carried on a *projectile* of enormous speed. Whereas coach travel allowed passengers to experience details of landscapes through which they passed, 'the railway put an end to this

Saltash Bridge, also known as The Royal Albert Bridge

intensity of travel', in Schivelbusch's words. He noted that 'projectile' was the word that was used regularly and typically in railways' early days to denote this loss of continuity (i.e. where spaces and particular landscape forms are skipped over and blurred). As one travelled by train, one was being 'shot through' landscapes, as well as into a new, exciting future.[23] The idea that railways, because of their speed, shrank distances was also characteristic of early nineteenth-century writings. However, the effect, according to Schivelbusch, was

> a dual one: space was both diminished *and* expanded. The dialectic of this process states that this diminution of space (i.e. the shrinking of transport time) caused an expansion of transport space by incorporating new areas into the transport network.

Kilvert's pride in the achievements of railway engineers emerges in his description of his journey to Cornwall in July 1870. When he travelled this line, he was especially keen, as the Dillwyns were, to see Brunel's viaducts, 'famous for their dramatic construction of timber beams on stone piers'.[24] Because the train was re-routed, 'I had after all missed seeing the Ivy Bridge viaduct',[25] Kilvert wrote, but, he consoled himself, 'there are some viaducts further on, quite as lofty and remarkable'. (He followed this remark with a detailed technical description of their construction.)[26] Timber bridges and viaducts were widely used in Britain's railways well into the 1860s, particularly by

Brunel. Kilvert would have been familiar in his childhood with the engineer's timber Lacock viaduct near Chippenham in the Thingley Junction-Westbury section of the Wiltshire, Somerset and Weymouth Railway.[27] Timber bridges and viaducts were introduced in the second stage of railways in the 1840s because wrought iron was too expensive, though Brunel sometimes combined its use with timber. Journeying to Cornwall in 1870, Kilvert knew that 'undoubtedly [Brunel's] finest achievements in timber were his massive viaducts in Devon and Cornwall completed between 1848 and 1859'. Lewis also noted that these 'impressive structures fired the public imagination [and] became well known', and were often photographed.[28] The longest was the Truro one (1,392 feet) and the highest was St Pinnock (151 feet), among the 51 of them on the West Cornwall and Cornwall Railways.

Even more spectacular and thrilling to Kilvert about the railway into Cornwall was what he called 'the great Saltash Bridge' which, in Binding's words, 'stands supreme today to remind us of the vision and talents of this exceptional man'[29] (i.e. Brunel). The Bridge's significance to Kilvert as the gateway to Cornwall can scarcely be over-emphasised.[30] A bridge over the Tamar would make Cornwall easily accessible for the first time and when Kilvert crossed it, also for the first time, on 19 July 1870, his excitement was considerable; partly because the Saltash Bridge was barely ten years old. An Act of Parliament in 1846 sanctioned its building and its story culminated in its Royal Opening on 2 May 1859. It crosses the Tamar at Saltash at a height of 100 feet. Its construction (1853-1859) coincided with Kilvert's teenage years and he no doubt followed its progress. Its massive cylinder, 100 feet high, 37 feet in diameter, 300 tons in weight, forming the base of its central pier, was floated and sunk on 24 May 1854. The granite pier that sat on this cylinder was completed by November 1856. The Bridge's two huge spans, each weighing over 1,000 tons, were floated out into the river on pontoons in August 1857. The spans, once positioned between the piers, had then to be lifted, three feet at a time, to the top of the piers 100 feet above by massive hydraulic jacks, one of several astonishing engineering feats involved in the construction. The *West Briton and Cornwall Advertiser* (25 February 1859) was writing as the Bridge neared completion that to leading engineers from Britain and Europe it was 'a subject of wonder for its lightness in appearance, yet great strength. . . . [It] is of all others the viaduct [that] is second to none in the world'.

The Royal Train bearing Prince Albert, who was to perform the Bridge's opening ceremony (marred by Brunel's absence – he was desperately ill) left Windsor at 6 a.m. and passed over several timber viaducts in Devon. (He got out to examine the one at Coombe.) The address of the Railway's directors that was read to the Prince stated that his presence was further proof 'of that truly enlightened spirit which . . . originated the Great Exhibition of 1851, and fostered the arts, manufacture and social progress of this great country'. In his reply, Prince Albert emphasised that the Bridge linked Cornwall for the first time with the rest of the Kingdom. There were indeed two main benefits resulting from the Cornish Railway and the Saltash Bridge: the introduction of a Night Mail service, providing a daily postal delivery between Penzance and the country's industrial centres, and telegraphic communication between some stations in Cornwall.[31] Kilvert was conscious of both of these, noting the 'Cornish mail carriage [bearing] the Prince of Wales' plume and motto' and the telegraph cable that now continued to the Scilly Isles.

Kilvert knew the history of railways and thrilled to the achievement they represented, especially to that of Brunel for he had created the GWR, which might be said to be Kilvert's main line or his 'home' line.[32] Kilvert took an interest in every aspect of the railways, enjoying in equal measure their enjoyable and inconvenient experiences. He made room in his diary to recount stories of lost luggage, of interminable waits on stations, of being on the wrong train, of missing his stop. They reflected what it meant to a man of his background and temperament to be alive in the 1870s, when railway journeys and railway experiences had become part of the very fabric of life. One aspect of Kilvert's love of railways was his eager appreciation of the wonder of the electric telegraph, 'the most important technological addition to railways', in Schivelbusch's words, their 'nervous system'.[33] It relieved train drivers of the responsibility of scanning the line ahead for obstacles or approaching trains, each section of the line having its own telegraphic transmitter which signalled when the line was clear.

The safety of railways had been of deep public concern from their beginnings when opposition to them predicted exploding locomotives and spectacular, grisly derailments. Statistics of accidents in 1841 were a cause for alarm: 29 accidents with 24 deaths and 71 injuries. However, by 1851 – in its last six months when roughly four times as many lines existed as in 1841 – there were only 36 accidents causing 38 deaths and 230 injuries.[34] Thus, 'the public's astonishingly speedy acceptance of this fearsome new form of transport was largely due to its excellent safety record'. More people were killed by stagecoaches in railways' early days.[35] Francis Mewburn, looking back in 1876 on forty years of railways, stated that of nearly 39 million passengers, only 96 lost their lives.

As is often the case with Kilvert's accounts of railway matters, there is

a good deal of considered detail in the 7 January 1872 *Diary* entry about
an accident on the GWR line between Swindon and Wootton Bassett.[36]
A passenger train had run into a goods train. Kilvert understood the
reason for there being no serious casualties: 'The goods train was very
heavy with Portland stone . . . [and] the passenger train would have
dashed into a lighter train, crumpled up the trucks and made a general
ruin'. The driver of the passenger train ended up in a hedge and the
stoker 'was hung up in the ruins'. Kilvert was particularly critical of the
guards' 'extraordinary negligence in not running back to stop the next
train. . . . The driver could have pulled up his train in five hundred
yards'. The guards were, he noted, 'properly discharged'.

On 19 September 1873, Kilvert was writing: 'I was talking to old
Mrs Matthews about the great number of railway accidents that have
happened lately'. He was himself fortunate on 11 June 1874 when a
train he was in was derailed just as it was leaving Shanklin station and
moving slowly. 'No harm was done, a screw jack was brought and by
this marvellous implement the carriage was lifted on to the line again.
It appears to me that if you had anywhere else to rest it a screw jack
would lift the world'. Did some of his ecstatic appreciation of the
screw jack's power derive from recollection of Brunel's stupendous
achievement of raising each of the 1,000 ton spans of the Saltash Bridge
one hundred feet? Screw jacks rescued Edward, Kilvert's brother, when
his train met with an accident: 'The facing points were wrong and the
train was cut in two'.

Kilvert made the Thorpe and Sittingbourne railway disasters
the theme of sermons on 4 November 1874 and 8 September 1878.
Both disasters presented to a Victorian mind dominated by the idea
of Providence and keen on life-improving technology much food
for thought. At Thorpe (which is near Norwich) around 10pm on
10 September 1874, two trains, late and trying to make up time, met
head-on on a single line as a result of misunderstandings between a
telegraph clerk and other officials. The telegraph system, so much
admired by Kilvert, was only as good as its human operators. The
Illustrated London News (*ILN*) for 19 September 1874 carried a
full account of the accident, including a striking engraving of 'the
pyramid . . . of locomotives, shattered carriages, and the wounded,
dead or dying passengers' referred to in the account. Graphic stories of
railway disasters appeared regularly in the *ILN* for readers to whom the
large numbers of dead and injured had great interest.[37] At Thorpe, 25
were killed, including both drivers and firemen, and 75 were injured.
The other disaster took place on 21 August 1878 when a train full
of day trippers returning to London from the Kent coast collided in

Sittingbourne station with the back of a train of trucks being shunted. Five people died and the two guards of the shunting train were charged with manslaughter. Again, the *ILN* provided the detail enabling Kilvert to draw out technological, moral, and spiritual issues in his sermons.

A landmark in the development of railways for the Kilvert family would have been the building of the Box Tunnel, which occupied three years. It was Brunel's stiffest challenge on his GWR line, requiring the blasting of a route one-and-three-quarter miles in length, through the solid limestone of Box Hill near Bath. One hundred tons of gunpowder were used, and an army of navvies – 4,000 of them – invaded the area, living in shanty towns. They removed 250,000 cubic yards of earth and laid 30 million bricks. It was this kind of undertaking that moved Coleman to state: 'The engineering of the early railways was like nothing before. Only the cathedrals were so audacious in concept and so exalted in architecture'. But, he added, there were few cathedrals and many railways.[38]

In 1835, Kilvert's father became Vicar of Hardenhuish, a village on the northern edge of Chippenham, barely six miles from Box Hill. He married Thermuthis Coleman in 1838 and, since work began on the Box Tunnel in June that year, the newlyweds must have felt they were living in the midst of a GWR building site. Brunel's nine-arch viaduct was, at the same time, rising up through the centre of Chippenham. Reports of the Tunnel's progress filled the local papers, including details of fatalities among the navvies (there were 100 deaths in all). The *Bath Chronicle* (24 May 1838) reported the crushing to death by a fall of earth of John Howel from Mrs Kilvert's home village of Kington St Michael. From the outset, the Tunnel was controversial. It opened in June 1841. At the time, it was the world's longest. Many said it should not be built at all, that it would fall in, that increase in air pressure as trains went through would collapse passengers' lungs. No means was found of lighting it for the benefit of passengers, gas lights being considered too expensive.[39] This was still the situation when Kilvert took an excursion train to Bath Flower Show on 18 May 1870: 'In the Box Tunnel as there was no lamp, the people began to strike foul brimstone matches and hand them to each other all down the carriage'. Each journey through the Tunnel for Kilvert and other locals must have been a reminder of its history and its cost in human lives.[40]

No less a figure than John Britton, whose significance for the Kilvert family as local hero and moral exemplar was noted in chapter two, was one of railways' most passionate advocates. An accomplished draughtsman himself, he was excited by 'the tide of lithography, steel engraving and wood engraving which between them virtually drove

out almost all other methods of reproducing pictures' in the early
1830s.[41] The 'world of wonders' (in Knight's phrase) that excited the
Kilverts was mediated importantly through pictures, which at the time
were 'wonders' themselves'. Britton, like Knight, wanted engravings to
represent the wonders of the new age of steam. Klingender noted that
Britton 'combined a love of ancient buildings with a passion for the
products of industry'.[42] This passion led the latter to back the building
of the London-Birmingham Railway. He became sponsor in 1832 to
the eighteen-year-old John Cooke Bourne, who, knowing of Britton's
interest in railways, sent him specimens of his London-Birmingham
drawings. Britton admired them so much that he felt their publication
(in four parts – September 1838 to July 1839) would both win support
for the project and counter prejudice against it. One can see why he
was fired by them. The drawing of Euston Station juxtaposes its portico
and other buildings at the entrance, looking like ancient Rome, with
stagecoaches and top-hatted and bonneted figures. The massive Camden
Town cutting, showing navvies building a retaining wall, is pictured
in a panoramic view. Another panoramic view depicts the building of
the stationary-engine house there. A *Rocket*-type locomotive is seen
emerging, a triumphant jet of smoke issuing from its funnel, from the
engine-house, with a figure alongside changing the points.

One Bourne drawing of the Watford Embankment silhouettes
a locomotive with a viaduct a hundred yards behind it, contrasting
dramatically with a rural landscape containing a meandering stream,
unchanged for centuries. The Colne Viaduct near Watford is reflected
in the river it crosses, sheep on one side and horses on the other,
suggesting that the new structure is already part of the present – and
the past. Several pictures provide details of the engineering involved.
Most suggestive of the sheer scale and effort required are the views of
Box Moor and Tring Embankments, which show navvies guiding large
barrows of earth up long, precarious wooden walkways ('runnings'),[43]
assisted by ropes over pulleys, to the top of the Embankments. And
there is the inside of Kilsby Tunnel, one of the most iconic images of
the early railway age.[44] In it, a shaft of light beams down from the roof,
sixty feet above, near the top of which is a figure, ethereal in the light's
beam, in a bucket of spoil suspended by a chain, while at the bottom
are two apparently exhausted horses in silhouette. Some have noted
the spiritual, cathedral-like atmosphere of the image and its suggestion
of man approaching heaven by dint of his enterprise and labour, the
horses already acknowledging that their time is done.

Britton's words, introducing Bourne's dramatic pictures, were equally
dramatic. 'Amongst all the changes of the civilised and commercial

world, there has never been one so eventful and prodigious as that effected by the agency of the Steam Engine,' he wrote; its 'superhuman power' and 'wonderful effects' had subverted all 'former modes of travelling'. Railways were, he said, one of the 'scientific wonders' of the age, signifying 'the rapid march of intellect' and men and nations competing for 'pre-eminence in art, science, and literature'. He linked railways to the ultimate final cause, 'the "end and aim" of creation – human happiness'.[45] Steam navigation facilitated the same end.[46] This was the vision of human progress shared by Charles Knight, Samuel Smiles, and the Kilvert family.

Britton had campaigned on behalf of the GWR in Bristol in 1833. He gave a lecture at the Bristol Scientific Institution on its 'desirableness and utility' at a time when Bristolians were lukewarm about it.[47] The Bristol Quaker and friend of Lewis Dillwyn (senior), John Harford, was among its supporters. The GWR was first proposed (by Bristol merchants, not London ones) on 27 December 1824, nine months before the Stockton-Darlington Railway opened. Bath's citizens proposed the Bath and Bristol Railway Company on 4 January 1830. One early suggestion was that the line would start from Monmouth Street in Bath. Ironically, it was in this street that Kilvert's grandfather ran his coach building business from November 1780 until August 1793. The *Bath Chronicle* for 27 August 1840 wrote enthusiastically that 'the good folks of Bath and Bristol will be whirled between those two cities in . . . twenty minutes – a revolution in travelling which . . . "would make our forefathers stare if they could witness it"'.[48]

John Bourne also produced a book of drawings to commemorate the GWR: *The History and Description of the Great Western Railway including the Geology and the Antiquities of the District through which it passes.*[49] It was his intention in the book to show railway features such as bridges, viaducts, and cuttings, normally unseen or unnoticed by passengers. These features, the result of railways' need for straight and level lines, isolated passengers to a degree from the existing landscape, and in effect created a new landscape. Among the drawings, many of which have a dream-like quality, was a view of the massive bridge over the Uxbridge Road, contrasting with stage wagons and flocks of sheep driven by smock-frocked figures; the huge Sonning Cutting with timber-supported bridges; a collection of locomotives in Swindon Engine-House; an unlined section of Box Tunnel; the line being constructed through Sydney Gardens in Bath; Bath Station, showing Brunel's broad gauge; and Chippenham Viaduct, through the arches of which are passing cattle, sheep, and farm wagons.

The Kilvert family background gives evidence of involvement in an engineering scheme as daring in character, though not in scale, as the London-Birmingham Railway and the GWR. The story of this scheme is another reminder of the Quaker influence shaping the Kilvert family's outlook. Kilvert's aunt Sophia was born Sophia Adelaide Leopoldina de Chièvre in 1789. Her father, Count Leopold of Buchlau, Moravia, was then attending Marie Antoinette in Paris and, in danger of execution himself, sent Sophia in 1793 to England disguised as a fisher-boy in an open boat. She was met at Dover by Mr Thomas Woodruffe Smith, a Quaker merchant, who was befriending French refugees. He became her guardian. She was married to uncle Francis Kilvert on 10 December 1822 from the Clapham home of Sir Robert Inglis (1786-1855).[50]

Thomas Woodruffe Smith (1747?-1811) was not a Quaker by birth but both his wives were. His second marriage (8 May 1789) was to Ann Reynolds. They originally lived in Stockwell, but on the death of her husband in 1811 she moved with her daughter Ann and Sophia de Chièvre to Acre Lane, Clapham, which presumably brought them into contact with Sir Robert Inglis. Inglis was involved with various philanthropic and educational societies, interests to which uncle Francis Kilvert was referring in his poem when he pictured Inglis 'at that social board where side by side,/ Votaries of Letters, Art, and Science vied'.[51] In 1815, Inglis became guardian to the orphaned children of Henry Thornton of the famous Evangelical family of Battersea Rise, Clapham. One of those children, Isabella, then aged eighteen, was a witness at Sophia de Chièvre's wedding to uncle Francis Kilvert in 1822. The other witnesses were Inglis's wife and younger sister, Mary Louisa. The presence of these witnesses indicates Sophia's intimacy with the occupants of Battersea Rise.

In 1798 Sophia's guardian became involved in a scheme to build a tunnel under the Thames from Gravesend to Tilbury, one of the schemes of improvement which stirred men of vision at the time. Ralph Dodd (1756-1822), the engineer behind the scheme, expressed its 'great public advantages' in terms of 'military communication' and 'increased facilities for intercourse between Essex and Kent'.[52] Woodruffe Smith was on the Committee chosen from the scheme's first patrons. Difficulties were encountered from the outset. Water continually flooded the workings and a steam-engine, supplied by Boulton and Watts's famous Soho Works in Birmingham, was needed to pump water out. Woodruffe Smith, in his capacity as Treasurer of the Proprietors of Gravesend Tunnel, was in correspondence with James Watt (junior) about money owed to the Soho Works for the steam-engine.[53] Fire destroyed the engine-house on 10 October 1802 and Rennie, the engineer, was called in to inspect the works that year. Eventually, the scheme was abandoned, its failure due in large part to the circumstances in which it was generated. Sophia de Chièvre was growing up in the Woodruffe Smith household throughout the Gravesend Tunnel episode, vicariously experiencing its successes and failures.

In order to appreciate the extent to which Kilvert's forebears embraced developments in public transport, we need to return to Bath's history around the turn of the century. It has already been noted that Kilvert's grandfather Francis was involved in coach travel; his coach building business was supplied with iron by George Stothert, who obtained it from the Coalbrookdale works. The two men were related through marriage to each other and to the Falkner brothers. The Falkner brothers, George Stothert, and coachbuilder Francis Kilvert were all involved in a Bath development epitomising the entrepreneurial and progressive culture which characterised the Kilvert family's early history. This was the Sydney Gardens scheme, which provided an exclusive promenading area, with green open spaces among elegant terraces, and an hotel.[54] Lewis Dillwyn (senior) showed its labyrinth to his daughter Fanny on 20 July 1823. First proposed in 1791, the scheme was financed by subscribers each of whom purchased a £100 share, and the Gardens opened in 1795. That the scheme manifested the skills of the modern world is confirmed by the fact that two of its four designers were the canal engineer John Rennie (1761-1821) and Brunel (at a later stage of its development). Directly behind the Widcombe (Bath) home of the Kilverts was the Kennet and Avon Canal, surveyed in 1790 and finished in 1810 by Rennie.[55]

In December 1795 the Kennet and Avon Canal Company wanted to push the canal through the nearly completed Sydney Gardens, offering £2,000 to its Proprietors for the privilege. It seems that the Gardens made large profits, which fuelled the expansion of Stothert's business. If Kilvert's grandfather had been able to remain a shareholder, the story of the family's life in Bath would have been very different, but his bankruptcy in 1794 debarred him from further involvement. At the end of 1822, the list of Gardens Proprietors still showed the names of Francis Henry Falkner (son of the original Francis) and of George Stothert (junior). The enterprise of these men did not end there. Brunel's GWR was nearing Bath by the late 1830s and he wanted to drive it through Sydney Gardens, destroying some of its choicest parts. However, the Proprietors did not object. At their annual dinner in March 1839, a toast was drunk to the GWR's success. The success of Brunel's Steamship Company and his *Great Western* was acknowledged by Mr J. Stothert and Mr Falkner.[56] Brunel's ambition was to see his GWR as the first leg of a service that would culminate in New York, and accordingly he had built a steamship, with a wooden hull and engines driving paddles, to make transatlantic crossings. The ship was the *Great Western*, then the biggest ship in the world, and it made its maiden voyage from Bristol on 8 April 1838, taking fifteen days.[57] The Sydney Gardens Proprietors had recognised that a new phase in the application of steam power in this age of wonders had begun. They had glimpsed a horizon beyond that of Bath. What did the loss of a few flowerbeds and arbours from their scheme matter if they could be associated with Brunel's much grander vision, a vision that was bridging the world?

The number of entries in *Kilvert's Diary* recording trips he took on steamboats is of course small compared with those recording railway trips. Kilvert was interested on 6 September 1878 to find that an old parishioner recalled the first steamboat on the Thames (this was the *Margery*, which operated daily from 1818 between the Dundee Arms, Wapping, to Gravesend and back). Kilvert had read about it in *Old England*. His interest in steamboats shows itself in a concern with accidents at sea that mirrors his concern with railway accidents. The entry (20 July 1870) recording the wrecking of a cargo ship, the *Scottish Queen*, off the Lizard in Cornwall is linked to lighthouses indirectly because he mentioned its 'two great twin white lighthouses'. In accounts of shipwrecks, Kilvert was often driven to ask of captains or ship-owners whether they had discharged their duties conscientiously, whether organisation and equipment were adequate. (It was the attitude he adopted to rail accidents.) Thus he recorded on 4 December 1874 that the captain of the *La Plata*, a telegraph cable-laying ship, which 'foundered and went down off Ushant in the Bay of Biscay with sixty souls', had always regarded it as 'an unseaworthy vessel' and inclined to be overloaded. Kilvert was especially outraged to hear of a Spanish steamer, the *Murillo*, which had run into the *Northfleet* and deserted her, 'leaving 327 souls to perish'. 'It is to be hoped,' he fumed, 'the Captain of the *Murillo* will be hung'.

Kilvert's local papers provided extensive coverage of disasters at sea, illustrated by 'the burning of the emigrant ship *Caspatria* near the Cape of Good Hope bound for New Zealand', referred to by him on 28 December 1874. ('*Caspatria*' is a transcription error for '*Cospatrick*', a sailing ship of 1200 tons.) The *Devizes and Wiltshire Gazette* for 31 December 1874 carried various accounts of the disaster: the *Times* report ('Railway Slaughter and Fire at Sea'), the *Daily Telegraph* report ('The Burning of the Cospatrick'), the report of the *Daily News* Special Correspondent at Madeira, as well as another piece ('Dreadful Disaster to an Emigrant Ship'). What stands out here, apart from such full coverage in a provincial paper, is the reports' reliance on telegrams, a main means of news-collecting by this time, making the world into the global village of today. Kilvert's own account begins 'Today we heard by a short telegram . . .'[58] All the accounts in the *Gazette* mention telegrams that first reported the disaster. One reviewed the circumstances of it from 'the concensus [*sic*] of telegrams' received. The 'Dreadful Disaster' article expressed satisfaction at the safety record of emigrant ships to New Zealand: 'They have landed many hundreds of passengers . . . with a freedom from disaster that, considering the distance – more than half of the entire circumference of the globe – has been really wonderful'. The shrinking of distance by steamship travel was still a wonder in 1874. Its shrinking by telegram was still something of a wonder for Kilvert. However, the *Times* took the view that, in such an age of progress, 'modern machinery' should have made impossible the 'cruel incongruity' of the destruction of a ship by fire when surrounded by water.

Kilvert took a steamboat in Weymouth harbour on 11 October 1872 to tour HMS *Hercules*, a wonder ship of the Royal Navy. His friend Arthur Dew was a midshipman on board. The *Diary* entry about Kilvert's tour is filled with patriotic pride that his country could produce such a symbol of power. He called it a 'splendid ship'. Launched in 1868, it was a screw-driven ironclad of 8700 tons, the first to mount a main armament of ten-inch calibre guns. A little boy's excitement is reflected in Kilvert's observation that he climbed aboard 'in the teeth of one of the great 400 lb stern chasers'. The ship's organisation was, he wrote, 'a little world [whose] beautiful order, regularity, cleanliness and smartness . . . are wonderful'. It typified the mid-Victorian ideals of industrial efficiency and achievement with which he had grown up.

The story of Grace Darling has a place in this Victorian vision of progress. The *Diary* entry of 28 September 1872 is a very cryptic one: 'The dream of Grace Darling' (the original entry may have been longer, and other entries may have referred to it – '*The* dream', instead of '*A*' dream', may mean the dream was recurrent). The entry's date provides some clues to its understanding. It was not the anniversary of her heroic feat of rescuing survivors from the wrecked steamship *Forfarshire*; that was 7 September 1838. Nor was it the anniversary of her death – 20 October 1842. However, September was the month of her feat and 1872 was the thirtieth anniversary of her death. She had set out during a storm in an open boat with her father from their home, the Longstone Lighthouse, an exploit that made her an icon for Victorians.[59] William Howitt interviewed her for his book in 1841 and represented her as a simple, devout, Quaker maiden.[60] The public regarded her as a pious Christian devoted to the service of humanity. She was also seen as a child of nature because she shared her father's love of natural history and her childhood was a time of burgeoning interest in the subject.[61] Grace's natural theology was founded in 'the wonders round her: in the sea birds, rocks and waves she found evidence . . . of a great Creator.'[62] She was also, importantly, a woman. Jessica Mitford stressed that she became a 'role model for the Victorian girl'.[63]

Her peculiar significance lay in the fact that she lived in a lighthouse, and a lighthouse symbolised her devotion and achievement. Uncle Francis Kilvert may have been responsible for holding her up as an example to his nephew and other of his pupils. He paid tribute to her in a poem, picturing her as 'a truly Christian heroine'. Lighthouses evidently held much meaning for him. He wrote a poem, *The Lighthouse*,[64] in 1859 – in September, the month of Grace Darling's famous rescue, and of Kilvert's *Diary* entry. The lighthouse uncle Francis urged readers to picture was 'raised by skilful hands' and its 'fiery column' was akin to 'the pillar of fire by night' which shed on Israel's 'faithless Tribes its wondrous light' as they journeyed through the 'wild desert'. Though man-made, the lighthouse itself was a wonder. Those 'whose deed of mercy fixed [the lighthouse] there' were rewarded by the 'fervent prayer' of mariners. The poem graphically illustrates the way in which a technological achievement could be transfigured by a Victorian mind that was both pious and progressive into a religious symbol, equating the creation of such a useful edifice with a Christian act of the highest order.[65]

The Lighthouse was, uncle Francis noted, written at the request of his 'valued friend', Captain Thomas Pickering Clarke. Clarke's naval career began in 1800 and by 1809 he was a lieutenant. In a letter to Admiral Edward Campbell Owen, under whom he served 1810-1813, he discussed the construction of the Bell Rock Lighthouse.[66] He himself managed, on behalf of Trinity House, a lighthouse on the rock called The Smalls, 21 miles off St David's Head, Pembrokeshire. Kilvert, on his visit to St David's Head on 17 October 1874, did not refer to The Smalls, but was anxious about 'dangerous treacherous black rocks' he could see a mile from the shore. The fact that Clarke, a former lighthouse keeper, was a 'valued friend' of uncle Francis is further confirmation of the Kilvert family's interest in technological achievement.

Again, we can turn to Knight's *Old England* and its place in Kilvert's upbringing to see how a respect for lighthouses and lighthouse builders and keepers was instilled into him. Several engravings of Eddystone Lighthouse are followed in Knight's book with notes on its construction by John Smeaton (1724-1792) in 1759; uncle Francis's poem was written on its 100th anniversary. Various previous attempts to build one on the small but deadly rock ended in disaster and thus Knight's account is a story of faith and perseverance and a desire to benefit mankind. His achievement in the eighteenth century is cited, with that of Brunel's Thames Tunnel in the nineteenth century, as works of 'moral grandeur' which overshadowed even their 'physical grandeur'.[67]

The *Diary* entry that Kilvert wrote of his visit to Liverpool on 20 June 1872 provides the clearest reflection of his passion for technological and commercial progress. The urge to see its docks may have taken root when he was ten and visiting the Great Exhibition where a model of them appeared in the civil engineering section. One of the sub-themes of the entry was Britain's Empire and maritime supremacy. The Mersey was, he wrote, 'almost crowded with vessels of all sorts . . . ships, barques, brigantines, schooners, cutters, tugs, steamboats, lighters, "flats", everything from the huge emigrant liner steamship with four masts to the tiny sailing and rowing boat'. His sense of Liverpool as a port that exported people as well as goods was strong: he referred several times to emigrants and 'the hundreds of sorrowful hearts on board'. At this point, his thoughts must have returned to his aunt Sarah and uncle Herbert, emigrants to Canada, and to Marryat's 'Settlers in Canada', who embarked from Liverpool. His excitement and pride in the achievement the port represented included this reference: 'We saw a large screw steamship in a graving dock being repaired and we had a good opportunity of examining her gigantic screw', the invention of Charles Pettit Smith (1808-1874).[68] Brunel, having learnt of the successful trials of Smith's screw-driven ship, *The Archimedes*, adopted screw propulsion for his revolutionary SS *Great Britain*. Kilvert's sense of progress, during his Liverpool visit, recognised however that Brunel's ship belonged to a bygone age: 'I was very much disappointed in this famous ship. She was painted black and white and looked like a collier beside the modern huge steamships'. Kilvert had grown up with the *Great Britain* from its departure from Bristol in 1845, its first transatlantic sailing on 26 July 1845, its record-breaking trips to Australia, its transporting of troops during the Crimean War and the Indian Mutiny.[69] Once a wonder, it had been superseded by other wonders, which was the story of the nineteenth century, and he was impressed by what was modern.

The 'modern huge steamships' with which Kilvert compared the *Great Britain* unfavourably were Cunard's ships *Batavia* and *Cuba*. The liners of Samuel Cunard (1787-1865), Quaker entrepreneur from Halifax, Nova Scotia, had been leading the way in transatlantic travel since Kilvert was born. Cunard's steamship the *Britannia*, sailing from Liverpool to Boston, via Halifax, was the first regular passenger and cargo service. Cunard came to Britain and won the British transatlantic steamship mail contract and for the next thirty years (1840-70) his ships

The *SS Great Britain*

were leaders in terms of speed. In the years following Cunard's death in 1865, great rivalry developed between his line and the British Inman line to achieve the quickest crossing, a rivalry marked by the introduction in both companies of screw-driven propellers. Awareness of all this colours Kilvert's account of Liverpool Docks. He noted that the *Batavia* was 'one of the Cunard liners' (in 1870 it had completed the transatlantic crossing in twelve days; in 1845 the *Great Britain* took eighteen). He actually went on board the *Batavia* and regretted he didn't have time to tour the *Cuba*, 'a magnificent ship, one of the finest of the line'.[70]

The day after he inspected Cunard's *Batavia*, Kilvert went by steamboat to Birkenhead to see the shipbuilding yard John Laird's. It was founded in 1824, built its first screw-propeller steamer in 1839, and also manufactured gun-boats for the Crimea. Of special significance to Kilvert would have been the fact that Laird's made the *Ma Robert*, a small river steamer for Dr Livingstone. It also built the naval ships that filled Kilvert with pride and patriotic fervour. He was proud to be able to talk with one of the yard's engineers who epitomised work and dedication: the yard was so busy that 'he himself had to be there at 4 o'clock a.m. and did not leave off till 9 p.m.' It is 'the largest ship-building yard in the world and they employ some 4,000 men,' Kilvert enthused. It was inevitable to one with his background that Laird's and the port of Liverpool should present a stirring image of business efficiency, of exciting technology, of booming trade, of Empire, and of a dynamic society that was leading the world.[71] The Gwatkins, who provided Kilvert with his Liverpool tour (20-21 June 1872), shared his values. 'I like the Gwatkins exceedingly,' he wrote. Mrs Gwatkin was the daughter of Kilvert's uncle, Dr John

Kilvert, of whom more will be said later. The Gwatkins were the kind of
forward-looking middle-class people the Kilverts cultivated, as can be
seen in tributes uncle Francis paid to the Stotherts. Of George Stothert,
son of the Bath ironmonger, he wrote: 'he had a sound and vigorous
understanding and a correct taste . . . cultivated by travel and commerce
with the world'. Of the widow of the first George Stothert, uncle Francis
noted that 'as the wife of a tradesman she [represented] those old-
fashioned virtues of modesty, industry and economy, which form staple
excellencies . . . particularly in the middle class'.[72] These same virtues
were largely what drew the Kilverts to the Kearys.

Another *Diary* entry concerning the Kearys needs to be noted here:

> Miss Mewburn whom I met at the Kerrys this evening lent
> me a pamphlet by Edward Hine[73] on the identity of the
> English nation with the ten lost tribes of Israel. It is a grand
> idea and an interesting and exciting surmise. We "stared
> at each other with a wild surmise". I only hope it is true. It
> would be a glorious truth.

The Miss Mewburn, whom Kilvert met on 29 November 1872 at the
'Kerrys' (a misreading for Kearys), was Frances Anne, eldest sister to
Lucy, who had married Alfred Keary. It is clear Kilvert found Hine's thesis
enormously thrilling. Why? Hine declared that his aim was to convince
people that they were 'heirs to the greatest temporal, political and social
blessings . . . ever vouchsafed to any one particular. . . . Nation . . . as a
result of being "Heirs to Israel"'. The blessings would come when the
English 'recognised' their identity with Israel. When 'Israel was restored',
which was imminent, the Gospel would truly triumph throughout the
whole world. Hine's thesis was that the Lost Tribes of Israel were identical
with the ancestors of the English and it rested on the recognition that the
one people of Israel was composed of two houses – that of Judah (the
Jews) and that of Israel – two peoples 'as distinct as France from Russia'.
The people of Israel became wanderers but eventually made their home
in the British Isles.[74]

What particularly excited Kilvert about this extravagant thesis
was its emphasis on England's central involvement with missionary
endeavour. Hine argued that the success of Christ's mission on earth
was that 'the English have been more highly favoured with divine
light above any other existing nation: Our race alone have the great
missionary work in hand'.[75] The idea that Christians had a divine call
to convert the rest of the world to their faith had existed for centuries
and Kilvert showed himself a true Evangelical when he registered on
27 October 1874 how much he was struck by the illustration a CMS
speaker, Mr Barne,[76] gave of the task facing the Church: 'If 5000 should

pass through Langley every day it would take 400 years for all the 800,000,000 [heathen] to go by'. The size of the task was a wonder; achieving it would be a greater wonder. Hine had envisaged a people for whom spiritual progress went hand in hand with material progress. It had been prophesied that the Isles to which the Israelites had migrated would become too small for them. Hence the expansion of England into her colonies, the so-called 'desolate heritages' of the earth. One of Israel's great characteristics was her 'pushing propensity', which meant that she dispossessed the original inhabitants of countries into which she expanded.[77] Hine was advancing a rationale for imperialism.

One particularly significant element of Kilvert's entry about Hine's pamphlet is his response to its central thesis as 'a grand idea', the response of a man to whom *ideas* – almost for their own sake – were important. Another particularly significant element, and one illustrative of the context in which Kilvert placed the 'grand idea', is his quoting of Keats's sonnet *On First Looking into Chapman's Homer*. Kilvert slightly misquoted a line from the following passage:

.... Then felt I like some watcher of the skies
When a new planet swims into his ken;
Or like stout Cortez when with wond'ring eyes
He stared at the Pacific – and all his men
Looked at each other with a wild surmise –
Silent upon a peak in Darien.

By suggesting that he and Miss Mewburn 'stared at each other with a wild surmise' at the thought of what Hine was proposing, Kilvert was recalling with Keats other momentous occasions when the barriers of knowledge were extended: the changing of man's conception of the earth through exploration, and of his viewing of the solar system through patient study of the skies. Later chapters will show how exciting such occasions were for Kilvert. Importantly, these occasions grew out of, and provoked, a sense of wonder; Cortez[78] stares at the Pacific with 'wond'ring eyes'.

The way in which pioneering technology – steam-engines, hydraulic jacks, electric telegraphs, bridges, viaducts, steamboats, screw-propellers, tunnels, lathes,[79] lighthouses, telescopes, microscopes – were sources of excitement for the Kilvert family has been the main theme of this chapter. Knight, Britton, Smiles, and others had been telling the romantic story of the achievements of the steam age from the time Kilvert's father was born in 1804. A significant part of this story had been conveyed through pictures, to which several Kilverts responded passionately. Bourne's often dream-like images of railways, juxtaposed with what had been for most people the only past – the rural one, may have haunted Kilvert's imagination from his childhood. He was prone to represent his experiences of railways in pictorial forms marked by imagination and wonder. In one entry, he wrote: 'The station lights glanced and trembled in the river and the train came down the Wye side sweeping round the curves and blazing with white and green lamps'. He was also intrigued when, because of 'some peculiar effect of atmosphere, the lights of Hay looked as if they were in the sky, and the train seen with its moving lamps at the end of the vista of trees . . . appeared to be travelling along in the clouds'.[80] Kilvert conveyed a sense of the new landscapes that railways had created.

This chapter has emphasised that the religion of the Kilvert family – particularly its Quakerism and Evangelicalism – was far from being hostile to science and industry. For the Kilverts, the pursuit of technological improvement was as religious and as altruistic as preaching – or teaching. We have seen how they became involved in industrial schemes, swept along by the atmosphere of new technology and entrepreneurial flair. In those stirring times, they were ready, even eager to be stirred. Kilvert's grandfather had left agriculture and eastern Shropshire, that crucible of the Industrial Revolution, to set up a coach building business in Bath. If it had flourished and he had been able to participate in the Sydney Gardens scheme, his sons, instead of becoming churchmen, might have been businessmen, as the Stothert and Falkner sons had, or professionals, like the Mewburns and Kearys, on the fringe of business. Noticeably, Annie Keary's brother William became, like Francis Mewburn, a railway solicitor, to the North Staffs. Railway Company in 1845. Annie herself, while at boarding school, collected 'out-of-the-way scraps of knowledge'. The school's headmistress once asked what Annie and sister Eliza were discussing so eagerly 'during the English-speaking hour'. Eliza replied: 'Oh, madame! Annie was telling me all about gravitation and the stars'.[81]

Kilvert's diary entry for 16 March 1872 encapsulates his own understanding of what had changed with the advent of the railways and of what railways had achieved. Kilvert was late for a train and he needed Venables's dog-cart to get him urgently to the station. The horse did the 5½ miles in 20 minutes. 'As we dashed up to the Three Cocks station the train glided up to the platform. . . . [It] was exactly punctual. Well done, old Rocket'. Venables's horse had been named to commemorate the locomotive, built by George Stephenson, whose winning of the Rainhill locomotive competition heralded a new age. Kilvert's affectionate tribute to old Rocket contained nostalgia for the age when the horse was still king. However, like the horses in Bourne's Kilsby Tunnel image, old Rocket could still play a part in the new age.

Chapter 5
Kilvert and Science and Technology

Little boys must take the trouble to find out things for
themselves, or they will never grow to be men.
Charles Kingsley, *The Water Babies*

Alfred rather prided himself on his scientific knowledge.
Mary Howitt, *The Children's Year*

Commentators on *Kilvert's Diary* have dismissed the idea that its
author had any real interest in science. William Plomer, its original
editor, stated that his 'delight in the workings of machinery' was
'aesthetic, not scientific', referring to Kilvert's visit to the Birkenhead
ship-building yard where he saw iron being made and cut.[1] Note needs
to be taken of the context of this *Diary* entry in order to understand it.
To Kilvert, Liverpool was another Bristol, full of 'life, movement and
work', and his mood was correspondingly excited and expectant: 'I was
in dancing spirits'. The sense of Liverpool as a foremost city of Empire
is deepened by the reference to the 'vast commerce of the country' on
the docks. It was the visit on 21 June 1872 to Laird's ship-building yard
that he enjoyed most:

It was very interesting to see the forging of the iron. . . . The
working of the machinery was beautiful, especially the
drills . . . boring a hole through a thick plate of cold iron as
if it had been cheese. Then the knives worked up and down,
shearing off the ends of thick iron bars as if they had been
bars of soap. The lathe too was wonderful, peeling off the
outer rusty skin of great iron cylinders and leaving them
bright and shining.

There is aesthetic appreciation in this description, but the aesthetic
is a common element in the experience of scientific discovery and
experimentation. The lathe that Kilvert saw was a wonder because its
operations were efficient and useful as well as beautiful.

Another commentator adopted Plomer's approach, asserting that
Kilvert rejected the industrialism of the Welsh valleys 'with a literary

shudder'.[2] Can this be reconciled with his declared intention on 11 March 1870 of visiting 'the iron works of Glamorgan'? In addition, he visited industrial sites in his extended tour of Cornwall, as the editors of *Kilvert's Cornish Diary* underlined.[3] Then we have his fascination with the electric telegraph: 'Miss Watkins took me into her telegraphing room and initiated me into the mysteries of the craft'.[4] It was presumably *his* interest that prompted Mrs Gough to show him round the Chippenham silk looms where she worked (24 May 1873). And, on 27 December 1871, two young men who worked in a Dundee iron-works told him 'of a new invention, iron paper, as thin as the thinnest tissue paper. The sheets of iron are rolled so thin that 3,000 sheets together are only an inch thick'. It is not true therefore that his writing focused only on conventionally beautiful scenes and objects: he was also typically Victorian in responding to the amazing transformations that science and technology were making in his world and he described them in vivid detail. This was, after all, the way he had been taught from an early age.

It is important at this point to clarify the nature of the Victorian understanding of 'science'. Keynes stated: 'science meant knowledge and understanding in the broadest view.... [It] was not seen as a narrow method of learning [but] shared concerns with metaphysics, religion, and art'.[5] Victorians viewed science and culture as 'inextricably linked'.[6] What scientific knowledge meant in the early nineteenth century, when Kilvert's uncle Francis (b.1793) was coming to maturity, can be seen in this statement: 'it was in demand as a form of rational amusement, as theological edification, polite accomplishment, technological agent, social anodyne, and intellectual ratifier of the new order'.[7] Science had not yet come to be what it later became – a discipline with its own objective aims and methods, separate from other forms of learning.[8] (The word 'scientist' itself was not coined until 1833.) In the early nineteenth century, it had close affinities with Romanticism:

> Romanticism as a cultural form is generally regarded as intensely hostile to science, its ideals of subjectivity eternally opposed to that of scientific objectivity. But I do not believe this was always the case, or that the terms are so mutually exclusive. The notion of *wonder* seems to be something that once united them, and can still do so. In effect there is Romantic science in the same sense that there is Romantic poetry, and often for the same enduring reasons.[9]

It has already been ascertained that Kilvert was drawn to Romantic science.

As Kilvert was growing up, natural history and science, which for

Francis Kilvert (the diarist's uncle)

centuries were one and the same, had begun to grow apart. Chapter
three has indicated the basis of the split between them: the naturalist
observed and admired; the scientist analysed. Both studied natural
objects but in different ways. Merrill noted that modern historians
of science are very ready to dismiss natural history: 'All Victorian
naturalists did was collect rocks or bugs in their spare time; thus they
are easily dismissed as dabblers; they did not practise science'.[10] The
closed, blinkered world of natural history books, their disinclination
to undertake real scientific investigation, was underlined by Barber.
Their authors, she stated, continually reproduced each other's facts,
anecdotes, and assumptions while ignoring 'all the great scientific
controversies that were raging in the world outside, even though these
were ones that directly concerned natural history'. This was because
their approach was dominated by natural theology. The conservative,
complacent stance of natural history books can be illustrated by
reference to one: Bellairs's book on ferns. Her introduction declared
that there was no need to fear that man's study of nature would
discover any flaws in it, even via the microscope. The book ended:
'Every created thing has something good and pleasant to say to us if
only we will listen aright' and looking for 'nature's beauty will 'lead us
to that high communion with the Most High'. Darwin found 'nature's
beauty but he also found, instead of the 'good and the pleasant', a story
of 'nature's appalling cruelty. Nona Bellairs shied away from this to
embrace a natural history that involved 'long walks in pleasant places

with cherished friends, a little speculation, a little argument. . . . '[11] In Victorian times this kind of natural history yielded slowly to the kind of professional science we have today. The former's 'salient qualities – subjectivity, collecting, classification, description – were spurned by the sciences that supplanted it'. It was in the matter of causes that natural history differed fundamentally from science: 'Natural history studied appearances; natural philosophy [physics] investigated relationships'.[12]

Morrell and Thackray trace the emergence in the 1820s and 1830s of 'men of knowledge' eager to apprise themselves of new discoveries in all areas of learning. One form of organisation into which they formed themselves were the Lit and Phil societies. This chapter gives an account of uncle Francis's involvement in one. A particularly significant institution, in relation to the development of science, was Trinity College, Cambridge, the 'spiritual home' of a group of liberal Anglicans, or Broad Church advocates of liberal reform. Adam Sedgwick was a leading figure in this group. Its mouthpiece was the British Association for the Advancement of Science (BAAS), a peripatetic organisation whose first Meeting was in York on 26 September 1831. It held a particular view of science: 'the ways in which nature and nature's laws transcended man's experience, yet opened the way to common feeling, and a common approach to nature's God'. This liberal Anglican position embraced the position of natural theology:

> The liberal Anglican position asserted the mutual autonomy of science and of theology, yet insisted on the ultimate congruence of natural with revealed religion. When rightly understood, the book of Nature and the book of Scripture were in accord, for their Author was the same. By investigating the regularities of natural phenomena, by inferring general laws, by revealing the evidence of design, and by referring design to a Designer, the natural philosopher could reinforce Christian faith.[13]

Kilvert's uncle Francis, by endorsing Sedgwick's *Discourse*, identified himself with this position, as will be seen.

Although uncle Francis was not a 'gentleman of science' as Sedgwick was, he was one of the early century's 'men of knowledge'. His own interests were mainly antiquarian, literary and historical. However, his collection of Latin inscriptions, *Pinacothecae Historicae Specimen*, celebrated men and women eminent in all fields of learning. Its title means roughly 'A Historical Portrait Gallery' but the word 'specimen' is suggestive. He intended his historical figures to be 'specimens', i.e. individuals exemplifying a particular class, as natural history specimens did. The class comprised bishops, kings, statesmen, orators, philosophers, churchmen, writers, historians, philanthropists, painters, dramatists, scientists, and astronomers.

Henrietta Joan Fry wrote a poem *A Character, for my friend Francis Kilvert, 1844*, in which she pictured him as a 'man of knowledge' and as a teacher. We are told that 'He deeply drank of wisdom's lore' and that 'Saints and Sages' were the 'Companions of his nightly toil'. She herself was one of 'a graceful female band', to whom uncle Francis's 'study door is opened wide'; books were 'supplied' and a 'mental banquet' prepared. The explanation for her membership in this group is most likely to be the fact that she was, like Sophia Kilvert, a Quaker. She did not live in Bath but came from the Fry family of Bristol, founders of the famous chocolate-making firm, and once again the social and religious ethos of Quakerism can be seen in the Kilvert family story.[14] Henrietta pictured Francis Kilvert as a 'specimen' of exactly the kind of person who found a place in his own Portrait Gallery: churchman, teacher, and savant.

It seems certain that Sophia Kilvert would have been the 'fair presiding grace' of the 'female band' that met in her husband's study, which prompts the question of her involvement in scientific things. 'Women were routinely excluded from scientific societies in the 1830s . . . [however] the cultivators of science or friends of science were assumed without question to be women'. Science was considered to be too technical and abstract, as well as too coarse (because of its exploration of physical matters), for women. Women were, however, regarded as central to the BAAS's aim of presenting science as a 'public resource', and also as a source of income, and eventually were admitted to some sections of its Meetings.[15]

The BAAS Meeting came to Bristol in 1836 with Lord Lansdowne as its President. Bristol recommended itself in the view of W.D. Conybeare[16] because 'There we should equally command Bath, where John Shute Duncan would zealously work for us'. Duncan was, he said, 'the leading spirit of the Bath Literary and Scientific Institute' (BLSI).[17] In March 1844 Murchison wrote to Whewell, Master of Trinity College, Cambridge, about future BAAS meetings and stated that Bath, 'which has invited us warmly to visit her in 1845, would be a good venue'. However, Bath had to wait another twenty years before the BAAS arrived. Sophia Kilvert's enthusiasm for science may have led her, in company with her husband, to attend BAAS Meetings. We know, for example, that in 1864 she donated to the Bath Literary and Scientific Institution (BLSI) the Report of the BAAS Meeting held at

Newcastle-on-Tyne the previous year.[18] Her donation came after her husband's death in November 1863. As a member of the BLSI, he was entitled, by BAAS rules, to become a BAAS Member and to receive free copies of its Reports, which could explain why Sophia had a copy of the 1863 one.

Kilvert grew up with the wonder of the electric telegraph. It is represented in *The Children's Year*, published in 1847, as a thing of enchantment to seven-year-old Herbert: 'It was wonderful to him . . . he kept his eyes fixed on those marvellous wires'.[19] Kilvert's interest in the 'wires' was no doubt stimulated by Herbert's. The former was only eight when 'half the country's railway tracks had telegraph wires running alongside them'.[20] *The Leisure Hour*'s article 'Electric Wires' (13 November 1856) explained that, a hundred years before, the idea that a man could transmit information to friends in any part of the kingdom in a few minutes would have been ridiculed. The public might not appreciate, the writer remarked, that the electric telegraph 'had its romance as well as its practical utilities . . . summoning one to a marriage feast, another to a grave-side'. However, the invention was of particular value to commerce. It gave Kilvert satisfaction to see in Liverpool's Exchange screens 'covered with the latest telegrams [detailing] stocks and shares lists, cargoes, freights'. (The word 'Telegrams' was coined by the early 1850s to mean telegraph messages.)

In 1856 a telegraph cable had been laid under the sea from New York to Newfoundland, and in July 1857 an abortive attempt was made at laying a transatlantic one. After four attempts it was achieved on 5 July 1858, only to fail a month later. When Brunel's *Great Eastern* succeeded in laying it on 13 July 1866 the feat, compared by the *Times* with the discovery of the New World, was made possible by the use of gutta percha, known as 'the wonder material of the age', as insulation. A sample of it had been shown in 1843[21] to Charles Mackintosh, maker of waterproof clothing. Charles Hancock, brother of Mackintosh's partner, could see its value as stoppers for bottles and in 1845 founded the Gutta Percha Company. The firm adopted it for insulation of wires and it coated the cross-Channel cable of 1851 and was displayed at the Great Exhibition of that year. Derived from the sap of Malayan trees, gutta percha was waterproof like rubber, but its great virtue was that, unlike rubber, it didn't rot in water; its great triumph was that it was used to coat the transatlantic cable.

It says much about Henry James Bodily, St Helena missionary, that in 1875 he took charge of the industrial parish of Silvertown in London,[22] named after Stephen Silver, whose vast India Rubber, Gutta Percha, and Telegraph Company (IRGPT) employed most of its working population. While Bodily served the parish, 2,500 of its people worked for IRGPT. Charles Hancock joined the Company in 1860, bringing his knowledge of gutta percha with him. The Company had developed the technique of extruding gutta percha into tubes to cover wire and this was the basis of the cable-making / laying industry that was pioneering submarine cables throughout the world as Kilvert grew up.[23]

He showed strong interest in the Scilly Isles cable when holidaying in Cornwall, referring to it twice in his Cornish diary. On the excursion to Land's End on 27 July 1870, he commented: 'The Scilly telegraph wire accompanied us along the road'. At Land's End, he could see 'the Telegraph House where the Scilly Cable leaves the mainland'. This point was the critical one because cables were in danger from coastal ships and from damage caused by storms tossing them against rocks. Consequently, they had to have thicker insulation. The day before Kilvert's excursion, a local paper, the *West Briton*, had reported on the benefits provided by the Scilly Cable. He could also have read about it in the 9 July 1870 *ILN*, which showed a picture of the Telegraph House he saw. The accompanying article told of the Cable's 'great utility' to ship owners as a means of reporting accidents. It was another technological achievement – with Silver's IRGPT Company supplying the gutta percha cable insulation – and it attracted Kilvert's attention.

The influence on Kilvert of his aunt Sophia, with regard to science and technology should not be underestimated. She was the author of *Home Discipline* (1841), an educational treatise and, since he was a boarder in her home for seven years, she should be included with his other teachers. Her treatise begins with the assertion that she regarded the 'religious, moral and domestic care of [her] husband's household' as a sacred trust. Pupils of her husband's school living in her household were to her extensions, along with the servants, of her family, and as such legitimate objects of her educational influence. That influence bore the imprint of her upbringing in the Quaker home of Thomas Woodruffe Smith. In her book, Sophia praised Quakers' 'habits of patient industry', which induced them to support 'the most useful institutions in the kingdom'. She castigated procrastination because it destroyed our 'usefulness'. It was these values that led to the involvement of Sophia's patron in the Gravesend Tunnel scheme.

She was also concerned about the reading material available to the lower classes, including those living in homes like hers. Crime in society was, she believed, attributable in part to 'the scandalous contents of our daily Newspapers . . . through the circulation of cheap publications and pictures, we may trace the fertile source of half our crimes'. The boon of increased literacy was unfortunately part of the problem: 'book-learning has added a weapon, for good or evil, in the war of passions,' she wrote, 'Books are our worst, or our best, private companions'. One thing employers could do was to repress 'the perusal of more than doubtful publications'. It was, Sophia wrote, the duty of the 'wise and prudent' to put before servants 'the imperishable materials of wisdom and experience', in the form of popular publications, so as 'to repair the breaches made in bulwarks of virtue'. To such employers, it was 'an incalculable good collecting and distributing . . . from unseen and distant mines, gems of various kinds and of infinite value'.[24]

The publication called *The Friends' Monthly Magazine* (*FMM*), that appeared at the end of the decade in which Sophia was concerned over popular reading material, must have given her intense satisfaction, especially as it emanated from her own Quaker community. Its second issue (December 1829) was introduced by a letter from a correspondent – 'Observations on the Probable Advantages of a Periodical Miscellany adapted to the Society of Friends' – whose ideas and words might have been Sophia's own:

The circumstances of the times seem to require that the press should be enlisted as much as possible on the side of piety and virtue. This is a reading age. . . . The mass of the community is taught the means of acquiring knowledge, and according as this knowledge is well or ill applied, will it advance or retrograde in a moral and religious course.

The letter was everywhere informed by the sense that a new age was dawning:

. . . progress [was] accelerating beyond all former experience. . . . The prodigies of the steam-engine in the material world, may be surpassed in the regions of mind and morals, by the combined operations of the press and popular instruction.

No Quaker periodical existed then and the 'present state of intellectual cultivation' in the Society of Friends warranted the launch of one.

Some examples of material from the magazine during 1830 will illustrate its nature. Among 'Miscellanies' in the March issue was an article on the proposed Clifton Suspension Bridge. Improvements in the design of iron bridges had resulted in the Suspension or Chain bridge – 'a bridge at once useful, beautiful and economical'. An engraving of Telford's design accompanied the article. It noted that the combination of iron and 'neighbouring coal mines' was responsible for 'the high station we hold among nations'. There was also a piece on 'Novel and amusing Electrical Experiments'. The May issue reviewed *A Sketch of the Life of Linnaeus* and *Rudiments of Conchology*, both 'for young persons'. The July article, 'Observations on Galvanism', began: 'The works of God . . . are calculated to excite admiration, astonishment, and delight, and the more so as they are the more attentively . . . investigated'. The 1830 issues featured a dozen articles on education and eleven meteorological reports.

The *FMM* was one manifestation of what O'Connor has called 'the explosion of new and cheaper forms of printed science' that occurred in the second quarter of the nineteenth century.[25] It would have circulated among largely middle-class Quakers. Copies of it may have found their way into the hands of uncle Francis's pupils. Sophia Kilvert was keen, however, that new discoveries in science and technology reached working-class people. The *FMM* preceded the *Penny Magazine* and *Chambers's Edinburgh Journal* (both appeared in 1832), one sign of the progressive nature of the Quaker mind. The SDUK, through its *Penny Magazine*, sought to introduce science into working-class homes as 'rational amusement', an alternative to (often cruel) sports, gambling, and the public house. However, its main readership was middle-class. Knight, the editor of the *Penny Magazine*, rejected the objection that such a 'desultory habit of reading' encouraged by it did no service to 'the cultivation of the popular mind', and produced no 'real or lasting knowledge'. Working people had, because of their small leisure time, little other means of gaining knowledge. On the *Magazine*'s national committee in 1833, lending their reputation to its endeavour, were such figures as Dr John Elliotson, physician and pioneer of mesmerism,[26] Rowland Hill, responsible for postal reforms and the postage stamp, James Mill, Lord John Russell, and Dr Roget, physician and inventor of the *Thesaurus*. On the 1833 Cambridge committee were Professor Henslow, Leonard Jenyns, and Professor Sedgwick. Josiah Wedgwood was on the Etruria committee.[27] The national committee in 1836 boasted such figures as H.T. de la Beche, the geologist, and John William Lubbock, supporter of progressive causes and friend and neighbour of Charles Darwin at Downe, Kent. In 1840, George Birkbeck, founder of the first Mechanics' Institution in 1823, and of Birkbeck College, now part of London University, served on the national committee, along with the geologist and explorer, R.I. Murchison.

The *Magazine*'s eclectic mix of 'printed science' resembled that of *The Leisure Hour* and the *FMM*. In 1833 there were articles on the Aurora Borealis, the Bass Rock, fire-damp and the Davy Lamp, modes of flying in birds, a visit to De Fellenberg's progressive school in Switzerland, two pieces on the 'Commercial History of the Penny Magazine' from the pen of Knight himself. 1836 issues told readers about St Helena (noting the visits of Halley and Dr Maskelyne), the Steam-Engine and Steam Navigation, and the giraffes at the Zoological Gardens – 'their appearance forms an era in the annals of natural history'. 1840 issues featured a series called 'Domestic Chemistry' (cooking methods, starch, the making of tea, bread, and soup).

Kilvert's mother's Quakerism, as well as that of his aunt Sophia, may have been one source influencing his response to science. Three years after he was born the *Friend* magazine was founded, described by Cantor as the 'unofficial organ of the Religious Society of Friends'.[28] Its aims were to impart information about philanthropic initiatives and about science, and to improve the living and working conditions of the working class. The *Friend* had a middle-class, educated readership which had 'a long tradition of participation in science'. Quakers encouraged science for two reasons: some knowledge of it, especially of botany and mineralogy, enabled Quakers to earn a living and 'the study of God's creation was deemed a serious and morally worthwhile activity'.[29] It is easy therefore to imagine Kilvert's mother as an avid reader of the *Friend*, because of her intellectual capacity and piety, as it is to imagine Sophia as an avid reader of the *FMM*.

Sophia Kilvert's aim of the 'reformation' of working-class morality via wholesome, instructive reading was shared by the editors of many miscellanies of the period. However, publishers recognised that their main market was the educated and expanding middle class: 'writings aimed at working men had their better-off readers constantly in view'.[30] Hence, those writings combined literary with scientific material, a fact of central importance: 'Rhetorical tropes and aesthetic forms did not merely decorate the science presented, but helped to constitute it. . . . Polite science cannot be separated out into distinct components of "scientific content" and "aesthetic form".[31] The periodical miscellanies which figured strongly in the outlook of the Kilvert family 'aimed to serve up a little bit of everything' (O'Connor's words). He pointed out that we too easily think of Victorian literature as

> . . . a dignified succession of single genre works: novels, . . . poems, dramas. In fact more than half of the literature published in the early Victorian period appeared in the generically promiscuous setting of a periodical. . . . Hence science rubbed shoulders with the full range of literary modes. . . . [31]

This was the way Kilvert experienced science.

His predilection for periodicals marked by this sort of cultural hybridity is clear in his choice of the *Cornhill Magazine* for regular reading. This periodical was at the forefront of the boom in magazine publishing that was occurring when Kilvert was coming to maturity in the late 1850s. Dawson wrote of the appeal of the *Cornhill*, among other magazines, to 'an unprecedentedly large . . . middle-class readership':

> From the very outset, the *Cornhill* included prominent articles on scientific subjects alongside its usual diet of serialised fiction and poetry, often tackling topical issues, such as engineering, manufacturing or surgery, that addressed the professional concerns of its largely middle-class readers.

Furthermore, these issues permeated its serialised fiction, with novelists such as Thackeray and Trollope commenting in their pages on controversial scientific topics. The result was that 'subjects pertaining to science, technology and medicine were discussed and debated extensively in all the different genres published in the *Cornhill*, both fictional and non-fictional'.[33]

Adelaide Sartoris (*c.*1814-1879), born Adelaide Kemble and sister of Fanny Kemble who rode the Liverpool-Manchester railway, was one of the minor novelists whose work often appeared in Victorian periodicals. Her *A Week in a French Country House* (*FCH*), which Kilvert was reading in September 1870, is a good illustration of the novels Victorians read which 'lived out the issues of the day' (see Introduction). The novel appeared first in the *Cornhill*, though Kilvert read it in book form. One of several reasons for his enjoyment of the book is that the Woman Question is at its heart, epitomised by the artistic, outspoken Ursula (Kilvert called her 'Dear Ursula'). The double bind that the intellectual Victorian woman was in is seen in the episode in which the 'male energy' of Ursula, in contrast to the 'tender, trembling, little woman' preferred by men, is found 'repellent and unattractive'. Did Kilvert warm to Ursula because he had encountered women of similar stamp in his mother, his aunt Sophia, and Henrietta Fry? In essence, the woman debate in *FCH* is about the science of the mind and typifies other concerns in the novel with scientific issues. For example, one character is seen 'rubbing the points of his fingers at the end of his nose'. He explains that he is copying the way flies clean their bodies. Ursula teases Berthier by telling him that women's delicate touch, their 'sensitive epiderme', was essential to the rolling of cigars, and thus justified their existence. Sartoris teases scientists by describing a conversazione attended by 'men of science with dowdy wives'.[34]

It has already been noted that Sophia Kilvert, like Pestalozzi, made nature the focus of education. The introduction to her *Home Discipline* noted that its ideas dated from the mid-1820s, which was the time that

Pestalozzi's influence was being felt very strongly in Britain. His ideas are evident in her statements on the instruction of children and domestic servants. She too gave a central place in teaching to the mother's role, deploring the 'culpable neglect of maternal education'. Similarly, Silber wrote of Pestalozzi: '[his] new education has its starting-point in Gertrude's living room'.[35] Both aunt Sophia and Pestalozzi made much of the mother's example of *behaviour*, instead of teaching and preaching, with regard to moral and religious education. The domestic sphere was the key area of learning: 'The general tendency apparent [in Pestalozzian doctrine] is the preference given to practice over theory, to the family over the school, to near objects in the home over remoter ones in the world'.[36] Sophia's aim – 'our children should be rendered independent as early as possible' – matched Pestalozzi's – 'they must be trained for early independence'. Both educators believed that children had to contribute by their work to the family and to society.

Kilvert was encouraged to take an interest in natural processes and objects at his uncle Francis's Claverton Lodge school, where again evidence of Pestalozzian influence is strong. The school's emphasis on pupils' independent learning originated in Pestalozzi:

> The most important and the essentially new principle for his time is that of spontaneity or self-activity. It demands that all knowledge should have 'its origin in the child himself' . . . that the fruits of perception should 'bear the mark of freedom and independence'. It implies that the child should not be given ready-made answers but should arrive at solutions himself. . . . [37]

One of Kilvert's fellow pupils at Claverton Lodge was William Warde Fowler, born in 1847 in a village near Wellington, Somerset, of a family whose men worked in the law, the Church, and the army. As a boy, Fowler was taken by his teacher for country walks and learned about flowers. Claverton Lodge school lay further up Bathwick Hill from the house where Fowler lived with his aunt and grandfather and he attended from spring 1857 to 1859, overlapping with Kilvert during 1857-8. In describing the school as 'in every respect utterly unlike a private school of today', Fowler was describing a Pestalozzian education. The main theme of his account was the freedom enjoyed by pupils: 'It was an entirely new life of freedom that my brother and I lived there'. Pupils' studies arose largely from their own curiosity, particularly in the area of natural history. 'We began with immense enthusiasm,' he wrote, 'to collect butterflies and moths'.[38] Pupils were also allowed to roam at will on Sham Castle Hill, beyond which were the Hampton Rocks, collecting specimens. The former was the folly built by Ralph Allen, entrepreneur of Bath. The latter is a site of geological interest, where Pleistocene rocks are delineated into clear strata.[39] In view of what is said in a later chapter about Kilvert's knowledge of geology, it is important to note that Hampton Rocks would have been part of his Claverton Lodge experience. The school's pupils enjoyed other kinds of freedom remarkable for the period. Fowler valued most 'the entire absence of any pressure or cramming,' including the total absence of written exams. He felt, slightly guiltily, that he 'shirked all the work [he] possibly could' while not feeling he 'wasted his time'. He was tasting the real learning which for Pestalozzi began and ended in pupils' own experience.

    Independent learning was the norm at uncle Francis's school. Pupils 'read all the books we could lay our hands on in the house,' Fowler wrote,[40] a statement adding weight to the claims made in earlier chapters about Kilvert's wide reading. In addition, pupils were able 'to explore together the whole city of Bath, . . . the Roman remains; the Museum we knew of course quite well' (the 'of course' refers to the fact that the Museum belonged to the BLSI, uncle Francis's links to which gave them access – see later in this chapter). Independent research existed in the form of class newspapers pupils produced, as Fowler noted: 'I may call to witness the [weekly] *Chatterbox*, the one surviving number [of which] opens with an article on the feathers of butterflies' wings, written by me, with another of my brother's about some story of Greek mythology'. Pupils were emulating the general knowledge magazines pioneered by the Chambers brothers and Charles Knight. Fowler remembered other subjects 'awakening for youthful minds': the Indian Mutiny, two Parliamentary elections, a total eclipse of the sun, and the 'great comet' of 1858 – all topics in which Kilvert had a marked interest. No wonder Fowler concluded: 'The two years [at Claverton Lodge] were perhaps the happiest and most fruitful of my life'.[41] No wonder too that in adult life 'he had a genuine enthusiasm for natural science'[42] and was so interested in birds that he published several studies of them. Fowler was a representative product of uncle Francis's school; Kilvert, who spent *seven* years there (to Fowler's two) was another, and similar one. We may well ask whether Lewis Dillwyn, with his passion for birds and geology, was another representative product.

    Feeding into Francis's approach to pupil learning was his work with the Bath Literary and Philosophical Association (BLPA), of which he was the mainspring. Natural theology, of which the BLPA was a vehicle, was so important to uncle Francis that he put his name, in probably his first publication, to a work entitled *Evidences of the Being of God and of the Truth of Christianity* (1827). Its preface refers to 'Evidences of Natural Religion' that were to follow, 'masterly treatises by some of our first theological writers'. Uncle Francis explained that he had 'extracted and arranged' the treatises 'for the use of my pupils' and that they were most suited for those aged fifteen and older. It can be assumed that Kilvert was taken through this material by his uncle and the same might be said of young Lewis Dillwyn, who became uncle Francis's pupil a few months after the publication of *Evidences*.

The treatises are *On the Nature, Existence and Unity of God* by Dr M. Hole and *On the Evidences of Christianity* by Dr S. Clarke. Uncle Francis merely wrote the preface to them. Matthew Hole (1640-1730) was an Anglican clergyman and religious writer with local (for uncle Francis) connections: Vicar of Bishop's Lavington (Wilts) and of two Somerset parishes up to 1711.[43] Samuel Clarke is the more significant figure in relation to uncle Francis's views of science and religion. Clarke (1675-1729) discovered Newton's *Principia Mathematica* at Cambridge at the age of sixteen and henceforth resolved to advance Newton's theories against the rationalist ones of Descartes, which encouraged irreligion. Clarke was 'the most important British philosopher in the generation between Locke and Berkeley . . . [he] was a leading figure in Newton's circle'.[44] His Boyle Lectures, established by Boyle to promote natural religion, were *A Demonstration of the Being and Attributes of God* (1705-6) and *The Verity and Certitude of Natural and Revealed Religion* (1705).

The title of uncle Francis's book was largely a paraphrase of Clarke's Boyle Lecture titles. The fact that it figured in Kilvert's education is of the utmost importance. Firstly, it confirms the rigour of his uncle's teaching. Secondly, it shows how the early and mid-nineteenth century debate about science and religion was carried on in Claverton Lodge school. Thirdly, it shows that uncle Francis, in a book about natural religion, was quite easy about endorsing one of the ablest scientific minds of the eighteenth century. Fourthly, it supplies further evidence (i.e. in addition to Sedgwick's *Discourse* – see chapter one) of the way in which Kilvert was encouraged to reconcile science and religion, by 'looking through Nature up to Nature's God'. The existence of a divine creator of the universe is built on the following arguments from Clarke's first treatise. It cannot be conceived 'without much absurdity that so glorious a fabric as that of the world should have been raised . . . without the interference of an all-wise and all-powerful architect'. The writer then pointed to 'the admirable order and beauty of the universe, the wonderful usefulness of all the creatures in it, the ample provision made . . . particularly for mankind, and the curious structure of mineral, vegetable and animal bodies'. 'Miraculous occurrences' are also cited as proof of God's existence.[45] We can recognise here the theological view of 'wonders' and 'curiosities' with which the Kilvert children were raised.

The learning that went on at Claverton Lodge was complemented by the learning available for its pupils at the BLPA. The BLPA was a sister association of the Bath Literary and Scientific Institution (BLSI); members of one could become members of the other for a small fee. It is important to know the origins of the BLSI because its history is very closely intertwined with that of the Kilvert family in Bath. Kilvert's grandfather came there in autumn 1780, his marriage making him brother-in-law to Francis and Robert Falkner, as was noted earlier. Francis Falkner was the father of the Frederick Falkner to whom Kilvert's uncle Francis had given Sedgwick's *Discourse* in 1835. Robert Falkner's partner in a corn and seed business was William Matthews. It was Matthews who linked the Falkners and Francis Kilvert to the BLSI because Matthews attended the public meeting on 8 September 1777 called to set up in Bath an 'Institution . . . for the encouragement of Agriculture, Planting, Manufactures, Commerce, and the Fine Arts'. This body was the brainchild of Edmund Rack, a draper and Quaker (as Matthews was). The body that emerged from the September meeting was the Bath Agricultural Society and Rack was its first secretary. In 1780 it acquired land near Bath which became Britain's first experimental farm. Its interests were by no means confined to agriculture as its records show: there are articles on meteorology, chemical analysis of soils, and steam-engine trials. Thomas Curtis, a governor of Bath General Hospital, suggested to Rack in 1779 the founding of a 'select Literary Society for purposes of discussing science and Philosophical subjects', and on Boxing Day that year it was formed. Rack became its first secretary and continued as secretary of the Agricultural Society. Its next secretary was William Matthews. The scientists Joseph Priestley and William Herschel were among its early members, as was John Arden, a great populariser of science of the time.

The vision of the first Bath Philosophical Society, shared by Matthews and Curtis, was of a club for gentlemen keen to discuss intellectual topics in the pattern of the Lit and Phil Societies that had emerged at the turn of the nineteenth century, noticeably in the new factory towns and older provincial centres. The driving force behind them was summed up thus by MacLeod: 'Provincial towns, through their Literary and Philosophical Societies, were creating important new traditions, effectively uniting mercantile, literary and philosophical interests'.[46] Fawcett described their ethos: 'They offered Dissenters and Anglicans alike a tolerant, intellectual forum for debate and self-improvement where only merit counted. [They] signalled a curiosity about all the humanities and sciences'. Although the Bath Society's 'combined expertise ranged from mathematics, astronomy and physics to geology, botany and . . . medicine',[47] enthusiasm waned quickly, key members left, and it died c.1787. No replacement followed for a dozen years, but in December 1798 the second Bath Philosophical Society was inaugurated on the initiative of two doctors, John Haygarth and William Falconer. By 1805, the second Bath Society had failed. The third one, open to the public by subscription, was established in January 1816, providing lectures on science and technology, but it only lasted till 1821, though revived in 1830 as Bath Philosophical Society for the Diffusion of Knowledge, with lectures on electricity, the mechanism of the eye, and Pestalozzi's educational system.

The successor to the various Bath Societies was the BLSI, which opened on 19 January 1825. In the list of original proprietors, each holding a twenty guineas share, were the names of uncle Francis Kilvert and Francis Henry Falkner (brother of Frederick Falkner); uncle Francis was on the Committee in 1825. The 17 January Committee minutes noted the setting up of a museum and a laboratory for 'Experiments in . . . the Sciences of Chemistry and Natural Philosophy' (i.e. physics). The museum's collection of local natural history and geological specimens were collected and catalogued by William Lonsdale, a geologist with a strong interest in Bath's geological strata.[48] Sir George Smith Gibbes[49] assured his audience in his inaugural address that 'the study of natural history, geology and comparative anatomy did nothing but reinforce belief in a beneficent, divine creation'.[50] Kilvert's uncle Francis could feel easy about the thrust of the scientific study pursued by the new body. He remained a Proprietor of the Institution until his death in November 1863. It is likely that he advocated a larger literary dimension in the BLSI, which the BLPA had, although in its early days it showed in its lecture programme a strong bias towards scientific topics.

This account of the Institution's origins indicates that its ethos was the same as that of the Kilvert family: improvement, usefulness, science, and technology. It assumed that trade was both a necessary and an honourable activity, and significantly the energy, initiative, and humanitarianism of Quakers played a key role, as did the idea of self-improvement, because such moving spirits as Edmund Rack, William Lonsdale, and William Matthews came from humble Quaker backgrounds. The ethos was largely a middle-class one, as the membership lists of both the Agricultural Society[51] and the BLSI show. When both these bodies were being founded to stimulate the cultural life of Bath, they formed a significant backdrop to the beginnings of the Kilvert family in the city. The BLPA was the central focus of uncle Francis's life in Bath.

The first regulation of the BLPA stated that its object was 'mutual communication, either orally or in writing, of Literary and Scientific Information.' This aim was refined and elaborated by the Annual Report of 1859: 'Its object is not the giving of lectures – they may be easily obtained elsewhere – but the bringing forward of subjects which lectures do not generally touch on, and the illustration of such subjects by discussion'. It may be assumed that these were the Association's objects as seen by uncle Francis, since he had become its Chairman that year.[52] The Association's lectures were for its own members (and often delivered by members or guest speakers), whereas the BLSI's lectures were public. Meetings were fortnightly on Monday at 7.30pm and the annual subscription was a mere 5s. The 1834 list of BLPA members included uncle Francis's brother, the Rev. Edward Kilvert; the name of Kilvert's father does not appear at any time among the membership. There is no record of Kilvert as a member. It was agreed that members could introduce visitors whose names were to be entered in a visitors' book and Kilvert may have been one.[53] Unfortunately, these records have not survived. The membership always included numerous clergymen, doctors, army and navy men, and the occasional lord and baronet.

Some details of the BLPA's lecture programmes over the years will indicate its nature. They do not manifest the popular appeal evident in those of the BLSI, which featured in 1851 such scientific topics as 'The Chemistry of Cooking', 'Photography', 'An Imaginary Voyage in an Aerial Ship', 'The Sciences of Sound and Light', 'The Locomotive Steam-Engine', 'Electricity', and 'The Microscope and its Wonders'. 1853 saw a three-lecture course on 'The Electric Telegraph' (so popular that it was repeated the next month).[54] Such courses represented an effort to popularise science, partly by appealing to the public's appetite for 'wonders'. The BLPA's science lectures, on the other hand, feature more esoteric topics: 'On Creation' (1828), 'On Physiology' (1829), 'On Portable Gas obtained from Resin' (1829), 'On the History of Plants' (1829), 'On Aerolites' and 'On Comets' (1832), 'The Dreams of Chemistry' (1857), 'Natural and Supernatural' (1860), and 'Meteorology' (1862).[55] There was a lecture on 'Darwin's Poetry' in 1859, the year of the publication of *The Origin of Species*; evolution was perhaps considered too controversial (Regulation VII of the Association outlawed 'subjects embracing polemical divinity and politics').[56] Mesmerism was absent from the lecture programme of both the BLPA and the BLSI, probably for the same reason. No details of the BLPA's programmes are cited here for 1836-56 because the body lapsed in that period. (Illness and deaths of key members were cited as causes.) It revived in autumn 1856 with 135 members.

The BLSI's museum was a significant element in its functioning and note should be taken of it as another influence on Kilvert with regard to his interest in natural history. It has been suggested that the museum (any museum), as both a physical entity and as an intellectual stance – the mind-set of collecting and arranging 'specimens' – figured strongly in his upbringing, and played an important part in disposing him towards enjoyment of 'curiosities' and 'wonders' in the culture of the first half of the nineteenth century. The development of the BLSI's museum as a result of donations is recorded with great pride in reports over the years as, for example, in 1834 when it acquired 'A Pair of Shoes and other North American Curiosities', '30 Specimens of Shells', 'A Rhino Horn', 'An Alligator's Head' and (bizarrely) 'A New Zealander's Head'.

In May 1853, the BLSI proposed that part of its building 'be sublet to the administrators of a new "city museum"'. The proposal found no favour and the BLSI decided to expand its museum, encouraged by the acquisition of a collection of minerals and of a substantial geological collection donated in 1854 by Charles Moore, an expert on Bath geology. All of this was opened to the public, three days a week, from 1856. This was the museum that Warde Fowler and others of uncle Francis's pupils, including Kilvert, visited as a regular part of their studies. Fowler's life-long fascination with birds (and indeed Kilvert's) was no doubt stimulated by the museum's collection of over 1,000 stuffed birds, acquired just before he became a pupil at Claverton Lodge. The Association felt its own status was enhanced by the museum and expressed satisfaction that it was 'rapidly enlarging and freely laying open its stores to the public'.[57]

Kilvert was very fortunate to have as his teacher a man whose range and depth of knowledge was exceptional. However, behind uncle Francis and his teaching was a whole group of men, all prominent figures in the BLPA and the BLSI, who made the local tradition of natural history and science in general, on which Kilvert could draw, a very rich one. One of them was Leonard Jenyns (1800-1893), who was on the Institution's museum committee from 1860. Educated at Eton, where he had a passion for chemistry (although it did not figure in the school's classics-dominated curriculum) he went on to St John's College, Cambridge in 1818. In Cambridge, he met John Henslow (collaborator with Benjamin Maund on *The Botanist* – see chapter three) and they were involved together in various natural history projects. Jenyns was invited in 1831 to become the naturalist on HMS *Beagle* but declined the offer and his place was taken by Charles Darwin.[58] Jenyns was one of the many scientists who visited Lewis Weston Dillwyn as, for example, on 15 August 1842.

Philip Bury Duncan (1772-1863) was a member of the BLPA from its beginning and one of its earliest and most regular lecturers. For example he spoke on 6 March 1826 on 'The Balance of Destruction and Preservation of Animal Life'. In 1856, he was the BLPA's president. His main occupation, however, was the care of Oxford's Ashmolean Museum, of which he became curator in 1829. Finally, we come to the Rev. Harry Mengden Scarth (1814-1890), who was at Cambridge during Simeon's last years there. Described by the *DNB* as 'one of the best English authorities on Roman antiquities', he published a series of books and gave many talks to the BLPA. The Roman remains that uncle Francis's pupils went to see no doubt included many that Scarth had discovered. His closeness to uncle Francis is signalled by the fact that he preached the latter's funeral sermon.

This chapter and earlier ones have documented various aspects of Kilvert's interest in science and technology. Lightman's observation 'signs of interest in science are evident in all realms of Victorian culture'[59] is borne out in the account that has been given of Kilvert's attitudes and their origins: his mother's Quakerism, the periodicals that appeared in his household, his own predilection for the *Cornhill* magazine, his schooling by uncle Francis and aunt Sophia, the influence of the BLSI and BLPA. An important part of Bath's culture was its tradition of public lectures. It was one of the first venues outside London to have public science lectures.[60] The BLPA, to which uncle Francis devoted his life, continued this tradition and reflects once again the extent to which the story of the Kilvert family is a story of teaching and teachers. The importance of teaching to uncle Francis is seen in this statement in his sermon 'On the Fear of God', addressed to school pupils: 'Your next duty is to your Instructors . . . namely obedience and love . . . your Instructors are the parents of your minds. They are both able and willing to teach you what will make you good and useful'.[61] Sophia Kilvert showed her dedication to teaching by urging that upper servants in gentry households should become teachers to both masters and mistresses and their children. She encouraged the idea of 'scientific amusements' such as 'Astronomy, Chemistry, Botany, Geology and Architecture' becoming 'domestic sources of pleasure' for all.[62]

The immensely valuable testimony of Warde Fowler about the Pestalozzian ethos and curriculum of Claverton Lodge school explains much of Kilvert's interest in natural history and science. A later chapter shows Kilvert teaching geography in a Pestalozzian way at Clyro School. Our knowledge of the teaching at Claverton Lodge and of its pupils' visits to the BLSI museum does much to explain Kilvert's preoccupation with museums, which will be developed later. The freedom he enjoyed in uncle Francis's care must be responsible in large measure for the wide knowledge, wide interests, freshness, directness, curiosity, and sense of wonder of his mind evident in his writing.

Chapter 6

Natural Law and the Mind

Through demonstrations and face-to-face encounters, mesmerism gave meaning to the mind's powers. It could provide a forum for people to make new assertions about human relationships.

Alison Winter, *Mesmerized: Powers of Mind in Victorian Britain*

I have myself seen one case, of a young and pretty girl, whose countenance became, in the mesmeric sleep, lovely and heavenly in expression. Her face beamed with a spiritual ethereal beauty, such as I had previously never even conceived.

William Gregory, *Animal Magnetism or Mesmerism and its Phenomena*

Kilvert's poem, *The Pilgrimage*, is one of his most carefully structured poems: it advances a series of religious and intellectual arguments; its basic premise being that individuals are destined to meet each other during their lives, not by chance but by 'the Hand and Thought of God'. Thus he was endorsing the idea of a God who was capable of suspending natural laws and intervening in human destiny, capable, in other words, of miracles. We have absolute confirmation that Kilvert believed in a God whose design for Creation included control of natural laws from the 7 October 1873 *Diary* entry in which he recorded his response to the sermon preached by Dr Alexander (1824-1911), Bishop of Derry, at the Bath Church Congress. There is no record in what has survived of the *Diary* that Kilvert attended any other Church Congresses;[1] his attendance at the 1873 congress was no doubt due to its being local and to its main theme: the Church's role in relation to working men.[2] At the Bath Congress there was a separate Working Men's Meeting, at which speakers addressed the audience on pre-selected topics 'of practical importance to the class involved'.[3] Dr Alexander's sermon, which Kilvert thought 'admirable', was about the 'successive Decadences, Revivals and Triumphs' of the Church. Kilvert was particularly impressed by this statement in the sermon: 'natural laws are not chains bound about the living God, but threads which He holds in His hand'. Especially significant here is the fact that Dr Alexander did not actually refer to 'natural laws'; his words were 'law is not a chain coiled round the Living God, but rather a thread which He holds'.[4] He had signalled the context of his use of 'law' by stating that one of the Church's current needs, with regard to reviving itself, was 'to adjust the boundary lines between science and faith'. Kilvert was therefore quite clear which kind of 'law' was meant. Furthermore, it was quite normal for him to think in terms of science and 'natural laws'.

The Bishop went on to underline that a key issue in the dispute between science and faith was *miracles*: 'The age is impatient of miracle,' he observed, 'whereas it is patient of fact'. He then portrayed the modern man of science as one who consigned 'the very elements of religion – prayer, the soul, immortality, God' – to the past, who pictured man exposed, without God's comfort, to 'the enormous machine of the universe, and the whirl and hiss of its jagged wheels, amid the crash and thud of its iron hammers' – a striking analogy between the terrifying machine of a Godless universe and the engine symbolising his age's industrial progress. To Dr Alexander, religion resided in 'the affections, imagination, emotions and conscience' but modern scientific man was 'fast becoming passionless intellect'. The result would be that religion would wither and die and be replaced by Comte's 'Positive Philosophy'.

The issue of science and faith, raised by Dr Alexander in 1873, had been an issue before Kilvert was born in 1840. A host of other challenging issues pressed round him as he grew up and, as earlier chapters have shown, his family, though strong in faith, was particularly open to science because of its belief in education and progress. Frederick Robertson, Kilvert's chief guide through challenging issues, was acting in this role to one of his Brighton congregation in spring 1851, the year of the Great Exhibition, which in many ways focused these issues. His advice to his Brighton friend was characteristically robust and fearless: 'to refuse to examine when doubts arise is spiritual suicide'. Yet he also cautioned against reading 'controversial' books. 'In this bewildered age of "Yeast" . . . an age in which . . . all are crying out loudly, the greater part not knowing why, or what the questions really are, it seems to me that the more we confine ourselves to simple duties the better'.

Robertson's reference to *Yeast* was a reference to Kingsley, whose novel of that name had appeared in 1848 in *Fraser's Magazine* and in book form in 1851. Robertson admired Kingsley (a 'generous and unselfish' man, he called him) and other Christian Socialists such as F.D. Maurice, but complained that the author of *Yeast* 'ought not to cry about fermentation, unless he can show how it can be made into bread.'[5] The novel drew attention to the plight of the rural poor, one of those questions which made the period in which Kilvert grew up a 'bewildered age of "Yeast"'.[6] A mere twenty pages of Robertson's letters, written between March and May 1851, raised the following controversial questions: Comte's 'Positive Philosophy', the education and political rights of the working class, the Woman Question, European revolutions, Italian independence, the threat of Catholicism, socialist doctrines, scepticism, Indian affairs, mesmerism, scientific discovery, and the Great Exhibition.

One of the many questions that Kilvert was curious about was the workings of the human mind. This curiosity manifests itself in the interest he had in mesmerism, the supernatural, and folklore. So serious was this last interest that on 21 February 1873 he approached the British Museum in the hope that the Society of Antiquaries would publish his collection of folklore in the *Archaeologian*. A large number of supernatural incidents in the *Diary* further confirms the interest. There is a *Diary* entry that indicates that he was aware of the idea of laws applied to the growth of the mind and of civilisation. It illustrates again the 'iceberg' nature of the *Diary*. The entry concerns Kilvert's visit to 83 year old James Jones of Clyro, who was very ill, and the diarist was touched by the old man's resignation, which stemmed partly from the fact that 'he had emerged from the atmosphere of charms, incantations, astrology and witchcraft'. Jones had practised these to the extent that he was known as 'the old wizard'. The transition that he had experienced in his long life Kilvert saw in terms of an historical process: 'The days of magic and necromancy had gone by. . . . ' It is one of those intellectual statements that seems to have come from his reading. The source can be identified as *The History of Civilisation in England* by Henry Thomas Buckle (1821-1862). The first volume appeared in 1857, the second in 1861, and they were as controversial as *The Origin of Species*. The *History* 'made a huge splash with the public but met with strong criticism from both Christian thinkers and academic historians'.[7] Buckle became a literary sensation and was introduced to such giants of the intellectual establishment as Thackeray, Herbert Spencer, Huxley, and Darwin.[8] Middle-class families such as the Kilverts admired Buckle's liberal, radical outlook, especially his belief in progress. His Victorian biographer, Alfred Huth (1850-1910), wrote of Buckle's delighted response to the Great Exhibition with its 'bright promise of reward to man's genius, and of continued triumph over the blind powers of Nature'.[9]

In volume one of his *History*, Buckle argued for 'the deductive application of laws which must be discovered historically' in order to produce 'a science of history'. The application of statistics to the study of history (e.g. of the rates of murder, suicide, natural deaths, marriage) confirmed that people's behaviour resulted from 'large and general causes'. Since behaviour resulted from motives that had 'antecedents', all of it 'must have a character of uniformity'. Four main 'physical agents' – Climate, Food, Soil, and the General Aspect of Nature (earthquakes, storms, diseases) – affected the human race. The last of these often gave rise to 'those innumerable superstitions which are the great obstacles to advancing knowledge'. Buckle proposed 'such a comprehensive survey of facts' as would reveal 'the great law of nature', which was that of *progress*. Progress was two-fold: Moral and Intellectual. 'This double movement . . . is essential to the very idea of civilisation, and includes the entire theory of mental progress'.[10] It is unsurprising that views such as these appealed to Charles Darwin: '[Darwin] revelled in Henry Buckle's breath-taking *History of Civilisation in England*. The first volume, with 500 fancy-footnoted pages, caused a sensation'. It is 'wonderfully clever and original', Darwin thought.

> [Buckle] hitched history to the capital's mid-Victorian mood. Barbarism, priestcraft, superstition were on the way out – "the signs of the time are all around," he announced. True religion was to believe in the one "glorious principle of universal and undeviating regularity" taught by physical science. . . . Social improvement and morality were statistically and scientifically explicable without recourse to divine caprice.[11]

The statement in Buckle's *History* that finds particular echoes in Kilvert's account of the changes in James Jones's outlook is this: 'The knowledge of men, gradually advancing, made them indignant at superstitions which they had formerly admired'.[12] In his folklore manuscript, Kilvert had expressed the same idea, with Radnorshire peasants like James Jones very much in mind: 'In many parts of the country the people are ignorant; everywhere they are credulous, highly imaginative and superstitious, but they are generally intelligent, and very much alive to the advantages of education'.[13] This statement, in turn, has echoes in Buckle's *History*. He explained that Western man did not leave his superstitions behind at the end of the Dark Ages because they were 'turned into a fresh channel'. He then told of the 'pagan ceremonies' of Catholic churches, 'not only the mummeries of idolatry, but likewise its doctrines'. He then used the words that Kilvert used about Radnorshire peasants: in the Dark Ages, 'men were *credulous* and *ignorant*' and thus they produced a religion that 'required great belief and little knowledge'. Although much credulity and ignorance persisted in the sixteenth century, the need was felt then for a new religion, one 'more favourable to free inquiry; a religion less full of miracles, saints, legends, and idols' and with fewer ceremonies.[14] Buckle was emphasising here that religious doctrines needed to be accompanied by 'intellectual culture', by enlightenment, by progress. After several centuries, the European intellect did rouse itself, Buckle noted, and 'Christianity slowly emerged from these corruptions'. Kilvert had used 'emerged' with the same point and the same force to mark James Jones's rejection of the toils of superstition. He also used, as Buckle did, the idea of emergence into a *simple*, radical Christianity. With superstition behind him, Jones became 'a simple humble childlike Christian man'. Buckle had written that Christianity had always 'taught a simple doctrine, and employed a simple worship'.

The year in which Kilvert attended the Bath Church Congress – devoted to the issues of strikes and labour – was also the year he took up *Alton Locke*. He was reading it (and was 'delighted' with it) on 24 March 1873;[15] the Congress was in October 1873. It was barely two years later that he was recording: 'So Charles Kingsley is dead. "His body is buried in peace but his name liveth for ever more." We could ill spare him'.[16] The problematic question of miracles, on which Kilvert had heard Dr Alexander expatiate at the Congress, is tackled head-on in *Alton Locke* in a chapter entitled 'Miracles and Science'. Here the Dean recalls with Alton a talk they had had earlier about natural and revealed religion. At that time, the Dean could not reconcile miracles with 'nature's laws' yet continued to believe in miracles. This was because 'Nature's deepest laws, her only true laws, are her invisible ones'. Scientific investigation, he argued, even using the most powerful microscopes, failed to reveal 'true causes [which] remain just as . . . unfathomable as ever' and which were attributable to a 'great primal law' that was in essence 'spiritual'. He then asked Alton to consider whether Christ's miracles were not in fact breaches of, but restorations of, natural law. (He focused chiefly on those miracles that restored health.) He yoked this understanding to the new insights that modern science was daily providing:

> Every new wonder in medicine which this great age discovers – what does it prove, but that Christ need have broken no natural laws to do that of old, which can be done now without breaking them . . . ?

Christ's healing power came from his 'vital energy'. The Dean claimed that the electric telegraph, by demonstrating scientists' refusal to accept the limitations represented by the laws of time and space, constituted a 'miracle'. Kingsley's chapter advancing a thoroughly up-to-date scientific conception of miracles ends with the example of the mesmerist, who cured patients by his own 'vital energy', thus demonstrating that 'Christ's miracles were but mesmeric feats'.[17]

Dr Alexander showed in his Bath Congress speech his hostility to Comte's 'Positive Philosophy'. Wadham College, which Kilvert attended from 1859 to 1862, was the home of Comte's Positivism in England. Richard Congreve (1818-1899), Wadham tutor in the new history course that Kilvert took, enthused a group of students with Positivism in the early 1850s. Though Congreve left Wadham in 1854, his influence persisted. His books were in Wadham's library[18] and 'no student, it was claimed, could "pass through the 'sixties untouched by curiosity about the new philosophical system"'.[19] Comte intended his philosophy to replace the idea of God with the concept of humanity and thus he spoke of a 'Religion of Humanity'. Kilvert showed awareness of this in the *Diary* entry of 25 June 1876 (only a month after dining at Wadham), recording his visit to St. Paul's Cathedral when the singing of the huge congregation 'brought the tears to one's eyes with an *enthusiasm of humanity*' (my italics).

A more specific source for Kilvert's 'enthusiasm of humanity' phrase can be identified, which not only provides further evidence of his thinking, but underlines again the systematic, cohesive nature of his reading. Gilbert Sutton's *Science and Faith* (1868)[20] contains the essay, 'English Positivism', which saw Buckle as the main means of publicising Comte's ideas in England. It also contained the essay, 'Robertson of Brighton', an evaluation of the preacher revered by Kilvert. In it, he stressed Robertson's 'power of assimilating the facts and results of science with higher religious conclusions'. His faith did not rely, Sutton wrote, on miracles, which he saw not as supernatural events, but as 'visible signs of the spiritual power . . . the very essence of [God's] law'. The discoveries of science tended daily to undermine faith. Man's 6,000 year history paled into insignificance when it was known that he was '20,000 years old at the least'. Similarly, 'miracles are not so miraculous when read by the light of the telegraph'. However, Robertson's faith was not subverted by these facts because his stance was: 'Your laws do not affect me. Science is one thing; religion is another'. His teaching was founded on 'human goodness imbibed from Divine love' and consisted in extending love to family, friends, and mankind in general.[21]

Brooke confirmed this view of Robertson's ministry: 'the fixed basis for his teaching . . . was the Divine-human life of Christ', quoting in support one of his sermons:

> Christ was the Son of God . . . because the Son of Man . . . and must be loved as the Son of Man before He can be adored as the Son of God. . . . Begin with Him as God's character revealed under the limitations of humanity.[22]

These ideas lay behind much of Kilvert's preaching, seen most clearly in his 26 November 1871 sermon, the theme of which he expressed as 'the High Priest of Humanity'.[23] Teaching of this kind could, Sutton said, reanimate man's hope and optimism 'by replanting . . . the enthusiasm of humanity, in a sense rarely understood before'. Thus, the phrase Kilvert settled on to express the deep joy aroused by the St. Paul's congregation emerged from a context in which the writings of Sutton, Buckle, Comte, and Robertson all came together on the theme of science and faith.

It is important to accustom ourselves to the idea of the Kilvert who sat through Dr Alexander's sermon (an hour long, Kilvert noted) and its review particularly of science's challenge to the Church. It is further confirmation of the fact that he was fully au fait with his age's urgent questions and dominant ideas. A man could not, would not, read Brooke's *Life* of Robertson unless he had a real relish for ideas. Kilvert was indebted to it for a review of science's challenge to faith during the first half of the nineteenth century. Of the *Life* Chadwick wrote:

> It was important in the development of the broad church school. It was a drama of the intellectual conflict of the age. In October 1865, when it was published, the argument was raging between an incredible Christian orthodoxy and a scientific . . . materialism. The *Life* represented this conflict within a single soul of twenty years before.[24]

Robertson emerged at the end of the conflict 'triumphant with the banner of a Liberal Christianity'.

Troubled as he always was by spiritual doubts, Robertson found reassurance in science: 'Positive science, such as chemistry, natural philosophy, mineralogy and geology, rests on facts: and the effect of certainty which it produces on the mind is always a healthy feeling'.[25] Science did not, however, provide him with all he needed. He had been enjoying Ruskin's *The Stones of Venice* and remarked that such books were 'precious – more precious than even works which treat of scientific truth such as chemistry, for *they* do not feed the heart'.[26] (Later, we will encounter a scientist, John Tyndall, known to Kilvert, whose books might fairly be said to 'feed the heart'.) The scientific mode of looking at things had strict limits, in Robertson's view: it could only 'dissect' and not create, nor could it account for the effects produced by objects. 'It is like attempting to explain the ecstasies of music by mathematics. . . . So with electricity, phrenology, etc.; they can tell us phenomena, but what lies beyond those they cannot tell. . . . Christ told us, but by the intuitions of the soul, not by science'.[27]

It will be shown later that Kilvert was interested in phrenology and its offshoot, mesmerism, so it is necessary to be clear what significance these things had for those who lived in the early and mid-nineteenth century. Chambers's *Vestiges of Creation*, a key work in the evolution debate, had grown out of the phrenological movement and challenged religious faith because it was materialist.[28] The idea of evolution embraced the human mind in its account of natural laws, as Chambers had asserted. Mind, he said, 'being proved to be under law, passes at once into the category of natural things'.[29] This was the view of George Combe, from a Scottish Calvinist background, the man mainly responsible for making phrenology into 'the nineteenth century's most popular and popularised science,' in Cooter's words.[30] Parsinnen referred to it as 'the most important popular science in the early nineteenth century', and as 'an essential prelude to mesmerism'.[31] It began to appear in the 1820s in the lecture courses of the Mechanics' Institutes, which were sponsored by the middle class, and was spread nationwide by an army of lecturers. Cooter identified over 200 before 1860, most between 1825 and 1845 – more than for any other science subject. Most phrenology lecturers came from 'the vanguard of the professionalising lower middle class'.[32]

Combe, in his *The Constitution of Man* (1828), argued that a theory of the mind was an essential element in examining the relations between the natural constitution of man and external objects. Phrenology was, he wrote, 'the true philosophy of mind . . . [and] the key to the true theory of the divine government of the world', which was regulated by 'the natural laws of Creation'.[33] As a young man, he had watched the dissection of brains at Edinburgh University, where notions of faculty psychology were prevalent, and he developed a theory of hierarchical mental powers, whose quality could be deduced by studying the shape of skulls. Human psychology could therefore be read from the surface of the cranium, a claim which, as Cooter pointed out, constituted 'a total assault on traditional thought and society', which insisted that worthwhile things were deep and hidden: 'Phrenology had everything to do with outer reality and nothing at all to do with inner structures of thought.[34] This idea frightened elites because it meant their human character could be read by others.

Phrenology was popular partly because of its simplicity and accessibility. Working people, especially those of the self-improving kind, relished the idea that complex emotions and the meaning of life itself could be clarified by the analysis of mental faculties. Combe himself recommended people meet together in order to exercise 'the several faculties of Benevolence, Veneration, Hope, Ideality, Wonder, and Conscientiousness'.[35] Through phrenology, individuals had the freedom to chart their own progress by encouraging some faculties while discouraging others, their choices predisposing, rather than predetermining, their human nature. Middle-class people warmed to this idea, especially when contemplating the physical and moral degradation of the working classes. Cooter saw this as the main reason for their support for the science 'well into the 1840s and 1850s'. He also noted that British phrenologists sought to mould 'the supposedly sensual, irrational, and fragmented minds' of the lower classes.[36] In this respect, phrenology gave some support to the more orthodox educational motive underpinning Brougham's SDUK. '*The Constitution of Man* was in reality a scientistic prescription for daily living', wrote Cooter, and 'Among the virtues it preached were temperance, cleanliness, regular habits, work discipline, the nuclear family, individualism, property rights, and free trade'.[37]

Alton Locke is concerned with the question of raising the working masses, preserving order and avoiding revolution, and the means to these ends are education and science. Alton speaks for the labouring man: 'Give us the same air, water, exercise, education, good society [as the gentleman], and you will see whether [our] "coarseness" . . . be an accident or a property'.[38] The process of 'improving' Alton is seen to benefit from his contact with the Scottish phrenologist, Sandy Mackaye, who on first meeting Alton 'began to feel his head all over' with approving comments: 'a vara gude forehead. Causative organs large, perceptive ditto. Imagination superabundant'. The novel's theme of self-improvement is centred both on Alton, for whom books offer 'a world of wonder', and on working people for whom self-education and the perception of 'Nature's will in the phenomena of matter' are the keys to progress.[39]

The most important aspect of phrenology was its endorsement of rationalism. Cooter emphasised that the new science helped to revive the rationalism and faith in science and progress of the eighteenth century, and to sustain them into the industrial and technological society of the nineteenth. Inevitably, one of its targets was superstition, systems of which, Combe argued, were 'inseparable attributes of human existence'.[40] He was in this respect driven by the same understandings that drove reformers such as Harriet Martineau, Herbert Spencer, and Henry Buckle. The fact that Kilvert was attracted, as we have seen, to Buckle's *History of Civilisation*, which posited natural laws channelling Man's development from superstition towards enlightenment and progress, suggests that, in spite of not living during phrenology's heyday (1830s-1840s), its vision of future society would have excited him. Earlier chapters have traced the backing that Kilvert's family gave to campaigns to encourage rational amusements among the working class. Writers that Kilvert admired – Martineau, Marryat, Knight,

William and Mary Howitt, Ballantyne, Kingsley – encouraged the spread of education and bourgeois values among the working class. Mary Howitt was applying Combe's *Constitution of Man* to her own children in 1833: 'I can trace out our children's characters to influences which Combe shows to be operative,' she wrote.[41] The Howitts and the Kilverts were typical of 'the reform-minded in both the middle and the working class [who] enthusiastically received the *Constitution of Man*'.[42] Generally, those attracted to phrenology opposed the idea that an individual's social worth depended on his place in the social hierarchy; they favoured a meritocratic society. Phrenology's opponents were much more wedded to existing forms of social organisation. *Kilvert's Diary* provides illuminating entries in which meritocratic values conflict with traditional ones based on rank.

Supporters and opponents of phrenology were also divided in terms of the generation to which they belonged: typically, the former were young, the latter were older. Again, Cooter supplies the data: 'In 1818 . . . the average age of the sixteen antiphrenologists for whom we have dates was forty-one, while the average age of the fifty-one phrenologists for whom we have dates was twenty-four'. One phrenologist of the time declared that it was 'the rising generation' who supported new doctrines.[43] One young supporter (born 1802) was Charles Wheatstone, inventor of the electric telegraph.

A vital issue concerning the possible stance of Kilvert and of his family towards phrenology was its materialist tendency. Although Cooter stated that 'phrenology championed a material practical world in which there was little room for the spiritual', he also insisted that *Constitution of Man* 'was not entirely a godless book'.[44] In his book, Combe asserted that phrenology 'was capable of combining harmoniously with religion'. He also urged the study of nature in terms akin to those used by Sedgwick in his *Discourse*. Combe quoted the *Discourse* in his preface – 'God seems to govern by natural laws'. Data about the religious views of phrenology's supporters and opponents is in short supply but Cooter was able to conclude that the latter were largely committed to orthodox faith and natural theology.

Mesmerism had a long history before Dr Mesmer, graduate of the Vienna Medical School, revived it in the 1770s under the name *Animal Magnetism*. Some authorities claimed that the physician Paracelsus invented it early in the sixteenth century; others that it was known to the ancient Egyptians. One authority noted that the magnet was an obsession with sixteen-and seventeenth-century scientists for whom it was 'the one universal cosmic force'.[45] Mesmer had begun from 1773 to use magnetised iron rods in the treatment of disease. An

Englishman named Perkins was at about the same time using rods, known as 'tractors', on patients, stroking diseased parts and producing remarkable cures. Mesmer later came to believe that the curative power of the magnet was in fact produced by the hand that held it; thus the idea of *animal* magnetism as opposed to *mineral* magnetism was born. Born too was the crucial idea that the power involved was the product of the mesmerist's *will*.

In order to grasp the appeal of mesmerism in the early decades of the nineteenth century, it is necessary to recognise that the public were excited then by the idea of electricity, much as, in more recent times, it has been excited by television, space-travel, and computers. William Howitt told how he and other children were entertained by Dr Dally's electrical 'exhibitions which, though well known to all better acquainted with scientific principles, appeared to our young eyes as actual magic'. Howitt encountered similar experiences at school in Tamworth from a visiting 'philosophical lecturer', whose 'exhibitions were full of the most intense wonder and delight'. The lecturer explained that he had demonstrated 'the most wonderful discovery of modern times' – electricity.[46]

Inevitably, one effect of electricity's appeal was that electrical terms were assimilated into the language (just as the word 'mesmerise' was). Brooke resorted to such terms when he wanted to convey the effect of Robertson's address at the opening of the Brighton Working Men's Institute: there was in the hall, Brooke said, 'a sort of electricity of excitement . . . as if a magnetic power flowing from the speaker had united [the audience] all to himself'.[47] Kilvert used the idea of electricity to register the preaching style of the curate of Glascwm: 'Mr Nathan electrified me by acting over again some striking passages he had met with in a book of Welsh sermons'. Kilvert described the contrast between the snow-capped Black Mountain and the brown landscape below as 'electrifying'. When one of his Langley Burrell parishioners, Farmer Lessiter, was recovering from illness, he told Kilvert that he thought he (Kilvert) 'must be a very strong man [because] when I was in bed the other day and you shook hands with me I felt as if an electrifying machine had gone all through me'.[48]

Mesmer believed that the processes involved in his healing stemmed entirely from natural laws and that he was simply assisting them.[49] He thought of the healing power as a fluid that was distributed throughout the universe, which 'insinuated itself' into the nervous system of human beings. Some individuals could change its movement by moving their hands in patterns around the person's body and thereby restore him to health. It had properties similar to those of a magnet.[50] William Gregory, professor of chemistry at Edinburgh University and a leading

Victorian advocate of both phrenology and mesmerism in Britain, said it may be regarded as a fluid or force like the force of chemical action or of gravity.[51] The mesmerist, it was assumed, transmitted his mesmeric power through his hands or his eyes to his subject. The power was directed to treating such diseases as rheumatism, sciatica, gout, paralysis, skin and eye problems, and various nervous diseases.

However, mesmerists' experiments had produced other more challenging effects that concerned the mind. Operations, including amputations, had been performed with patients in a mesmeric trance. Subjects in mesmeric trances could not only say what other so-called 'sympathetic' individuals were thinking and feeling, but could produce learned information on every conceivable subject, however unlearned they were in the waking state. Much attention was given to the 'mesmeric sleep', as it was called. Gregory described it as 'a state of somnambulism . . . or more correctly sleep-waking', in which 'the lower or animal propensities were laid to rest while the intellect and higher sentiments show forth'. A great deal of importance was attached by mesmerists to the *sympathy* between mesmerist and his subject, which Gregory defined as 'an attraction towards the mesmerist, or . . . obedience to his silent will'.[52] The Scottish doctor, James Braid, coined the term 'hypnotism' to describe the power which enabled one human mind to dominate another. Some have even claimed Mesmer to be the father of modern psychotherapy.[53]

Why did these ideas and experiences make such an impact on the Victorians? Mesmerism first came to Britain in the wake of the French Revolution when interest in superstition, magic, dreams, artistic imagination, and other special states of consciousness was at its height. However, mesmerism failed to gain acceptance then because it was associated with France at the time of the Napoleonic War. By the 1830s, interest in it revived in Britain. Dickens, for example, was drawn to it in 1838 in the work of Dr John Elliotson, professor of medicine at University College Hospital in London, the wards of which Dickens used regularly to visit. This was exactly the period, as Ackroyd pointed out, when Faraday was exploring the forces of magnetism and electricity.[54] Mesmerism could flourish at a time when science appeared to be emerging as the authority on the nature of the world and natural laws. 'The 1840s were characterised by a heady optimism about the powers and achievements of scientific enquiry [which] suggest . . . an ever-increasing mastery of nature.[55]

Kaplan noted that mesmerism represented a utopian vision of the future which appealed to both heart and head. The fierce debate and scandal that accompanied its discovery 'made the terminology and assumptions of mesmerism part of the air the early Victorians breathed'.[56] At its height in the 1840s and 1850s, it would have had particular interest for Kilvert's parents and his uncle Francis. It has been noted that Quakerism, in which Mrs Kilvert was raised, was marked by a preoccupation with the nature and potentiality of the physical world. Since it was a perennial topic in the newspapers and conversation of the day, it seems inevitable that it would have been a focus of enquiry for Kilvert and his fellow pupils at uncle Francis's school, which was 'progressive' in important ways. For religious families like the Kilverts, mesmerism held special fascination, chiefly because 'the question of whether the effects were natural or supernatural made experiments a testing ground of faith and doctrine'.[57] (Chapter eight shows Robert Kilvert's close concern with precisely these issues.) There was also the fact that 'the pseudo-scientific movement [of phrenology and mesmerism] was a new kind of evangelicalism'.[58]

Mesmerism was able to take a firm grip on the public's imagination partly because of the state of scientific knowledge early in Victoria's reign. Winter emphasised that

> definitions of science were malleable during these years. Society could not agree about what could be said about natural law. . . . What counted as a proper science . . . remained open to dispute. Similar ambiguities surrounded the human body. There were no definitive medical orthodoxies. . . . [59]

Another authority on the state of medical science at this period wrote: 'For decades after 1800, the causes of most diseases were embarrassing enigmas'.[60] Even by the 1870s the view taken by Victorians of illnesses and their treatment was a curious mixture of the traditional, the bizarre, and the downright alarming. One *Diary* entry (22 February 1878) tells of an old woman suffering from cancer of the eye and of a Dr Giles whose proposed treatment was 'to drive a needle through her nose and work it backwards and forwards'. Kilvert evidently thought such treatment both extreme and suspect because he noted that another doctor considered it 'the most inconsistent thing he ever heard of'.

Diary entries about Marlborough College show Kilvert looking forward to a period of more enlightened medical treatment based on sound knowledge. His brother Edward had been a pupil at Marlborough in the 1861-1866 period when there were six deaths from scarlet fever (60,000 people in Britain died from the disease in 1863-1864.) Kilvert knew that the College's earlier history was marked by outbreaks: 'How they do get it. . . . The place never seems free of it,' he remarked on 31 March 1870, when the College was once more in its grip, adding 'Now they have 60 cases, 3 deaths, and the school entirely broken up for the time'. Bad drains were often seen as the cause of the disease. Kilvert was always conscious of the dangers of the disease, expressing amazement on 18 November 1870 that a Clyro family reacted casually when their daughter was diagnosed with it.

Science, in a state of flux at this time, could not resist or discredit wild theories and practices. Only by 1870 were clearer lines of division drawn between various branches of science as a result of university reforms, new laboratories, and the emergence of professional bodies and proper regulations. Earlier in the century the vague relations between physical forces in nature and the mind were a tantalising area of study. Animal magnetism appealed to so-called 'progressive' doctors, natural philosophers, and intellectuals because it seemed to shed light on their questions about the relationship of physical forces to life, about the way in which mental and spiritual elements were governed by natural laws. Victorians were constantly bombarded by new discoveries, and were excitedly aware that theirs was a time of enormous change. Alison Winter expressed the Victorian situation thus: 'Because they felt themselves to be living in a dramatically and mysteriously altered world, Victorians were attracted to the notion of altered states of mind'.[61] Part of mesmerism's appeal lay in the idea that people's minds and souls were, or could be, in touch with each other in mysterious ways. It fascinated too because it was based on exploration of strengths and weaknesses, or superiority and inferiority in society. The mesmerist was assumed to have superior mental or moral powers to those of his subject. Mesmerism raised the possibility of achieving influence over the sinful, the sick, and the suffering and in this bore similarities to forms of possession and divine inspiration. 'The testimonies people gave to their mesmeric experiences often read like narratives of religious conversion'.[62] The activities of both preacher and mesmerist were concerned with God's influence through the natural world.

Knowledge of science was disseminated at this time in a wide variety of ways: through amateur naturalists' field trips, classes at Mechanics' Institutes, erudite lectures to gentry audiences, popular lectures in provincial halls, and reviews of science in periodicals. Kilvert experienced some of these. According to Parsinnen there was, especially in the 1840s and 1850s, 'a small army of mesmeric performers' who made a living out of the 'New Science' by presenting an act that appealed to the public. While they resembled scientific lecturers in certain ways, 'they diverged from them by offering a subject which, unlike chemistry or even natural history, was accessible to their auditors'.[63] Thus, its appeal was to all classes, and was 'improving' in the way popular publishing of the kind pioneered by the Chambers brothers and Charles Knight was seen to be.

Kilvert had the advantage of Robertson's commentary on, and evaluation of, mesmerism when it was at its height; several passages in Brooke's *Life* deal with it in some detail. When the mesmerist and clairvoyant Alexis Didier came to Brighton in 1849, Robertson went to see his performance but there were no startling revelations, which delighted Robertson. "'My close observation confused the charlatan'", said Robertson of Didier. "'His want of faith dimmed the mesmeric vision'", said Didier of Robertson. In 1851 he was advising a friend who was entering London life:

> Gavazzi's Exeter Hall orations and this electro-biology are of the exciting class of stimuli which I reckon dangerous and useless. The first leaves nothing behind, morally or intellectually; the second belongs as yet to the witchcraft and mesmerism class, which may hereafter be reduced to calm rules and become scientific.[64]

Robertson was acutely conscious that people whose religious faith was waning might turn to mesmerism. He felt that there was only one place to repose faith, and that was in Christianity. Mesmerism and other pseudo-sciences were not the answer, nor was true science, although he had a lot of respect for it because it depended on reason. However, truth could not be based on reason because 'it is not by reason – meaning, by reason, the understanding – but by the spirit, that is, the heart'. And he rejected the attempt to rest Christianity upon miracles as 'the vilest rationalism'.[65] Robertson's observations are valuable for registering the atmosphere, emotional and psychological, surrounding the public's reaction to mesmerism.

The foregoing account of the nature and significance of phrenology and mesmerism for Victorians introduces the *Diary* entry that records Kilvert's visit to a lecture on them at the Assembly Rooms, Weston-super-Mare, on 3 September 1872. The fact that lectures on mesmerism were still popular in 1872 is further testimony to its hold on the public imagination long after the period when it was at its height. Kilvert described Mr Hume's exhibition as 'a lecture on craniology and phrenology and mesmerism'. That it was billed as a 'lecture' indicates something of Hume's purpose and intended audience, although it is clear he aimed also at popular appeal because his advertisement in the local paper referred to his 'exceedingly amusing illustrations in mesmerism', as well as to his 'celebrated Lectures'.[66] Kilvert's account is detailed and careful as though he meant to evaluate mesmeric claims seriously; he was not expecting mere entertainment. From the outset, Kilvert's attitude towards the lecture was critical, especially the element of phrenology, which he seemed mentally to have already rejected.

Some skulls had been arranged on a table on the platform. 'Mr Hume,' Kilvert wrote, 'talked a good deal of wild nonsense and examined the heads of two or three of the audience whose moral and mental qualities he appraised highly'. Kilvert's observation showed both a familiarity with the pattern of such lectures and some amusement that no person's qualities were deemed deficient. Phrenology had of course had its critics from its beginnings: various reviews before 1820 dismissed it as 'crude, shallow, puerile, dull, dogmatic, absurd, and foolish'.[67] Kilvert may have been aware that it had featured in the lecture programme of the BLSI.

In attempting to assess Kilvert's attitude to phrenology as he sat in 1872 listening to Mr Hume's 'wild nonsense', a number of factors need to be examined. Cooter described *The Constitution of Man* as 'one of the most esteemed and popular books of the second third of the nineteenth century' and noted that by 1860 100,000 copies had been sold in Britain, twice as many as *The Origin of Species* (1859) had sold by the century's end. He also observed that 'phrenology in the second half of the nineteenth century became . . . more deeply entrenched than ever in everyday thought and expression', and that it was revived by the British tour in the 1870s of the American phrenologist Lorenzo Fowler.[68] We might also note that Charles Mackay's *Life, Literature, and Public Affairs*, which Kilvert was reading in 1878, a year after its publication, contained an entire chapter on George Combe. It is also relevant that, in spite of Kilvert's criticism of Mr Hume's comments on phrenology, he showed positive interest at the lecture's end: Hume showed 'a curious instrument for gauging the intellect of the human head by taking an angle and measuring from it'.[69] Finally, it is highly significant that a 'Mutual Improvement Society', established by Kilvert with some friends and his brother Edward, operated throughout the latter half of 1874 and was almost certain to have involved phrenology because '[it] was one of the few subjects pursued by nearly every mutual improvement society'.[70]

To return to Kilvert's account of Hume's lecture:

Then began the mesmerism. A number of men came up on the platform. . . . They were placed in a semi-circle on chairs sitting with their faces to the wall and their backs to the audience. A young lady went to the piano and began playing low soft dreamy music. The mesmerist passed between his victims and the wall and after making a few passes over their faces and arms and looking intently into their eyes he soon had 8 out of the 10 prostrate on the floor in a mesmeric sleep. He took them by the hand and drew them after him, holding his hand against the side of their heads. 'Come,

come,' he said authoritatively, and they followed as it seemed to me unwillingly, but unable to help themselves, though the mesmerist used no violence but appeared to draw them after him by the influence of a stronger will.

The emphasis on the mesmerist's stronger will is significant. The exertion of strong willpower was considered to be the explanation for mutual attraction or sympathy between individuals. Professor Gregory had identified Sympathy and Clairvoyance as the 'Higher Phenomena' of mesmerism. Clairvoyance, or 'lucid vision', was the capacity possessed by some, in trances or out of them, of seeing and describing absent persons or objects, and of predicting future events.[71] Signs that Kilvert gave some credence to this power exist in the *Diary* entry (26 May 1873) in which he recounted how Miss Bland, the Langley Burrell schoolmistress, coming home at twilight, was passed by a young man running 'swiftly without a sound', his feet not touching the ground. She couldn't see the young man's face but was sure it betokened that her brother, who was ill, had grown worse. She learned later that exactly at the time when she saw the running man, 'her brother was struck for death'. Kilvert was inclined to take supernatural events seriously and he was also a firm believer in the significance of dreams.[72] The similarity between dreams and the mesmeric trance was of considerable interest to advocates of mesmerism.

Other controversial aspects of mesmerism are highlighted in Kilvert's account, which continues thus:

> The young men and lads (all apparently of the shopkeeper class) were now lying asprawl upon the floor in all attitudes and wrapped in a deep mesmeric sleep. They lay like dead men and as still as death, with a ghastly unnatural look in their faces and at the mercy of the Mesmerist. One by one he raised them up, stiffened them by a pass and wave of the hand and stamp of the foot and left them swaying to and fro, unable to fall down or lift a foot from the ground, telling them sternly as he turned away, that they could not move.

Mesmerism was all about differences and inequalities, not only between individuals but different social groups, hence Kilvert's observation that the mesmerist's subjects were of 'the shopkeeper class'.[73] These young men were then told they were cocks, whereupon they crowed and flapped their wings. One was given a shawl, which he was told was an infant he had to nurse. Kilvert's comment on this young man's reaction is most revealing: 'But here a curious trait in his character came out. No sooner had the Mesmerist left him than a fury of hatred seemed to seize the lad and he dashed the child's head against the back of the chair. Perhaps he had a real hatred to infants which he could not conceal'. In the mesmeric sleep, just as in dreams, deep latent elements of a person's psyche manifested themselves, according to mesmerists. Thus, it was a means of insight into the origins and structure of the individual self. It is in this way that we can see mesmerism's closeness to psychoanalysis. Victorians were deeply interested in the way in which the circumstances of a person's life shaped their character and the progress of their life: 'Victorians were fascinated by the idea that one person's mind could reach into the immediate parts of someone else – the mind, the body, the home, or the past'.[74]

At the end of his account of Hume's performance, Kilvert noted that the mesmerist's subjects all denied any previous acquaintance with the mesmerist and said that they had no power to resist him. All in all, Kilvert seemed convinced by what he had seen and relieved at the absence of vulgarity – which was just as well because he had taken his mother to Mr Hume's lecture. Kilvert had attended the lecture to make up his own mind on the controversial subject of mesmerism because, as Houghton pointed out, in Victorian times 'one was expected to have an opinion about everything . . . the Oxford Movement or democracy or evolution or mesmerism and phrenology'.[75] To Kilvert the matter of meeting other individuals, of the possibilities and problems of 'knowing' them, of achieving a sympathetic relationship with them, was deeply compelling. The sense in which *Kilvert's Diary* is a 'collection' is particularly strong with regard to this compulsion. The *Diary* is a record of scores of meetings, most of them casual and inconsequential, but there is a consistent motif of a search for individuals with whom special rapport could be achieved. To an extent it simply represents Kilvert's interest in the opposite sex and his desire to find a wife. However, the search embraces men too and it is more than a mere relish for congenial company.

In his encounters with individuals, Kilvert was pursuing an enquiry that is the subject of his poem *The Pilgrimage*. The poem begins: 'It is a strange and solemn thing to mark/ How our paths cross each other in this world,/ And then diverge for ever'. 'Strange' is used very often in the *Diary* to indicate events or experiences with a supernatural dimension that is both fascinating and disturbing.[76] In his poem, however, he attributed the 'chance-called meeting' to God's influence, God's Providence,[77] a disturbance, therefore, of natural law. The purpose of the meetings envisaged in *The Pilgrimage* is the exchange of sympathy, the opportunity 'To look as sadly into those sad eyes/ That seek our own'. The idea of looking into another's eyes with more than ordinary intensity, as the mesmerist and his subject did, is caught in the insistence that the eyes of the stranger '*look and look*' into our own. Kilvert emphasised that the recognition of a significant encounter between strangers was effected through the eyes in the episode in which he met the 'angel child' on the Wootton Bassett train: 'How strange' (that word again) 'is this *seemingly* chance crossing of paths', he wrote. 'It was not chance, I know by the way the angel child looked into my eyes and soul . . . that she was "God's sweet unconscious messenger"'.[78]

A stranger appears in another *Diary* entry (19 June 1872) which features very heavy emphasis on eyes' beguiling power. It was another seemingly chance meeting on a train, this time with a girl Kilvert christened 'Irish Mary', who entertained the people in the carriage 'with her merriment, laughter and songs and her antics with a doll dressed like a boy'. In order to understand what the Irish Mary and angel child episodes have in common, we need to remember that Kilvert was greatly influenced by Wordsworth's mysterious Lucy Gray poems.[79] Lucy Gray qualities characterise the angel child and Irish Mary. Both exhibit her spontaneity and vitality: the eyes of the angel child 'expressed a thousand emotions'; Irish Mary's 'merry grey eyes sparkled'. Both girls exhibit Lucy's dramatically changeable moods, the former is 'by turns arch and laughing sweet, reproachful and grave', while the latter has 'merry laughter [but] suddenly she became grave and sad'. Irish Mary also possesses Lucy Gray's power to haunt listeners with her singing. We are told she has 'a magnificent voice' that can entertain with comic songs as well as with plaintive love songs. She is no 'ordinary' woman just as Lucy Gray and the angel child are not 'ordinary' children. Kilvert insisted that the angel child was 'singularly' beautiful and emphasised the 'singular' beauty of Irish Mary's eyes. Something of Lucy Gray's *mystery* attends them both. Her mystery resided partly in the fact that she is not depicted as a real person but as a quality of *mind*, of imagination. Kilvert forgot to ask the angel child's name, and never learnt Irish Mary's real name. The former's social origins are as puzzling as the latter's. The child, accompanied by a *lady*, has a 'distinguished air and manner', yet was in a third-class carriage. Though 'saucy' and a street hawker, Irish Mary is modest, 'blushes', and her voice has the 'sweetness and softness' of a lady's voice. There is also the suggestion about her, as about the angel child (and Lucy Gray), that she is not fully human; we are also told she 'fascinated' Kilvert 'strangely'.

This last emphasis is most telling and takes us back to Kilvert's poem *The Pilgrimage*, which is all about strange meetings, meetings with strangers. There he wrote: 'We cross the path of many travellers and stand a moment *face to face*'.[80] Furthermore, Kilvert very deliberately expressed the secret influence behind these encounters in terms both familiar and fascinating to him – in *mesmeric terms*: 'There is an influence irresistible that steals into life, and *draws and draws*' (my italics). The notion of magnetic force in this last phrase is very striking and is the key to the episodes involving the mysterious girls on trains, as well as to Hume's mesmeric performance. All three epitomise the power one individual can exercise over another, power that is expressed through *eyes*. It was the angel child's 'eyes of the deepest blue' that drew Kilvert's attention, eyes that looked into 'his eyes and soul'.[81]

The suggestion that Irish Mary is controlling Kilvert by mesmeric power is unmistakable. She alighted from the train at Chester; Kilvert stayed on it as he was going to Liverpool, and he and she were thus 'face to face' through the carriage door. 'Her look grew more wistful, beautiful, imploring. Our eyes met again and again. My eyes were fixed and riveted on hers. A few minutes more and I know not what might have happened'. All the social barriers and constraints were in retreat at this moment – 'a porter and some other people were looking wonderingly on' – so Kilvert ended the conversation. He knew that he and the girl were communicating at a level that made 'respectability' meaningless, because 'there was an attractive power about this poor Irish girl that fascinated me strangely'. 'Attractive' here means more than that she was beautiful; it means that she *attracted* as does a magnet, as Kilvert confirmed when he wrote: 'I felt irresistibly *drawn* to her' (my italics). Such was her power that 'A wild reckless feeling came over me. Shall I leave all and follow her?' He was acutely aware that his career and social position were in jeopardy.

He summed up her power as 'the power of a stronger over a weaker will and nature'. The similarity of idea and phrasing between this account and his account of his visit to the mesmerist is extremely close. Describing Hume's power over his young shopkeeper subjects, Kilvert wrote: 'He appeared to *draw* them after him by the influence of a stronger *will* . . . they *followed* unwillingly, unable to help themselves' (my italics). It was precisely this kind of influence which, in *The Pilgrimage*, drew individuals to each other: 'They cannot choose but go'. Kilvert was similarly unable to resist the 'message' of Love of the angel child and of Irish Mary. The strong sense in both cases that he was under a 'spell' makes it appropriate to view them as experiences of 'enchantment'.

Kilvert's summary of the nature and meaning of Irish Mary's *power* could stand as a summary of the power of Lucy Gray and the angel child, the power glimpsed in *The Pilgrimage* and in the Weston-super-Mare mesmerist. In Irish Mary, Kilvert perceived 'a certain intensity and power and richness of life'. All of his meetings that have been focused on, including the ones envisaged in *The Pilgrimage*, concern experiences of an unusual kind, in essence ones that yielded special insight into truth. In the case of the mesmerist, it was psychological insight, the revelation of hidden aspects of identity; in Irish Mary's case, it was insight into creative, imaginative power and the power of beauty; in the case of the angel child, it was insight into love and sympathy, a religious experience, which was of course how mesmeric experiences could appear: 'mesmeric states were so similar to religious ones; the relationship between the two was tantalisingly ambiguous'.[82] Kilvert was, in typically Victorian fashion, exploring the relationship between nature and the mind. And mesmerism was for him, as for many Victorians, the phenomenon which most powerfully reflected that relationship. Sympathy, which mattered so much to Kilvert, is the common denominator of his meetings with Irish Mary and the angel child; ecstatic experiences also played a significant part in them. In terms of the possibilities of human relationships, they were wonders.

One of the problems implicit in mesmerism was its sexual dimension. Fears that vulnerable people, especially young women (mesmerists' chief 'subjects') would be exploited by mesmerists informed this statement by a member of the Royal College of Surgeons: 'The principle on which the success of mesmerism depends is the subjugation of the will. . . . The subject becomes [the mesmerist's] captive. . . .His judgement is perverted and destroyed'.[83] In August 1861, the Royal College forbade any of its members to offer to cure diseases by homeopathy, mesmerism, or 'any other form of quackery'. In spite of such opposition, mesmerism flourished because it responded to the needs and preoccupations of the Victorian period. Ackroyd, in his biography of Dickens, said it was 'an aspect of the guiding principles of the age'. 'It was,' said Ackroyd, 'intimately associated with other leading ideas of the period – notably the belief in work, in progress, in the force of industry, in the dynamism of society itself'.[84] It also appealed to Victorians at a time when, in the view of many, orthodox religious belief was beginning to wane.

Kilvert was a man of curiosity, interested in anything and everything. He was intelligent enough and concerned enough to evaluate the Weston-super-Mare mesmerist himself, partly because he had been

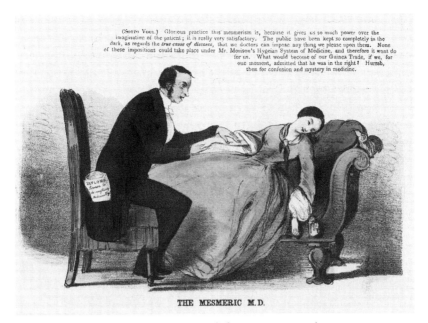

(Sotto Voce.) Glorious practice this mesmerism is, because it gives us so much power over the imagination of the patient; it is really very satisfactory. The public have been kept so completely in the dark, as regards the *true cause of diseases*, that we doctors can impose any thing we please upon them. None of these impositions could take place under Mr. Morison's Hygeian System of Medicine, and therefore it wont do for us. What would become of our Guinea Trade, if we, for one moment, admitted that he was in the right? Hurrah, then for confusion and mystery in medicine.

THE MESMERIC M.D.

The 'Mesmeric M.D.' says, *sotto voce*, 'Glorious practice this mesmerism is, because it gives us so much power over the imagination of the patient . . . We doctors can impose any thing we please upon them.'

brought up with mesmerism, partly because it was controversial, and partly because he was interested in science and natural laws. In all of this, he appears as that which he essentially was – a highly intelligent man who was concerned with the key questions of his time. He was interested in different kinds of power – spiritual, moral, artistic, scientific, emotional – and mesmerism was seen, especially given the amorphous nature of science at the time, as involved with the power of the human mind in relation to natural phenomena. Though interested in and enthused by notions of power and their use for good, he was uneasy at the way in which individuals lost control and freedom in the Weston-super-Mare and Irish Mary episodes. But mesmerism was filled with excitement and potential for him as it was for Victorians in general. It also seems likely that he tended to side with Dickens, one of a number of writers who defended mesmerism because it helped to prove the existence of the soul, and thus combated anti-Christian materialism.

This chapter has shown a Kilvert exposed to the controversies of his day, to the 'age of *Yeast*'. His own diary contains much of its 'fermentation'. Raised in a tradition of popular journalism dedicated to curiosity, knowledge, free enquiry, and progress, he inescapably engaged with controversies. Progressive influences in his background drew him to the highly controversial 'science' of phrenology and its rationalist, democratic, improving thrust. Perhaps nothing intrigued him quite so much as the potentiality of the human mind, glimpsed by contemporary writers, especially when they held out the possibility of increased sympathy among people, because that was a concept that fired him. On 10 August 1872, among several female parishioners distressed that he was to leave Clyro, was one who burst into 'bitter lamentations' and he marvelled at his own power: 'What have I done? What am I that these people should so care for me?' Sympathy was the centre of his faith and he responded to it when he encountered it in his parish work, in literature, in Positivism, and in mesmerism. It was the centre of his poem, *The Pilgrimage*.

Although committed to a simple faith, he had the curiosity and the courage to face the age's difficult questions, to read the controversial books by Buckle, Kingsley, and Comte. Committed as he was to the traditions of the past, he nevertheless found the challenge of the future mesmerising. When it beckoned, he was one of the individuals pictured in *The Pilgrimage*: 'They cannot choose but go'. When Irish Mary beckoned, he had just enough will to resist and didn't 'leave all and follow her'.

Chapter 7
Kilvert and Tyndall

For great numbers of educated Victorian laymen, Tyndall
personified both the most exciting and many of the most
disturbing elements of the new science.
Joe D. Burchfield, *John Tyndall – A Biographical Sketch*

It is the function of science, not as some think to divest this
universe of its wonder and its mystery, but, . . . to point out
the wonder and the mystery of common things.
John Tyndall, *Matter and Force, lecture to the working men
of Dundee* given in 1867

When William Plomer dismissed the idea that Kilvert had any interest
in science, he also chose to ignore his interest in John Tyndall. Kilvert's
admiration for Tyndall emerges in the *Diary* entry for 10 May 1875
when he 'fell into a pleasant talk about Professor Tyndall's discoveries
in science and sound, Swiss mountaineering, etc., with an agreeable
clergyman, a Mr Burns of Clifton, going up to London for the May
Meetings'.[1] The 'agreeable' clergyman was Lawrence Henry Byrnes
(Kilvert wrote his name as 'Burns' because he heard it that way) and
he came from the Nonconformist background that has been found
significant in this study of the diarist. He was born in 1822 of Roman
Catholic parents, who had 'a great dislike to the Established Church; but
having the idea that the Independents were "less bigoted" they allowed
the boy to go to the Independent Sunday School'.[2] Byrnes entered
Cheshunt Dissenting Academy in 1845 and then proceeded to London
University, obtaining a B.A. with first-class honours. When Kilvert
met him he was Pastor of the Pembroke Chapel, Clifton, where he was
known as 'a man of culture and refinement'.[3] His obituary recorded
that 'His sermons were thoughtful and instructive, evangelical in
matter . . . and he was deeply interested in Christian Missions'.[4] While
at Kingston-on-Thames Congregational Church, he found a YMCA, a
Tract and Visitation Society, and a Sunday School.[5] This was the man
who, to Kilvert's delight, shared his enthusiasm for Tyndall.

From the time when Kilvert was
growing to maturity, Tyndall was a
famous and controversial figure in
Britain as a populariser of science
through his Royal Institution
lectures (widely reported in the
press), his journal articles, and
his books. It seems that Kilvert
knew his *Fragments of Science for
Unscientific People*[6] (*FSUP*), which
'were aimed at making intelligible
all of the dominant ideas of the
century'.[7] Tyndall stressed science's
value in terms of education and
practical benefit in justifying his
work as a populariser: 'Science has

John Tyndall, a mid-career portrait

produced . . . immense changes – vast social ameliorations, and vast
alteration in the popular conception of the origin . . . of natural things'.[8]

We ought to know what kind of man this John Tyndall was who
both fed and reflected Kilvert's interest in the exciting developments
that were ushering in the modern world. Tyndall was born in 1820 at
Leighlinbridge, Co. Carlow, Ireland, to parents who were firm believers
in advancement through education. His father was a shoemaker and
staunch Evangelical Protestant; his mother was descended, like Kilvert's
mother, from a family of Quakers. Although his family was poor, he
received a good education at the Ballinabranagh National School where
he developed a love of learning under a gifted teacher who taught him
book-keeping, surveying, mathematics, English and other practical
knowledge. This enabled Tyndall to find a job with the Irish Ordnance
Survey. At this stage of his life he was influenced by the radical ideas of
the Chartists and of Thomas Carlyle (1795-1881). His radical bent is
further illustrated by his acceptance of a teaching post at Queenwood
College (Hants). It had begun in 1839 as Harmony Hall, a socialist
community founded by Robert Owen (1771-1858), industrialist and
educational and social visionary.[9] Education based on the theories of
Rousseau was an important part of Owen's vision of a new society.
'Owen and Pestalozzi provided much of [Queenwood] College's
philosophical foundation'.[10] It had a school for junior boys and also
trained 20-year-old youths in vocational skills. Its principal was George
Edmundson, a Quaker who had attended Ackworth Quaker School
in Yorkshire, where vocational/practical education was carried on, a
system 'not unlike that of Pestalozzi'.[11] One of Queenwood's principles

was to give pupils as much freedom as possible in an atmosphere of research and experimentation:[12] 'This was the first school in England to adopt practical and laboratory work in the teaching of applied science'.[13] Tyndall, appointed to the college in 1847 as superintendent of the engineering laboratory, proved himself a great teacher and in his farewell address 'claimed he was mainly moved to know the meaning of the book of nature and to penetrate the spirit of its author'.[14]

The approach to education of Kilvert's uncle Francis had much in common with that of Queenwood where Tyndall learned to teach: both combined study of natural objects with a sense of wonder. This was the reason, in Turner's view, for Tyndall's appeal to the Victorian public: to Tyndall 'a thoroughly naturalistic interpretation of nature according to the laws of contemporary science did not necessarily remove any of the wonder of nature that the clergy found there because of the presence of God'.[15] Kilvert warmed to Tyndall for exactly this reason – the scientist approached nature with both imagination and reverence (as all Kilvert's nature teachers had). Tyndall devoted an entire lecture to *The Scientific Use of the Imagination*.[16] Reason and imagination were, he said, continually combining to explore 'nature's mysteries, and 'imagination is the mightiest instrument of the physical discoverer'.[17] In one Address[18] he contrasted traditional classical education with modern scientific education; the two tended to be in conflict (something he deplored). It was the latter that sought to 'reverently uncover the inner workings of the universe'; such study was 'a worthy discipline' and employed not just the mind: '[man] feels as well as thinks; he is as receptive of the sublime and beautiful as well as of the true'. The best teachers needed 'to feel the mystery of the universe without tending to give it a rigid form'.[19] Although Tyndall was feared as a 'materialist', especially by religious people, he was forever insisting that science could never explain the ultimate mystery of the universe, for example: 'the real mystery of this universe lies unsolved, and . . . is incapable of solution'.[20]

Tyndall was the kind of scientist Dawkins would admire: one whose investigations of phenomena did not simultaneously empty them of mystery and wonder. Mystery was for him an inevitable dimension of nature, a permanent challenge to his intellect and understanding. *Kilvert's Diary and Landscape* has emphasised the diarist's fascination with mystery – of ancient stones, castles, barrows – and his desire that their mystery should remain unexplored, lest it lose its power to enchant. However, at the same time he was driven to learn all he could about natural phenomena by close observation, and admired Tyndall's unrivalled ability to demonstrate natural wonders in public lectures.

The scientist's appeal to Kilvert may be understood from the following statement by Gillian Beer: 'John Tyndall was probably the most important single figure among the scientific community for those concerned with the relations between ordinary human perceptions and science'.[21]

Tyndall's belief in the imagination as a means of education and a pathway to emotional and spiritual truth marked him out as a Romantic, as McMillan and Meehan recognised: 'Tyndall was considerably affected by the Romantic movement . . . in particular its worship of nature'.[22] His lectures always contained an imaginative or aesthetic dimension as, for example, when he told the working men of Dundee that 'the commonest substance in Nature [is] a miracle of beauty' and, with his great skill as a teacher, showed them 'the beautiful forms of splendid branches of ice-crystals' by illuminating them on a sheet of glass using a microscope and a lamp.[23] Successful popularisers knew that their audiences expected to be entertained as well as educated, and accordingly Tyndall made use of the most stunning visual techniques available. His lamp, or 'magic lantern' as contemporary newspapers liked to call it, was a key part of his lectures. It was a very powerful carbon arc lamp, which displayed images on a large screen. His presentations, like those of Pepper, were important stages in the progress from magic lantern to cinema. The zoetrope that children were looking through at a party on 19 January 1872 at the Clyro home of the Crichtons caught Kilvert's attention. It was a device that gave the illusion of moving pictures, and consisted of a stand supporting a cylinder inside which were painted pictures. As they were viewed through slits in the side while it was rotated, they appeared to move. Members of the Kilvert family were typically Victorian in their enthusiasm for pictures, as technology presented more and more of them to the public. Tyndall went in for other arresting visual tricks, as Lightman recorded: 'In his 1862 Spring Lecture [he] lit a cigar at the invisible focus of a beam of infrared radiation'.[24]

He enthused about Switzerland's 'system of glaciers [to which] belong the sublimity and beauty of mass, form, colour and grouping. And still the outward splendour is by no means all because the physical is the substratum of the spiritual'.[25] Tyndall's imaginative language enthralled audiences and readers. He wrote of 'lovely bits of pasture – bright emerald gems set in the bosom of the woods', 'clouds becoming ever blacker, until finally they were unlocked by thunder, and shook themselves down on us in furious rain' and, referring to the origin of life, he said that not only all natural forms but 'the human mind itself – emotion, intellect, will – were once latent in a fiery cloud'.[26] Cosslett noted that Tyndall regularly used analogies (metaphors in essence) in order to convey natural processes and that this was central to his work as a science populariser. She noted too that his 'popularising works' were permeated by human values: 'Science is continually being related to our sense for conduct and beauty, and touched with emotion'.[27] It is unsurprising that Kilvert was drawn to a man who could describe natural objects so exquisitely; later we shall see descriptions of Kilvert's that seem to derive from Tyndall. Thompson summed up Tyndall's approach by saying that he took his audience into 'the fairy land of science' by his blend of the poetic and imaginative with factual content.[28]

Tyndall's popularity was due in part to the topics on which he lectured and wrote. The first lecture in his *FSUP* is 'The Constitution of Nature', in which he examined the origin of the universe, the nature of space, and the origin of light and heat. Lectures on 'Matter and Force', 'Radiation', 'Radiant Heat', 'The Structure of the Light of the Sky', 'Dust and Disease', and 'Magnetism' also appear in *FSUP*.[29] The public's interest in him stemmed largely from the fact that his research areas directly affected people's lives or were, or became, controversial, as in the case of germ theory and disease or evolution.

It is noticeable that Kilvert singled out Tyndall's work on *sound*. He had given his Royal Institution lecture on it in summer 1857; his main findings appear in his *On Sound* (1867).[30] He was Scientific Adviser to the Elder Brethren of Trinity House, the body that provides lighthouses, and he experimented to ascertain the effect of wind, rain, fog, and snow on the transmission of sound. Mariners' safety depended on sound signals in weather conditions when light from lighthouses could not be seen. It was believed that sound signals did not travel well through rain, fog, and snow but Tyndall disproved the idea. Lighthouses had particular interest for Kilvert, as was noted in chapter four; they are mentioned a dozen times in his *Cornish Diary*, often with strong awareness of the danger of the coasts where they are located.[31] He seemed relieved to catch 'the brilliant flash of the revolving light of Godrevy'; near the Wolf Rock lighthouse he was uneasy because 'we could not hear the solemn incessant tolling of the bell [buoy]'.[32] This awareness of sound's transmission through the air, which seems to owe something to Tyndall, who did many experiments on the opacity and transparency of the atmosphere to sound, is in Kilvert's frequent references to sounds (often church bells or voices) heard at a distance in various weather conditions as in these examples: 'At five minutes to midnight the bells of Chippenham Church pealed out loud and clear in the frosty air'; 'The Chapel bell tolled out sharp and sudden through the white mist'; 'A white mist gathered in the valley and distant voices and laughter of children at play came floating at intervals across the river'; 'Then in the silence the Hay Church bell for evensong boomed suddenly out across the valley'. 'I could hear [the men's] voices quite distinctly across the fields in the silence of the frost'. Tyndall's influence seems particularly clear in this entry: *For the first time I heard today* the sweet bells of Clyro chiming down in the valley just before I reached the Chapel. *I could even hear* the three bells chime change for the single bell. *The west wind brought the sound of the bells up the hill so clearly that it arrested me even while I was walking*.[33] The viewpoint in these examples is factual, objective, analytical. This is particularly true of the last example, whose italicised portions (italics supplied) show that sounds' capacity to be heard in varying weathers had been a subject of study for Kilvert for some time. He was intent on precise recording, not picturesque description.

If Kilvert's awareness of sounds was strong, his preoccupation with the blue of the sky was almost obsessive and this too owes much to Tyndall's work and writing. He is credited with discovering why the sky is blue.[34] In a laboratory experiment, he produced 'a blue which shall rival . . . that of the deepest Italian sky'.[35] Laying bare the reasons for the phenomenon of blue skies in no way destroyed the wonder they held for him. His deep, almost spiritual enthusiasm for the blue of Alpine skies communicated itself to Kilvert, who responded with his own fervency in such passages as: 'There was not a cloud in the deep wonderful blue of the heavens' and 'Another dense white fog which cleared off to cloudless blue'.[36] Both Kilvert and Tyndall were especially captivated by the contrast of intense blue sky with the whiteness of snow. This is evident in the former's case by this entry: 'The morning frosty and exquisitely clear and lovely with a brilliant blue sky meeting the dazzling white slopes'.[37]

There is a *Diary* passage and a passage in Tyndall passage which have such a similar tone and outlook and such similar phrasing that it seems likely that Kilvert was half remembering Tyndall's words as he composed his own.[38] The essence of both passages is the contrast of blue sky and white snow, suddenly illuminated by the sun. Kilvert's begins with the Black Mountains invisible, 'being wrapped in clouds, . . . till a clearer burst of sunlight revealed the truth. This brilliant white cloud that I had been looking at . . . was the mountain in snow . . . and the mountains stood up in the clear blue heaven, a long rampart line of dazzling glittering snow. . . . '[39] In this description we find verbal echoes of Tyndall's Snowdon passage and of other passages in his *Mountaineering in 1861*. The latter wrote: 'The scene [from the top of Snowdon] would bear comparison with the splendours of the Alps themselves'. Kilvert, 'overwhelmed at the extraordinary splendour of this marvellous spectacle', said 'I never saw anything to equal it . . . even among the high Alps'. The latter part of this last statement has its counterpart in Tyndall's book. Of the Weisshorn mountain he wrote: 'I had never seen anything to equal it'. Another echo of Tyndall's Snowdon passage is to be found in the *Diary* entry for 24 March 1872: Tyndall's Flintshire mountains were 'flooded with glory'; Kilvert's Black Mountain was 'bathed in glory'.

Both men were also taken with the colours of sunset on the snow of mountains. Tyndall wrote of some mountain peaks: 'They seemed pyramids of solid fire . . . stretches of crimson light . . . over the higher snow-fields . . . the eastern heavens assumed a deep purple hue, above which was a belt of red and zones of orange and violet'. Kilvert wrote of 'primrose light . . . deepening into rose and crimson . . . an intense brilliant yellow light deepened with the sky to the indescribable red tinge that snow-fields assume in sunset light'. For both men, the moment was unique. Tyndall wrote of the Weisshorn: 'I had never before witnessed a scene which affected me like this one', while Kilvert wrote: 'it seemed to me as if one might never see such a sight again'. And finally, both men conceived of their experiences, which were essentially experiences of enchantment, in religious terms. Tempted to make notes in his notebook, Tyndall 'soon relinquished the attempt' because he thought it 'profane . . . where silent worship seemed the "reasonable service"'. Kilvert's 'first involuntary thought . . . [was] to lift up the heart to God . . . for having made the earth so beautiful'.[40]

Mountains were important to Kilvert partly because he had grown up with the Alpine climbing movement. A love affair with Swiss mountains began in the middle of the eighteenth century, stimulated largely by the rediscovery of nature led by Rousseau, and the British were in the vanguard of this trend.[41] Englishmen went to the Alps in the 1850s and 1860s in the golden age of mountaineering. The British Alpine Club was formed in 1857, establishing 'the playground of the Alps as a preserve for English gentlemen and scholars'.[42] Of its members, almost 30% were barristers and solicitors, while 16% were clergymen and dons. Newspapers steadily recorded their exploits as peak after peak was conquered.

Kilvert loved stories, and the story of the Matterhorn disaster had all the ingredients he enjoyed: drama, heroism, poignancy, scandal, and violent death. He recorded telling the story to a child sweetheart, along with some of his 'adventures in Switzerland', on 13 May 1874. The Matterhorn was in 1865 the one unconquered peak of the western Alps – 'a towering physical confirmation of inaccessibility' – and the expedition to conquer it that year resulted in 'the most dramatic and famous disaster in the history of mountaineering'.[43] The famous climber Edward Whymper, Lord Francis Douglas, and their Swiss guides teamed up with

a party consisting of the Rev. Charles Hudson, Robert Hadow, and their
guides. Whymper had already made seven unsuccessful attempts on the
mountain. He and the others reached the Matterhorn summit on 14
July 1865. However, on the descent, Hadow slipped carrying Douglas,
Hudson, and a guide to their deaths. The party were all roped together
but the others were saved because the rope broke.

The three English victims were newsworthy before the disaster.
Douglas was the handsome son of the 8th Marquess of Queensbury.
The *Times* called him 'the heir presumptive of one of our noblest
titles' and said that all three were 'just the men that England is proud
of . . . scholars and gentlemen'.[44] Linking Douglas and Hadow was their
extreme youth: the former was eighteen, the latter nineteen. Hadow had
significance for Kilvert on two counts. He was from a local family. His
mother was Emma Nisbet, daughter of Robert Nisbet of Southbroom
House, Devizes, twenty miles from Kilvert's home near Chippenham.
Furthermore, Robert Nisbet had been Chippenham's M.P. from 1856
to 1859. In addition, Hadow's father, Patrick Douglas Hadow, was
Chairman of the P. and O. Steam Navigation Company. The young
Hadow was the protégé of Charles Hudson, who was likely to have
been a heroic figure in Kilvert's eyes. Hudson, an Anglican clergyman
from Lincolnshire, born in 1828, was 'a splendid example of muscular
Christianity'[45] (in the Kingsley tradition). Controversy surrounded the
cause of the disaster. Hadow was inexperienced and had worn boots;
the two groups of climbers did not know each other; the rope that
broke was old. There was even a suggestion that Whymper's guide had
cut the rope. The *Times* regarded the Englishmen's deaths as a waste – a
throwing away of the 'gift of life . . . in an emulation which [is shared]
only with skylarks, apes, cats and squirrels'.[46]

Kilvert remembered the disaster for another reason: the dimension
of wonder and spirituality it possessed. When he recounted the 'sad
story of the Matterhorn accident' to Georgie Gale and her family in
1874, he told of 'the appearance in the air of the three mysterious
crosses'. Whymper described what he and his Swiss guides saw as,
utterly disconsolate over the loss of their companions, they descended
the mountain:

> When, lo! a mighty arch appeared. . . . Pale, colourless, and
> noiseless, but perfectly sharp and defined, . . . this unearthly
> apparition seemed like a vision from another world; and
> we watched with amazement the gradual development of
> two vast crosses, one on either side. . . . It was a fearful and
> wonderful sight.[47]

Whymper believed it was a spiritual vision commemorating the victims. However, he sought explanation of it in terms of a 'fog-bow' and also noted that Italian guides descending the mountain a few days later had seen 'the phenomenon commonly termed the Brocken'. A modern weather expert, Paul Simons, explained the crosses were "'sundogs" created by microscopic ice crystals in . . . cirrus clouds, bending sunlight like glass prisms so that a pair of "ghost" images of the sun appeared alongside the real sun'.[48] An odd postscript to the Matterhorn tragedy is that Tyndall was thought to be one of its victims. He was with his

The Matterhorn Crosses

friend Hirst and, as they were leaving Gadmen, a guide approached Tyndall and asked him whether he knew 'Professor Tyndall who was killed upon the Matterhorn. I then listened to a somewhat detailed account of my destruction'.[49]

To the Evangelical mind of Kilvert, ready to see God's interruption of natural laws, the three crosses, commemorating deaths of heroes, would have had an irresistible spiritual significance. (His reference to them as 'mysterious' is telling; he wanted them to be a mystery, a miracle.) However, he was also capable of adopting a scientific, objective viewpoint to a similar natural phenomenon. His sister Thersie had told him of an odd experience. Lying inw bed in the morning with the bedroom shutters closed, light entering only through a small square hole cut into them, she noticed at 6.45 just as the postman came to the door, 'the figures of two little men or a man and a boy, very small, walking up the ceiling'. After the postman had gone, 'the shadows went down the ceiling again and disappeared'. However, as the postman reached the curve of the drive, the two little figures appeared briefly on the ceiling again. Kilvert commented: 'It was a curious optical effect and one difficult to account for as there was no light behind or below which could throw upon the ceiling of this room the shadow of any figure upon the drive'.[50] We have here the same intense interest and detached observation that marked Kilvert's stance at the Weston-super-Mare mesmerism lecture.

In this effort to map Kilvert's general cultural awareness and understanding, note has been taken of the literary periodicals he read, and this is fruitful in relation to his knowledge of science and of Tyndall in particular. It is worthwhile examining the kind of periodicals they were to see why he may have chosen them. Those he regularly read were three in number and they together provided him with an in-depth knowledge of cultural affairs. *Macmillan's Magazine* featured critical reviews as well as serial novels (he read Keary's *Castle Daly* in it) and it also had a strong interest in science.[51] The *Saturday Review*, founded in 1855 by A.J. Beresford Hope,[52] was edited by John Douglas Cook, as Kilvert knew because he referred to 'the house where Mr G. Venables used to stay with Mr Cook of the Saturday Review'.[53] The dominant force behind the *Saturday Review* was James Fitzjames Stephen (1829-1894), a very close friend of George Venables, who wrote leading articles for the paper.[54] The *Saturday Review* under Stephen's influence stood for England's traditional institutions and the rights of the governing classes.[55]

The *Saturday Review* was sympathetic to liberal tendencies in society while simultaneously being critical of them. It was particularly scathing of books and theories that encouraged ordinary people to indulge facile dreams of social improvement. 'A relentless critic of Victorian cant' was Briggs's description of it.[56] Before considering what the *Cornhill Magazine* offered Kilvert, three further points about the *Saturday Review* ought to be noted: first, that it set out to review *Science* as well as Literature, Politics and Art; second, that Horace Moule, whose tragic history was known to Kilvert, was one of its writers;[57] and third, that it was not the kind of journal to appeal to the soft, sentimental, uncritical, and unintellectual man that is the received picture of Kilvert. Its tone was 'cynical, sceptical, hypercritical, malicious, and destructive' and 'was not ready to accept without question the reforms of enthusiasts whose emotions outrun their intellects'.[58] Kilvert could warm to the journal's endorsement of the political status quo, its hostility to democracy, and its acceptance of religious scepticism.

If the factors drawing Kilvert to the *Saturday Review* were numerous, they were exceeded by those drawing him to the *Cornhill*. Described as 'the most important magazine of the latter half of the century',[59] it was founded in 1860 by George Smith (of the publishers Smith and Elder), with Thackeray as its first editor. Selling (like *Macmillan's Magazine*) at one shilling, it combined critical reviews with serialised novels – by Thackeray, George Eliot, Trollope, Mrs Gaskell, Hardy, and Henry James, as well as by more popular authors.[60] The *Cornhill's* editor from 1871 was the Evangelical Leslie Stephen (1832-1904), younger brother of James Fitzjames Stephen. The father of Leslie was at Trinity

College, Cambridge in 1806, during the reign of Charles Simeon.[61] Leslie's mother was Jane Venn, daughter of the Rev. John Venn (of the Clapham church where Kilvert's uncle Francis was married); Venn was one of the leaders of the Evangelical Clapham Sect.[62] With this background, it is not surprising that the *Cornhill* under his editorship had an Evangelical tone. He was 'a severe moralist' and the tone of his magazine was 'consciously serious, and even earnest'.[63] He had initially entered the Church (ordained in 1859) but inclined towards teaching as his faith declined.[64] The *Cornhill* work enabled him to follow his literary tastes, his flair for writing, and to encourage right conduct. He said he wanted 'to provide healthy reading for the British public'.[65] He also wanted to encourage useful work and learning, as is seen by his book *The Life of Henry Fawcett*, social reformer and the first pupil at Queenwood College.[66] Leslie's *Free Thinking and Plain Speaking* (1873) is another sign of his radicalism.[67]

A further aspect of Leslie Stephen's character that made him important to Kilvert was the love they shared for mountains. After his visit to the Bavarian Tyrol in 1855, Leslie became an enthusiastic pioneer of mountaineering. He wrote articles on his Alpine exploits for the *Cornhill*, which Kilvert would have seen. Leslie spent winter holidays in Switzerland[68] and Easter ones in the Lake District. Mountaineering is the link between Leslie and the physicist John Tyndall because it was this (and their radicalism and youthful Evangelical persuasion) that made them warm to each other. When the Alpine Club was formed, Leslie joined 'along with John Tyndall'.[69] The *Cornhill* fostered interest in science with a series of articles called 'Our Survey of Literature and Science', usually written by George Lewes, partner of George Eliot. The December 1862 article in this series mentioned Tyndall, while one entitled 'Notes on Science' (7 March 1863) by Lewes recorded that Professor Tyndall 'had made some curious revelations of the invisible' when lecturing on Radiant Heat at the Royal Institution.[70]

The third journal that Kilvert saw regularly, *Macmillan's Magazine*, did not feature science articles as frequently as the *Cornhill* and the *Saturday Review*, but its owner, Alexander Macmillan, had a particular interest in science that involved Tyndall. Macmillan launched his magazine in 1859 in order to bring science, literature and the arts together in one publication. When he moved from Cambridge to London in 1863 he made contact with men of science, one of whom was the brilliant Norman Lockyer, amateur astronomer and editor of *The Reader*, a science journal. Macmillan invited him to become science adviser to his publishing house as *The Reader* was struggling financially. Tyndall, whose interest in publishing was wide, was one of a group of scientists who established the journal *Nature* to replace it.[71] It was owned by Macmillan and edited by Lockyer, and first appeared on 4 November 1869 with the declared aim of 'placing before the public the grand results of scientific discovery and work'.[72] Tyndall wrote many articles for it. It also contained reports of meetings of scientific societies, including the Woolhope Naturalists' Field Club.[73]

Kilvert did not read such journals specifically to feed an interest in science; he read them because he wanted to keep up with the culture of his society, of which science was an increasingly important aspect. He read them because he loved ideas and books. This so-called 'unbookish' man was *always* reaching for a book – or for journals that had to do with books. And if the question still lingers about his reading largely 'ephemeral' novels, we should reflect on the words of radical intellectual Victorian, Frederic Harrison, about the *Cornhill*: 'It contained a great body of excellent and permanent literature'.[74] That would have been Kilvert's attitude; to argue otherwise is to fail to see his reading in its contemporary context.

One of the 'Fragments of Science' touched on by Tyndall for the interest of 'Unscientific People' was the electric telegraph. Tyndall's imaginative description of it would have aroused Kilvert's imagination: 'Who put the soul into the telegraphic body?' he asked, 'Who snatched from heaven the fire that flashes along the line?' It was, he said, 'the standing wonder of the age'[75] and a significant element in Kilvert's childhood. Developed in Britain by William Cooke and Charles Wheatstone, it obtained a patent in 1837. A line from London to Slough was connected in 1842 and by 1851 it was being used by officials of the Great Exhibition to keep in touch with the police. (Kilvert may have first seen it there.) Some 4,000 miles had been installed by 1852 and a cable was laid under the Channel in 1851. Kilvert's enthusiasm for the telegraph reflected the general public interest. His aesthetic response to the actual instrument – 'It is a beautiful simple instrument' – was wedded to appreciation of its utility and efficiency; the new instrument he saw made transmission easier than 'the old method'.[76] His sense of the instrument's beauty was enhanced, typically for him, by the fact that a 'dazzling fair-haired beauty' was operating one at a table! The 1870s was 'a notable period for other, new applications of physics – the microphone, telephone and phonograph'.[77]

It was easy for Kilvert to accept Tyndall's endorsement of the telegraph but what of the latter's formidable reputation as a materialist? In his lecture 'Matter and Force', delivered to the working-men of Dundee, Tyndall asserted that man shared his 'celestial pedigree with the meanest living things', an idea which, by its 'apparent tendency towards what is called materialism', might frighten some of his audience. But, he continued, 'the physical philosopher must be a pure materialist'. Kilvert had to come to terms, not only with these statements, but also with the fact that the *Record*, his father's newspaper, had linked Tyndall specifically with the atheist, Louis Buchner (1824-1899) and his work *Force and Matter* (1855), one of the most popular books in the materialist movement.[78]

> The arguments of the book . . . all derived from its central claim . . . that there is no matter without force and no force without matter. Force is inseparably bound to a material substrate and thus cannot be regarded as a kind of supernatural, transcendent entity. All changes and events follow mechanical laws. These laws are not imposed on nature from outside, but are built into matter itself. Matter is eternal. . . . It is ruled by rigid and universal laws which do not allow for miracles.[79]

We have noted that Kilvert would have been reassured that Tyndall approached nature with reverence, imagination, feeling, and that he sought spiritual experiences in landscape. Nevertheless, he 'constituted himself the hammer of theology, wherever it impinged on physical nature'.[80] The issue of evolution was the key area in the nineteenth century, where science and religion met head-on, and was the most potent threat to religious faith. Tyndall stated that evolution theory was not to be 'denounced as wicked . . . but approached with a reverent freedom' such as had been shown by the London clergy, who had 'nerve enough to listen to the strongest views. . . . With the country clergy I am told the case is different'.[81] Apparently it was not the case with the country clergyman of Clyro.

Tyndall attracted Kilvert's attention because of his articles in *FSUP* on such topical and controversial issues as the efficacy of prayer and the credibility of miracles. He had submitted a letter to the *Contemporary Review* (vol. XX, July 1872) introducing the article by the London surgeon, Sir Henry Thompson. The article was entitled 'The "Prayer for the Sick" – Hints Towards a Serious Attempt to Estimate Its Value'. It proposed that a particular hospital or hospital ward containing patients whose diseases had been well studied and their mortality rates well known, should be made the object of special prayers by religious people for three to five years. At the end of this period, the mortality rates should be compared with previous rates to see what difference prayer made. The article aroused much controversy in other journals, and in newspapers. The July 1872 issue of the *Contemporary Review* also included Tyndall's article 'Prayer as a Form of Physical Energy'.

It was common practice in the society in which Kilvert grew up for prayers to be authorised locally and nationally for relief from particular ills. In 1831, 1832, 1833, and 1849, prayers were approved for relief from cholera. Special prayers of thanksgiving were issued in 1846, 1847, and 1854 for abundant harvests. It seems likely that Kilvert would have backed the enlightened view taken by Kingsley in 1854 that 'God had answered previous prayers for relief from cholera by revealing through the labours of scientists the origin of the disease'.[82] While Kilvert was a student at Oxford in 1860 there was a very wet summer and the Bishop of Oxford, Samuel Wilberforce, instructed his clergy to include prayers for good weather in their services. Kingsley expressed his opposition to this in a sermon. Tyndall gave his support in his article 'Prayer and Natural Law' to clergymen 'wise enough and courageous enough' to reject 'delusive reliance on supernatural aid'.[83] To him and other scientists of the day 'Prayers on special occasions represented a concrete form of superstition whereby clergy with the approval of the state could hinder the dispersion of scientific explanations of natural phenomena'.[84]

Tyndall had also noted in his 'Prayer and Natural Law' article that those people who believed that 'the miraculous is still active in Nature' were likely to join in prayers for good weather and for rain. Was Kilvert distancing himself from such people when he noted on Midsummer Day during the drought of 1874: 'Blessed blessed rain fell all the evening upon the parched . . . ground. . . . In many churches there have been prayers for rain'? He didn't add that he himself had joined in the prayers. However, the fact that he referred to the rain as 'blessed' and quoted 'Thou sendest a gracious rain upon thine inheritance' suggests that he believed the rain was God's response to prayer.

When the Prince of Wales was mortally ill in late 1871 a cabinet committee and a committee of the Privy Council issued a call for a special day of prayer. The Prince suddenly began to recover and 'all manner of claims were made in the religious press for the efficacy of prayer'.[85] Kilvert seemed to fall in with this praying initiative. On 10 December 1871, he recorded that the Rev. Venables 'prayed "that it may please Thee . . . to bless Albert Edward Prince of Wales". It was very impressive'. Kilvert noted that before the afternoon service a form of prayer for the Prince came down by telegraph from the Archbishop of Canterbury, 'the first prayer that I ever heard of as coming by telegraph'. His remark may be seen either as his unease at the incompatibility of ancient, superstitious faith in prayer with such a symbol of the modern, scientific world as the telegraph, or his satisfaction that the telegraph could – strangely – be put to the service of prayer. On 14 December, when the Prince was better, he thanked God for it, as though the prayer had helped. The government proclaimed on 27 February 1872 a day of national thanksgiving for the recovery – an event Kilvert recorded.

Kilvert's faith, and his faith in Tyndall, faced another test following the latter's Belfast lecture to the BAAS on 19 August 1874.[86] What became known as the 'Belfast Address' 'sparked the most intense debate of the Victorian conflict of science and religion'.[87] Tyndall chose that centre of the fiercest religious beliefs in the kingdom to declare that science was bound to take over from religion in all speculation about, and explanation of, the origin and meaning of the universe. 'Acting otherwise proved disastrous in the past,' he insisted, 'and it is simply fatuous today'.[88] Before arriving at this conclusion he had conducted his audience on an historical tour: from the growth of science in ancient times, to the Middle Ages ('when acceptance of mere authority led, as it always does in science, to intellectual death'), the persecution of scientists by the Church in the sixteenth and seventeenth centuries, and the philosophers of the Enlightenment. By the early nineteenth century, traditional belief had been challenged by naturalists and geologists who had shown that the earth had not existed for sixty thousand, nor even for sixty million years, but for 'aeons embracing untold millions of years'. They had shown too that species evolved from simple to complex. Then came Darwin's *Origin of Species* in the present day, along with other 'grand generalisations' illustrating the 'law of causal connection which . . . asserts itself everywhere in nature'.[89] Herbert Spencer had cast light on the science of the mind. Tyndall said he believed Buckle had erred when he had detached man's intellectual achievement from 'moral force'; a serious limitation of materialism was, Tyndall thought, its lack of a moral dimension.[90]

This last point brought Tyndall to the climax of his Address. Just as the intellectual and the moral were inseparable, so were science and literature: 'The world embraces not only a Newton but a Shakespeare. . . . They are not opposed, but supplementary – not mutually exclusive, but reconcilable'. (Dr Alexander, in his 1873 Bath Church Congress lecture, thought them irreconcilable – see start of chapter six.) Man's development, said Tyndall, was a journey from ignorance to knowledge, from superstition to reason. In man's texture there were feelings of 'Awe, Reverence, Wonder . . . the love of the beautiful, physical and moral, in Nature, Poetry and Art'. Man would always 'turn to the Mystery from which [he] has emerged'.

'There is also,' Tyndall told his audience, 'that deep-set feeling which [had always] . . . incorporated itself in the Religions of the world'. The 'problem of problems at the present hour' was to yield this sentiment 'reasonable satisfaction'.[91]

Tyndall closed his Address with a quotation from Wordsworth's *Tintern Abbey*, which concerned mystery apprehended in nature:

And I have felt
A presence that disturbs me with the joy
Of elevated thoughts; a sense sublime
Of something far more deeply interfused,
Whose dwelling is the light of setting suns,
And the round ocean and the living air,
And the blue sky, and in the mind of man:
A motion and a spirit, that impels
All thinking things, all objects of all thought
  And rolls through all things.

Kilvert used Wordsworth's poem to convey his experience of visiting the Wye (the poem concerns that river) at Aberedw, twenty miles from Clyro, the moment when he first recognised the region's beauty and felt the release of his own creativity. It was a moment of 'enchantment', 'a day never to be forgotten [when] every step was through an enchanted land'.[92]

It was typical of Tyndall to quote poetry which saw sunsets and blue skies as gateways to 'nature's mystery. His and Kilvert's passionate exultation in both these natural phenomena has been touched on earlier in this chapter. It is a coincidence, but a highly appropriate one, that in a *Diary* entry for 21 August 1874 (two days after the Belfast Address), Kilvert recorded the receipt of a letter (written on 16 August) from his lover, Katharine Heanley, in which she connected religious feelings of the kind Tyndall had mentioned at the close of his recent Address to blue skies and the changing colours of sunsets in an ecstatic expression of religious faith typical of the period:

About this time last year we had one of our lovely Lincolnshire sunsets. . . . A deep blue sky fading into light blue. Faith.
A lovely golden and orange. Hope.
Fiery red and lovely rose. Love.
Each and all melting and glowing into each other, making a perfect whole, and yet the rose of love and charity shining out above and over all.

It was with Katharine Heanley that Kilvert could share Tennyson's *In Memoriam*, the poem which for many Victorians presented the age's conflict between religion and science in an accessible and deeply enjoyable form, reassuring doubtful believers that 'There lives more faith in honest doubt,/ Believe me, than in half the creeds'. Kilvert referred to it on 1 October 1874 as a key element in his relationship with Katharine: it was 'our beloved *In Memoriam*' and they were in the habit of 'comparing notes' about it and 'showing each other our favourite passages'.

Tyndall, a friend of the poet, was an acceptable figure to Kilvert in a debate that went beyond the issue of faith and doubt. Turner emphasised that the issue raised by Thompson's proposal to monitor the efficacy of prayers for the sick was 'neither the physics nor the theology of prayer, but rather the nature and direction of cultural leadership in a modernised English society'.[93] Kilvert valued the way Tyndall was able to convey the miracles of beauty and complexity of natural phenomena in his lectures and his writing. From him, Kilvert learned how to incorporate precise physical details into his imaginative descriptions of the natural world. His account of the optical illusion experienced by his sister is notable both for its precision and for its effort to marshal evidence to explain it. These qualities are evident in the *Diary* entries concerning strange occurrences, examined in the next chapter.

Although Kilvert would always believe in the Church, traditional religious views, and 'the good old Bible stories' (as he termed them), he was nevertheless able to accept Tyndall's vision of a new society with new intellectual and cultural leaders, a significant number of whom were men (and women) raised in the culture of Lit and Phils. This was partly because as a clergyman with a strong leaning towards the culture of Nonconformity, he too had a radical stance towards society's traditional leaders.[94] Tyndall stood for progress. Kilvert was able to accept the scientist's views because they ran 'temptingly alongside the religious, even while they repudiated religious authority'.[95] It is of the utmost importance to note that when Kilvert enjoyed 'a pleasant talk' about Tyndall with the Rev. Byrnes it was 10 May 1875 – *after* the latter's pronouncements on miracles and prayer, *after* the Belfast Address. Thus, he was not unnerved by Tyndall's radicalism, but could maintain a balanced position, rejecting some elements of it while endorsing others – the sign of a sophisticated intelligence, not of an unworldly, shallow one.[96]

Chapter 8

Miracles and Wonders

Spirits, fairies, and ghosts . . . haunt Kilvert's landscapes.
John Toman, *Kilvert's Diary and Landscape*

Besides the phenomena [of Nature] which address the senses, there are laws and principles and processes which do not address the senses at all, but which must be, and can be, spiritually discerned.
John Tyndall, *Matter and Force, lecture to the working men of Dundee* given in 1867

[Kilvert] was acutely conscious, as ancient peoples were, of weather.
John Toman, *Kilvert's Diary and Landscape*

The theory of evolution would not have been seen by Kilvert as a challenge to his faith, nor prevented him from admiring Tyndall. However, other of the scientist's pronouncements on man's relations with nature may have caused him disquiet. He had been taught by his uncle Francis that miracles (which were a species of 'wonder') were one of the 'Evidences of the being of God', as chapter five noted. When Kilvert wrote, of the driver and stoker who survived a railway accident, 'their escape was almost miraculous', it was not an idle comment; the 'almost' indicates he was placing the event in relation to other extraordinary phenomena. Providence had saved them because, unlike the guards of one of the trains involved, they were blameless.

In 1865, J.B. Mozley, Regius Professor of Divinity at Oxford, delivered and published the Bampton Lectures *On Miracles*. His basic thesis was to 'prove' Christianity. The evidence of feeling and conscience was not enough; miracles were needed to prove it. The Preface to the first edition of his lectures stated his intention to address the problem of miracles' credibility, an aim 'most adapted to the particular need of the day'. There was a need to attempt 'a reconciliation [of miracles] with the laws of nature in the scientific sense' (Preface to second edition).

In Lecture I, he said he believed that the intellectual movement against miracles stemmed partly from the advance of science, which turned minds towards the physical and material, although even people without knowledge of science also rejected them. A miracle was a phenomenon for which no complete physical explanation could be given. Some extraordinary coincidences were called 'special providences . . . signs and tokens of the Divine will'. Special providences differed from miracles in terms of evidence, not nature, because the former were a matter of *degree* of coincidence. Where there was no violation of physical law, the amount of coincidence had to be considerable in order to constitute proof of Divine power. He gave the example of a cross appearing in the air (the Matterhorn crosses had appeared in 1865); such a phenomenon could not be seen as a miracle. Miracles were of supreme importance to a Christian, Mozley argued, even if he said that his faith did not depend on them; their truth or falsehood still mattered. 'Miracles and the supernatural contents of Christianity must stand or fall together'.[1] Throughout the *Lectures*, Mozley reiterated the idea that miracles were 'violations of the laws of nature', but, he asked, may not the Scripture miracles (he cited those concerned with healing) be instances of unknown laws?

In Lecture I, Mozley insisted that 'a miracle is not an anomaly or irregularity but part of the system of the universe'. It was the 'instrument of communication' between the two worlds, visible and invisible. Robert Kilvert indicated in his 'Memoirs', begun in 1866 – the year after the publication of *On Miracles* – that he held this belief about two worlds. When assured by a parishioner that she heard heavenly music in the cottage where her husband lay dying, Robert noted: 'we know there are attendant angels (Luke XVI, 22),[2] that there is celestial music, and . . . there is nothing to forbid exceptional communications from the other world. . . . ' It seems that Robert, when evaluating this episode in his 'Memoirs', made use of Mozley's book, especially Lecture III, which examined the nature of the sense of wonder. Imagination, said Mozley, was able to accept unlikely things, thus resisting its dependence on the idea that only the recurrent (the basis of a natural law) was believable, by 'two great counteracting influences . . . the wonders of the visible world . . . [and] the wonders of the invisible world'. The former appealed to the imagination even though they seemed to interrupt physical law. Thus, the sense of wonder contained an element of resistance in the mind, 'a resistance to the facts which excite it'. The mind experienced difficulty 'in taking in the new material' and assimilating it with received ideas. 'All wonder . . . is therefore a precedent for facts resisted and yet believed . . . all wonder therefore tends to dispose us to the supernatural'.[3]

Robert's careful evaluation of the celestial music in the cottage follows closely Mozley's account of the mental and imaginative processes involved. Robert registered what the latter had called 'resistance to the facts'. He questioned the wife of the dying man 'strictly in order to learn whether [the music] might be traced to some natural cause', but she assumed it had a 'supernatural' one. Other witnesses 'were persuaded in the same way . . . though they had never witnessed anything like it before'. Resisting their incredulity, they believed in what they thought they' had heard. And Robert, although observing 'How far the facts were real, how far imaginary, I have never been able to satisfy myself', nevertheless testified to his belief in 'exceptional communications from the other world'.[4] (Mozley used the phrase 'Any communication from the other world'.) The presumption that Robert was familiar with Mozley's book is reinforced by the fact that the former quoted, as did the latter, the lines from *Hamlet*: 'there are more things in heaven and earth, Horatio, than are dreamt of in your philosophy'. Robert was ready to believe the cottage phenomenon, which Mozley would have classified as a 'special providence', because the wonder of the celestial music was 'proof' that a man of faith would be received in heaven.

Kilvert would have known Tyndall's review of Mozley's *Lectures*, collected with other pieces in *FSUP*. The review, entitled 'Miracles and Special Providences', had appeared earlier in the *Fortnightly Review*.[5] Tyndall's main objection to Mozley's arguments was his tendency to place feeling above reason, invoking 'the affections [to] urge the reason to accept conclusions from which unaided it recoils'. Feeling was inappropriate, Tyndall considered, when approaching issues concerned with the credibility of physical facts, which needed 'the dry light of the intellect alone'. Mozley had urged the use of feeling because he wanted miracles to be true. The 'so-called spiritualistic phenomena of the present day' illustrated this tendency in Tyndall's view.[6]

The fact that Kingsley devoted a chapter to 'Miracles and Science' in *Alton Locke* in 1850 shows they were already issues of concern. They had become even more so by the 1860s when people who favoured miracles appeared anti-scientific.[7] Kilvert had only just arrived in Oxford when the publication of *Essays and Reviews* in April 1860 caused a furore. Its aim was to foster discussion of religious subjects, one of which was miracles, in a liberal atmosphere. Seven scholars and divines contributed essays to it. Baden-Powell, Oxford's Savilian Professor of Geometry, chose 'On the Study of the Evidences of Christianity' (a title recalling Paley's *Evidences of Christianity*) as his topic. Divine revelation had hitherto, he noted, formed the basis of Christian belief, accessible in Scripture. In setting out proofs of revelation in the seventeenth century, 'the appeal was mainly to the miracles of the Gospels'. Where scepticism was encountered, 'a brief reference to the Divine Omnipotence to work the miracles' was deemed enough of an answer.[8] This was uncle Francis's approach to the problem, as we have seen. Baden-Powell argued that the laws visible in nature were incompatible with belief in miracles and that in time science would be able to explain apparently anomalous natural phenomena. Such ideas outraged the Anglican establishment of the day. Houghton saw *Essays and Reviews* as both a characteristic product of the 1860s as well as one which 'intensified' the problem of belief. It was a time when 'a settled state of baffled judgement and a mind empty of beliefs [began] to appear'.[9]

The *Diary* supplies ample evidence that the issue of belief in miracles, and of other spiritual or supernatural beliefs, was of great importance to Kilvert. The entry for 29 November 1872 exemplifies the point: 'The Irvingites are all in a flutter of expectation and excitement. They believe that Christ has already come and is at Glasgow working miracles'. His remark reveals familiarity with 'Irvingites' over a long period and indeed his background was one in which they loomed large.

Edward Irving's birth in Scotland in 1792 made him almost exactly contemporary with uncle Francis Kilvert, and his career, and its place in the development of early nineteenth-century Evangelicalism, was of particular moment for him and his brother, Kilvert's father. Noted at Annan Academy for his critical and sceptical turn of mind by a teacher who also taught Carlyle,[10] Irving began studies at Edinburgh University at the age of thirteen. After early years as a schoolmaster, he moved in 1819 to Glasgow as assistant to the Presbyterian minister, Dr Chalmers, at St John's Church. Irving's 'keen spirituality, heroic faith, magical eloquence'[11] attracted attention and he was invited to preach at London's Caledonian Chapel, becoming minister of a Holborn chapel in July 1822, where he began to draw an enthusiastic congregation: 'a flood of noble and fashionable hearers poured in upon the little chapel'.[12] One of these hearers was the Evangelical leader, Zachary Macaulay; another was Henry Drummond (1786-1860), banker and M.P. In May 1824, Irving was chosen to preach an anniversary sermon for the London Missionary Society (LMS). His sermon, over three hours long, caused a sensation, partly because it had no relevance to that body and partly because he presented himself as 'an Apostle responsible to no man – a messenger of the Cross'.[13] It was the beginning of his severance from his Evangelical brethren, though not from Drummond, who became his friend and patron.

Irving emerged as a key figure in the 1820s when Evangelicalism

Edward Irving

was spreading rapidly through middle-class families like the Kilverts. It advocated renewed piety in response to anxieties of the time over the French Revolution, Catholic Emancipation, economic problems, increasing secularism, cholera, technological and industrial changes, and social unrest. Robert Kilvert's two breakdowns may be attributed partly to his perception that society was in crisis. At school, he showed the typical Evangelical tendency to interpret punishment and pain as proof of God's interest in his spiritual state. At Oriel College between 1822 and 1827 he was deeply pessimistic. Work pressures and tensions in his college were the main causes here but anxiety over the national scene, of which he was acutely aware, must have contributed.

Another breakdown followed five years later, during which time Robert had been curate at Keevil, Wiltshire. In his 'Memoirs', he hinted vaguely that the three months spent after Keevil as curate of Melksham were the cause of his second breakdown: 'the work was too much for me . . . and my health broke down'. This explanation is hardly convincing. At Melksham, Hume, its vicar and Robert's close friend, shared the work; at Keevil, as he himself emphasised, 'there was no one . . . to give me the smallest scrap of direction', in what was a large, difficult parish. Noticeably, he made no mention of the Swing riots and other national convulsions (e.g. the Reform Bill of 1832), which would have made a profound impact on a man like him,[14] who took notice of 'public affairs' as he himself noted. 'Public affairs' troubled him not only because he was a devout Evangelical but also because he had a sensitive nature, as Anne Falkner testified when she made the interesting observation that uncle Francis Kilvert too was prone to breakdowns: 'Francis Kilvert, nervously constituted like his brother Robert, had one of his breakdowns early [in 1817]'.[15] Anxiety over family finances and over his father's deteriorating mental state may account for Francis's collapse at this time but apparently he had several in this period.

The religious controversies of the time, some of which centred importantly on Irving, would inevitably have contributed to the unease of two such intense Evangelical clergymen as the Kilvert brothers. 'The period after 1820 was for Evangelicals . . . a time of acute crisis', Newsome stated and he continued:

> A growing rift can be discerned between the older and more responsible Evangelicals, whose organ was the *Christian Observer*, and whose major spokesmen were Simeon, Daniel Wilson, and the members of the Clapham Sect, and the younger, more fiery elements who were attracted towards Edward Irving and Henry Drummond.[16]

The older leaders insisted on 'sobriety and regularity' among Evangelicals whereas Irving represented 'individualism and peculiarity' and emotionalism. Hilton expressed the rift as one between 'the respectable Clapham Sect and its followers . . . and the Pentecostal, pre-millenarian, adventist, and revivalist elements'.[17] In other words, it was between moderate Evangelicals and extreme ones. Moderates despised 'enthusiasm' in religion because it overpowered reason. The rift may also be said to be one between moderate and extreme Calvinists. Simeon had rejected the Calvinism of preachers like Whitefield because it insisted that only the elect would be saved. The extreme views of Irving were promulgated by the highly Calvinistic *Record*, which was favoured by Robert Kilvert. Alexander Haldane was its editor and used it to advance both his extreme Evangelical opinions and those of his uncle Robert, encouraging 'the growth away from the views of Simeon and Wilberforce to a Calvinistic orthodoxy', in Hennell's words.[18] The Recordites might be described as 'the party of the Haldanes and Irving', Hennell added.

Alexander Haldane wrote that 'the hope of the second appearing of our Lord was one which ever occupied [my father's] thoughts' but he considered the current state of the world too 'wicked and unholy' for it to be likely.[19] Irving's increasing emphasis on the humanity of Christ was too much for Alexander's father.[20] This doctrine was central to the split between Irving and Recordites on the one hand and more moderate Evangelicals on the other. There is little doubt that this split placed some distance between the ideologically extreme Kilvert brother (Robert) and the moderate one (Francis). The poem by the latter attacking the *Record*, cited in the next chapter, is clear evidence of this. However, sermons with strong Calvinistic traits by both brothers show that their spirituality was fairly similar. Robert's supposedly un-Evangelical brother once regaled his congregation of elementary school children (aged 5 to 13) with the Calvinistic terrors awaiting them for such 'sinful pleasures' as cruelty to animals, truancy, and Sabbath-breaking: 'being in torments, they will curse . . . that folly and wickedness which has plunged them in the fiery lake, "where their worm dieth not, and the fire is not quenched".'[21]

Uncle Francis's sermon (from 1827) reflected the Calvinism which experienced a revival at this time, an element in the 'fiercer, darker Evangelicalism of the 1820s and 1830s'.[22] Its revival was due in part to Dr Chalmers,[23] patron and friend of Edward Irving. Chalmers, with a national reputation built partly on his popular 'Astronomy Lectures' (1818), toured parts of England in 1822, arriving in London in autumn after visits to Bristol and Somerset. His aim was to obtain first-hand information on the English Poor Law. His 24 September letter to his wife in Bristol described meetings with 'men of parochial management' and dining with Irving, who was sharing his lodgings, and who was building his own reputation in the capital. On the following day, Chalmers went by coach to Clapham at the invitation of the vicar of Holy Trinity Church, the Rev. Dr William Dealtry.[24] 'Dealtry had a large party of parishioners to dinner, whom he wanted to impregnate with my views', wrote Chalmers, adding 'Mr Dealtry . . . a most active, sensible, and enlightened man[25] . . . is to attempt the imitation of my pauperistic processes even in the face of existing laws'. Chalmers singled out among the dinner guests 'Robert Grant, brother of Charles',[26] as 'the most distinguished'. 'There were additional' [i.e. to those at dinner] 'ladies at tea, among whom Miss H, daughter of the deceased Henry, was the most remarkable'. This lady was presumably Henrietta Thornton, daughter of Henry Thornton; she was then only fifteen. Sophia de Chièvre must have been among these ladies in what Chalmers called 'an assemblage of pious and highly cultivated individuals'.[27] Her piety and aristocratic background would certainly have entitled her to a place. One other Thornton daughter, Isabella, would be a witness at Sophia's wedding two months later, which suggests they were friends. The wedding was conducted by Dealtry. Chalmers was fêted in Clapham not only by its leading Evangelicals but also by the Quaker families, such as the Frys and the Gurneys, with whom Sophia associated.

Sophia's *Home Discipline*, begun in the year following Chalmers's London visit, is marked by the stern Evangelicalism of the time, which he typified. The pessimism she felt about emergent industrial society, referred to earlier, led her to the conviction that 'mournful traits in our national condition tell us too plainly that ours is a country passing through some extraordinary crisis'.[28] Chalmers was a follower of the Rev. Thomas Malthus (1766-1834), whose *An Essay on the Principle of Population* (1798) went through six editions up to 1826. In it, he argued that ever-increasing population would inevitably outstrip food supply – a notion that contributed to the pessimism of the early nineteenth century. Poor Rates had soared in the depression following the end of the Napoleonic War. Chalmers condemned poor relief as an automatic right because it encouraged idleness and dependence.[29] Poverty was, he thought, disgraceful and should be countered by hard work, self-respect, and restriction of family size. He instituted his schemes of parish organisation in St John's, Glasgow, from 1820, dividing it into sub-sections of 60 to 100 families. Each inhabitant was to be personally known to the parish's minister and, although the parish authorities were to exercise care for the poor, help in the form of charity was expected from the better-off. This approach was urged strongly by Sophia in her *Home Discipline*, which condemned liberal approaches to the problem of poverty. Charity was, she insisted, a neighbourly obligation, based on exploring 'the distresses of those around us'.[30] She may have meant Chalmers when she stated in her introduction that 'Much has been well written of late years, on the minute details of family management', and she recommended that each person fight against 'the tempers and habits' that led to bad management. While recognising that 'feudal ties' were dissolving in a society that was changing, she pictured a community that was basically traditional and rural, as Chalmers's St John's was: 'His answer to middle-class fears of an . . . immoral and irreligious under-class was to recreate an idealised rural parish community'.[31] Sophia was, it seems, one of Dealtry's parishioners, who had been 'impregnated' with Chalmers's views.

In the parish of Clapham in autumn 1822, Sophia may have met not only Chalmers but his protégé Irving. The latter was a focus of interest and amusement in the Clapham circle later, as Forster explained; Irving was keen to 'advertise' himself by talking 'constantly' at May Meetings in 1825. He dined at Sir Robert Inglis's home on 10 December 1827, in company with Charles Simeon. Marianne Thornton was fascinated by his 'strange personality' and went in 1832 to a service at his church where people 'spoke in tongues'. His prayer 'winds them up to expect a message from Heaven,' she wrote. There was nothing 'supernatural' about the phenomenon of 'Tongues': it consisted of 'little short words such as cry, cry, cry, repeated' and 'cries and shrieks'.[32]

Irving became obsessed by prophecy, especially the Second Coming. He once stated: 'The Second Coming of the Lord is . . . the vantage ground . . . from which, and from which alone, the whole purpose of God can be contemplated'.[33] Robert Kilvert may have warmed to Irving on this issue too because 'it was once a characteristic of Evangelical churchmanship',[34] especially of the more extreme kind and was commonly to be found in the *Record*. Drummond, Irving's patron, shared 'the convictions that knew no middle course' which were 'stirring the hearts in men's bosoms' at this time from Irving's pulpit.[35] The furthest limit of the extraordinary views held by Irving and Drummond was the prophetical conferences held by the latter at his Albury Park (Surrey) mansion. Divine judgements were expected at the conferences followed by Christ's appearance and the Millennium – the thousand-year period of earthly happiness.

Just as moderate Evangelicals saw Providence as the means of showing men that pain and tragedy were the results of their sinful behaviour rather than as punishments from an angry God, so they also believed with Simeon that Irvingites were harming the Church by spreading gloom and terror through their obsession with sin and damnation. Both Kilvert's father and uncle showed tendencies towards this obsession, although they were relatively moderate Evangelicals, like their friend, the Rev. Harvey Marriott.[36] His *Eight Sermons on 'The Signs of the Times'* not only provide insights into a man greatly admired by the Kilvert brothers, but also a reaction to Irvingism. They were written at its height and published in 1828.[37] Marriott was certain it was a unique period, marked by six distinctive features: the French Revolution, the rejection of the slave trade, the recognition of 'Papistical errors', the growth of Evangelicalism, increased sympathy for Jews, and the appetite for religious knowledge. He was disposed as Evangelicals generally were to scrutinise events for signs of God's purposes: 'we are summoned to more than usual watchfulness for the divine will'.

However, as if with Irving's extremism in mind, he cautioned: 'avoid all matter merely speculative . . . seek of God that lesson only which it is intended we should learn'. He too was drawn to see in recent events signs of the 'Great Tribulation' perceived by extremists. Events of the last 35 years were, he emphasised, 'peculiar' and furthermore had come 'in quick succession', not witnessed in any period 'since the world began'. In Marriott's sermon on Prophecy he came closest to rebuking Irving and his Apostles. It was right to study the pattern of history that showed 'God's government over the world, but exceeding diffidence' should be applied to its interpretation. And he warned that 'no prophecy of the Scripture is of any private interpretation'. The true Apostles spoke only under the influence of the Holy Ghost, 'so those who come after must never dare to appropriate a prophecy to an event, unless amply borne out by the manifest providence of God'.[38] It would not have been hard for Irvingite Apostles to recognise themselves in this characterisation.

It is noticeable that the period – 1827 to 1828 – in which Marriott was writing anti-Irving sermons was exactly the period when Robert Kilvert was recording and analysing cases of 'miraculous' events. The cottage where the celestial music was heard was in the parish of Keevil, which he took over in 1827. He had carefully dated the music episode: 22 November 1828. That case was one of three such that he noted *at that time* (his 'Memoirs' record no others). In one episode, the 'spiritual truths' he related to a dying woman produced 'a most remarkable change . . . from an overwhelming dread to a rejoicing confidence in the Divine mercy'. Always suspicious of 'sudden impressions', he believed nevertheless that this change was 'a phenomenon which I never witnessed in any other'. The woman's face became 'radiant'; the effect on witnesses was 'awful and thrilling'. The other episode was less dramatic: a parishioner who had always rejected his ministrations suddenly sought them.[39] One can readily imagine the two ardent Evangelical clergymen – Robert Kilvert and Henry Marriott – discussing the alleged wonders of Irvingism and making the responses to it that we have seen.

It seems inevitable too that the story of Irving would have been reviewed frequently in the Kilvert family, partly because of its interest in the phenomena and doctrines he represented and partly because of the contact uncle Francis and aunt Sophia had had with his patron, Dr Chalmers. Kilvert showed clearly that Irvingite phenomena and doctrines interested him. The November 1872 *Diary* entry about Irvingites noted that they believed 'Christ has already come'. They had been disappointed before that the Second Coming had not materialised.

Russell told how on 14 July 1875 a thousand of Drummond's followers (Irving had died in 1834) gathered in the Irvingite church in London's Gordon Square to greet the Lord on his return. However, 'before that date and since, expectations . . . have been equally disappointed'.[40] Interestingly, Kilvert's entry for 14 July has an apocalyptic tone: 'Rain all day. . . . The accounts of the storms and floods from all parts of England are desperate . . . whole districts flooded by sheer force of incessant rain. . . . . There has not been such a time for fifty years'. Perhaps the entry originally contained an allusion, explicit or implicit, to Irvingites' expectations. Can we detect in the entry Kilvert resisting the conclusion that the disturbed weather was connected to Irvingite prophecy? Was he seeing it as 'a sign of the times' like Harvey Marriott fifty years before? Was it God's hand registering disapproval of self-appointed Apostles prophesying the Second Coming?

Kilvert referred in his entry of November 1872 to miracles as the other characteristic belief of Irvingites. Irving had declared that 'Spiritual gifts ought to be exercised in the Church' and that such gifts had fallen out of use 'because of the Church's great ignorance concerning the work of Christ at His Second Coming . . . but things are taking a turn'. Unless men assert that God no longer testified to the work that Christ performed, 'they have no ground for believing that the age of miracles is past'.[41] Miraculous events in Scotland in 1830 became identified with Irving. The 'gift' of speaking in tongues and of healing were reported in the parish of Roseneath and the town of Port Glasgow. Mrs Oliphant described the events in detail, while declining to judge the truth of these 'marvellous phenomena', by which Irving was captivated. Mary Campbell of Roseneath was the first speaker in tongues. Highly pious, 'fair and delicate and young, this inspired creature . . . is one which nobody can turn from without wonder and interest'. The wonder of healing occurred in the 'devout and prayerful home of the Macdonalds' in Port Glasgow. James Macdonald had an invalid sister who had heard of Mary Campbell. James was assured on one occasion by his sister that he was endowed with the Holy Spirit. 'Almost instantly, James calmly said, "I have got it". He went to his sister's bedside and commanded her to walk and she did. James then wrote to Mary Campbell, who appeared then to be dying, commanding her to get up and she, like his sister, was cured. Mrs Oliphant summed up these events as 'unresolvable wonders' like others that have 'perplexed the world'.[42]

The record of biblical texts Kilvert chose for sermons shows a regular focus on miracles: the feeding of the 5,000 (used twice), Daniel, who had a gift for interpreting dreams and visions, being saved from the furnace by his faith, God making the shadow of the sundial move backwards (the story of Hezekiah, told on two occasions by Kilvert: to his Bredwardine school pupils and to two Langley Burrell parishioners), and Christ restoring the sight of a blind man. 'The Evangelical God is a God of miracles,' Annan observed,[43] and Evangelicalism generally encouraged belief in supernatural events. In this respect, Kilvert junior was like Kilvert senior. *Kilvert's Diary and Landscape* noted that the childhood of the latter was steeped in supernatural stories. We have seen that he believed in 'attendant angels'. Kilvert confirmed he did too in this 28 April 1870 (NLW edition) entry: 'I heard the great sudden flap of an unseen wing. Angels were going about the hill in the evening light'. The matter-of-fact tone here suggests he was not indulging a mere fancy. Of course, he *wanted* to encounter an angel, as appears in the following entry for 21 July 1873: 'I thought I saw an angel in an azure robe coming towards me across the lawn, but it was only the blue sky through the feathering branches of the lime'. Angels shared with women the attribute of physical beauty and Kilvert's adoration of women included the tendency to identify particularly lovely women and girls with angels. On 10 October 1873, he noticed 'a very beautiful young girl' in the assembly hall at the Bath Church Congress. However, to him she was not simply a girl who resembled an angel but rather 'an angel [who] had taken the form' of a girl. It was the angel that was real, not the girl, though she was real enough to provoke lustful thoughts, for which he rebuked himself. He was much taken with the idea of angel-children as in his meeting with the 'angel-child' on a train on 24 April 1873. She had golden curls like the girl in the assembly hall. To register the moment's 'great happiness' – of religious/romantic ecstasy and of revelation – he quoted St Paul's second Letter to Corinthians: 'I knew a man in Christ . . . caught up into paradise, and heard unspeakable words'. We are in the world of Irving's church services here, of speaking in tongues and of miracles.

The presentation of angels in both his poems and in his diary confirms that he believed in their reality. His belief in them had not been destroyed by the 'cold philosophy' which Keats had said 'will clip an angel's wings'. *Kilvert's Diary* is full of examples of people expressing belief or disbelief in apparently supernatural phenomena. We have already focused on the 'old wizard' of Clyro, who rejected witchcraft, and on Kilvert's own rejection of the 'ludicrous naïve simplicity' of Edmund Jones's belief in Providence. The issue of belief in angels is raised explicitly in the 8 September 1875 entry in which Kilvert's sister Fanny (Frances) told him of a Langley Burrell parishioner who was afraid of the dark. She had tried to comfort him by saying that 'angels were always near and would take care of him', reassurance he rejected. "'I don't believe there are any angels", he said. "I don't see them". Kilvert knew that Buckle had recommended a religion 'more favourable to free inquiry' and 'less full of miracles' and other supernatural beliefs (see chapter six). Kilvert's exploration of these issues of belief may also have been informed, as his father's apparently was, by Mozley's book *On Miracles*.

Kilvert loved to listen to the stories of old Hannah Whitney because he had a deep respect for them and for the folklore contained in them. 'Hannah is a very wise woman,' he wrote in the 20 October 1870 entry in which she told of the strange circumstances surrounding the death of her mother. His account of her story is carefully constructed. Hannah's observation at the start of it that 'There was one cruel flash of lightning yesterday' is not directly relevant to it yet helps to set its tone. Kilvert then takes the reader into the world of Gospel miracles by remarking on her shining eyes as 'she took up her *parable*' – an apt word for a story full of moral and spiritual implications. It was New Year's Day when Hannah's mother was 'seized suddenly with putrid fever'. She had been horrified to be visited early that morning by two of her neighbour's girls. To be visited before noon on that day was considered very unlucky, and she 'screamed. . . . Sure as fate something will happen before twelve months are out'. Hannah's grandfather protested against such forebodings. However, from that moment she began to feel cold. 'She went to bed and died in a fortnight'. Hannah's father and sister also died. In response to Kilvert's considered question, 'What gave her the fever?' she replied: 'It was something as God sent'.

Kilvert's preoccupation with strange beliefs reflected in folklore appears in many entries, a number of which concern ghosts or spirits. On 4 October 1871, he comforted a woman whose stepson had died after seeing a ghost on a bridge over a local stream. She believed it was the spirit of his dead mother and was 'his death warning'. As though to assert reason over superstition, Kilvert ended his account by stating breezily that after leaving the woman he crossed the same bridge where the spirit had been seen.[44] On 19 December 1870, Kilvert heard of a strange 'waking dream' in which a woman saw in her arms a child, 'like a little angel'; it was wearing grave clothes. Science appears triumphant over superstition in the 18 January 1871 entry describing Kilvert's visit to the royal home of Claremont. The renowned Dr Jenner, hearing of its haunted room, insisted on sleeping in it. Kilvert observed with some satisfaction: 'he has been in possession ever since'.

All these stories of supernatural events illustrate Mozley's statement: 'Nature *borders* everywhere on the supernatural' (his italics). He distinguished between the wonder inherent in nature and the wonder of a miracle. The wonder of the former resided in the power exhibited in such things as lightning or floods, as well as in beauty and grandeur. These were visible features. The wonder of the latter was invisible, inherent in the reality behind it – the existence of another world. Miracles spoke of God's existence, giving them special 'awe and wonder'. Nature's wonders nevertheless pointed to God's wonders in the sense that physical wonders introduced the idea of the supernatural.[45] The *Diary* provides examples of events in which both kinds of wonder merge or complement each other. Mozley referred to manifestations of animal instinct as natural wonders. Kilvert did too. Bees were buzzing around Langley Burrell Church's windows on 26 May 1870. 'My father says this has happened on several Ascension days,' Kilvert wrote. On 2 June 1870 he wrote: 'I am told Mrs Preece's bees swarmed the day she died'. He heard a tale of the Black Mountains on 8 December 1870, of a house built where a crime had taken place and it was consequently 'accursed'. A greyhound refused to enter the house, which its master took as a warning, and that night an avalanche of snow engulfed the house, killing all its occupants.

One of the epigraphs to this chapter noted Kilvert's responsiveness to weather, particularly weather extremes that illustrated 'nature's power'. The floods around Clyro in late January 1872 provide a good example. The 24 January *Diary* entry stressed that the event was unusual: 'Something very extraordinary must have happened in the hills last night. A waterspout must have burst' (a 'waterspout' is a tornado). Details are then given of brooks overflowing, houses flooded, in an account that treats the wildness and strangeness of the phenomenon as though it were supernatural. Two days later, Kilvert enjoyed discussing the 'extraordinarily wet weather and floods' with Edward Williams, who spoke of the Wye as 'a very *wild* river' (Kilvert's italics). The man's memory went back to a similar, but even worse, event: 'He remembered the water spout bursting on the Epynt hills above Builth and Brecon, when the Dihonwy swept away Mrs Lawrence's cottage'. The entry for 7 July 1872 gives full details of another demonstration of 'nature's power: 'a fearful storm of thunder, lightning, rain and hail. . . . All night the rain poured, not like rain, but as if streams of water were being emptied out of buckets'. Again, emphases create the sense of strange, malign, destructive power: rain that was not like rain, one tremendous lightning flash, and such a crack of thunder that Kilvert feared the church had been struck. The 'red raging furious waters' of the Dulas brook became 'a water demon in full power'. A reference to the Epynt floods placed the 7 July event in the context of local memory: 'This afternoon . . . there was the highest summer flood that there has been for exactly 19 years when Mrs Lawrence's house at Aberdihonwy was washed away'.

This latter event actually occurred on 9 July 1854 when, after a period of humid weather, a storm broke. Torrential rain was followed by hail which covered the ground to a depth of five inches. Rivers couldn't cope with the water, much of which drained into the River Dihonwy, by which stood the Lawrences' house. Trees and dead animals blocked the river, forming a dam, sending a tidal wave onto the Lawrences' smallholding. 'Soon flood waters were pouring through the upstairs windows ... and the house collapsed into the raging torrent'. Mrs Lawrence, her daughter, two grown-up grandchildren and two maidservants were drowned.[46] Mrs Lawrence's body (with only one arm, according to Edward Williams) was found in the Wye eighteen miles away. It was the kind of event which gripped the imagination and feelings of country people: nature at its most savage and awe-inspiring. A superstitious mind would seek meanings in it, especially in the mid-nineteenth century when rational, scientific explanations were less readily available. Kilvert's mind certainly dwelt on it because he included another reference to it in the entry for 31 December 1877. He talked then with an old woman, 'full of strange stories of the countryside', who was apparently psychic for 'she had felt beforehand and predicted the coming of the great rainstorm and waterspout which fell on the Epynt Hills'. No doubt she felt some guilt at its terrible outcome: the ability to prophesy it implied some responsibility for it. However, like Cassandra, she was powerless to prevent the catastrophe she prophesied.

1872, with its storms and floods, was a year that particularly challenged Kilvert's persistently curious mind, which ranged over events far and near, seeking comparisons by which to measure their strangeness. On 25 November 1872 he referred to a storm of 21 December 1821, 'The night Madam Ashe, the old squire's wife, died [when] there was a dreadful storm. Whole groves of elms . . . were uprooted'. A few days later, he was recording that the Irvingites were celebrating the Second Coming, and though the entry's tone is sardonic, the event must have contributed to his almost obsessive sense that 1872 was momentous in disturbing ways. As 1872 neared its end (7 December) he was reflecting: 'They say there has not been such a rainy season as this for 50 years. In this year up to November we have had only 31 . . . days without rain'. Kilvert's local paper imagined the reaction of the mythical 'oldest inhabitant' of the district to the year: 'What can you write about 1872 but rain, rain, rain, nothing but rain?'[47] Kilvert's keen interest in the recurring pattern of extreme weather events may have been fostered by his brother Edward, who had come under the influence at Marlborough College of the Rev. Preston, leading light of its National History Society. Preston specialised in Phenology, the study of recurrent natural phenomena in relation to climatic conditions. In addition, 'It was common then [the 1860s] for naturalists to have an interest in meteorology and weather patterns'.[48]

If Kilvert had not already been convinced that 1872 was a year of portents, he might have been on 8 December when 'the Great Storm of 1872 began'. Two lengthy entries give copious details of the storm's power and effects. It began disturbingly enough on a Sunday, in the middle of the Langley Burrell church singing practice. The first entry is given a religious significance suggestive of the Great Tribulation preceding the Second Coming: 'the storm shrieked and wailed and howled like multitudes of lost spirits'. Kilvert's quoting of the Prayer Book (104.3) – 'the Almighty was making the clouds His chariot and walking upon the wings of the wind' – contributes to this end-of-the-world theme. That the storm was divine in origin, constituting a warning to mankind, is suggested by Kilvert's statement 'the very world itself must [it seemed] give way and be shattered to atoms'.

Behind many of the storm and flood entries lies the question: why is this happening? And Kilvert tended, like Harvey Marriott in disturbing times, to exercise 'more than usual watchfulness for the divine will'. In the next entries to be considered, Kilvert can also be seen adopting his father's approach to marvellous occurrences, trying to ascertain 'how far the facts were real, how far imaginary' – a more scientific approach. One of his Bredwardine parishioners was 'much terrified' by a recent violent thunderstorm: 'She thought the end of the world might be come'. In this case there could be little review of 'evidence'; he simply had what he called 'a serious talk' to reassure her because she was afraid of dying spiritually unprepared. He himself was intrigued on 14 March 1872 by the 'strange fit of nervous restlessness' he experienced, 'something like the peculiar restlessness that comes shortly before death'. He had a presentiment of death on 13 May 1874 as he set out to pick flowers with young Georgie Gale: 'a shadow fell upon my mind. What if she should be dead?' (It was to this girl that he told the stories of the Matterhorn crosses and of Father Lyne's monastery.) The 29 November 1873 entry concerned 'a terrible dream. I dreamt that Cissy Bryant died in my arms'. He sought explanation of this in the fact that he was aware that two young girls of the parish had recently died and were unburied. He had no explanation for the events described in the entries (1/2 October 1871) in which a dying child had seen 'a beautiful bright place, a garden', but only the question: 'How is it that dying people so often see a beautiful place and beautiful little children that it has come to be an almost certain sign of approaching death?' Children, though not dying ones, appear in the 30 April 1874 entry when Kilvert was visiting the Rev. William Barnes. The poet explained that he had 'a curious second-sight about a house', a real house that he had seen earlier and that 'haunted' him. Though he knew nothing of it nor of its occupants, he saw 'in a vision' a boy and girl playing there. Later, he learned that 'just such a boy and girl did live in that house'.

Did Kilvert believe that 'special providence' was the explanation for the strange episode of his aunt Sophia's death? When she was ill, her daughter Anna got her some mutton, believing it would 'do her good'. The nurse said she was unable to eat it because she was dying. Anna, hearing this, put the mutton on the floor and quickly went to her mother. 'At that moment Aunt Sophia died and Anna turned round to see the cat running away with the mutton and the Epiphany Star shining in through the window'. Noticeably, Kilvert emphasised that Anna herself, an educated woman, gave this account of this occurrence which, because of its high degree of coincidence, Mozley would not have categorised as a miracle but as a special providence. The Epiphany Star, also known as the Star of Bethlehem, represents Jesus' birth and incarnation, and Anna's emphasis on it at her mother's death may have been a tribute to the latter's piety.

Joining the Catholic Church was one of the ways in which some people responded to the period's scepticism. One such person was Father Lyne who embarked on the building of a monastery near Clyro. Once again, we can find in Kilvert's reading elements that shaped his approach to this attempt to revive monasticism. He was typically Victorian in his need for heroes but struggled to find one in Father Lyne. A large number of heroic figures appear in *Kilvert's Diary*.[49] There are writers like Wordsworth, Barnes, Tennyson and Kingsley; clergymen like Henry Moule and Robertson; veterans like John Morgan and John Gough; engineers like Brunel and George Stephenson; labourers like John Hatherell; missionaries like Henry James Bodily and explorers like Livingstone and Speke.[50]

Houghton has emphasised the importance of heroes to Victorians: 'hero worship is a nineteenth-century phenomenon'.[51] Carlyle had written of the age's need for true heroes in *Heroes and Hero-Worship* (1841) and developed the theme in *Past and Present* (1843). The latter work examined medieval history and its heroes to show the poor quality of the nation's leaders in the political/economic crisis of the early 1840s. 'The manner of men's hero-worship . . . is the innermost fact of their existence' he wrote.[52] Kilvert found Carlyle's analysis relevant to the case of Father Lyne, and that analysis centred on the concept of work, a key concept for Kilvert as earlier chapters have shown. Evangelical morality had permeated attitudes to work in the early nineteenth century: 'work was the chief sphere in which moral worth was developed and displayed'.[53] Kilvert's poem *Honest Work* reflects this understanding and has echoes in it of Carlyle's *Past and Present*. The former argued that 'In the milking of the cows,/ In the sweeping of the house,/. . . . There are meanings sacred, deep'. To the latter, 'All true Work is sacred; in all true Work, were it but true hand-labour, there is something of divineness'. To Kilvert, working people were 'Nobles through [their] workful days' while Carlyle declared 'All work is Noble'.

On Kilvert's 5 April 1870 visit to Lyne's monastery, the sight of 'a hearty healthy girl' washing clothes represented 'living naturally in the world and taking a share of its work, cares and pleasures' in contrast to the 'unnatural' life of the monks, who shut themselves away from the world to pray for it. He then added 'Laborare est Orare' (i.e. to work is to pray). He endorsed the monks' work and the holiness of it, but wanted it to be *in* the world. Similarly, Carlyle had asserted: 'On the whole, we do entirely agree with those old Monks, *Laborare est Orare* . . . true Work *is* Worship'.[54] 'Laborare est Orare' was one of the sayings of St Benedict, whose order stressed the equal value of study, prayer, and work. Father Lyne's Order was Benedictine. Carlyle's purpose in exploring medieval monasticism was to contrast it with nineteenth-century religion. Like Kilvert, he urged that the latter period was not one for monasticism's 'tight lacing' but demanded 'a certain latitude of movement'. Monks were 'a strange extinct species of the human family', though there were 'live specimens' still to be found. They demonstrated not the 'personal religion, self-introspection' typified by Methodism, but 'serene Religion . . . a great heaven-high Unquestionability', quite different from the nineteenth-century's 'horrible restless Doubt'. To illustrate this thesis, Carlyle examined the book by Jocelin de Brakelond, a monk of St Edmundsbury, who was a mixture of unworldliness and worldliness. He was 'a simple-hearted soul' with 'a beautiful childlike character'. At the same time, however, his was 'a wise simplicity' and he showed 'much natural sense'. He was also 'quick-witted' and looked on the world 'in a really *human* manner' (Carlyle's italics). This balance appears in Kilvert's portrayal of Lyne in his 2 September 1870 entry. He had 'gentle simple kind manners' and 'thinks that everyone is as good as himself and is perfectly unworldly, innocent and unsuspicious'. Kilvert highlighted his unbusinesslike nature, the way he had been cheated by a builder working on the monastery. However, his close study of Lyne ('I had a good deal of conversation with him,' he remarked) included details counterbalancing his unworldliness. He had a human outlook as did Carlyle's Jocelin: '[Lyne] allows that a man must be of a very rare and peculiar temperament to become . . . a monk. A monk he says must either be a philosopher or a holy fool'. He was also realistic and shrewd in his view of his monastic dress and able to get the better of the Bishop of Gloucester and Bristol in evaluating it. Furthermore, he had managed to earn £1,000 by his preaching.

Carlyle also based his analysis of monks on Abbot Samson, whose story was told by Jocelin. We find close parallels between Carlyle's picture of this other monk and Kilvert's picture of Father Lyne. 'Singlemindedness' was a characteristic of Samson picked out by Carlyle for admiration and by Kilvert in his evaluation of Lyne: 'His manner gives you the impression of great . . . singlemindedness'. Samson had a 'devout grave nature', Lyne had 'great earnestness'. Samson's devoutness showed in 'his clear eyes flashing into you',[55] which was how Lyne impressed Kilvert: 'The face is a very saintly one . . . the eyes earnest and expressive. . . . When excited they seem to flame'.

Kilvert was of course interested in Lyne's beliefs, in which miracle played a part: '[Lyne] said that once when he was praying Gerald Moultrie[56] who was present saw the crucifix roll its eyes, then turn its head and look at Father Ignatius [Lyne]'. Although Lyne hadn't seen the crucifix move, he believed Moultrie had and commented, commonsensically, that Moultrie 'was not at all an excitable imaginative man'. Here again, as in the cases of marvellous occurrences examined earlier, Kilvert was setting out the facts, the 'evidence'. Perhaps he felt disposed to raise the question of miracles here because Carlyle had observed that the Middle Ages, for all their superstition, was a time when 'all the Earth's business was a kind of worship', when 'glimpses of bright creatures flash in the common sunlight;[57] angels yet hover doing God's messages among men. . . . Wonders, miracles encompass the man; he lives in an element of miracle'.

Kilvert was interested in the doctrine of the 'Real Presence'. Lyne told him that his father 'did not believe in the Real Presence' and so declined to kneel at the altar. The 'Real Presence' refers to the sacrament of the Eucharist and Christ's presence at it. Belief in the doctrine means believing that the body and blood of Christ are actually, physically, present in the form of bread and wine, rendered so by 'transubstantiation'. In the 1552 Prayer Book a change was introduced stating that kneeling implied 'no adoration . . . of the Sacramental Bread or Wine there bodily received, or unto any real or essential Presence of Christ's natural Flesh and Blood'.[58] Kilvert knew of course the Thirty Nine Articles of the Church of England, partly because as a pupil at his father's Hardenhuish school he was made to memorise them, and partly because Anglican churchmen had to formally assent to them.[59] Article XXVIII rejects transubstantiation: 'the body of Christ is given, taken, and eaten in the Supper only after an heavenly and spiritual manner'. The Catholic doctrine of transubstantiation was unacceptable to Lyne's father. The Catholic Apostolic Church of Irving and Drummond accepted transubstantiation, as Russell noted: '[it] came to accept . . . the Real Presence . . . and a worship embellished with vestments, lights, incense and holy water'.[60] Kilvert discussed similar issues on 10 May 1871 with a group of clergymen, one of whom, Mr Winthrop, to Kilvert's dismay, denied 'the gift of the Holy Spirit at Ordination and Baptism, . . . the presence of the Saviour with His Ministers, denied everything in short'.

The period in which Kilvert lived, in the view of many, was one of religious faith in which science, rationalism, secularism, scepticism, and materialism were making steady inroads. He was acutely aware of this process and his diary documents a wide-ranging response to it. The world of nature, which scientists like Tyndall and Darwin were analysing, is in large measure the subject matter of the *Diary*, and the relationship between nature and man may be seen as its main theme. The diarist's preoccupation with unusual states of consciousness makes better sense in the context of nineteenth-century concern with the grounds for belief in Christianity and the debate about miracles, which has been the particular focus of this chapter. Those who believed in miracles did so because they were a convincing demonstration both of God's existence and of God's power. Kilvert was interested in the debate because it had emerged as a testing-ground in the conflict between religion and science. By the time he was an adult, 'The problem was not whether or not God governed the universe but how. And the answer became, increasingly, "in the manner of law, not by meddling"'.[61] This chapter has examined *Diary* entries concerning natural phenomena in which Kilvert glimpsed 'meddling'. He believed firmly that God had made the world and continued to intervene in its working, agreeing, as we have seen, with Dr Alexander that 'natural laws are . . . threads which [God] holds in His hand'. Kilvert also believed, as his father did, that the world was filled with spiritual presences. His writings about folklore originated in part in a fascination with the fact that superstition could co-exist in his age of progress with scientific and technological wonders. In addition, his own superstitious nature felt an affinity with country people who continued to find meanings in tragic events and strange weather patterns. However, he was aware, as Buckle and Tyndall were, that the age of superstition and witchcraft was past. Nevertheless, his insatiable curiosity steadily drove him to record and analyse, producing a narrative filled with accounts of strange phenomena. Sometimes, as in the extraordinarily wet year of 1872, he was troubled by irrational fears that the world was moving towards some cataclysmic event reminiscent of the time of Edward Irving and his millenarian visions, a time his parents and his uncle Francis and aunt Sophia had lived through.

Kilvert knew that Irvingites in his own day continued to believe in miracles and the Second Coming. He distanced himself from them as he distanced himself from Edmund Jones of Aberystruth. Although he found Father Lyne admirable as a man, he rejected his attempt to revive monasticism. There could be no going back to that past either. He was intrigued by the variety of beliefs people could hold in the context of what he called 'the prevailing scepticism of the day'. In the long talk he had with Mrs Venables on this topic (20 November 1870), he found comfort in asserting that he would continue to teach his children 'to believe in the dear old Bible stories'. It is a poignant moment in the *Diary* partly because he was to die childless five weeks after his marriage on 20 August 1879 and partly because he perhaps perceived that soon that's all the Bible stories would be – stories.

His faith was reaffirmed on 21 May 1873 when he was overwhelmed by 'the great sight . . . of the now world-famous picture of "Christ leaving the Praetorium"' by Augustus Doré.[62] He added: 'There seemed to be a Real Presence'. The evidence he gave for this minor miracle was that 'Men took off their hats before the picture and spoke in subdued tones'. In the painting, Christ, all in white and as though in a spotlight, moves humbly yet majestically down steps through an excited crowd. Before him, blocking his path, is a large black cross. The juxtaposition of this entry with the next is another poignant moment in the *Diary* because in the later one, headed 'Holy Thursday' (i.e. Ascension Day), he wrote: 'To me afresh with each Ascension Day there comes again a sense of loss, and it seems as if one had left the world and left it for the present comfortless'. There must be a misreading of the original text here; 'one' must refer to Christ who had left it 'comfortless' after ascending to heaven. The tragic image of Christ leaving the Praetorium on his First Coming may have remained in Kilvert's mind as he made the later anguished entry. Disappointment that the Second Coming had not happened in the November of that portentous year of 1872, as the Irvingites claimed, may have compounded Kilvert's anguish.

Chapter 9
Kilvert and Teaching

Any system of Education which does not recognise the
Supreme Authority of the Word of God, which gives
prominence to human rather than divine knowledge, and
which aims at cultivating the mind rather than reinstating
the heart, is unsuited to the state of man as a sinner.
Cheltenham Chronicle, 2 November 1837, report of an
Evangelical meeting on infant education

For Pestalozzi, geography and natural history were the
foundation subjects of history, politics, the wider sciences
and a range of other subjects.
P. Elliott, S. Daniels, *Pestalozzi, Fellenberg and British
nineteenth-century geographical education*

It was noted earlier that Tyndall's approach to teaching was influenced
by Robert Owen and Pestalozzi, on whose principles Queenwood
College was built. In directing the focus towards Kilvert as a *teacher*,
their names will now recur. It has been shown that Kilvert's earliest
teachers embraced Pestalozzi's idea that the infant mind was a plant to
be nurtured and that natural objects had a key role in infant education.
Owen too had embraced this view: 'His educational principles could
be summed up as Rousseauism applied to working-class children'.[1]
He is credited with having established the first infant school at New
Lanark in 1816 and was a leader of the early infant school movement.
That movement attracted religious 'outsiders' – Evangelicals, Quakers,
Plymouth Brethren, Unitarians, Swedenborgians – so inevitably its
progress would have interested a household like uncle Francis Kilvert's,
which combined Evangelical and Quaker elements. Elliott and Daniels
noted that it was reformers, dissenters, and Evangelicals who were
Pestalozzi's most enthusiastic supporters.[2]

Apart from Owen, the other great British pioneer of infant education
at this time was Samuel Wilderspin (1791-1866), whose name and
reputation would have been known to the Kilverts due to the fact that he

lived in nearby Cheltenham (from 1829) and was actively involved with the town's influential Evangelical clergymen, the Rev. Francis Close and the Rev. Charles Jervis. He not only gave public lectures there on his work but gave two sets of lectures in Bath in April and May 1831. Furthermore, the meeting he instigated in London on 3 June 1824 for people concerned to develop infant schools had as speakers William Wilberforce and Lord Lansdowne;[3] it was also attended by many Quakers. It resulted in the founding of the Infant School Society, which had twelve Evangelicals on its 25-strong committee and the aim of raising the infant poor to be virtuous. Lord Brougham, leading figure of the new body, had (like Owen) visited Pestalozzi's school at Yverdon in Switzerland. At this time, the infant school movement was thoroughly permeated by Pestalozzi's ideas. Wilderspin became the movement's missionary, travelling all over the country and Ireland (he visited Richard Edgeworth's progressive school at Edgeworthstown), preaching the cause, the essence of which was that children learned through the senses; observation (particularly of natural objects), and practical tasks. His ideas owed much to Pestalozzi's *Letters on Early Education*, published in Britain in translation in 1827.

Wilderspin realised that the dissemination of his principles required properly trained teachers and would progress with the help of the Home and Colonial Infant School Society (HCISS), which emerged in 1836, founded by the Evangelical John Stuckey Reynolds[4] (1791-1874), in company with two other Evangelicals, the Rev. Charles Mayo and his sister Elizabeth. This body aimed to train teachers in Pestalozzian principles. Evangelicals were very powerful at this time and notably extreme in outlook, including their educational outlook. Their mouthpiece was the *Record*, the newspaper taken by Kilvert's father. Uncle Francis had a clear view of the satisfaction the *Record* gave its readers as he showed in this poem he wrote in November 1847, comparing its editorial policy with that of the *Times*:

Some good folks, to show their abhorrence of crimes,
Say, "Take in the *Record* instead of the *Times*;
The latter foul scenes of iniquity fill,
Which lessons of lust, theft and murder instil":
Most true – but mark well the polemical rage,
The slanders that sully the *Record*'s dark page;
How it "damns with faint praise", assents with a leer,
And the fair fame it injures is backward to clear!
On the whole these compeers being placed side by side,
This seems the sole question we have to decide,
Which savours least strongly in point of demerit,
The filth of the flesh or the filth of the spirit?[5]

It seems that Francis's very strong antipathy to the *Record* and the 'good folks' who were its readers must have had some effect upon his relationship with his brother,[6] because the core of his antipathy to the paper was its lack of human sympathy, which was the very foundation of his own moral outlook. Frederick Robertson, angry that the *Record* charged him with holding socialist opinions, wrote: 'The Evangelicalism (so-called) of the *Record* is an emasculated cur, snarling at all that is better than itself, cowardly, lying, and slanderous.'[7]

The HCISS initiative was enthusiastically reported in the *Record*. After initially welcoming Pestalozzi, Evangelicals condemned him in the early 1820s because his view of child-nature was too benign: 'Evangelicals saw infant education in terms of the preparation of young children for God and Jesus'. The HCISS 'saw the infant primarily as a sinner to be saved rather than as a delinquent who needed . . . sympathetic instruction'.[8] However, the established Church's hostility to the HCISS at this time meant that the latter's teacher-training college struggled to attract Anglican candidates so it played down its extreme curricular demands and made much of Pestalozzi. He now became 'an honorary Evangelical'.[9] This helps to explain how and why Kilvert's father became involved with Pestalozzi to the extent that he did. The HCISS came into being on 23 February 1836; Robert Kilvert became Rector of Hardenhuish in 1835, and married in 1838. Thus the HCISS foray into elementary education would have provided an uplifting accompaniment to the setting up of his Hardenhuish school. Of course, his school was for young gentlemen whereas the HCISS was concerned with educating the poor.[10] Robert Kilvert's school was therefore a compromise: it provided the training in piety his Evangelical conscience demanded along with the Latin deemed essential for gentlemen.

It was a compromise too in its curriculum and teaching style. The *Record* (15 July 1841) stated that the aims of the HCISS were 'the extension of the Infant-school system on Christian principles [which] are embodied in the Articles of the Church of England'. This was what Augustus Hare, one of Robert's pupils, recalled of his Hardenhuish school experience: the learning 'by heart' of Psalms and the Articles of the Church of England. Hare had other criticisms. The lessons were, he said, 'trash' and he learned 'next to nothing'. Even the Latin instruction was poor.[11] However, some aspects of the school derived from Pestalozzi, via Wilderspin. The latter had urged that Nature should be studied outside the classroom, 'in the garden, in the lanes, in the fields', and that 'museums' of natural objects should be created in schools.[12] Robert Kilvert had built this element into his school as is evident from Mrs Hare's letter of 17 August 1844 to Augustus, who had been a pupil there for one year: 'I daresay Mr Kilvert is today giving

you some useful lessons to learn from the harvest-fields around you, as
he did last year when I was at Harnish.' Augustus Hare himself recorded:
'From 12 to 1 we were taken out for a walk, when we employed the time
collecting all kinds of rubbish – bits of old tobacco-pipe etc. – to make
"museums".'[13] Evidently Robert Kilvert had not convinced his pupil of the
worth of the philosophy behind the study of natural objects. However, that
philosophy and especially its preoccupation with museums, had been fully
assimilated by the Kilvert children.

On 15 November 1870, Kilvert quoted an affectionate letter to his
parents from Augustus Hare, full of recollections from Hardenhuish
schooldays, including 'our "museums" of bits of tobacco pipe picked up
in the roads, . . . the geography book which taught us about Crema and
Cremona (such extraordinarily obscure places!)'. This *Diary* entry would
have been the opportunity for Kilvert to reminisce about those days;
noticeably, he didn't. (Again, one feels Plomer would not have cut such
reminiscences.) Was Kilvert avoiding any comments because he had critical
ones, as we know Hare had? And did he avoid commenting on either of
the schools he attended because he would have favoured his uncle's and
betrayed his father? These omissions may be connected with the omission
from Robert Kilvert's 'Memoirs' of any reference to his relationship with
Augustus's mother. Perhaps Robert felt guilty about his teaching and his
'reign of terror' (Augustus's phrase) at Hardenhuish school.

The uneasy mixture of pedagogic elements in Hardenhuish school
reflected the uneasy relationship of Samuel Wilderspin, pioneer of infant
education, with the HCISS. The latter adopted many of the former's
ideas without acknowledgement. Wilderspin rejected the teaching of
creeds and catechisms to infants, urged by the HCISS, because they were
beyond their understanding and bred shallow lip-service. He clashed with
Evangelicals especially over their belief in the innate sinfulness of children
and their overloading of the curriculum with scriptural knowledge:
'Where Wilderspin had seen moral education in ethical and secular terms,
the Society identified moral education with vital Christianity. . . . '[14] The
HCISS view of the curriculum was endorsed by the Rev. Charles Mayo
(1792-1846), who had spent the years 1819-1822 at Pestalozzi's Yverdon
school, teaching its English boys and studying its methods. Mayo was
later headmaster of the Pestalozzian Cheam School, helped out by his
sister Elizabeth (1793-1865). She left later to become adviser on infant
education at the HCISS College, where she pioneered the object lesson.[15]

The confusions of Hardenhuish school curriculum stemmed in some
measure from Pestalozzi himself as Mary Hilton explained: 'Pestalozzi's
pedagogy – the teaching methods and the philosophy on which they
were based – was essentially contradictory.'[16] He believed in the organic

model of child-nature held by Kilvert's early teachers – a plant to be nurtured through a series of experiences that corresponded to the organisation of the child mind. Early nineteenth-century educators were searching, as were the phrenologists, for a 'theory of the learning mind',[17] a subject that interested Kilvert, as we have seen. The organic model of learning inevitably conflicted with the model of instruction in vogue at the time, which emphasised factual information, rote-learning, question-and-answer classroom exchanges, and scriptural knowledge. To Pestalozzi, children's chief characteristics were 'imitativeness, curiosity (the "inquisitive spirit"), and liveliness'.[18] The elementary school's curriculum and teaching style – epitomised by Mary Hilton as 'catechistical' – signally failed to take note of these characteristics.

The HCISS experienced the same conflict because, though under its influence 'children were freer and less subject to drilling, the interpretation of Pestalozzi's methods was still contradictory and incoherent', (Hilton's words). Pestalozzi intended children to respond to objects through their senses and to explore nature at first hand via observation and reason. The lessons of Charles Mayo on the other hand usually lacked first-hand experience and were abstract and information-based, so that children were not encouraged to think for themselves. Elizabeth Mayo was aware of this weakness. She cited an objection which had been made to her object lessons: 'that they put fine words into children's mouths, and give them an air of pedantry'. She also warned teachers against telling pupils too much about objects in case '[their] minds remain almost passive'.[19]

Robert Kilvert showed, in a revealing reference to his earliest reading, that he was attracted to a pedagogical approach based on reason and children thinking for themselves. He recalled going with his mother when he was seven (in 1811) to Claverton Rectory, home of the Rev. Harvey Marriott. The two youngest Marriott girls showed him some of their books, which 'proved to be quite new to me'. One was about snakes, liked by Robert 'exceedingly'. The one he enjoyed most was 'that delightful story in the "Evenings at Home" of the "Transmigrations of Indus"'. ('Indus' is an error for 'Indur'.)[20] He was referring to *Evenings at Home; or the Juvenile Budget Opened* by Anna Letitia Barbauld (née Aikin, 1743-1825) and Dr John Aikin (1747-1822).[21] It consisted of 'a variety of miscellaneous pieces for the instruction and amusement of young persons', and the idea was that the pieces could be randomly selected from a 'budget', meaning the contents of a bag. Barbauld's co-author was her brother and they were Unitarians and saw education, as most Victorians did, as the means of improving society.

Anna Aikin and her brother were born in Kibworth Harcourt, Leicestershire, where their father was headmaster of its Dissenting

Academy, as well as minister of its Presbyterian church. In 1758 he became a teacher at the famous Dissenting Academy in Warrington, known as 'the Athens of the North', which boasted Joseph Priestley and Thomas Malthus as alumni. Mrs Barbauld and her French Huguenot husband also became teachers – at Palgrave Academy, Suffolk, its excellent reputation attracting both Anglicans and Dissenters. Instead of traditional classical studies, it provided a practical curriculum of science, modern languages, geography, history, and composition.

Evenings at Home consists of almost 100 short pieces, divided into 31 chapters called 'evenings', on a variety of subjects and genres, combining instruction with amusement. Though there is significant moral content, it is not overdone. The piece 'On Things to be Learned' deals with the education of both boys and girls, and is one of several pieces in the form of a conversation. The daughter is told by her mother that reading for both instruction and pleasure is necessary, as were housekeeping skills. Geography, history, French, and astronomy are recommended and, we are told, 'It is very useful to know something of the value of plants, and animals, and minerals'. Girls were to study science and maths although, unlike boys, they would not use them in professional work. Usefulness is the watchword in this and other pieces. The conversation between Harry and George emphasises botany for boys for both professional and recreational purposes. Boys' education was to differ from that of girls, signalled in the book by the fact, as Fyfe has pointed out, that 'most of the specifically scientific conversations took place between Harry and George, and their tutor'.[22] The scientific conversations cover natural history (especially botany), chemistry, and astronomy. In another (conversation) piece, 'The Colonists', Mr Barlow and his sons engage in a play in which he is the founder of a colony while they represent trades and professions offering their services to him. They take on the roles of farmers, millers, carpenters, blacksmiths etc. while he explains the nature of their work and its value. High valuation is placed on teachers. 'Manufactures' complements 'The Colonists' by exalting Britain's trade: 'We could not be a manufacturing, unless we were also a commercial nation'. Britain's manufactures needed 'productions from the different parts of the globe'.[23]

Indur, in the Barbaulds' *Transmigrations of Indur*, is noted for his 'humanity towards all living creatures' and his 'insatiable curiosity' about them. Once while observing animals, as was his habit, he saw a huge snake about to devour a small monkey which had fallen from a tree. Though he rescued it, he was bitten by the snake and was close to death. The fairy Perezinda, who had taken the form of the monkey, appeared before him, telling him she could not save him from death but would grant him a wish respecting the new existence he would shortly inhabit. Indur's wish was this: 'In all my transmigrations may I retain a rational soul'. In addition he asked to retain all his adult 'powers and faculties' without becoming a child again.[24] The story traces Indur's various 'transmigrations' as different creatures, each providing opportunities to describe in detail their habitats, feeding and breeding patterns, and other characteristics.

Robert Kilvert had warmed to the Aikins' book as a child and still approved it when writing his memoirs as an adult. When he stated that the Marriott girls' books were 'quite new to me', he was registering more than their unfamiliarity. He was recognising a different approach to education, one in large measure distinctively Nonconformist. It shows itself in Indur's wish to retain 'a *rational* soul'. It is there in 'On Things to be Learned' when the mother tells her daughter that education should cover 'everything that makes part of the discourse of rational and well-educated people'.[25] The importance attached in *Evenings* to the learning of science, especially by girls, and to other practical, useful things, is also distinctive of the Aikin background. The book's secular feel made it distinctive, as did its concern with trade and manufacturing. Fyfe laid great emphasis on the fact that the book was 'identifiably different', that its 'potential purchasers . . . would be likely to associate it with dissent'. Not only was it the production of 'a well-known Unitarian publisher [but] the majority of his children's books were by authors connected with the dissenting academies'.[26] The Marriotts and the Kilverts would have known this when they exposed themselves to it.

Robert Kilvert's positive feeling for *Evenings at Home* was part and parcel of his positive feeling for the Marriotts. He stated that he had spent 'many happy days' at their home, recalling particularly their 'family room', large enough to accommodate the Rev. Marriott, his mother, his three brothers and seven sisters. To Robert they were 'a delightful set of people'. The mother was 'refined and autocratic . . . the girls amiable, lively and thoroughly natural, though used to the best society; the younger sons excellent fellows. . . . In all my life I have scarcely ever met with so pleasant a household'.[27] That he could so idolise this family means that he did not have the deep distrust of worldly knowledge typical of the *Record* reader. The Marriott sons, all older than himself, stimulated him intellectually: they were his teachers, their home a centre of enlightenment and reason, in touch with the new society that was emerging.

There seems no doubt that the Kilverts warmed to the Claverton Rectory family as fellow Evangelicals. Anne Falkner referred to them as a 'deeply religious family'. Uncle Francis Kilvert not only went to the same Oxford College (Worcester) as Harvey Marriott,[28] but became his curate in 1817. One can picture uncle Francis (and his brother) joining in the reading aloud in the Marriotts' family room that so impressed Robert – 'a really good and comfortable room of twenty-five by sixteen feet'. Reading aloud was practised in Claverton Rectory, as Anne Falkner recorded. She pictured convivial evenings at Claverton Rectory shared by the Marriotts and William and Frederick Falkner, Robert's cousins, who farmed an estate – Claverton Manor Farm – 'a few yards' from the Rectory, where books were read aloud by the gentlemen.[29] Harvey Marriott wrote four *Courses of Practical Sermons expressly adapted to be read in Families* (1814, 1819, 1824, 1829).

Evenings at Home was also designed to be used in this way. The Edgeworths praised it for its 'conversations' because they encouraged discussion of the text between parents and children. Unitarian parents were particularly keen on using discussion 'to broaden the child's education and encourage curiosity', in Fyfe's view:

> *Evenings at Home* contained conversations in which the children were not merely passive receptacles for the teacher's knowledge. They thought for themselves, were curious and asked questions based upon their past experiences. Most of the conversations began with curious children asking for an explanation of something which puzzled them, rather than with the parent choosing the topic.[30]

There is a random feel to the topics in the Aikins' book, masking the sense that it is teacher-directed, while replicating the haphazard nature of children's attention.

Reading aloud within the family circle is another instructional method featured in *The Children's Year*: the father of the children loved 'to talk or to read to them in the evenings'. He told them about the animals he saw during his childhood in the country and about the pets he kept. And always a story would be read aloud: 'In this way a great many charming books had been read'. He read *Masterman Ready* and *The Settlers in Canada*. 'There was a great deal of talk whilst they were reading the *Settlers*', Mary Howitt emphasised, 'about "suppose" they themselves should go and live in America'.[31] There are good reasons to believe that the examples of the Marriotts, *Evenings at Home*, and *The Children's Year* induced the Kilvert parents to establish the habit of reading aloud to their children, with accompanying talk, as part of their home instruction. Emily Kilvert recalled her father's reading of the *Waverley* novels. She also noted the reading aloud of missionaries' reports and letters by 'Mama' at the working parties held at the Kilvert home. On weekday evenings Mama 'would sometimes read to us' (Emily remembered Aguilar's novels). Sunday evening lessons were more serious: 'exercise books taken in to Papa in the drawing room, Mama teaching in the dining room'.[32]

When Charles Mayo returned to England, he embarked on the popularisation of Pestalozzi's views. One means of doing this was through lectures, for example the lecture he gave at the Royal Institution in May 1826. The fact that the lecture was published (in 1828) by James Augustus Hessey (1758-1870) has particular importance because he and his partner John Taylor (1781-1864) were closely linked to the Kilvert family and its friends.[33] Catherine Falkner, sister of Kilvert's great uncle Robert Falkner, had married Hessey. Taylor and Hessey established their firm in 1806, achieving fame by bringing out the works of De Quincey, Lamb, Clare, Coleridge, and Keats.[34] Taylor also became involved in the educational book market that was expanding in the 1820s as a result of 'urbanisation, mechanisation and Sunday schooling'. This popular demand included 'the thousands of private schools and adults who wanted to teach themselves'.[35] On 11 December 1827, Taylor became official bookseller and publisher to the new University of London. Lord Brougham had supported Taylor's application for this position and in addition his SDUK backed Taylor's publications.

Especially enjoyable to Taylor and Hessey, as a rest from their publishing labours, were visits to Claverton Manor Farm, the home of William and Frederick Falkner. Taylor pictured his partner there: 'He is thin, dresses principally in black, . . . his conversation is good, his manner lively, . . . His reading has been serious but not very deep'.[36] Anne Falkner pictured Hessey always 'with some new publication in his pocket', at the Rev. Marriott's Claverton Rectory.[37] Two volumes of uncle Francis's sermons became Taylor publications through his contacts with the publisher at Claverton. *Sermons Preached at Christ Church, Bath* appeared in 1827. *Sermons Preached in St Mary's Church, Bathwick* is to be found, priced at 7s.6d., in a Taylor and Walton catalogue of educational books of 1839, alongside *The Cheam Latin Grammar* (i.e. a work emanating from Mayo's school), Clare's *The Shepherd's Calendar*, the Rev. Henslow's *Principles of Botany*, and Dr Lardner's *The Steam-Engine, familiarly explained*.[38] The assembly of literary-minded, pious, progressive folk under Marriott's roof also included Henry Moule. One book circulated at the Rectory, the owner of which 'must surely have been Frederick Falkner',[39] was *The World before the Flood* (1813) by James Montgomery (1771-1854), a long poem in heroic couplets containing a 'fictitious narrative' of the world from the Creation to the Deluge. Montgomery, son of a Moravian pastor and missionary, lived in Sheffield and, according to his biographers, contributed to the 'March of Intellect' in the town through newspapers he edited and his membership of its Lit and Phil.[40]

One of John Taylor's main interests was Locke, particularly his ideas about the organisation of knowledge. He published Locke's *Classical System*, a set of interlinear translations of Latin and Greek authors. Taylor had withdrawn from publishing by 1828, the date he published Mayo's *Memoir of Pestalozzi*, and was running his own private school. Pestalozzi's approach to learning was related to Locke's principle which postulates that reason is developed by the practice of reasoning. Mayo's account of the Swiss educator's ideas suggests other ways in which they would have appealed to the Kilverts. Reason was to be developed in the study of objects which, as we have seen, figured in the schools of uncle Francis and Robert Kilvert. Mayo stressed that 'accurate observation' of objects came first, followed by 'correct expression of the results of observation'. A significant aspect of the teaching pursued by uncle Francis, aunt Sophia, Robert Kilvert, and Harvey Marriott was that it was domestic, a feature of Pestalozzi's system heavily emphasised by Mayo. That system conveys 'the pure and gentle influence of domestic life', Mayo stated. Furthermore, the liberty allowed by the system 'must be directed by an influence essentially *parental*'; Pestalozzian teachers were to act in the roles of mothers and fathers. Even though Pestalozzi encouraged mutual instruction, this 'was an engine very different from the machinery of the Madras system.[41] It was founded on . . . the affectionate feelings of domestic life, not on the principles of political institutions'.

This brought Mayo to two other main features of Pestalozzi's system. Elementary education was usually 'a mechanical inculcation of knowledge; on the Pestalozzian system it is an *organic* development of [all] of the human faculties'. The second feature emphasised by Mayo was that 'education should be essentially *religious* [and] . . . essentially *moral* . . . its principles derived from the precepts of the gospel'. He added: 'The instructor must regard himself as standing in God's stead to the child'. And Mayo's conclusion was that 'the method of Pestalozzi is, in its essence, the application of Christianity to the business of Education'.[42] As an Evangelical, Mayo was very ready to emphasise the Pietistic elements in Pestalozzi's religious outlook. Krüsi referred to the latter's 'consciousness of sin' and enjoyment of suffering as a means of 'self-improvement'.[43]

Evidence of this educational background and of the infant school movement's influence can be found in what can be gathered of Kilvert's teaching methods at Clyro School. It was a blend, as his father's was, of Evangelical and Pestalozzian principles and methods: there was the Catechism, Scripture Knowledge, Church doctrine of the one, with the object lessons, natural history, and geography of the other. We may assume that much of the philosophy behind his work came also from his 'teachers' whose attitudes to natural phenomena have been examined earlier. He worked for sixteen months (spring 1865 to summer 1866) at Clyro School alongside Miss Henrietta Coleburn, who had trained at the HCISS College. Her six months' training included Scripture Knowledge (heavily represented), lessons on objects, use of coloured pictures, natural history, arithmetic, and geography. Students were also inducted into Pestalozzian theory. Candidates for the course had to have 'sound moral and religious principles' and capacity to withstand a hard regime.[44]

Her background would have made her a very congenial colleague. Roughly the same age as Kilvert (she was born in 1844), Henrietta was the daughter of Henry Coleburn, who was a parish relieving officer in 1851 in Runcorn, Cheshire. By 1861 he was Registrar of Births, Marriages and Deaths. Two other facts stand out from the Census record of that year when Henrietta was seventeen: the family home is given as 'Literary Institute' (on New Lane, Runcorn) and Henrietta's occupation, and that of Mary, a younger sister, is given as 'pupil teacher'. Runcorn's Literary and Philosophical Institute was founded *c.*1835 and held a collection of minerals, fossils and shells. Thus, Henrietta sprang from a background of socially useful occupations and was surrounded in her childhood by the objects of natural history, as Kilvert was.

Clyro School was a National (i.e. Anglican) school and its pedagogic tradition was the 'catechestical' one favoured by the Church. The Vicar of Clyro, the Rev. Venables, stated in his summer 1866 Visitation Return that either he or his curate (Kilvert) catechised the children and in his 1869 Return that it was 'chiefly done' by Kilvert. Kilvert also taught such aspects of Church doctrine as the Nativity and the Crucifixion.[45] Josiah Evans, the teacher who replaced Miss Coleburn in autumn 1866, taught the Catechism, as is clear from the HMI inspection on 1 July 1870:

> The schoolmaster was asked first to examine the children in the Church Catechism and ask them to explain part of it. They said it very accurately as far as to the sacraments and explained the duty to our neighbour fairly. The Liturgy is not so well known.[46]

Emily Kilvert recorded that the Kilvert children always repeated the Church Catechism with her father's pupils on Sunday evenings. That Kilvert believed in the importance of this kind of instruction in piety and drilling[47] is confirmed by the fact that he continued it when he was in charge of his own parish (Bredwardine, Herefordshire). On 8 February 1878 he recorded his pleasure that some written exercises he had given to his pupils on 'What makes a true Sacrament?' were 'nicely done'.

Other evidence of Kilvert's teaching reveals the basic contradiction in the interpretation of Pestalozzi's methods referred to earlier. When Kilvert 'asked the children . . . what an embalmed Egyptian body was called', receiving the answer 'a life preserver' from one pupil and 'a muffin' from another, and persisted with the question 'What is a muffin?' only to be told it was 'a bird', it is evident that there were too many scraps of information in the curriculum divorced from the actual objects, the observation, and the real enquiry recommended by Pestalozzi. (Hare resented having to learn about Crema and Cremona for exactly this reason.) Of course, it was not easy for Kilvert to produce such objects as Egyptian mummies and puffins in his classroom for first-hand study.

It seems Kilvert intended to follow Pestalozzi in studying Nature with his pupils. This is confirmed by the *Diary* entry for 28 January 1870: 'Bought *Phenomena of Nature . . .* at the SPCK Repository'.[48] The book's full title, *The Phenomena of Nature Familiarly Explained. A book for parents and instructors and especially adapted to schools* (1832) by Wilhelm Von Türk, indicates its aims. Not only was such knowledge 'useful', but 'admirably calculated to draw out [the child's] powers of observation'. Kilvert no doubt saw it as a handbook for his teaching. Born in Germany, Von Türk (1774-1846) gave up his work as a lawyer and spent three years with Pestalozzi, studying his methods, after which he set up a school for orphans and became known as the 'Prussian Pestalozzi'.[49] He was obviously a disciple of Wordsworth because the preface to his book paraphrases the *Immortality Ode.* Nature is 'God's book', a source of deep pleasures and spiritual insights.[50] He also noted that the child possessed, in addition to innocence, great capacity of observation: 'every worm, every pebble, . . . every echo from the hill speaks visibly to the child'.

In spite of its Wordsworthian preface, Von Türk's book (favourably reviewed in the *Journal of Education* that was published by the SDUK) is scientific and inductive rather than imaginative and religious. He said he proposed using the child's power of observation to develop understanding of natural objects and natural laws, a method that placed him firmly in the Pestalozzian tradition.[51] Von Türk's book explored common phenomena – 'it treats only of such things as are daily before our eyes' – through an approach combining the application of reason with a sense of wonder and beauty. Such phenomena as sunrise, the return of spring, 'the wonders of the storm and the frosts of winter . . . all offer important lessons to the mind'. In effect, this approach completely revolutionised the teaching of geography and became the basis of the modern approach to it as a school subject.[52] For Pestalozzi, geography and natural history were the foundation of most other subjects, including science. At the HCISS College founded by the Mayos, 'geography was regarded as the third most essential component of the curriculum' (after English and maths).[53] This was the approach too of the Religious Tract Society, which argued that Christians had a moral duty to study geography, natural history, and biography.

In Pestalozzi's approach, geography merged easily into science as it did for Wilderspin.[54] Von Türk's book too might be said to be a blend of geography and science with its sections on (for example) 'The Earth and its Nature' and 'Of Light and Luminous Bodies'. Its guiding principles are the displaying of 'a chain of cause and effect in nature' and its verification by 'actual experiment'. Some details of the book's section 'Of Water' will illustrate the kind of teaching manual that Kilvert chose to buy. The preface urges the teacher to 'reply as far as possible to children's questions'. However, although the lessons are framed as dialogues between master and child, these are much more mechanical and teacher-dominated than the conversations of *Evenings at Home*. Children are first asked (as they are in all sections) to recall their everyday observations, in this case of water – in streams and rivers, in caves and hollows after rain, in condensation on window panes, and in steam from cooking pots. The properties of water are then explored. The master points out that though water is a 'fluid body', some heat is needed to maintain its fluid state. Focus shifts to the (apparent) transparency of water then to its specific gravity, which is explained through experiments showing that the heavier a piece of wood is that is floated in water, the more water it displaces. Water's ability to mix with other liquids and with mud in rivers is discussed. It is noted that water in the form of steam can work machinery. Mists and clouds at the tops of mountains are used to explain condensation of water, and icebergs, glaciers, and avalanches to show how at low temperatures it can form into ice and snow.

No *Diary* entry shows Kilvert using the book in school, although Plomer might have omitted it (the only other surviving reference to it records that Kilvert lent it to his literary farmer friend, Lewis Williams). Kilvert could, however, in his own informal Sunday School, follow Pestalozzi to the letter. In the summer of 1875 he recorded a pattern of conducting these classes on the lawn of Langley Burrell Rectory on sunny days. On 8 August he said his 'little scholars' were amused at what he called 'the green drawing room' under the shade of the lime trees. He had taught them outside two weeks before, though the lessons were on conventional religious subjects, as was the case on 8 August. However, on Sunday 5 September he taught them on the lines laid down in Von Türk's manual: 'I taught them lessons from the nuthatch tapping in the tree overhead, the woodpigeon cooing in the elm and the flowers that grew around us'.[55] His approach has an exact counterpart in Pestalozzi's own. He noted in his diary: 'Lead your child out into nature, teach him on the hill tops and in the valleys . . . should a bird sing . . . [the bird] is teaching him'.[56]

It is noticeable that Kilvert had a reputation at Clyro School for being a geography specialist: 'There'll be no one to teach us now. Mr Kilvert do come and tell us about all parts', said one boy, heartbroken that Kilvert was leaving Clyro.[57] Mrs Gore of Whitty's Mill showed Kilvert, presumably because she knew it was his special area of interest, 'with great and lawful pride a very nicely drawn and coloured map of England and Wales, which Carrie [Gore] had done at Clyro School'. His particular interest in maps appears in the 4 May 1876 *Diary* entry in which he took the opportunity to show some St Harmon's school children an ordnance map: 'I read out . . . the names of familiar places to the great delight of the children.' We have good evidence that Clyro school prided itself on its geography work, including Kilvert's contribution to it. He showed particular concern for the older pupils' performance during an HMI inspection in a 'special subject' – geography – of which he and Josiah Evans had high hopes.[58] The HMI, however, was not impressed, 'the children not being quite accurate enough in their knowledge'. Kilvert's subsequent comments show not only that he knew what good teaching was, but also that he was aware of the differences between the conventional approach to geography in elementary schools and the Pestalozzian approach. By 'special subject' he meant what the Revised Code (1862) called 'specific' or 'extra' subjects. These included history, geography, algebra, geometry, various sciences, English grammar, and foreign languages. Matthew Arnold (an HMI) stated that these subjects were 'very valuable' because they constituted real knowledge, as opposed to the 3Rs, which were merely the means to knowledge.[59] The Revised Code's aim was better teaching of the 3Rs but the result was that teachers concentrated largely on them to the detriment of other subjects. Inspectors' reports recorded the neglect particularly of history and geography. Where those subjects were taught 'Considerable emphasis was placed upon their factual [content]'.[60] Unfortunately for Kilvert and Evans, this was what the HMI wanted: 'The questions he asked were rather hard, e.g. about the Pennine, Northern, Cambrian and Devonian mountain ranges, more catch and cram than practical questions'.[61] Kilvert was contrasting the parading of mere information with deeper understanding based on children's own experience and insight.

Kilvert's own school experiences, his childhood reading, Pestalozzi and the infant school movement, and Miss Coleburn all seem to have played a part in making him into something of a geography specialist. Professor Blunt too was an influence. The minister can circulate through his school, Blunt said, 'whatever information he sees fit . . . [can] put his Tracts in motion'. The tracts the professor recommended were those that reflected missionary work overseas such as those published by the Society for the Propagation of the Gospel (SPG), because they 'combined in themselves many topics of popular interest – the manners of savage tribes, the habits of new settlers, the produce and scenery of distant lands, the geography of the world – a subject of more curiosity to the poor than some would suppose'.[62] Noticeably, it was exactly these kinds of topics that attracted Kilvert to Mr Bodily's SPG St Helena Lecture (see chapter one). The information in Kilvert's teaching had to come from somewhere and the Church missionary field advocated by Blunt was one likely source. The considerable overlap between what the latter recommended, in terms both of content and Christian approach and tone (the blend of information and piety), and the RTS policy suggests that magazines such as *The Leisure Hour* was another likely source. Typical articles from 1858 *Leisure Hour* issues illustrate this overlap: 'British Columbia – our youngest colony', 'A Visit to Chittagong', 'Curious Customs in China', 'Glimpses of Delhi', 'The Republic of Liberia', 'An Evening with Dr Livingstone', 'Henry Martyn the Missionary', 'Traits of Savage Life' (about the botanist Robert Brown in Tahiti).

In this account of Kilvert's cultural background, Brighton connections have been identified in his uncle Herbert, Grace Aguilar, and Frederick Robertson. Further, such significant Irish elements figure in his background – the Edgeworths, Lord Lansdowne, Annie Keary, Tyndall – that it is appropriate to speak of an Irish connection. The number of elements constituting a Swiss connection is even greater. Switzerland mattered to Kilvert because he had himself been there and retained fond memories of it. In summer 1869 he had taken a continental holiday, visiting France, Germany and Switzerland, just as Robertson had done in 1841 and 1846. By the time of his holiday Kilvert had read Brooke's *Life of Robertson* so he knew of his Swiss experiences and particularly his recommendation: 'A man ought to go [to Switzerland] to feel intensely at least once in his life'.[63] It was advice Kilvert followed. He had a memento of walking tours in Switzerland: 'got out my old Swiss haversack. . . . ' It was 27 April 1870 and the haversack was for his clothes on an overnight stay at Whitney Rectory. His European holidays enabled him to tell his pupils about foreign 'parts'. His itinerary took in places Robertson had visited – Strasburg, Geneva, Heidelberg (where the latter had been chaplain in the English church). Switzerland had produced a great educator in Pestalozzi and Kilvert's journey there may reasonably be viewed as, in some respects, a form of homage to him and the progress he represented, as well as to Robertson.

Kilvert was eager to talk about Switzerland with anybody. A dinner was made more enjoyable because Louise Wyatt 'talked Switzerland and saved me the trouble of finding conversation'. Presumably Kilvert had recounted Swiss 'adventures' to Janet Vaughan, daughter of the Vicar of Newchurch, near Clyro, because she had a 'Geneva brooch' – no doubt a present from him. Mrs Webb, wife of the Hardwicke clergyman and astronomer, had been to Switzerland and she and he were accomplished painters of Alpine scenery. Kilvert praised her watercolours and showed familiarity with some of the mountains depicted – the Matterhorn, Schreckhorn, Monte Rosa[64] – all of which figured in Von Türk's textbook and Tyndall's book on mountaineering.[65] The scientist's experiences in Switzerland were in part what hallowed it for Kilvert. Its mountains, clouds and glaciers influenced Tyndall to become 'profoundly impressed with the majesty and mystery of matter'.[66] The same might be said of Kilvert.

For Kilvert, as both priest and teacher, no members of a community were more important than its children. Their moral, spiritual, and educational development was a sacred task, as the *Diary* everywhere confirms. His deep pleasure in being the means of bringing understanding to (especially female and beautiful) pupils emerges in the 4 July 1870 entry, just after the HMI inspection of Clyro School. The 'indescribable beauty' Gipsy Lizzie had now been put in his reading class. When she raised her eyes to his, he was enchanted by their 'clear unfathomable blue depth of wide wonder and enquiry'. His joy in those blue eyes, and in the 'fearless blue eyes' of the angel child (see last chapter), owed much to Tyndall's ecstatic exploration of blue skies. His joy also stemmed from a deep sense of children's capacity for seeking and absorbing information, their drive to *know*. On another occasion, we find him emphasising Gipsy Lizzie's 'rapt observation'. In the entry for 2 May 1876, he told a story to another girl (and former pupil) with 'bewitching' blue eyes, like 'the windows of heaven', Florence Hill, and underlined her 'rapt' attention and wonder as she followed the progress of his story.

We shall never know whether Kilvert was aware that Tyndall's teaching career began in a Nonconformist Pestalozzian institution. His importance to Kilvert as an inspirational teacher has been underlined in an earlier chapter. When Kilvert bought Von Türk's *Phenomena of Nature*, he was identifying himself with the educational mission of both Pestalozzi and Tyndall. Tyndall's lectures to the public, especially to audiences of elementary school teachers and working men, identified him with 'the march of intellect' represented by Lord Brougham and Charles Knight. Tyndall was another of Kilvert's teachers, not least in the development of his own literary style. Tyndall inspired through his ground-breaking work, by his fearless exploration of natural phenomena (especially in Switzerland) and confrontations with the establishment, by his rich and imaginative presentations, and by his fostering of an appreciation of miracles of science rivalling those of Scripture.

That Tyndall was one of Kilvert's heroes is further confirmation of his own broad vision, intellectual stature, and engagement with the challenging questions of the day. He was able to admire a scientist who found the origins of life in Matter, and not in a divine designer, because his science was approached in a spirit of reverence and wonder. Kilvert no doubt sought to bring that spirit to his own teaching about natural phenomena. However, the catechistical mode of elementary school instruction worked strongly against it. Von Türk's manual had the question-and-answer format characterising most textbooks of the period and the Pietistic strain of the English elementary school. Its preface stated that in nature could be discerned 'the irrefragable testimony of a presiding Providence', and that its 'eternal laws' revealed 'the beautiful harmony in the ordinances of the ruler of the universe'. The study of nature could be relied on to 'restore the confidence in God' of one whose faith was failing. It was therefore a textbook in which religion and science co-existed in mutual support.

In the book's expressions of natural theology can be glimpsed 'the unease in Anglican circles about the nature of popular science in this period – particularly the theory of evolution', referred to by Mary Hilton. She linked this unease to the question of why it took so long 'for English elementary education to abandon the "catechism mode"'. The doctrine of original sin was central to the Church Catechism. Thus a good deal of the answer to the question lay, she believed, in another contradiction in Pestalozzi himself: 'Clearly an educator and lover of humanity such as Pestalozzi, who believed in the process of "unfolding" a child's mind, could not' [Pietist though he was] 'hold strictly to a notion of original sin'. Anglican admirers of Pestalozzi recognised his failure to endorse this latter notion and this was the reason for his ultimate rejection in Britain.[67] It was particularly Evangelicals like Kilvert who clung most closely to the doctrine of original sin.

His was typical of other Evangelical families, like the Marriotts, who were able to educate their children under 'the pure and gentle influence of domestic life'. Behind their education would ideally lie a pious family, united in faith and sympathy; Kilvert was reproducing it when he conducted his Sunday School among Nature's wonders on the lawn of Langley Burrell Rectory. That vision also lay behind his notion of an ideal society.

Chapter Ten

Museums and Picture Galleries

Visiting museums could be nearly a devotional exercise for
Victorians.
Lynn Merrill, *The Romance of Victorian Natural History*

The Polytechnic was one of the favourite destinations
in London for those Victorians who wanted to visit an
institution of science.
Bernard Lightman, *Victorian Popularizers of Science*

This study of Kilvert has laid great emphasis on what he read, and what
he made of what he read, in order to recreate the culture in which
he was raised and to give some idea of the characteristic cultural
furnishings of his mind. This has entailed an examination of books, but
also pictures, a concern extended here in the context of the nineteenth-
century popularisation of science and technology. It has been shown
that pictures mattered a great deal to the Kilvert family. Emily Kilvert
testified to the importance to her of Charles Knight's *Old England,*
with its hundreds of steel engravings, and the lovely engravings in her
copy of Kirke White's poems. She also showed detailed knowledge of
the early photographs of Fox Talbot. She told how the Kilvert children
had large pictures of birds and beasts, and how she never forgot the
picture painted by her mother in *The Children's Year.* Her beloved
Playmate book had especially good pictures. The Kilvert family knew
Maund's *Botanic Garden,* which was full of them; Britton's *The Beauties
of England and Wales,* so important to the family, is full of engravings.
Kilvert's knowledge of steamboats and railway viaducts and bridges
had come partly from pictures. The Pestalozzian educational tradition
that shaped the schools run by Kilvert's uncle Francis and by Robert
Kilvert made much of museums and pictures. And finally, *Kilvert's
Diary* is full of references to paintings, to landscape forms expressed in
pictorial terms, and to visits to art galleries and museums.

Robert Kilvert loved pictures and brought his children up to
love them. The period of his childhood was dismissive of pictures:

'the written word was felt to be the most reliable vehicle for calling up . . . pictures in the mind's eye', and this was true even of 'urban visual culture which, for all its pictorial novelty, was rooted in reading'.[1] Robert Kilvert had assimilated this outlook: 'Pictures are the books of an unlearned age', he wrote. However, when he was eight he was convinced that 'Nothing that I ever read or heard was so successful in giving me an idea of [Napoleon's] miserable retreat [from Moscow]' as the pictures in the window of Salmoni's shop in Bath.[2] Accordingly, his children's nursery was well supplied with pictures, as Emily recorded. The walls 'were covered with pictures of all shapes and sizes, but almost all brightly coloured ones' she wrote.[3] To the Kilvert children, pictures were a means of education and a source of pleasure and interest.

Kilvert had had this message reinforced in Kingsley's *True Words for Brave Men* (*TW*), a collection of sermons and addresses aimed particularly at soldiers and sailors involved in the Crimean War. Clear evidence that Kilvert had assimilated from *TW* the message of its 'God's Beautiful World' sermon appears in a *Diary* entry full of Kingsley's ideas and phrases.[4] The latter had subtitled his sermon, 'A Spring Sermon', which is what Kilvert's 24 May 1875 entry essentially is. Kingsley referred to walking through 'golden meadows', Kilvert referred to walking through 'green meadows'. Kilvert's moment of joy was 'a deep delicious draught from the strong sweet cup of life'; Kingsley's moment was 'a charmed draught, a cup of blessing'. The *Diary* moment was 'one of the flowers of happiness . . . found by the wayside of life; the moment in the sermon was 'a wayside sacrament'.[5] Kingsley knew that working people did not have the leisure to admire beauty in the countryside, so in his address 'Picture Galleries' he included the 'God's Beautiful World' passage but recommended the National Gallery or South Kensington Museum, 'or any other collection of pictures' as substitute. Those work-dominated individuals, inhabitants of the 'grim city-world of stone and iron', could emerge 'into the world of beautiful things' by this means. 'Go to the British Museum', Kingsley urged, ' . . . there at least, if you cannot go to nature's wonders, some of nature's wonders are brought to you'.

Kilvert chose to begin[6] the record of his 'curious and wonderful' life (it was 18 January 1870) with a visit to the kind of institution Kingsley recommended. It was two weeks after Christmas so a festive air informs the entry but its excitement reflects the fact that Kilvert was himself a child again, beguiled by the displays: 'Walked about the Palace, bought various things, salt cellars of green glass, brooches (German stags in ivory) and saw in a cave old Father Christmas'. Not only were 'stalls and shops dazzling' but 'chameleon and flying tops [were] glittering and flying through the air overhead, returning like boomerangs to the spinner's hand'. This world of wonders induced nostalgia and he relived his visit fifteen years before when he was fourteen, much the same age as his charges. Regular pilgrimages to the Crystal Palace were a feature of his life. He had visited first in 1851, the year of the Great Exhibition. The visit when he was fourteen took place in 1855. He was there with the Thomas boys in 1870. He visited again on 26 June 1874 for the Handel Festival.

Another key institution in the nineteenth-century popularisation of science was William Bullock's Egyptian Hall in London's Piccadilly. It was completed in 1812, the year that Robert Kilvert was enjoying being horrified by the Moscow pictures. So-called because its design resembled an Egyptian temple, it would have been a place of wonders in Robert's childhood, when it was devoted to natural objects. Admission cost 1s and the Museum was 'a popular attraction [which] played on the confusion between entertainment and education'.[7] In 1819, Bullock sold the Hall and it was converted into an exhibition hall.[8] It continued to be a talking point throughout the nineteenth century and Kilvert was familiar with it as a place of 'wonders'. The Hall's tradition of entertainment and sensation was to the fore when he visited on 23 June 1876 and wrote: 'Psyche is wonderful, and so are Maskelyne and Cook in the cabinet'. John Nevil Maskelyne (1839-1917) had taken over the Hall in 1873 and Kilvert's reference to the 'cabinet' probably meant the 'spirit cabinet' that Maskelyne and his friend George Alfred Cooke (a cabinet maker) built in order to discredit the stage performance of the fraudulent spiritualists, the Davenport brothers.[9]

The regular delivery of periodicals at the Kilvert home, remembered by Emily Kilvert, almost certainly would have included the *Illustrated London News* (*ILN*), the world's first illustrated weekly newspaper. (Kilvert would have known that Charles Mackay became one of its reporters in 1848 and its editor from 1852.) Emily Kilvert remembered reading about the funeral of the Duke of Wellington in a 1852 issue of it, when she would have been ten. Kilvert recorded (29 November 1870) that his brother Edward read it. Another significant entry (29 November 1871) shows Daisy Thomas, a girl Kilvert hoped to marry, bringing him a copy of it to read as though she knew it was a favourite of his. It was founded by Herbert Ingram in 1842, with Mark Lemon, editor of *Punch*, as his chief adviser. The first issue of 14 May cost sixpence and had sixteen pages and thirty-two wood engravings. In addition to crime reports, it covered the current war in Afghanistan, as well as the kind of events that always drew Kilvert's attention: a train crash in France and a steam-boat accident on the Chesapeake. Dodds called the *ILN* 'the most phenomenally successful paper of the time' because, within a year of its launch, it had a circulation of 66,000, rising to 100,000 by 1851.[10] Mary Howitt clearly approved of it because she noted that the walls of

Egyptian Hall, *Maskelyne and Cooke's Marvellous Entertainment*

her children's garden playhouse 'were adorned with large pictures from the *Illustrated London News*'. It aimed to be a family newspaper, treating topical events in a lively, intelligent way. Though aimed at the middle class, it appealed to working-class readers too. Wordsworth, however, was contemptuous of 'this vile abuse of pictured page!'[11]

In the 1840s there was a large readership for almanacs, the 'respectable' elements of which were 'ready to be schooled in a proper appreciation of natural knowledge'. The *Illustrated London Almanac* (*ILA*), published by the *ILN* from 1845, targeted this element. Kilvert's father was one who saw it regularly, as the *Diary* entry for 24 February 1871 confirms: 'Wrote to my Father for his birthday and sent him an *Illustrated London Almanac* as usual'. This was a regular pattern: he despatched another copy of it on 26 February 1870. The *ILA* was a folio, eight by eleven inches, with 64 pages, and priced at 1s. After 1858, issues were illustrated, with eye-catching colour engravings on the covers. Obviously, Robert Kilvert had never lost his appetite for pictures. The first issue of the *ILA* covered history, folklore, scientific material, sport and leisure, domestic matters, and statistics. Meteorology featured in it but by its second year this had given way to astronomy, 'with regular discussion of discoveries of new planets and comets'. There were always large sections on natural history. 'The most striking feature of the *Illustrated London Almanac* was . . . its scientific content', Henson observed.[12] Since it is reasonable to assume that copies of this periodical appeared regularly in the Kilvert household because of Robert Kilvert's predilection for it, its contents must have contributed to the diarist's stock of knowledge about natural history and science.

In the following account of further visits Kilvert made to museums, the British Museum and South Kensington Museum have a special place. He was able to entertain the exciting prospect of having his folklore collection published by the British Museum in a learned journal, with the help of Reginald Poole, a Keeper there.[13] Kilvert had met the Pooles at the Bredwardine (Herefordshire), home of Miss Newton in August 1872, and they invited him to call on them in London. He called to see Poole at the British Museum on 21 February 1873 and he, having seen Kilvert's MSS, pronounced 'the matter interesting and valuable'.[14] The Poole/Newton families represent one element in Kilvert's intellectual network, similar to the scientific one glanced at in chapter five. The former network was concerned with archaeology, museums, and anthropology. Its manifestation in provincial Bredwardine was a reflection of its metropolitan self. While in the British Museum seeing Poole, Kilvert noted excitedly: 'I saw . . . the drum of one of the columns of the Artemision, the Temple of Diana at Ephesus. Upon this very column St Paul's eyes may have rested'. (He could not resist inserting a slight note of sensation.) He continued:

'The Artemision was discovered in 1871 and is now being excavated under the direction of Mr Charles Newton.' Kilvert's information on this occasion was wrong. This site was actually found on 31 December 1869 by John Turtle Wood, who bought it for the British Museum. Newton's great achievement was the discovery of the Mausoleum of Halicarnassus, one of the Seven Wonders of the Ancient World, as the Artemision was.[15] He became Keeper of the British Museum's Greek and Roman Antiquities; Kilvert was to meet him at Miss Newton's on 23 August 1878.[16]

The Polytechnic, where Kilvert took the Thomas boys the day after their Crystal Palace visit in January 1870, had from its early days staged popular lectures on chemistry and physics aimed at young, mainly working-class men, eventually making a particular target of middle-class families. We can sense that his visit there was a re-acquainting of himself with an institution which, like the Crystal Palace and the Egyptian Hall, was part of his family tradition. This is evident in the note of familiarity with which he referred to its programme: 'Arrived just at the beginning of the Dissolving Views, showing natural phenomena, the Northern Dawn, avalanche, earthquake, lightning, then Pepper's Ghost multiplied and revolved, and Christmas in the Olden Time.'[17] The Polytechnic, opened in 1838, represented 'the attempt to afford to the real castaways of Victorian London the merest minimum of literacy and decency.'[18] Sir George Cayley (1773-1857), landowner and aeronautical scientist, was the force behind it originally. An 1839 description of it stated: 'The objects of this truly valuable institution are "the advancement of practical science in connection with agriculture, the arts and manufactures".'[19] To Secord, it was 'a commercial showcase for invention and ingenuity.'[20] Lewis Dillwyn senior wasted no time in introducing his children to it after its opening in 1838: they visited on 13 May 1839 and made several visits in June 1843. Lewis junior was regularly taking his children there in the 1850s.

The Polytechnic was always associated with exciting *spectacle*. The 'Dissolving Views', familiar to Kilvert, were from its beginning 'the main reason for its reputation as a favourite haunt of children.'[21] The Views showed landscapes, exotic fantasies, and the interior and exterior of famous buildings. The Polytechnic's continuous programme of popular lectures had steady appeal for visitors. It also provided teacher-training classes in the sciences. However, it was later given over entirely to 'exhibits, demonstrations and lectures for laymen.'[22] Its aim was to combine education with entertainment, but found this increasingly difficult while remaining economically viable. It sought to give its exhibits topicality by relating them to events reported in newspapers, for example on the development of the electric telegraph. When Kilvert visited in 1851, the theme of its lectures was the adulteration of food and drink, which had featured in *Lancet* articles.

John Henry Pepper (1821-1900), a graduate in chemistry, became lecturer at the Polytechnic in 1848 and its owner in 1854. Described by Lightman as 'among the most well-known popularizers of science in the second half of the nineteenth century,'[23] Pepper exploited the public's hunger for spectacle by the use of elaborate and revolutionary visual techniques, the most famous of which (and familiar to the Kilvert family) was 'Pepper's Ghost'. It was an illusion that made objects disappear and reappear by means of plate-glass, hidden mirrors, and lighting. It featured in the programme Kilvert saw in January 1870, and was in fact invented by Henry Dircks in 1862, though always associated with Pepper. Emily Kilvert remembered that 'Professor Pepper's Ghost [was] an entertainment in which my children used to delight.[24] 'Pepper's fame as the producer of an ingenious and exciting spectacle known as Pepper's Ghost quite eclipsed his real and serious intent in making science attractive to young people'.[25] Pepper honed his lecturing skills over the years, imitating Tyndall's use of thrilling images and often referring to Tyndall in his lectures and books. Pepper gave audiences 'the most elaborate and sophisticated lantern shows ever exhibited', with the aid of large slides painted by a team of highly skilled artists,[26] one of whom, Edmund Wilkie, emphasised Pepper's Christian faith and his belief that science and unbelief were not mutually opposed.

This theme was reiterated in one of Pepper's books, the popular *The Boy's Playbook of Science* (1860), which aimed to bring the wonders of science to the young. One chapter deals with the electric telegraph, describing it as 'this important instrument'.[27] The book's chapter three on astronomy may have fed Kilvert's interest in that field, while chapter twenty-two, 'The Refraction of Light', could have provided the knowledge he showed in the entry he wrote about the optical illusion seen by his sister Thersie (see chapter seven).

The other institution (in addition to the British Museum) recommended by Kingsley in 'Picture Galleries', where the working class could see 'the wonders of Nature', was the South Kensington Museum (SKM), which was a particular favourite of Kilvert. Perhaps this was because it was not devoted to profit but was more of an educational institution: '[It] was the first non-commercial London museum not explicitly intended for use by the general public . . . but was actually devoted to public service'.[28] It was free on Mondays, Tuesdays, and Saturdays, 6d on other days. In addition it was open two nights a week for the benefit of working people, though most working-class districts were too far away for them to make use of it. It was praised by Pepper as the foremost science museum because of its superior collection of

Royal Polytechnic Institution, Professor Pepper's Ghosts

models and works of art. The original SKM, opened in June 1857, was
intended to house a number of heterogeneous collections that had been
displayed separately or not at all. It was a series of 'sub-museums', each
of which represented the ideal of industrial education that had been
the theme of the Crystal Palace, including an exhibition on schooling,
museums of building materials, architecture, animal products, and
ornamental art. Later, these collections became the Victoria and Albert
Museum. Prince Albert had promoted the South Kensington area as a
cultural centre for London since 1851, making its museums 'one of the
truly significant products of the Victorian period'.[29]

After Kilvert had left the Thomas's house in Mitcham on 25 January
1870, he went to London and two days later was at the SKM. As though
driven by Kingsley's urging, he recorded: 'I went upstairs at once to
the picture galleries'. He admired the 'splendid collection' of paintings,
'especially of Landseers'.[30] The next afternoon, Kilvert was again at
the SKM and the Horticultural Gardens, particularly enjoying the
Conservatory and its 'beautiful Ferns'. Two years later (4 January 1872)
he was at the Museum once more looking at paintings.[31] The excitement
of spectacle drew him on 28 May 1872 to Kensington Gardens to see the
International Exhibition, after which he wrote: 'Some good pictures,
especially in the Belgian Gallery'. At the International Exhibition a
year later (22 May 1873) his attention was on industrial processes: silk
looms weaving and the striking of medals.

Another branch of the SKM was the Bethnal Green Museum,
which attracted Kilvert on 24 February 1873 (a few days after meeting
Reginald Poole at the British Museum). The Bethnal Green Museum,
owing much to the efforts of various workers among the East End
poor, was opened on 24 June 1872 by the Prince and Princess of Wales.
It can be seen as another product of the movement for the education
of the people, together with the Great Exhibition, the Crystal Palace,
the Polytechnic, and the Zoological Gardens. Its permanent display
illustrated the sources of and chemical composition of food. For three
years it housed the outstanding art collection of Sir Richard Wallace,
with which Kilvert said he was 'delighted'.

In the midst of sorties to picture galleries during his May 1875
London visit, Kilvert found time for further visits to SKM on 11 and
12 May. His appetite for curiosities still unsatisfied, the afternoon
of 12 May found him paying his first visit to the Alexandra Palace
in Muswell Hill. Named after Princess Alexandra of Denmark, who
had married Edward, Prince of Wales, it opened in June 1873 as 'The
People's Palace'. Part of Kilvert's morning had been spent '[marking]
the Royal Academy catalogue and pictures yet to be seen and studied

according to the *Daily Telegraph* notice and critique'. However, he intended to devote his afternoon to more popular attractions. 'The People's Palace' had only been reopened eleven days before, after being totally destroyed by fire, when he visited 'by Westbourne Park train and King's Cross, . . . a long roundabout journey, but a very pleasant and pretty place quite worth going to see'.

The apologetic, defensive tone of this last statement is reinforced by what follows. He quoted Mary Howitt's poem *The Spider and the Fly*, which begins: "'Will you walk into my parlour?"'/ Said the spider to the fly'. The next lines are: "'The way into my parlour/ Is up a winding stair;/ And I have many curious things/ To show you when you're there'". Kilvert substituted 'palace' for 'parlour' in order to fit his Alexandra Palace outing. Was he making a slightly guilty acknowledgement of the seductive power of the Palace's popular appeal, in contrast to the serious study of the morning in preparation for his visit to the Royal Academy? The fly in Mary Howitt's poem, though initially wary of the spider, is eventually won over by its 'wily, flattering words', and the poem's moral is a warning against falling victim to facile appeals. Routledge's *Popular Guide to London* (c.1873) told of the Palace's 'concerts, collections of scientific and art objects, flower and fruit shows, theatrical and other entertainments daily'.[32] Kilvert acknowledged some of its popular attractions. The 'great organ in the fine concert Hall' was, he wrote, 'a high treat',[33] though it played 'variations of popular airs', including *The Last Rose of Summer* which, he insisted, 'was beautiful'. His comments are a reminder of his father's defence of pictures (as compared with books) – 'unlearned' perhaps but effective in arousing interest. They are a reminder too of the influence on both father and son of the popularising tradition that made use of sensation and spectacle.

Altick also noted that the early 1860s craze for 'sensations' coincided with the period when the new Crystal Palace was seeking to establish its policy, pressuring it to push entertainment at the expense of education.[34] This explains Kilvert's sardonic comment, in the entry about his visit there on 18 January 1870: "'Wild Rose", the blue mare spotted with pink, hairless and elephant-tailed, from Africa was exhibited . . . for the moderate sum of three-pence'. He recorded other examples of vulgar spectacle as, for example, the 'procession of horsemanship and circus riders' in Bath's main street on 30 September 1873. The riders, purporting to be Circassians and Tartars, were 'in spangles and tawdry tinsel'. A 'blasting' brass band was 'huddled in a gilt car dragged by miserable piebald horses'.

Kilvert, with his background of natural history and museums, would inevitably have been excited that the new University Museum of Oxford was just being finished when he arrived at Wadham College in autumn 1859. 'It signalled Oxford's determination to end the exclusive stranglehold of classical and religious studies'.[35] The Museum reflected the reform movement affecting the University at the time, announcing 'metaphorically [its] decision to set up an Honours School in Natural Science'.[36] The 1850 statute responsible for this initiative had also introduced another new school – Law and Modern History, which was the course that Kilvert had chosen. It was a significant choice because it is further confirmation that, though in many ways a traditionalist, he embraced a modern outlook. The history curriculum of his course was traditional enough: English history from the birth of Christ up to 1789. The law element 'resembled much less a modern law school than the modern School of Philosophy, Politics and Economics'. In the context of the time 'It was a school of modern studies', its purpose being to ensure that 'the average country gentleman should know something of the world about him'.[37] Kilvert's determination to know of the new world developing all around him, the theme of this study, is further signalled therefore by his choice of this challenging course.

Oxford's new Honours School in Natural Science was, like Kilvert's course, a compromise between old and new. It did not signify, Yanni stated, 'waning Anglican influence at Oxford; on the contrary, the study of natural objects was seen as part of the teaching about Creation'. Similarly, the new Museum was to be an expression of natural theology, its specimens, brought together from various Oxford locations, intended to demonstrate the manifold quality of God's work. The Museum was, however, more than a collection: 'it was more like the "science centres" of today's universities', with lecture rooms, professors' offices, a library and a laboratory.[38] The sculpture over its doorway also signified compromise or fusion. It showed the Angel of Life holding in one hand an open book (the Bible or the Book of nature) and in the other a biological cell.

Warde Fowler believed that the Oxford of 1866, when he was admitted, had yet to embrace 'the true idea of learning'. Its new museum heralded the growth of the idea but Oxford, like Kilvert, still had one foot in the past. Similarly, museums and shows Kilvert visited in the 1870s continued to retain links with a period when people, less educated and less sophisticated, expected sensation. It was national education, making significant strides in the 1870s, that steadily eroded the demand for sensational 'wonders'. People were growing up, but as they lost their innocence they also lost some of their capacity for curiosity and wonder. Kilvert and his family always had, however, a soft spot for the Polytechnic's wonders that managed to convey both entertainment and instruction, steadily stimulating in its earlier years a fascination with the age's scientific and technological development.

Chapter 11

The Christian Geographer

The Christian takes up the map of the world, prays for the
sheep of Christ in distant lands. . . . He surveys the vast
continents of Asia and Africa, and for the most part it seems
darkness visible.

Memoirs of the Rev. Legh Richmond

Our race alone have the great missionary work in hand.
Edward Hine, *The English Nation identified with the
lost house of Israel*

Previous chapters have shown that the Kilvert family embraced a
notion of progress: social, moral, and spiritual as well as scientific and
technological. The threat accompanying this latter form of progress, in
the view of men such as Dr Alexander, Bishop of Derry, and Frederick
Robertson, was materialism. To many in Kilvert's time materialism was
epitomised by John Tyndall, as Kilvert knew. However, the imagination
and reverence of Tyndall's approach to natural phenomena and
the liberal, Broad Church outlook of Robertson enabled Kilvert to
withstand the threat. We have also seen that the teaching of the Kilvert
men was geared towards the progressive movement in education
represented by Pestalozzi and the Dissenting tradition, which
emphasised usefulness, trade, and the extension of control over nature.
Kilvert had assimilated a vision of social and moral progress which
went hand-in-hand with scientific and technological progress from
the pages of the *Leisure Hour*, the *Penny Post*, and from the Howitts,
Robertson, Buckle, Kingsley, and Knight.

At the end of *Old England*, Knight reviewed some of the 'principal
events' of England's history of the last hundred years which had
important consequences for the 'social progress' of its people. He
dwelt on one that mattered a great deal to Kilvert: 'In January 1807
Lord Granville brought in a bill for the abolition of the slave trade'.
Reactionary forces – 'the slave faction, headed by the royal princes'
– opposed the bill but 'from that hour the slave trade was finally

condemned and prohibited'.[1] Kilvert's childhood reading also included Legh Richmond's *Annals of the Poor* (1816),[2] one story in which was entitled 'The Negro Servant'. It begins:

> If a map of the world . . . were to be painted with darker or brighter hues corresponding with the spiritual character of the inhabitants, what a gloomy aspect would be presented to the eye of the Christian geographer, by the greater portion of the habitable globe! . . . and what a mass of gloom would characterise the African quarter of the world!
>
> Here and there a bright spot would mark the residence of a few missionary labourers. . . .

The passage's last sentence presented the challenge facing Evangelical clergymen like Richmond: the conversion of Africa to Christianity. Sixty years later, Kilvert was excited by the challenge, dramatically illustrated by Mr Barne, the CMS speaker, in terms of the number (800 million) of 'heathen' that still existed. Richmond's negro servant was one success story.

This chapter will focus on Kilvert as a 'Christian geographer' and on his sense of geography, particularly vis-à-vis Africa, the heathen continent. It will examine the importance of missions and missionaries in his life, his awareness of the slave trade and of those who worked for its abolition. His geography teaching was informed by missionary tracts, as has been noted. The St Helena lecture in Hay-on-Wye attracted him because Bodily was both a clergyman and a missionary, and Kilvert knew that the island had long been an East India Company possession, and that its destructive white ants had arrived there in the timbers of a Brazilian slave-ship. To the nineteenth-century Evangelical mind, these subjects were replete with 'wonders', every bit as exciting and inspiring as scientific, mechanical and natural ones. The writings of Evangelicals and of CMS missionaries regularly featured accounts of spiritual wonders: self-sacrifice of those who braved disease, dreadful climates, and savage animals and savage natives in order to spread the Word, amazing death-bed conversions after lifetimes of sin, supernatural piety in children and in patriarchs. *Annals of the Poor* contains some of these.

Richmond was one of the chosen preachers of the CMS. He was made a Honorary Life Governor of the Society in 1824 for his services. By late 1817 the CMS message had come to Bath. A public meeting took place in the Guildhall on 1 December in order to form the Bath Church Missionary Association (BCMA) in aid of the CMS in Africa. In the chair was Henry Ryder, recently appointed (July 1815) Bishop of Gloucester, the first Evangelical bishop in England.[3] Resolution one of the BCMA stated that its purpose was 'to call into action the zeal of her members for the civilisation and conversion of the Heathen'. Members were to subscribe one guinea a year; clergy members half a guinea a year, plus twenty guineas from their congregation.[4]

BCMA annual reports document the involvement of Kilverts, their relatives, friends, supporters, and patrons. Between 1819 and 1825 the names of John Stothert, Jane Stothert, and Philip Bury Duncan (stalwart of the BLPA) appear in the list of subscribers. Mrs Clutterbuck, wife of Thomas Clutterbuck the squire, neighbour, and patron of the Kilverts in Widcombe, Bath, appears as a subscriber in 1825-1826. In the collections for 1826-1827, we find the name of the Rev. Griffiths of Keevil, who had raised £6.12s.6d from his congregation. (Kilvert's father followed Griffiths as Keevil's curate in 1827.) The name of Mrs Griffiths is in the 1828-1829 list of subscribers, along with that of Mrs Harvey Marriott, whose husband regularly raised large collections. In addition, a collection of £2.11s.6d had been made by Robert Kilvert on behalf of his Keevil flock. In the years 1829-1838, the Stotherts, Duncans (*both* brothers from 1833) and Marriotts regularly appear, though no Kilverts. In 1838-1839 Robert Kilvert's Hardenhuish school pupils had contributed (one wonders with what zeal) 12s.6d and he himself paid an annual subscription of 10s. In the year 1840', Stotherts, Duncans, and Marriotts were subscribers but no Kilverts. The involvement of Robert Kilvert and his circle in the BCMA paved the way for the devotion to African missions central to Kilvert's experience from childhood. An earlier chapter noted the missionary working parties of his mother at Hardenhuish, recorded by Emily Kilvert, at which a group of spinster ladies, the Kilvert daughters, and other girls busied themselves with needlework articles for the heathen or for missionaries, while Robert Kilvert handed round buttered toast.

The absence of the names of uncle Francis Kilvert and Sophia Kilvert from the lists of supporters of the BCMA is notable. He perhaps shared her Quaker stance regarding missions, which Quakers did not favour partly because they opposed paid ministers and partly because they relied on guidance from the Holy Spirit instead of planned projects. When the movement against slavery began, Quakers were of course at the forefront. Thomas Clarkson began research into the slave trade encouraged by the Quakers' London Committee, and when the Committee for the Abolition of the Slave Trade was founded in 1807 it was led by the Quakers William Dillwyn (father of Lewis), Samuel Hoard, Joseph Woods, and James Phillips, along with Clarkson and Wilberforce. Support for the movement was particularly strong in south-west England. Sophia Kilvert indicated her attitude to missions in her *Home Discipline*, in which she asserted that 'Christian principle', the 'regulating power' on which all conduct was to be based, had its origin at home, 'its true centre'. In chapter seven, entitled 'Home duties to take precedence of public', she recommended 'relieving the circle around us' rather than 'remote regions'.

Sophia's outlook had been influenced by Dr Chalmers's visit to Clapham, especially by his visit to the home of her own minister there, William Dealtry. He took over Holy Trinity Church in 1813 after the twenty-year reign of John Venn. Many poor people settled in Clapham and she would have noted Venn's efforts on their behalf. He was a regular visitor at the Girls' School in Clapham where we can picture Sophia attending the Clapham's Young Ladies Society (a Bible class) that met in the School. Venn was one of the first visitors to the Battersea Rise home of Henry Thornton, whose aim was to start a 'Clapham System', i.e. an Evangelical community there. Sophia, although not at the heart of this community, was very much an insider. When she married from Battersea Rise in 1822, then Sir Robert Inglis's home, it was in effect the home of the Thorntons, of whose children he had become guardian. She married in Holy Trinity Church, Clapham's spiritual centre. Venn and his Evangelical and Quaker circle made Clapham 'the most important parish in England. Never have the members of one congregation so greatly influenced the history of the world'.[5]

The shaping force of the Clapham Sect on the outlook of the entire Kilvert family can scarcely be exaggerated. Sophia's *Home Discipline*, in its concern with individual morality and piety as the mainsprings of social action and amelioration, is a true product of Clapham's ethos. Unsurprisingly, she was a close friend of Elizabeth Fry, the most famous daughter of the Quaker Gurney family. (One of Elizabeth's sisters married the abolitionist, Thomas Fowell Buxton.) In his 'Historical Portraits', uncle Francis Kilvert paid tribute to Elizabeth Fry as one who 'cared for those who suffered', as well as to Hannah More, regular visitor to leading members of the Clapham Sect, as 'a friend of the poor'. When Emily Kilvert wrote of the 'awe' her family felt towards Sophia, it was partly because of her aristocratic background and manner. However, most of it must have emanated from the knowledge that she had known some of Clapham's great figures, like Thornton, Venn, and Wilberforce, included in the 'wonderful accounts of her people'.[6] In 1797, the year in which Wilberforce's hugely influential *Practical View*[7] was published, he got married at St Swithin's Church in Bath. His contact with Bath over a long period of time must have made him especially significant to the Kilverts. Perry Mead Villa, which he rented in 1791 with Henry Thornton, was in Widcombe where the Kilverts later lived.

The outlook of the Kilvert family replicated that of Clapham Sect members. What the latter stood for is apparent in statements made by Sir James Stephen (1789-1859), the Sect's legal adviser, who bought a house in Clapham in 1794: 'They mourned over the ills inseparable from the progress of society. . . . They were the sons of the great evangelical doctrine of faith'. However, their faith was broadened by 'a more elaborate education, greater familiarity with the world and human affairs, a deeper insight into science and history'.[8] The Sect's involvement in all areas of power, social and political, meant it could 'turn the great wheels of society', according to Spring. He noted too that it took the tasks of organisation seriously in its aim of reforming English religion and manners.[9] It was especially efficient in forming, with much Quaker assistance, voluntary associations such as the Religious Tract Society so important to Kilvert. The Sect was, Spring reminds us, in alliance with 'the enemies of the old order', which included, *inter alia*, dissolute aristocrats, dealers in slaves, M.P.s who regarded Parliament as a gentlemen's club, reactionary landed-gentry obsessed with aggrandising themselves, with family 'honour', and with game laws. Thus, the Sect constituted, as Kilvert did, a paradox: conservatism allied with radical innovation.

This paradoxical combination manifests itself in Quakers' role in the movement to abolish the slave trade. Their insistence that all men, including black men, were equal before God automatically made them radicals. However, some Quakers were slave owners. Sophia de Chièvre, linked by background to some of Europe's most aristocratic families, was rescued from the Terror in 1793 by Quakers who despised rank. The Quaker conscience, however, responded to all who suffered. Sophia's guardian, Thomas Woodruffe Smith, was a merchant. Barely half a mile from the business address of his father (Leadenhall Street), a group of men, including several Quakers as well as Granville Sharpe, a Clapham resident, and Thomas Clarkson, met on 22 May 1787 to form the Committee for Effecting the Abolition of the Slave Trade.

Thomas Woodruffe Smith's second wife was Ann Reynolds, daughter of Anna Barclay and Foster Reynolds, a Quaker linen-bleacher of Carshalton, Surrey. The names of Ann's brothers, Jacob and William, are found with that of her husband, Thomas, in the 1811 list of members of the African Institution, an anti-slavery body set up in 1807 by Wilberforce, Thomas Clarkson, and Zachary Macaulay. Thomas, then residing at Stockwell Park Manor, had paid the large subscription of £31.10s, equivalent to over £1,000 today. Such luminaries as the Marquis of Lansdowne, Wilberforce, Macaulay, and Spencer Perceval (the Prime Minister) had also paid £31.10s. Henry Thornton had paid £63. William

Dealtry had pledged £3.3s annually.[10] A shared outlook on slavery was one of the factors which united the Dillwyn and Kilvert families. Lewis Dillwyn was carrying forward the work of his Quaker father, William, when he attended a meeting in Swansea on 2 May 1825 'for a gradual emancipation of West India negroes'. William Dillwyn contributed £10 to the African Institution in 1811. No less than seven members of the Fox family of Falmouth appear with Dillwyn in the list of contributors.

In 1811 Thomas Woodruffe Smith died and his widow and Sophia moved to Clapham. Sophia was already used to mixing with prominent Quaker families because her stepmother was a Barclay, of the famous banking family, and was friendly with the Frys who had intermarried with the Gurneys.[11] All these family names, including that of Reynolds, appear in the 1840 list of contributors to the Society for the Extinction of the Slave Trade, established in 1839. Sophia's contact with these Quaker families would have increased when she settled in Clapham. The efforts of Quakers in the abolition cause perhaps became more significant to uncle Francis Kilvert after he, like Thomas Woodruffe Smith, married a Quaker. A bookplate showing the Quaker leader William Penn among the Red Indians was found among Francis's literary remains; the plate is from Thomas Clarkson's *Memoirs of the Public and Private Life of William Penn* (1813). Francis honoured Wilberforce and Henry Thornton in a poem, referring to them as 'this sacred pair'. Francis had written it in his copy of Thornton's *Family Prayers*, published posthumously and edited by Inglis.[12] Another of Francis's poems praises Wilberforce for 'liberating slaves from servitude'.

The solidarity with Clapham shown by Francis in purchasing Thornton's *Family Prayers* was reciprocated when he brought out his *Sermons Preached at Christ Church, Bath* in 1827, published by John Taylor of the London firm of Taylor and Hessey. The list of contributors to Francis's volume shows how far he had been received into Clapham's elite community. Copies had been bought by Sir Robert and Lady Inglis, Lady Dowager Inglis and two Inglis sisters, Henry Milnes Thornton (son of Samuel Thornton), Miss Thornton, and the Rev. Watson Thornton (son of Henry), Wilberforce and Mrs Wilberforce, and Hannah More (two copies). Support came too from Robert, Richard, and Francis Henry Falkner, John Stothert (four copies), the Rev. Harvey Marriott, and the Duncan brothers of the BLPA. Several members of the Moule family were contributors. Kilvert's father bought one copy, his mother bought four.

Clapham influence played a large part in the special interest, underlined by Emily Kilvert, that her mother's missionary working party showed in the West African areas of Sierra Leone and Abeokuta. Of societies spawned by the Clapham Sect, the most important to the Kilvert family was the CMS. When its originating committee of 16 clergymen and 9 laymen met, Venn was in the chair, later to become its first Chairman and author of its constitution. Wilberforce was its first President. In 1791, the Sect had formed the Sierra Leone Company (SLC), of which Henry Thornton was Chairman and Wilberforce and other prominent Sect members were directors. Slavery, pronounced illegal in Britain in 1772, left many negro servants unemployed and Granville Sharp proposed settling them on the Sierra Leone peninsula, purchased from an African chief. Four hundred British negroes, a thousand from Nova Scotia (their refuge from slavery in the USA) and some English farmers and craftsmen settled in Sierra Leone. The SLC aimed to safeguard the colony from attacks by surrounding tribes and from disease and to introduce trade, industry, and Christianity. Zachary Macaulay of the Clapham Sect became its governor and in 1816 the CMS established a mission there. Thomas Clarkson, one of SLC's earliest supporters, and his colleagues 'ambitiously imagined [it as] a beacon of commercial and moral energy radiating into the African continent'.[13]

To understand the idealism and zeal behind this initiative one needs to recognise what Africa meant at the time: it was seen as a challenge to men devoted to philanthropy, religion and reform. Sir James Stephen stated that the Sect perceived the earth as the scene of conflict between light and darkness: 'on one side, science and religion – on the other, war and superstition.'[14] Africa was also a mystery (India by contrast was very well known). Africa was the Dark Continent, morally as well as geographically, as emerges in these words of William Jowett, a CMS missionary: 'Even the geographer, whose task lies merely with the surface of the land and sea, confesses that all he has to show of Africa is but as *the hem of a garment!*'[15]

Emily Kilvert recorded that the missions of Sierra Leone and Abeokuta were of special interest to her mother. Stirring as the story of Sierra Leone was to a Moravian and Quaker like Mrs Kilvert, that of Abeokuta contained even more triumphs and disasters, heroes and villains, to keep her ladies' eyes on their needlework and their ears on the missionary reports being read aloud. In the 1830s, Egba tribes people, fleeing from slave-traders, took refuge around a high isolated rock called 'Olumo'; their settlement they called Abeokuta (meaning 'under the rock').[16] Some Yoruba tribesmen belonging to the Egba branch of the Yoruba people, who had earlier settled in Sierra Leone, emigrated to Abeokuta. A detailed account of its CMS mission, known as the Yoruba mission, established in 1844 and occupying 'a foremost place in the interest and sympathies of the Society's circle of friends',[17]

appeared in 1859. Mrs Kilvert may have known it. It was written by
Sarah Tucker, whose brother was the well-known Rev. John Tucker,
Secretary of the Madras CMS mission and later of the CMS itself.[18]
To Miss Tucker, the links between Abeokuta and Sierra Leone were
wonders in which God's hand was visible: 'The entire history of this
remarkable colony [showed] realities . . . more romantic than day-
dreams "that float in visions round the poet's head"'. Education and
civilisation had converted many 'enslaved and degraded negroes into
men of enterprise and intelligence'.[19]

For CMS workers and supporters the Abeokuta mission had almost
mythical significance. Ajayi noted its excellent situation: '[It was] a
town judged to be ideal for applying [Fowell] Buxton's principles. It had
good communication with large neighbouring towns'. Furthermore, its
backbone was the community of two to three thousand Christianised
Sierra Leone emigrants. It therefore promised 'conversions still to come
[and] the civilisation of Africa', and it 'soon became a symbol of the
hope of Christian missionaries'. Stock noted that in the 1860s 'it was
the most popular of all the [CMS] Missions'.[20] This was partly because
it seemed marked out for God's special favour. Abeokuta's people
had fought off an attack in 1851 by the slaving King of Dahomey, a
victory that seemed a wonder because his army numbered 15,000, far
exceeding that of the Abeokutans. The victory was 'widely reported in
England, as Abeokuta was now well known and regarded with affection
in many churches and homes', according to Ajayi.[21] Abeokuta promised
to be the springboard for further missionary work in Africa.

The Kilvert family obtained regular news of African missions
from the reports 'always read aloud by Mama during the work time,
and when she got tired she would pass the book on to someone
else', in Emily Kilvert's words. The 'book' was likely to have been the
Missionary Register, begun in 1813 by Joseph Pratt, CMS Secretary.
It gave information about all missionary societies and resulted in
bulky volumes (the 1820 one has 540 pages). 'From 1813 to 1855 one
could obtain from it almost all the materials for a General History of
Missions'.[22] Quoted in the 1842 *Missionary Register* was this statement
from the 41st Report of the CMS: 'The importance of interesting our
Youth in the cause of Missions has been strongly impressed on the
Committee'. To promote this endeavour, Juvenile Associations were
being recommended to Assistant Secretaries and a monthly journal,
the *CMS Juvenile Instructor*, was being produced.[23] This was the ethos
in which the Kilvert children were raised. African missionaries were
heroes, as Pratt emphasised in 1816: 'The devoted Missionary is the
greatest character in the Church of Christ'.[24]

Missionary reports gave details of the illnesses and deaths, including obituaries, of missionaries. The Kilvert children could therefore build pictures of these heroic men and women in their minds, a process assisted by the letters from missionaries or their wives that some members of Mrs Kilvert's group brought to be read aloud. Emily confessed that she liked those 'much better than the rather dry reports'. Evangelicals generally distrusted fiction, but factual accounts of missionary lives could possess all the drama and excitement of novels. Furthermore, these lives were interwoven consistently with tales of African explorers, with what Brodie called 'the magic lure of African exploration'.[25] That Kilvert had become fascinated by African explorers, particularly if they were also evangelicals, is clear from the number of references to them in the *Diary*. On his Cornish holiday, for example, he noted the statue of Lander, who discovered the source of the Niger in 1830.[26]

Another explorer in whom Kilvert seems to have had considerable interest was John Hanning Speke, whose family was a local one for the Kilverts since his elder brother, William, lived at Monk's Park, Corsham, six miles from Langley Burrell. Kilvert's interest appears in the *Diary* entry for 9 August 1871 when he was staying with his uncle Will in Hawkchurch, Dorset. In the 'Cups' pub in Lyme Regis, the barmaid told of several rooms booked there by George Fuller, Speke's cousin, who also lived in Corsham. As Kilvert left the pub he saw a 'drag with seven ladies and gentlemen on the roof'. Close familiarity with the Speke family informs his next observation: 'We thought they had possibly come by Ilminster and Jordans and that the Benjamin Spekes might be among the party'. Jordans was the parental home of the Speke brothers in Somerset and Benjamin was Rector of nearby Dowlish Wake. Some of this information came no doubt from Kilvert's uncle Will, who was with him, but some would have been Kilvert's own.

Interest in African exploration reached a new height in the 1850s and 1860s and the travels of Speke and Richard Burton were at its centre. The interior of Africa was an enigma, all the more tantalising because of reports by natives and Arab traders of huge mountain ranges and 'inland seas'. Stock wrote of 'a provisional map of Equatorial Africa' made by Erhart in 1855, which was full of uncertainties and which led to the 1857 expedition by Speke and Burton. Elements in Speke's background and character made him more of an explorer than Burton, who was really an ethnographer and anthropologist. Born in 1827, Speke's family was part clerical, part military, and part mercantile.[27] From the many natural objects he collected, he intended to create an extensive museum of natural history at home. In a letter of May 1857, at which time he was exploring Lake Tanganyika with

Burton, he stated that his interests in hunting, collecting, and mapping had led him 'instinctively' to geographical research.[28] During his 1856-8 journeys, he discovered a large lake he named 'Nyanza Victoria', a feat that won him the Royal Geographical Society's Founder's medal in May 1859.[29] He would have come to Kilvert's attention for these reasons but also because after his triumph he stayed at the Corsham home of his brother William between early September and early November 1859, some of which time was spent preparing articles on his exploits for *Blackwood's Magazine* (September-November 1859 and May-July 1860). Kilvert would have admired a man who wrote: 'The missionaries are the prime and first promoters of this discovery. They have for years been doing their utmost . . . to Christianise this Negro land'.[30] Speke not only had 'an urgent desire to expose the natives of central Africa to the Christian faith' but also saw the potentiality for commercial development; the region was a wonderfully 'fertile zone' that could be enhanced by trade and European know-how.[31] Developments at the Sierra Leone colony and Abeokuta, so important and inspiring to Mrs Kilvert and her family, were in a sense background to the drama of African exploration.

To believers in missions, such as Sarah Tucker, Abeokuta was self-evidently a triumph. She wrote of 1847 as a year of 'steady progress': a church was opened early on, with mud walls, floor, and seats, in which 150 to 200 could be accommodated; four other places of worship also existed. In 1850 Henry Venn, CMS Secretary, had sent out to an Abeokuta missionary cotton gins for natives and could boast in 1859 that 200 to 300 were then in use. Seven thousand natives attended public worship in Sierra Leone by 1842 and there were fifty schools with 6,000 pupils.[32] Miss Tucker was proud to record that presents had been sent by the Queen and Prince Albert to native chiefs in Abeokuta, who had earlier written to their majesties. The Queen's reply stated: 'The commerce between nations, in exchanging the fruits of the earth, and each other's industry, is blessed by God'.[33]

The substitution of lawful commercial trade for slave-trading had long been the cornerstone of the abolition movement. As the latter trade was suppressed in the Yoruba country, Lagos became such a thriving open port that it was likened at the time to Liverpool. Native chiefs were encouraged to persuade their people to cultivate the ground and products such as arrowroot, ginger, cotton, coffee, palm-oil, and pepper were shipped to Britain, facilitated by a London committee which included Lord Shaftesbury and Sir Robert Inglis. The Abeokuta mission thus appealed to the Kilverts because it fostered the arts of civilisation urged in *Old England, Masterman Ready*, and *Evenings at Home*.

It is quite common to find in the history of the CMS names of significance in the history of the Kilverts. For example, the list of CMS Vice-Presidents in 1841 who served alongside Inglis included Dr Symons, Warden of Wadham College when Kilvert was a student, Richard Lynch Cotton who entered Worcester College, Oxford, the same day as uncle Francis Kilvert and who became throughout his life 'his attached friend',[34] and Dr Macbride, Principal of Magdalen Hall, Oxford, friend and mentor of Kilvert's friend, the Rev. Thomas Webb. (Macbride was approached on 22 July 1822 by Lewis Dillwyn regarding a tutor for his son John.) Another example is William Walsham How, whose sermons (e.g. *Plain Words*) were favoured by Kilvert[35] and who offered him the Chaplaincy of Cannes in June 1878. How became Secretary of the Oxford CMS Association (founded 1825). The *Diary* entry for 23 January 1870 provides another telling example. Kilvert heard Dr Charles John Vaughan (1816-1897) preach at the Temple in London and expressed strong approval. Vaughan's father, the Rev. E.J. Vaughan, was described by Stock as 'one of the ablest of the Evangelical clergy, and his work for the missionary cause at Leicester became a pattern . . . for imitation'.[36] At Rugby School, Charles Vaughan's 'chief friend' was George Lynch Cotton, whose life Kilvert was reading on 20 March 1871, and who came from the same family as uncle Francis's 'attached friend'.[37] Cotton had significance for Kilvert chiefly for his development of schools in India as Bishop of Calcutta, a post he took up after his headmastership of Marlborough College, which he left in 1858, three years before Edward Kilvert became a pupil there.

If ever there was an African missionary or explorer whom Kilvert would have adopted as his particular hero as he was growing up it was David Livingstone. The life of the former ran in parallel with the African exploits of the latter. Throughout Kilvert's life, those exploits were controversial, exciting and, above all, were always in the news. Livingstone, from a working-class background of industry and Calvinistic piety, eager to advance himself by education and to bring Christianity to the Dark Continent, was of the heroic mould admired by the Kilverts. Only two references to Livingstone have survived in the Plomer edition of the *Diary*. On 4 November 1874 Kilvert reviewed 'the events of the last seven months' in a winter evening lecture at Langley Burrell school and dwelt on 'the funeral of Dr Livingstone'. Livingstone had been buried in Westminster Abbey on 18 April 1874 and it is hard to believe that Kilvert would not have commemorated the occasion.[38] (There are no entries between 15 and 21 April in the Plomer edition.) The other *Diary* reference to the explorer is 14 December 1874, when Kilvert took Langley Burrell schoolchildren to Chippenham's

Temperance Hall to see 'a Panorama of the African travels of Dr Livingstone'. The children's favourite picture was of his funeral when 'the Abbey was first shown empty. Then by a slight dioramic effect or dissolving view the open space in the Nave gradually melted into the forms of the funeral party'. Even in death, Livingstone continued to provide interest for the media of the day.

The Chippenham panorama was accompanied by a lecture from a missionary who, Kilvert explained, had been with Livingstone 'on his first journey from Kurumba'. 'Kurumba' is a transcription error for Kuruman, in South Africa's Northern Cape, where Livingstone arrived on 31 July 1841. His *Missionary Travels* (*MT*),[39] which Kilvert must have known, begins with his residence there, and was the site of a mission belonging to the London Missionary Society (LMS), Livingstone's employer. He stayed in the Kuruman home of Rogers Edwards (1795-1877), another LMS missionary, whose lecture Kilvert heard in Chippenham. From October 1841, Edwards and Livingstone embarked on two long journeys from Kuruman.

Potential for evangelising further north existed in the fact that its native chiefs welcomed Europeans, and Livingstone set off on a 700-mile journey, arriving back at Kuruman in late 1843. All the while he pursued scientific enquiries into native illnesses and their treatment, climatic change, flora and fauna, and diet. In May 1845 he was sending home geological specimens to Professor Buckland and anatomical ones to Professor Owen. A Victorian biographer of Livingstone stated: '[He] may be said to have initiated the scientific exploration of Central Africa by the European race'.[40] One of his greatest achievements in African exploration was the epic journey, beginning on 11 November 1853, when he pushed north to Linyanti, arriving at Loanda (now Luanda) on Africa's Atlantic coast on 31 May 1854, a journey no European had ever undertaken. Returning to Linyanti, he began exploring the Zambezi in late 1855 and discovered its tremendous falls, which he named the Victoria Falls, referred to by Johnston as 'one of the wonders of the world'.[41] Livingstone himself wrote of them:

> The whole scene was extremely beautiful. . . . It had never been seen before by European eyes; but scenes so lovely must have been gazed upon by angels in their flight. . . . The entire falls are simply a crack made in a hard basaltic rock from the right to the left bank of the Zambesi . . . the most wonderful sight I had witnessed in Africa.[42]

Livingstone's picture of the Falls as a glimpse of Paradise shows that he shaped his account for his audience.[43] From the Zambezi, he then travelled east, finally arriving at Quilimane on the Mozambique coast on 25 May 1856. He had crossed Africa from coast to coast, a journey of 11,000 miles, 'in Jeal's view today's equivalent of landing on the moon, with Livingstone as 'a kind of Victorian astronaut'.[44]

Kilvert, like everyone in Britain, was able to read in newspapers and missionary magazines reports of Livingstone's travels before he arrived in the country on 9 December 1856. His return visit must have been of overwhelming significance for the Kilvert family, bringing together as it did many of the events, movements, issues, and personalities of vital importance to it. The dates of his stay in Britain – December 1856 to March 1858 – coincided with an important period of Kilvert's adolescence. He was entering on the final phase of his schooling at Claverton Lodge which, though a small, closeted world, had always looked to distant horizons. Britain was to welcome as a hero a man who had journeyed to those horizons, and even extended them. If Kilvert had not already pasted into his scrapbook one of the pictures of Livingstone, widely available in journals of the day, he would do so shortly after December 1856, for it saw the emergence of the myth of the missionary- explorer.

Blaikie explained the 'remarkable effect' of Livingstone's return visit on British public opinion about Africa. Firstly, it caused 'a revolution of ideas as to the interior of the country . . . instead of a vast sandy desert, it was . . . a rich and productive land'.[45] This chapter began with Legh Richmond's African quarter of the world's map presenting 'a mass of gloom' to the 'Christian geographer', and Kilvert pictured as just such a geographer, who showed special interest as a teacher in geography and maps. Richmond's point is brought home by comparing two maps of Africa south of the equator: one from 1840, the year Kilvert was born, before Livingstone's journeys, and one from 1874 incorporating them. The former shows largely coastal locations – bays, mouths of rivers and parts of their inland courses – some lakes, very few towns. The latter shows the routes of Livingstone's journeys, numerous towns, extensive river networks, waterfalls, and several large lakes. Detail is still sparse but the overall advance is impressive. The 1840 map is from the *London Atlas of Modern Geography* by John Arrowsmith.[46] When, in 1845, Augustus Hare wanted to convey the boredom of Robert Kilvert's history lessons, he said they were what Arrowsmith's description of Central Africa *used* to be, that is, before Livingstone brought light into the Dark Continent: 'a barren country only productive of dates'. Peter Barber wrote of Livingstone: 'His surveys of previously uncharted lands caused major revelations in Britain, bringing the Victorian public such sights as the Victoria Falls and the Rwenzoris – the fabled "Mountains of the Moon".'[47]

MT, which Livingstone wrote at breakneck speed in 1857, was a vital component in the myth that developed around him. Louise Henderson emphasised that the book, being the product of several hands both in its writing and illustrations, was essentially a carefully 'packaged' account.[48] It was published in November 1857 to a reception almost unparalleled in the nineteenth century. 12,000 copies were sold immediately, rising to 25,000 by mid-December. Seven editions followed. Livingstone became a celebrity not simply by virtue of his achievements but of the efforts of 'Victorian myth-makers [who] made it their business to profit from turning individual explorers into heroes or villains'.[49] The key element in this process, Henderson stressed, was *print*, whose products could now reach a mass readership. Newspaper and journal reports shaped explorers' images during their travels as reports reached home but the shaping continued once they were home because explorers were expected to respond to reports already received. One main means to this end was the explorer's own account of his travels and Livingstone's *MT* 'created his reputation as a heroic explorer who made contributions to geography, medicine and science, the abolition of the slave trade, [and] missionary endeavours'.[50]

Although the book was 'a publishing sensation' (Henderson's words), sections of the public felt concern that it was more the work of a geographer or scientist than of a missionary, and hence its title was misleading. The Kilverts might have shared these concerns but would have been pleased by its wide range of information of a geographical and scientific kind, as well as by the exciting, sensational details of exotic creatures that were part of the book's popular appeal. It was that appeal which drew Kilvert to the lion and elephant of Wombwell's Menagerie (7 May 1872) and to the 'Blue Mare . . . elephant-tailed, from Africa' at the Crystal Palace (18 January 1870). Pettit underlined the varied appeal of *MT*: '[It was] a curious amalgam of heroic adventure story, scientific observation, anthropological encounter, quest narrative and campaign literature'.[51] It had affinities, therefore, with the novels of Marryat and R.M. Ballantyne that Kilvert enjoyed. Its sensational aspects led the *New York Courier and Examiner* to call it 'a wonder-book all through' (quoted by Pettit).

Livingstone was being fêted as a hero on this first return to Britain at a time when national morale badly needed a boost. The slaughter and incompetence of the Crimean War was a very recent memory and murmurs of rebellion were being heard in India. Various honours were lavished on Livingstone. On 15 December 1856, the RGS had a special meeting to welcome him; he was the key figure in the 1857 BAAS gathering in Dublin; Oxford University conferred the degree of LL.D on him, and he was made F.R.S. He gave speeches in several cities and his meeting in 1857 with Prince Albert was followed by one with the Queen in 1858. To the Kilvert family, this honouring of a missionary, a man they regarded as one of their own, must have been deeply gratifying. Their vision of what Africa might be, symbolised by Abeokuta, was that much nearer realisation because of him. 'Central Africa became a focus of national interest – political, mercantile and missionary',[52] because of him.

Livingstone had been impressed by the idea of combining trade with religion when he heard it from Fowell Buxton at the 1840 Exeter Hall meeting of the Society for the Extinction of the Slave Trade. The success Livingstone enjoyed in Britain in 1857 was a matter of timing in an economic, as well as a political, sense: Britain's industries were booming and his urging of manufacturers to trade with Africa was well received. 'Commerce and Christianity . . . together become civilisation' was his message to audiences in 1857 and his 'coupling of divine and economic virtues made him still more popular'.[53] Not only was this the message Kilvert had assimilated from the Abeokuta mission, *Old England*, *The Leisure Hour*, and the *Penny Post*, but it underpinned Hine's exciting thesis of Britain as the foremost religious and mercantile power, expanding into her colonies, always with 'the great missionary work in hand'.

Kilvert's support for missions was steady and consistent. There are no references to any CMS meetings at Clyro Church in his diary, probably because Venables vetoed them. In the 27 October 1874 entry, when Kilvert was acting as his father's curate at Langley Burrell, after a CMS meeting Kilvert expressed great pride, that they had raised £18.11s for the cause in the past year – about £800 'today. He was also delighted by the turnout – 'nearly 150 people must have been present . . . all most attentive', even the boys, who could be rowdy. These CMS meetings occurred regularly for 'Mr Barne spoke well *as usual*' (my italics). Four years later when Kilvert was Vicar of Bredwardine he could record, after a CMS lecture by his father, 'We have raised for all such missionary work this year . . . nearly £14'. Robert Kilvert appears in the role of Christian geographer (with his faith in the efficacy of pictures) in Kilvert's observation: 'Father spoke and showed the people some CMS pictures about missionary work . . . which seemed to interest them much.' A few days earlier Kilvert had attended a talk by Father Douglas, who was going out to a mission in Bloemfontein.

Soon British drawing-rooms would have another exciting topic to discuss in the wake of *MT*. Livingstone's speaking tour of British cities during 1857, on the theme of 'Christianity, Commerce, Civilisation', took him to Cambridge. The Rev. William Monk, curate of Christ Church in that city, had met the explorer in May 1857 and pressed him to visit the University. He duly arrived on 3 December 1857 – Kilvert's birthday. In the light of what ensued, Kilvert would have seen this as Providential. On 4 December, Livingstone gave a lecture to the University in the Senate House and stressed that the CMS was short of missionaries. The sort of men needed were those of his audience, and the lecture closed with this stirring appeal: 'I go back to Africa to try to make an open path for commerce and Christianity; do you carry out the work I have begun. *I leave it with you*'.[54]

When Emily Kilvert emphasised how long her family had supported the Abeokuta mission, she stated that it existed 'long before the Universities' Mission to Central Africa' (UMCA).[55] She was referring to the body that grew out of Livingstone's Cambridge University lecture. In fact the particular incentive to the UMCA's foundation came in the 1858 visit to Britain of Bishop Grey of Cape Town on a campaign to recruit missionaries for South Africa. He met Monk and heard of the support in the University for a mission in the area of Livingstone's recent travels. Out of the Cambridge Committee formed from their meetings emerged the UMCA. At a Cambridge meeting on 1 November 1859 Charles Frederick Mackenzie, then Archdeacon of Pietermaritzburg (Natal), was present and was invited to lead the UMCA Mission.

Livingstone meanwhile, having resigned from the LMS and having heard of the explorations of Burton and Speke, and eager to reassert his influence in Africa, had left Liverpool on 10 March 1858 to explore Eastern and Central Africa. He went on HMS *Pearl* by way of Sierra Leone and the Cape, on what was the beginning of his Zambezi Expedition, during which he was much more explorer than missionary. He was also under Government instructions to use guns to obtain natural history specimens. While one of his main aims was the establishment of an English colony, he also intended to survey the Zambezi for the purpose of commercial exploitation. His plan included that symbol of technological progress, the steamer. He could see steamers plying Africa's lakes and rivers, likening them in *MT* to Thames steamers. He had gone to the Zambezi with the *Ma Robert*[56] paddle steamer (carried in sections on HMS *Pearl*). It was an experimental vessel, built by Laird's, the Birkenhead yard visited by Kilvert in June 1872. It was badly designed. Johnston wrote of it: 'it was an unsuccessful experiment. She was built of thin steel plates . . . in which some chemical action of the water caused minute holes to appear. . . . The bottom of the ship soon became like a sieve.'[57] She consumed vast amounts of wood, was underpowered, and kept sticking on the bottom. The failure of the *Ma Robert* epitomised the failure of Livingstone's Zambezi Expedition. The river proved unnavigable, and neither the proposed colony nor the commercial exploitation of the region took place. Furthermore, the UMCA expedition ended in tragedy. Mackenzie and six missionaries arrived from England on 31 January 1861 and Livingstone helped to establish the mission during that year. However, the site chosen was unsuitable, food in short supply, and too far from a river for fresh supplies to be bought in. Little missionary work was done and the party struggled simply to survive. Mackenzie and others died of fever in early 1862.

To the Kilverts, the UMCA disaster and Livingstone's setbacks on the Zambezi, though disappointing, are hardly likely to have dimmed his reputation in their eyes. He would have remained the supreme Christian hero. It is important here to underline that the years of *MT*, the UMCA, the Zambezi Expedition, Livingstone's emergence as national hero and media celebrity were critical years for Kilvert. He finished his schooling, and spent three and a half years at Oxford. He was still at Wadham in mid-July 1862 when the Church Congress met in Oxford.

In the summer of 1864 Livingstone made his second visit home, 'to less than a hero's welcome'.[58] If Kilvert had been keeping his diary in 1864 he would have been able to record a local event of momentous significance: the BAAS Meeting in Bath. The programme began on 14 September with Lyell's Inaugural Address and ended on 21 September with the General Meeting. Section E of the Meeting – Geography and Ethnology – promised drama and controversy. Famous explorers featured in it: J.M. Stuart, the first man to cross Australia from south to north, Henry Bates, the Amazon naturalist, and Dr Livingstone himself. But the real draw was the confrontation on the 16th between Burton and Speke, the local man, over the source of the Nile, 'the holy grail of Victorian geography'.[59] The latter believed Lake Victoria was its source while the former argued in favour of Lake Tanganyika. Furthermore, 'it was common knowledge that the two men hated each other'.[60] Livingstone was interested in the question of the Nile's source and therefore felt a rivalry over this issue with Burton and Speke but was hostile to both men on other grounds.

People who were not BAAS members could attend the Meeting by becoming 'Associates' for the cost of £1. The *Bath Chronicle*, in one of its 'Special Daily Editions', stated that the total (record) attendance by Associates was 1,069, plus 1,036 ladies. The name of Kilvert's aunt Sophia does not appear in the lists of Associates that appeared in the *Chronicle*. Such friends of her recently deceased husband as

H.D. Skrine and the Rev. Scarth were Associates in 1864, as were John, George, and Richard Stothert. Francis Henry Falkner, cousin of Kilvert's father, is shown as a BAAS member. Kilvert's name is absent from both Associates and Members lists.

In his lecture on the 19th September, Livingstone intended to attack Portugal's role in the slave trade. This was controversial enough. What happened on the 16th, the date of the Burton/Speke debate, was even more so. The *Chronicle* report stated that at 11 o'clock, when the meeting should have begun, and the room was crowded with ladies and gentlemen 'radiant with the hope of seeing Dr Livingstone and calm in the assurance that Captain Speke and Captain Burton would be there', the platform was still vacant. The audience became restive. Then Murchison appeared accompanied only by Burton. The former announced that Speke had been killed the previous day in a hunting accident. It appeared that when climbing a wall and pulling his shotgun up after him, it had gone off with the muzzle close to his body. At the inquest the death was judged an accident, though rumours of suicide persisted.

The sensational events of the 1864 BAAS Meeting in Bath illustrate again the way African explorers had become media celebrities. Earlier chapters have shown that Kilvert and his family had welcomed technological developments which could provide the cheap books, journals, and pictures essential to the education of the masses and to the promotion of 'the arts of living'. Kilvert had taken particular interest in the electric telegraph and the undersea cable by which events in remote places in the world were transmitted instantaneously to the drawing-room. It was news reports of Livingstone's exploits in Africa that had made him and that continent the focus of public concern and excitement. Pettit asserted that 'without Stanley and the famous meeting, we would probably not remember Livingstone'. The meeting became important because it was 'the first sensational news story to break simultaneously on both sides of the Atlantic', made possible by the Atlantic cable, and making Livingstone into a 'global celebrity'.[61] Kilvert had grown up with tales of Livingstone's African journeys and with the story of the development of Abeokuta, conveyed with increasing detail and speed as the years went by, and together they fuelled his passion for the anti-slavery and the missionary causes. Devotion to them was far easier when information about missionary and explorer heroes was readily available via the telegraph to bolster faith and hope. It was easier to be a 'Christian geographer' when improved communication and improved maps facilitated the penetration of the Dark Continent.

Chapter 12

'Plunging into Ancient Chaos': Kilvert and Evolution

> Man is not a thing of yesterday; nor a thing of 6,000 years
> ago. Whether he came from stocks or stones, from nebulous
> gas or solar fire, I know not. But, however obscure man's
> origin may be, his growth is not to be denied.
>
> John Tyndall, Address to the Students of University
> College, London given in 1868

When uncle Francis Kilvert recommended his friend Henry Moule
as tutor for Lewis Dillwyn's son in 1823, Moule had yet to make
his reputation as a devoted and enlightened parish priest. Moule
campaigned for better sanitation in the cottages of his Fordington
(Dorset) parishioners, which was partly what Kilvert meant when
he referred to the 'improvements' Moule had made. He also knew of
Moule's selfless work during the outbreaks of cholera in 1849 and 1853
in the parish. His zeal for sanitary reform made him the forerunner
(he was born in 1801) of another campaigner in that field – Kingsley
(born 1819) – and another of Kilvert's heroes. Kingsley was a hard-
working, caring priest of the Moule stamp.[1] In this final chapter, which
will examine where Kilvert stood in relation to the most crucial issue
of his time – evolution, Kingsley will figure prominently.
When Kilvert wrote on Kingsley's death 'We could ill spare him', he was
acknowledging Kingsley's influence on him. Kilvert had just arrived at
Wadham College in 1859 when Kingsley, earlier seen by the Church as
a dangerous radical, began to be accepted by the establishment. That
year he preached before the Queen and Prince Albert and became one
of her chaplains. In 1860 he was appointed Professor of Modern History
(Kilvert's degree subject) at Cambridge. *Alton Locke* is the only Kingsley
book we know for certain Kilvert read, but we may assume that there
were others. His writings were important to Kilvert *inter alia* because
they expressed a middle-class identity. In Kingsley's *The Wonders
of the Shore* (1855), we find an Evangelical clergyman attempting to
reconcile science's findings with natural theology. He rejected scientific
materialism by insisting that 'a Mind presides over the universe, and not

a mere brute necessity, a Law without a Lawgiver'. Kilvert too approved this idea – that natural laws were threads in God's hands – when he heard it from Dr Alexander in Bath (and from Sedgwick). Kingsley believed that God created every new species; the theory that there had been any 'development of species was unsupported by experiment and induction'. However, each new species was 'a development of the idea on which the older species were created', Kingsley wrote, struggling to clarify his partial acceptance of evolution. Geology had, he said, disproved 'the old popular belief' that the universe was created 'by a single fiat, we know the work had to be gradual. . . . Let us say boldly that there has been "a progress of species" . . . beautiful enough to keep us our lives long in wonder'.[2] Later, we shall see how he presented an idealised picture of the evolution of civilised man.

We have seen that Kilvert wanted Africa to be opened up by missionaries and traders so that its unknown areas, which contained both wonders and horrors, could be brought within the realm of civilisation. When he gave Ballantyne's The Gorilla Hunters to ten-year-old Hugh Thomas, he was once more in the role of teacher. Ballantyne's novel, heavily influenced by Marryat's writing, reflects Kilvert's own interest in natural history in one of its heroes, Ralph, who declares at the start: 'I am a naturalist . . . only an amateur [but] . . . I have made one or two not unimportant discoveries'. Published in 1861, the book contains many of the key preoccupations and debates of the time and, though cast in the form of an adventure story, constitutes a programme of study, a main aspect of which is the issue of the animal-human boundary.[3] As a young person, Kilvert had lived through the stirring period that The Gorilla Hunters recorded (it was another period of 'Yeast') and wanted Hugh Thomas to experience it too.

Kilvert was only fifteen in 1856 when the famous anatomist Professor Richard Owen was attacking Huxley's scientific naturalism for encouraging a pagan response to Nature, thereby undermining natural theology. In Desmond's words: 'The moral purpose behind Owen's science is clear: to prove that Man was in the Divine Mind at the time of Creation'.[4] Owen was especially concerned to oppose the idea that creatures had evolved from simple to complex. His study of apes, particularly the gorilla in 1849, led him to deny that man could have apes as ancestors. The missionary, Thomas Savage, the first white man to have seen a gorilla, described it in 1847 as 'one of the most startling and important discoveries in the science of life on Earth, a disturbingly humanoid creature that would soon . . . play a key part in the coming debate over Darwinian evolution'.[5] Savage named the creature 'gorilla'; before that it was unnamed and known only by rumour.

No-one in England had seen a gorilla until 1858 when the corpse of a young adult male preserved in spirits arrived at the British Museum. Owen passed it to a leading taxidermist who stuffed it and it was put on display. Lewis Dillwyn (junior) went there to see what he called 'the gorilla ape' on 17 April 1859. An *ILN* article (9 April 1859) referred to 'a new specimen' exhibited at the Crystal Palace. The writer probed the similarity of its face to that of a human but eagerly pointed out that its 'most brutal character . . . entirely destroys the slight resemblance to the human countenance'. More savage characteristics are emphasised: its eyes 'flared with a baleful emerald light when its fierce passions were aroused'. Ballantyne was capitalising on this public interest when he published *The Gorilla Hunters* in 1861. He knew the *ILN* article because his book paraphrased that part of it which told of gorillas' alleged habit of lurking in trees and picking up men and strangling them. Peterkin, who insists that there is no such creature as a gorilla, argues that native stories of it have made him sceptical. Ralph however states that he has seen a gorilla skeleton in London. Peterkin believes that could have been a fake – 'a compound of the bones of a buffalo and a chimpanzee'. To Jack, the native stories only confirm the existence of gorillas' because in Africa, 'where so many wonderful and horrible animals exist, men are not naturally tempted to invent *new* creatures' (his italics). The stories of 'the huge baboon, the man-monkey' have made Peterkin 'determined to shoot a gorilla, or prove him to be a myth'.

Apart from myth and mystery, Ballantyne cleverly exploits other main elements of the gorilla issue for the entertainment and education of his young readers. Once our heroes have arrived in Africa, the crucial theme of the age and origin of man becomes prominent. The 'silence and solitude' of the jungle – where they are to encounter their first gorilla – elicit from Peterkin the reflection 'I feel as if we had got to the fag end of the world, as if we were about plunging into ancient chaos'. Attention is drawn to the primitive stage of development of African natives: 'all the nigger tribes are sunk in gross and cruel superstition'. Their capacity to learn is focused by the character Makarooroo, who has 'picked up something of English and a trifle of geography and arithmetic' at a missionary school, in spite of his 'thick skull'. This is part of a general discussion on man's capacity to make progress intellectually and morally. Civilised European values are generally contrasted with uncivilised native ones, and Christianity is seen as the basis of a truly moral nature.

Negroes are pictured in Ballantyne's book as human but more akin to animals. The son of a native chief is acknowledged to be 'a very fine little fellow, despite the blackness of his skin'. (Kilvert was sensitive to the

issue of blackness, noting on 29 February 1872 that Clyro folk thought
that the Indian Army husband of his sister Emily was 'a darkey'.)[6] One
discussion of the issue of differences between man and animals in *The
Gorilla Hunters* – sustained throughout by the running joke that Jack,
who is large, is really a gorilla – includes Peterkin's declaration 'men are
not beasts'; he then emphasises that a gorilla *is* a beast (and not therefore
an ancestor of man). It is pictured as 'a terrible creature', 'a possessed
brute', 'a monster with a satanic visage'.[7] When a gorilla is confronted,
Ballantyne stresses its resemblance to a man but one given over to evil:
it is 'a human fiend', yet Ralph finds affecting its resemblance to human
beings. He is also so affected by the care shown by a female gorilla to
her baby that he stops Makarooroo from killing the pair.

Fascination with similarities between the behaviour of man and
monkey appears in several *Diary* entries. Kilvert quoted a letter
from his sister Emily in India which pictured 'Chin Chin (the
monkey) . . . taking her accustomed constitutional at the end of her
chain' (2 February 1874). On 13 July 1875 he 'wondered at the antics of
the monkey which was chained in the middle of the lawn' at the Isle of
Wight home of Mrs Cowper Coles. Stories about the anthropomorphic
baboon at Maesllwch Castle 'grow more and more extraordinary',
Kilvert wrote on 16 August 1872. It had attacked visitors, dropped
kittens from towers (as though it was jealous of them), and was believed
to have a plan to 'serve the young heir in the same way'.[8]

The question of exactly how similar a gorilla was to a man tended
to resolve itself into a concern with sexual behaviour. 'From its very
first appearance in Victorian Britain, the gorilla was represented as a
rapacious sexual creature', wrote Dawson.[9] He was referring primarily
to the work of the French/American explorer and anthropologist Paul
Du Chaillu (1835-1903), who travelled West Africa between 1856 and
1859 observing gorillas. The area was almost completely unknown to
Europeans and he could present the gorilla as a wonder in his book
Explorations and Adventures in Equatorial Africa (1861), which caused
a sensation. Gorillas are the subject of eleven of its twenty-six chapters.
Its frontispiece showed a ferocious, snarling gorilla in the jungle, an
overhanging branch conveniently but suggestively hiding its sexual
organs. The stuffed gorillas displayed at his London lectures also had
their sexual organs removed.

Ballantyne's *The Gorilla Hunters* borrowed extensively from
Du Chaillu. Its emphasis on natives' low stage of development,
condemnation of their superstitions alongside a stance combining
affection with contempt, admiration for gorillas' maternal instincts,
portrayal of gorillas as human fiends – all appear in *Explorations*, often

'It had broken Jack's rifle across.'
R.M. Ballantyne's 'The Gorilla Hunters' (1863)

in very similar wording. Ballantyne also paraphrased Du Chaillu in a description questioning a gorilla's closeness in evolutionary terms to man. The former told how Ralph 'shuddered' as he looked at a gorilla's corpse 'for there was something terribly human-like about it, despite its brutishness'. The latter commented thus on a dead gorilla: 'There is enough likeness to humanity in this beast to make a dead one an awful sight'. He knew this was 'an error' but couldn't help it.[10] Ballantyne followed Du Chaillu too in remarking that killing gorillas made one feel like a murderer of one's own species. Ballantyne's firm declaration 'men are not beasts' corresponds to Du Chaillu's '[there is] a vast chasm . . . between even the lowest forms of the human race and the highest of the apes'.[11]

In the discussion of racial differences encouraged by the gorilla question, the case of the Irish loomed large. The establishment in Britain tended to blame the poverty of the Irish on their own lack of industry, initiative and moral probity. As a race, they were compared to negroes and portrayed frequently in cartoons as monkeys. On a tour of Ireland, Kingsley referred in a letter to his wife of seeing Irish 'chimpanzees'. An article in *Punch* in 1862 characterised the Irish as the 'Missing Link' and stated that creatures somewhere between the gorilla and the negro could be encountered in the poorest districts of London and Liverpool. In Kilvert's frequent references to Irish people there is an awareness of these issues. While dining at Venables's vicarage on 14 January 1872, he admitted to being 'convulsed by Captain Adam's stories of the manners and customs of the Irish'. Generally, the *Diary* entries about them are sympathetic, as on 21 June 1872 when he recorded how Liverpool had left him with 'an impression of ragged Irish bare-footed women and children'. On 14 September 1872 he travelled on a train with an Irish squire and 'a family of the fairest noblest looking boys . . . and a noble looking mother'. Here he was determined the reject the stereotype of the Irish as a degraded race. His admiration for Irish Mary – beautiful and capable of beautiful music, and of inspiring beautiful passion – becomes more significant in this context, as does the group of Irish people that was referred to in an earlier chapter as the 'Irish connection' in his life.[12]

An event took place at Oxford University in June 1860 which would have been a watershed in Kilvert's education, and indeed in his entire development, particularly in relation to his understanding of the nature and origins of man. He had just embarked on his course at Wadham (only two terms completed). Darwin's *Origin of Species* had been published during Kilvert's first term – in November 1859. What Browne and Messenger referred to as 'the gorilla craze [which] made Du Chaillu's name and brought those huge beasts into the Darwinian uproar',[13] had in many ways prepared Kilvert for the momentous event of 30 June 1860 – the debate between Bishop Wilberforce and Huxley during the BAAS Meeting (Botany/Zoology Section) in the newly finished University Museum, 'the shrine to nature's God'.[14] Professor Draper spoke first on a Buckle theme – the application of

Darwin's views to the progress of society. An audience of between 700 and 1,000, made up of clergy, dons, teachers of science, ladies, and undergraduates, eagerly anticipated the speech of Samuel Wilberforce, Bishop of Oxford, who had been contemporary at Oriel College with Kilvert's father,[15] because Wilberforce was expected to attack Darwin's *The Origin of Species*. Huxley, Darwin's close friend and supporter, shared the platform. The question of the descent of man from apes had been raised at a meeting on 28 June. That of 30 June shaped up to be a collision between faith and science and it was to occur in the citadel of the Anglican Church. We don't know if Kilvert was present but the thought of it must have excited him.[16]

It was rumoured that Wilberforce, known as 'Soapy Sam', had been primed the night before by Professor Owen, 'probably pushing Sam beyond Genesis miracles to a more enlightened view'.[17] Darwin's friend, Sir J.D. Hooker, related that 'the Bishop spoke for a full half an hour with indomitable spirit, emptiness and unfairness', adding that it was clear he had been 'crammed . . . and knew nothing at first hand. . . . He ridiculed Darwin badly, and Huxley savagely'.[18] The legend which grew up about the debate derived from the following alleged exchange between Wilberforce and Huxley. The Bishop asked: 'Is it on your grandfather's or your grandmother's side that you claim descent from the apes?' Huxley retorted: 'I would rather be descended from an ape than from a bishop'. Lucas, who has examined the encounter in detail, doubts that these were the words actually used,[19] as well as the legend's suggestion that Wilberforce was completely routed. The Bishop had, however, erred in introducing the idea of a grandmother as an ape, offending 'Victorian sensibilities about the sanctity of the female sex'.[20] Lucas's summing up of the encounter between Wilberforce and Huxley helps to show why it would have been a critical moment for Kilvert. It was an occasion when an attempt by the Church to dictate to scientists what they were to believe was 'decisively defeated'.[21] The exchange was 'the defining moment of the whole controversy about evolution because it harped on man and animal, bishop and baboon'.[22]

Professor Owen's resistance to the theory of evolution was based on his research with apes, dinosaurs, and the platypus, and his ideas were popular from the late 1840s to the mid-1850s. His Royal Institution lecture (19 March 1861) dealt with differences between the brain of a negro ('or lowest variety of the Human Race') and that of a gorilla. The brain diagrams he used had been shown at Du Chaillu's lecture there the previous evening. His main finding was that a small lobe, the hippocampus minor, 'is peculiar to man', and he insisted that there were 'unmistakable distinctions between the human and higher quadrumanal brains'.[23] These views were totally rejected by Huxley in a paper reproduced in Darwin's *The Descent of Man* (1871). The hippocampus was, Huxley declared, as well developed in apes' brains as in humans' and there was 'wonderfully close similarity between the chimpanzee, orang and man'.[24] Darwin, in *The Descent of Man*, was equally forthright: 'man is descended from a hairy, tailed quadruped' and 'there is no fundamental difference between man and the higher mammals in their mental faculties'.[25] Owen was completely mistaken about the hippocampus minor. He was keen to reject a materialistic theory of gradual biological change, advocating instead that God could create new species at birth, even using, for example, the womb of an ape to produce the first human. He was motivated partly by a belief in natural theology and partly by a desire to reassure gentlefolk that they were not descended from apes.

Kingsley built a vision of a society improved by the application of science, and a satirical account of the gorilla issue, into his novel, *The Water-Babies* (1863). Tom, the book's hero, is a creature of water. He has grown used, as a chimney boy, to being black but when he sees Ellie, a beautiful young lady, he yearns to be clean: 'What did such a little black ape want in that sweet young lady's room?' Kingsley continually identifies Tom with apes because of his benighted condition of dirt and ignorance, but shows the means by which it can be ameliorated. Tom hears the Fairy Queen saying 'Those that wish to be clean, clean they will be'. Kingsley's sub-title is 'A Fairy Tale for a Land-Baby'; Tom is transformed from the latter into a Water-Baby. A sceptical voice in the novel asserts 'But a water-baby is contrary to nature'; if one existed, it would have been sent, preserved in spirits (as a gorilla was), to be examined by Professor Owen. Kingsley pointed out that all kinds of wonders existed in nature, such as the elephant. Similarly, a savage might declare that there was no such thing as a locomotive 'because he had never seen one running wild in the forest'. Having given several examples of water animals that changed into land animals, he asked why the reverse could not be true. His vindication of evolution (and of natural history) concludes: 'may not man . . . undergo some change as much more wonderful than all the rest?' The birth of every human being involved transformation.

Kingsley's book is all about learning and teaching, about lessons people learn from the way they are raised, and about different ones they might learn if raised differently. Poor people caught scarlatina and diphtheria from being raised in 'nasty-smelling undrained lodgings'. He satirised the 'poor Paddy', whose habit of telling lies meant that Ireland 'does not prosper like England'. He told of St. Brendan's taming of 'the wild Irish', who did nothing but drink poteen and fight and would not learn to be 'peaceable Christians'. Those who refused to listen to St. Brendan became gorillas. Mrs Bedoneasyouwouldbedoneby gives Tom a book that shows 'what happens to people who do only what is pleasant'. These people, the Doasyoulikes, have abandoned the country of Hardwork and have become 'savages' and finally apes. They eventually died out – except for one 'tremendous old [ape]' shot by M. Du Chaillu. This was Kingsley's warning about mid-Victorian society that was embracing luxury and self-indulgence. Counteracting this degeneration were the lessons of Christianity. If Victorian society could avoid degeneration, materialism, and faithlessness, its future was bright in Kingsley's view. The *Water-Babies* employs fantasy to convey a vision of man's past and his future. The everyday world is left behind as Tom enters the world of Nature, a world of wonders in which anything can happen. He undergoes strange experiences and transformations, hears of strange places and peoples, and meets strange characters, including fairies.[26]

People in the early and mid-Victorian era struggled to conceive of 'deep time': Rudwick wrote of 'a timescale of humanly inconceivable magnitude',[27] a timescale that was without limits, without beginning or ending, and which had been glimpsed in rock strata. The visit that Kilvert said he made in 1855 to the Crystal Palace, in what was likely to have been a family outing, would have helped him to develop a conception of deep time. The Crystal Palace had moved to Sydenham on 10 June 1854, and whereas in 1851 it had housed industrial and colonial exhibits, in 1854 there were 'areas devoted to geology, ethnology, zoology and botany'.[28] Of most interest to the Kilvert children, no doubt, would have been the thirty-three concrete life-size models of dinosaurs, conceived by Professor Owen and constructed by Benjamin Waterhouse Hawkins (1807-1894).[29] What made them exciting was that they were situated on three islands, representing a time-line, and the level of the surrounding lake rose and fell to reveal dinosaurs belonging to different periods.[30]

To those people who believed in Genesis, Man had existed on the earth from its beginning. Had he existed alongside the dinosaurs whose bones were now being found? If not, a lengthy pre-human world had to be accepted, an idea deeply disturbing to those for whom the earth had meaning only because of man's presence in it. Paley's *Natural Theology* (1802) ignored all the evidence that had accumulated by the end of the eighteenth century confirming the great age of the earth. By about 1830, nearly forty years' research on fossils had established a huge timescale for the earth.[31]

Kilvert's preoccupation with the age of man surfaces in his account

Crystal Palace Dinosaurs, Benjamin Waterhouse Hawkins' studio, Sydenham

of his visit on 16 April 1872 to the Giant's Grave in Gower, 'a strange weird place – how old, no one could tell'. His visit was driven by previous knowledge, as in the case of visits to other key locations. 'These graves were uncovered a few years ago,' he noted, 'and there were found in some of them skeletons sitting upright'. 'A few years ago' must refer to the site's excavation in 1869 by Sir John Lubbock (1834-1913), whose report on it appeared in January 1871.[32] Mr Hussey Vivian, on whose property the tumulus stood, accompanied Lubbock during his excavation and recorded skeletons 'in sitting or crouching positions'. A number of factors suggest that Kilvert would have known of Lubbock. Lubbock's mother was Harriet Hotham (1810-1873), grand-daughter of Sir Beaumont Hotham, 7th Baronet. Shortly before going to Oxford Kilvert's father had tutored the son of Sir William Hotham. Furthermore, Lubbock's great-uncle John, a London banker, lived from 1787 at Clapham House, renamed Battersea Rise, home later of Sir Robert Inglis.

Kilvert knew Lubbock's *Pre-historic Times* (1865), the most popular archaeological textbook of the period. Evidence for this conclusion is the similarity between Kilvert's account of Stonehenge and Lubbock's account. The former's likening of the Stones to giants and to 'solemn and stately' dancers was likely to have come from the latter's quote from Giraldus Cambrensis: 'There was in Ireland, in ancient times, a pile of stones called the Giant's Dance'.[33] Kilvert's discussion of the age of Silbury Hill (15 April 1874) also seems influenced by Lubbock. Kilvert's friend Pinniger was keen to stress that the Roman road 'avoids Silbury Hill . . . showing that the Hill is older than the road'. This comment of Kilvert's and his additional one – 'This fact has been proved by excavation' – shows not only his grasp of archaeological methods, but also knowledge of Lubbock's observation that 'Mr Blandford, who opened the hill in 1849, came to the same conclusion'.[34] To Kilvert, Silbury Hill was a wonder: 'vast, mysterious, . . . the great problem, the world's puzzle'. He was curious about the people who had built this 'King of the Barrows'.

In Kilvert's effort to reconstruct the lives of the people buried in the Giant's Grave, he was disposed to imagine a time no older than that of the Bible. The Grave is in fact Neolithic, estimated to date from 3500 BC. However, he referred to 'the graves of the children of the people', a phrase from 2 Kings 23.6 describing how King Josiah of Judah[35] suppressed pagan cults, burnt all objects associated with them, and scattered their ashes 'on the graves of the children of the people'. It seems Kilvert wanted to associate the people of the Giant's Grave with Christianity. His curiosity about them may have derived partly from knowledge that some of them were giants.[36] Giants were a rich element in the folklore to which he had devoted much study and they surface often in the *Diary*. On 28 March 1870, he recounted a story about a fierce giant and '40 men each 7 feet high'. He prepared for his tour of Cornwall by reading Bottrell's guide to the county's legends, which frequently feature giants, one of whom in ancient times threw rocks at passing ships. The rocks eventually formed a reef thus determining the shape of the coast.

Kilvert noticed on his 16 April 1872 Gower visit, but did not enter, 'a large bone cavern' (known as Cat Hole Cave), 200 yards north of the

Giant's Grave. During his Gower holiday in June 1878, he prevailed upon his host, the Rev. Westhorp, to take him to it. The 13 June 1878 entry is very short and may originally have described the Cave more fully. All we have is Kilvert's comment: 'Westhorp could not see even "the outline of a female". The inverted commas suggest that he was quoting some source, that he could make out a drawing on the Cave wall and was irritated that Westhorp could not.[37] Even from this brief entry, the impression of the diarist's knowledge and interest is strong. The people he was trying to imagine were older than those of the Giant's Grave. A recent report states that the Cave contained Palaeolithic, Mesolithic, Beaker and Bronze Age remains, indicating long occupation.[38] There is a working area before the Cave entrance thought to have been used by hunters living 14,000 years ago. Kilvert may have known of the exploration of the Cave in 1864 by Colonel Wood, who excavated several Gower caves between 1849 and 1866. He was a friend of, and lived near to, Lewis Dillwyn (senior).[39] Kilvert knew of the Wood family, referring on 25 August 1870 to meeting Wood's son, Captain Wood, at Three Cocks Station, near Clyro.

Kilvert's preoccupation with the age of the earth was one facet of an interest in geology, which had been cultivated in his childhood. It has been noted earlier that his uncle Francis liked to spread knowledge of the *Discourse* of the geologist Sedgwick among his friends, and that pupils at uncle Francis's school were encouraged to take field trips to Hampton Rocks near Bath. Aunt Sophia Kilvert had also urged in her *Home Discipline* that geology should be one of the 'scientific amusements' of a good home. Several geologists were key figures in the BLPA, which featured geology frequently in its lecture programmes. 'The 1820s and 1830s were . . . a period of "Geological Mania"'[40] and literary and imaginative books with dramatic pictures were aimed at a predominantly middle-class readership in Kilvert's childhood. Their purpose was to 'excite a sense of wonder at God's works'.[41] Mrs Kilvert may have bought her children the enormously popular *Peter Parley's Wonders of the Earth, Sea and Sky* (1837), published by William Darton,[42] a fellow Quaker. Two of the six books Emily Kilvert listed as gifts from Mrs Hare, her godmother, were published by Darton.[43] *Peter Parley's Wonders* was just one of many geology books available at this period for children.

Another was *Caves of the Earth* (1847) by Thomas Milner, a writer for the RTS's 'Monthly Series', cheap non-fiction books launched in 1845. O'Connor has documented the strong interest shown in earth history by the RTS, *ILN*, and other periodicals Kilvert knew at the time he was growing up, constituting 'a torrent of geological prose' joined in the 1850s 'by a powerful spate of evolutionary writings'.[44] *Caves of the Earth* assumes that there had been a great flood and that the earth was unequivocally God's creation. The book deals with the geological features which, as we shall see, were focused on by Kilvert. His knowledge of geology manifests itself in two main areas: mineralogy and land forms. His awareness of such terms for mountain ranges as 'Pennine, Northern, Cambrian and Devonian' (used by him in connection with the HMI inspection of Clyro School) is one indication of his knowledge. Terms for rock strata and mountain systems were household names in the mid-nineteenth century.[45]

Mineral wealth linked to scenic beauty is the theme of Kilvert's 27 July 1870 entry about a visit to Land's End. It actually begins with a focus on industry (he knew that minerals were an important source of Britain's wealth): 'We came upon an old tin-stamping wheel and works'. Heringman noted: 'With the new demand for mineral resources, the earth's material presented itself as a foreign substance, provoking both sublime wonder and scientific curiosity'.[46] Both forms of response emerge forcefully in Kilvert's Land's End account. Its main theme is that the place's landscape is non-human, ancient, alien. He was particularly fascinated by the age of Land's End's granite and by the sea's power to shape and smash granite rocks which, as he knew, were some of the world's oldest and which endured because of their immensely hard, crystalline nature. His account incorporates an effort to take readers back to the time when the earth's surface was being formed by violent catastrophe. It presents cliffs rising there and then out of the sea as geologists pictured them doing in ages past: 'cliffs rising sheer from the ocean, rearing themselves aloft in wild fantastic masses and strange awful shapes'. The disturbing quality of this vision deepens as Kilvert dwells upon Nature's terrifying power: 'the iron granite rocks split, riven, wrenched, torn asunder, tossed and tumbled in huge piles and vast fragments'. The preoccupation with time becomes more evident: the cliffs seemed about to 'crash forward into the sea like falling towers, huge pinnacles and rocks like castle walls, rocking, staggering, . . . ruined, undermined by caverns'. Thus the very cliffs that reared up from the sea are now in danger of being cast down into it again, as in the endless cycle of change in land forms envisaged by Lyell. The sea is a force strong enough to erode even granite, reforming the coastline: 'waves wash boiling, foaming, wearing the granite away gradually and threatening to detach large masses of rock from the mainland'. He speculated on the changes that over time would be effected by the sea on the coast. 'Probably the bridge which spans the cavern will give way some day, and the present Land's End will be an island'.

Kilvert showed a concern with the evolution of the earth's surface in another entry that centred on the formation of a mountain top and on a particular kind of rock – basalt. Basalt was akin to granite because of its crystalline composition, which made it very hard. Sedgwick identified its constituent minerals as 'quartz, felspar and mica'.[47] Controversy over basalt's origin was intense in the first quarter of the nineteenth century. Lyell had argued that crystalline rocks, such as basalt and granite, were not remnants of an original molten state of the planet but could be formed at any time.[48]

Kilvert had both opportunity and reason to reflect on these issues while holidaying in North Wales in summer 1871, which he recorded in an entry of disturbing strangeness. On 13 June he ascended Cader Idris, which he depicted as a hostile place. The entry begins by recounting the death six years before of a Mr Smith, who fell to his death over a precipice (a horribly graphic description of his body – 'a skeleton in clothes' – follows). The weather was hostile: strong wind, rain and cloud so low that Kilvert and his guide were 'wrapped as if in a shroud'. Kilvert commented: 'It is an awful place in a storm'. Dominating the entry is the idea of alien rock: 'Cader Idris is the stoniest, dreariest, most desolate mountain I was ever on'. Central to this reality is *basalt*, the 'primitive materiality' (Heringman's phrase) out of which the mountain's top is made. Kilvert referred to struggling through 'wildernesses of slate and basalt' and of 'loose stone'; the basalt stones lay so close together that 'no grass could grow between them'. The mountain top he experience was a place of sterility and death. The basalt wilderness of Cader Idris was a wonder for him, though a grim one.[49]

Kilvert's interest in how the earth was formed appears also in the amazing regularity with which his landscape descriptions register the presence of streams, usually referred to as 'watercourses'. This concern was basically a concern with the question, a much debated one in geology, of what forces created valleys. It was, in turn, connected with the question of the changes wrought by *time* on the surface of the earth. To orthodox Christians, geology's finding that the earth had existed for untold millions of years challenged Genesis and diminished man's importance, giving rise to the question of whether he had progressed, intellectually and morally, in his short habitation of the planet. In this regard it is of the utmost significance that Tennyson's *In Memoriam* was one of Kilvert's favourite poems, the focus of passionate exchanges between him and his lover, Katharine Heanley. Written between 1833 and 1849, it was a poem that reviewed all the major ideas of geology current at the time. While at Cambridge (1827-1831), Tennyson had attended Sedgwick's geology lectures.

Dean wrote of Tennyson's poem: 'Once *In Memoriam* appeared, it became part of the literature of geological controversy . . . Tennyson became almost the centre of Victorian attitudes towards geology'.[50] Rupke wrote of him: 'Tennyson may be seen as the poetical exponent of the English school of geology'.[51]

The poem's geology represents, Dean stated, 'a debate between two contradictory earth-voices. One of these is the cyclic, non-progressive and wholly materialistic geology of poem XXXV'. The 'voice' of that poem insists that 'Man dies: nor is there hope in dust', and pictures streams washing dust endlessly and remorselessly down hillsides in order to 'sow/ The dust of continents to be'. Kilvert's steady noting of hillside streams was likely to have been informed by this awareness. The other earth-voice in the debate urges a view that is 'linear, progressive and teleological' (i.e. concerned with a final cause, indicative of design in the universe).[52] This latter view was based on the fossil record that provided some evidence of the development of species.

Discoveries in caves before and after Kilvert was born steadily developed their imaginative appeal. Buckland had explored Kirkdale Cave (Yorkshire) in December 1821 to study its fossil bones, a mixture of hyena, elephant, duck, and rhino. He advanced the astonishing theory that creatures now found in the tropics had actually existed in Britain before being drowned by the Flood. O'Connor underlined that this was 'a defining moment in the history of geology's imaginative impact'. The Cave was 'a time capsule', a venture into a pre-human 'deep past'.[53] So-called 'scriptural geologists' tried at the time Kilvert's father was growing up in the 1820s to reconcile the Flood with the earth's ancient origins revealed by geologists. Evangelicals were to be found on both sides of the debate. Kilvert had a gentle dig at scriptural geologists in the *Diary* entry for 11 September 1872 when he mocked 'two Antediluvian parsons' who (significantly) belonged to a group of clergymen archaeologists. One of the most important aspects of the Brixham, Devon cave, excavated in 1858 and widely publicised, was that evidence of tool-making man was found alongside, and apparently of the same age as, remains of extinct Ice-Age (1-2 million to 10,000 years ago) mammals.[54] Lubbock's *Prehistoric Times* refers to Brixham and has a chapter on cave men.

The extent to which Kilvert was imaginatively stirred by caves as 'portals of the past'[55] is amply illustrated in the *Diary* entry for 9 September 1873 when he visited what he called 'Cox's stalactite cave, the beautiful forest and fairyland of stalactites, one of the wonders of the world'. It had been discovered in 1837 by George

Cox, who ran it from then on as a tourist attraction for visitors to the Cheddar Gorge.[56] Kilvert was captivated (it is another moment of enchantment) by the 'wildest most fantastic forms' of the stalactites, by the 'bell-like sounds' they emitted when tapped, and 'beautiful and indescribable effects' created when the gas lights were raised or lowered. Again, Kilvert was moved to link the Christian with the pagan in his response to the cave. Its roof reminded him of 'the nave and aisles of a Gothic Cathedral'. This 'water sculpture' had taken 'countless ages' to achieve the forms it possessed. The frightening aspect that the deep past had for Kilvert is reinforced by his reference to 'the black and silent solitudes of these awful caves'. We can readily understand, from Kilvert's response to this cave's 'wonder', what Shortland meant when he wrote of a cave as 'a site of spiritual confrontation', of the capacity of a cave to 'unfetter the over civilised mind and thrust it forth on wild imaginings'.[57] The highly civilised mind of Mrs Moore in Forster's *A Passage to India* (1924) is profoundly unsettled by her experience of the Marabar Cave, notable for its echo which reproduced anything that was said as 'Boum'. 'The echo began in some indescribable way to undermine her hold on life', seeming to suggest: 'Pathos, piety, courage – they exist, but are identical, and so is filth. Everything exists, nothing has value'. This reductionist effect applied even to religion. She knew that all the 'divine words' of 'poor little talkative Christianity' only amounted to 'Boum'.[58] Kilvert's experiences of primitive otherness – in Cox's Cave, at Land's End, on the summit of Cader Idris – have much in common with Mrs Moore's Marabar experience.

Among all the books Kilvert read concerned with the issues of the evolution of the earth and of Man, it would be hard to overestimate the importance of Kingsley's 1850 novel *Alton Locke*, which contained a representative example of the visionary narratives depicting earth history of this period. It has been noted that Kilvert found it enormously satisfying and one reason must have been that it provided a synthesis of many of the key conflicts of his age: of materialism and spirituality, of education and ignorance, of rich and poor, of progress and tradition, and of science and faith. Towards the end of *Alton Locke*, which traces the collapse of the Chartist movement, Kingsley gives a shocking picture of the depths of urban poverty. We visit the slum of Jacob's Island where houses are built over a sewer. The starved bodies of a man's wife and children lie on the bare floor, dead partly as the result of having to drink sewer water. The so-called 'improvement' of the district illustrated, Kingsley explained, 'the law of competition' whereby 'great buildings . . . had already eaten up half the little houses;

as the great fish . . . eat up the little ones of their species'. The 'law' he was referring to was evolution, 'lately discovered to be the true creator and preserver of the universe'.[59] These bleak images of a social system bereft of sympathy for its weakest members give way to the visionary chapter 'Dreamland', in which Kingsley reviewed pre-Darwinian evolutionary ideas. It begins with Alton imagining himself to be 'at the lowest point of created life – a madrepore' (creature which produces coral). He then becomes a series of creatures hunted down by stronger predators. The essence of this meaningless, material, primitive world is caught in Kingsley's reference to 'Sand – sand – nothing but sand!' In turn, Alton becomes a predator himself, destroying weaker creatures. However, alongside 'mere animal destructiveness' there stirs within him 'the spark of humanity', which renders his behaviour more intelligent.[60]

In a later phase of development, Alton is an ape, in whom stir 'germs of a new and higher consciousness', but still his intellectual and moral promise is belied by 'animal faculties': 'I caught the birds and insects, and tore them to pieces with savage glee'. And the reflection of his face in a pool shows that of 'a negro child, with large projecting brow'. Characters from the novel make brief appearances among Alton's dreams. His cousin appears as 'a hunter missionary', talking of 'the new world of civilisation and Christianity which he was organising in that tropic wilderness'. Alton feels drawn upwards towards 'a mighty destiny' emerging in the West. Christianity appears as a new principle in the universe, based on Love, in opposition to the law of the jungle. Alton, in a dream, tells the rich and powerful that the 'All-Father meant neither you nor your children to devour your brethren'. The dream sequence ends with an emphasis on the blessedness of work and effort which would transform the original wilderness of the world into a garden where 'science and wealth, philosophy and art' flourish.[61]

It is unlikely that Kilvert made specific references in his diary to evolution, to *The Origin of Species*, or to the Huxley/Wilberforce debate. It is inconceivable that Plomer would have excised them. The issues raised by evolution would have been assimilated by Kilvert during his growing-up and would not be likely to provoke explicit comment when he began to keep his diary in 1870. The adverse reaction that Darwin feared to his *The Origin of Species* did not happen; the public greeted it positively because by then it was used to the idea of evolution.[62] Kilvert would have been aware that the father of Sir John Lubbock was a friend and neighbour of Darwin at Downe, Kent.[63] Darwin's daughter, Annie, attended the Lubbock children's parties. Lubbock junior, six years older than Annie, was from boyhood a keen collector of natural history specimens and received advice from Darwin. John gave his first lecture on natural history to Downe's villagers when he was fifteen. When the Huxley/Wilberforce confrontation took place, John was on the platform. In the audience was the Captain Fitzroy who commanded the *Beagle* when Darwin embarked on it in December 1831 and began the voyage that would take him into mankind's origins.[64] A deeply religious man, Fitzroy was horrified, as Sedgwick was, that the theory of evolution denied God's hand in man's appearance on earth. Fitzroy's intervention in the debate in Oxford was almost as sensational as the famous exchange between Huxley and Wilberforce. He seized a bible from a clergyman, waved it above his head, and beseeched the audience to believe in God rather than man. When Kilvert met Miss Fitzroy, a relative of the Captain, on 8 March 1876 at the Wiltshire home of Mrs Meredith Brown where she was like him a lunch guest, he felt no need to explain who she was, because he already knew. Her Christian name was Lavinia and she was Mrs Meredith Brown's cousin. What interested Kilvert about her at the time was that she was 'very pretty'.

In addition to Kingsley, Kilvert embraced other inspiring figures who could combine faith in God with faith in science. Robertson, whose views were examined in chapter six, was one. 'Science is one thing, religion is another,' he had asserted. Lubbock was another inspiring figure. In the last chapter of his *Pre-historic Times*, he reviewed the debate on evolutionary theory, 'which . . . is even yet very much misunderstood'. He quoted Herbert Spencer's words expressing satisfaction at 'the constant progress towards a higher degree of skill, intelligence and self-regulation' in man consequent on this theory. To Lubbock himself, 'the great principle of Natural Selection . . . illuminates the future with hope' and it was mistaken to see it 'as opposed to the . . . interests of true religion'. Science and religion constituted 'the two mighty agents of improvement', whose separation was 'the great misfortune of humanity'. Lubbock was giving expression to the vision of progress with which Kilvert had been brought up. He also raised the question of sin, of overriding importance to a fellow Evangelical like Kilvert. Some people would argue, the former admitted, that sin was the basic cause of human misery and that any moral improvement must be due to religion, not to science.[65] Sin arose, however, from ignorance and mistaken views of pleasure, and effort directed towards the study of science would, in Lord Brougham's words, 'make our lives not only more agreeable, but better'.[66]

We know that *In Memoriam* by Tennyson was for Kilvert a source both of inspiration and guidance in the area of science and religion. Charles Tennyson summed up the poet's religious position in that poem as 'a middle way between the narrow dogmatism of the Evangelicals and . . . extreme scepticism'. That position paralleled that of his friend Jowett, who believed that 'religion must be ready to adjust itself to any new facts or laws which science might establish'.[67] Tennyson dismissed scientific materialism in *In Memoriam*: 'I think we are not wholly brain/ Magnetic mockeries' (the last phrase indicating his rejection of the claims of phrenology and mesmerism). Science may prove that we are 'cunning casts in clay' but 'What matters Science unto men,/ At least to me?'[68] Even though science taught that a 'wiser', more highly developed human being would evolve from 'the greater ape', he himself was born to other things. The poem ends with a declaration of faith in humanity, in the worth of the individual who had 'moved through life of lower phase' and was no longer 'half-akin to brute' but who had an identity made up of 'all we thought, and loved, and did,/ And hope and suffered'. The sum total of these experiences would in the future yield 'a noble type' of man who 'lives in God', the God 'to which the whole creation moves'.[69]

Tennyson's rejection of the scientific materialism that portrayed Nature in a negative way is dramatically illustrated by an anecdote concerning a visit made to Farringford, Tennyson's Isle of Wight home, by Tyndall. Tyndall expressed disbelief in God, whereupon the poet's fist crashed down on the table and he exclaimed earnestly, 'Tyndall, there *is* a God'.[70] It is important to remember that Tyndall, feared as a materialist, brought a spiritual viewpoint to bear on Nature's wonders and was a close friend of men who combined faith in God with faith in science: Kingsley and Lubbock, as well as Tennyson. Tennyson, in turn, was an admirer of Frederick Robertson; he gave his wife a copy of Robertson's *Trinity Chapel Sermons* on 9 April 1856.[71] Robertson showed his admiration for Tennyson by writing a study of *In Memoriam*, which he dedicated to the poet.[72]

Robertson inspired Tennyson and Kilvert because he typified the sympathetic, self-denying clergyman pictured by Eleanor at the end of *Alton Locke*, of the class 'which God has appointed to unite all the others', leading the people into spiritual and moral reform in the footsteps of Christ, who knew what it meant to be a man. This Christ-like clergyman was not an impossible ideal, she insisted, because of 'the miraculous, ever-increasing improvement of the clergy'.[73] A major part of the appeal to Kilvert of Kingsley's novel must have been this vision of the clergy leading people through the problems of the new industrial, urban and scientific society of the mid-nineteenth century.

There is, however, one cryptic, enigmatic entry in *Kilvert's Diary* that implies that its author had doubts about his fitness as a clergyman. The entry is: 'An angel satyr walks these hills'. It has always been a puzzle to readers, partly because it stands on its own; Plomer may have omitted its context. Readers have inevitably wanted to know what Kilvert meant by it. Somehow, tantalisingly, it seems emblematic of him. The present study has emphasised that for him angels were real beings, caring and kindly intermediaries between God and man. Kilvert habitually likened those who cared for their fellows as 'angels'. It seems certain that he wanted to see himself, in his pastoral role, as one. But what of the satyr element of the duality which he used to characterise himself? *Kilvert's Diary and Landscape* examined this duality in the context of his near obsession with the sexual charms of young girls[74] and of the poem, *Angel Satyr*, written by Plomer. The poem shows insight into the relationship between religion and sex in the diarist's life. Plomer believed that the angel and satyr facets of Kilvert were interdependent and inseparable, partly because the diarist himself yoked them together. It is worthwhile in the context of the present chapter to consider them in terms of his awareness of the elements which made him a man and those which made him a beast.

The temporal and physical context of the angel/satyr statement has some relevance to this awareness. The entry containing the statement is dated 20 June 1871, the following day was the longest day, and 24 June was Midsummer Day. Hot midsummer weather always evoked a pagan response in Kilvert, as his diary very frequently records. Kilvert regularly met attractive young girls in the surrounding hills, and hills were also the location for his dutiful parish visits. The figure of the angel satyr walking the hills encapsulates Kilvert, the curate of Clyro. A suggestion of self-reproach seems to lurk in his cryptic 'angel satyr' comment. Was he expressing guilt over the lustful, beastly part of his nature, a part which undermined and made a mockery of the angelic, spiritual part? Was he doubting that Man, or at least the man that he was, had progressed beyond the ape?[75] Was he even confronting the possibility that his religious faith was declining, that the only reality was the here and now, that there was no immortality, that he would die like the Nature-worshipping pagans who had set up the Cross Ffordd stone near Clyro, which 'Perhaps could tell some strange *wild* stories . . . ' (Kilvert often used 'wild' with a sexual connotation)? Did all Christianity's fine words and promises amount to no more than 'Boum'? Was Tennyson in Kilvert's head when he pictured himself as an angel satyr? It was in Poem XXXV of *In Memoriam* that Tennyson referred to love appearing 'in his coarsest satyr-shape', without confidence in immortality.

When Kilvert's father was growing up, wonders to him were the picture he saw in a Bath shop window of Napoleon's retreat from Moscow and the experience of riding a stage-coach travelling at ten miles an hour. Kilvert's period of growing up included railway travel at forty miles an hour as well as even greater wonders, both those developed by Man and those discovered in Nature. These were exciting and challenging enough. However, behind many of them lurked ideas which threatened to subvert the very foundations of the society into which his parents' generation had been born. One of these was evolution which, although it had been a commonplace of people's thinking and talking in the years before Kilvert's birth in 1840, assumed its full, threatening potential by the time he went to Oxford. He had gradually adjusted to it throughout his life, and achieved that reconciliation between science and faith which many of his age, including figures whom he greatly admired, had achieved. Darwin found that evolution, though it helped to destroy his religious faith, did not destroy the wonder he experienced when exploring the natural world. Life continued to be, for him, as it always did for Kilvert, a curious and wonderful thing.

References

Introduction

1. Peter J. Conradi, *At the Bright Hem of God. Radnorshire Pastoral*, Bridgend, Seren Books, 2009, pp. 126-7.
2. *Tretower to Clyro. Essays*, London, Quercus, 2011, p. 36.
3. Norman Gash, *Aristocracy and People. Britain 1815-1865*, London, Edward Arnold, 1979, pp. 12-14.
4. Asa Briggs, *The Age of Improvement 1783-1867*, London, Longmans, 1967, p. 1.
5. David Thomson, *England in the Nineteenth Century*, Harmondsworth, Penguin, 1983, p.33.
6. Gash, *op. cit.*, p. 20.
7. Briggs, *op. cit.*, p. 3.
8. Kilvert Society publication, 2002, p. 1.
9. Louis James, 'The Rational Amusement: "minor" fiction and Victorian studies', *Victorian Studies*, vol. XIV, no.2, December 1970, Bloomington, University of Indiana.

Prologue
'Some Great Change Must Take Place'

1. This would be the effect on society of the railways in the view of Maria Hare, Kilvert's godmother (see chapter four).
2. Andrew Cobbing, *The Japanese Discovery of Victorian Britain. Early Travel Encounters in the Far West*, Richmond (Surrey), Japan Library (an imprint of Curzon Press), 1998, p. 120. Tosa is an island.
3. A few weeks after Kilvert's talk with Mrs Daniell, the five students went to live in Warminster (Wilts.) where Daniell had taken up a post as curate, which explains why Kilvert referred to Daniell (15 August 1871) living in Warminster. One of his five students was attending Lord Weymouth's Grammar School (Daniell's old school) in the town. In October 1871, Daniell lectured at the Warminster Athanaeum on 'Japan and its People'.
4. Cobbing, *op. cit.*, pp. 66, 70.
5. *The Autobiography of William Plomer*, London, Jonathan Cape, 1975, p. 367.
6. Introduction to volume two of *Kilvert's Diary*.
7. 'A Curate's Diary', in *In My Good Books*, London, Chatto and Windus, 1942, p. 108.

8. 'Reading Other People's Diaries', in *From the Headlands*, London, Chatto and Windus, 1982, p. 187.

9. R.L. Brett, introduction (p. 11) to *Barclay Fox's Journal*, London, Bell and Hyman, 1979.

10. It actually ends in October 1854, but is a daily record only until October 1844.

11. For an account of Brislington House, see J. Toman, '"A Grand City": Kilvert and Bristol', in *'A Grand City' – 'Life, Movement and Work': Bristol in the eighteenth and nineteenth centuries. Essays in honour of Gerard Leighton, FSA*, edited by M.J. Crossley Evans, Bristol and Gloucestershire Archaeological Society, 2010, pp. 336-39.

12. The editor of *Barclay Fox's Journal* stated that it was 'one of the most important foundries in Britain' (*op. cit.*, p. 299). It produced the largest (46 cwt) piece of wrought iron ever made for a machine to raise miners out of Cornwall's mines.

13. *'Under the Clee': the Falkner family in Shropshire, 1578-1766*, p. 9, Falkner Papers, D300, Dorset History Centre.

14. The outlook possessed by this family and the Falkners is seen in the fact that Thomas's cousin, Isaac Collett, and Frederick Falkner subscribed to *The Works of the late Thomas Wilson*, Bishop of Sodor and Man (*Bath Chronicle*, 9 November 1780). Wilson renovated the Island's churches, established libraries, schools, and medical services. He was also a supporter of foreign, especially Moravian, missions.

15. *The Falkners of Bath 1779-1818*, part I, p. 16, Falkner Papers. She also stressed the high cost of letters – average price 9d – and the six months a letter took from India.

16. *Ibid.*, pp. 22-3. The first letter (17 September 1783) was occasioned by Robert Falkner's forthcoming marriage to William Parsons's sister Elizabeth.

17. Simeon, the Cambridge churchman, had set up in 1817 a trust to purchase church livings for Evangelical clergy. The quoted words are Anne Falkner's.

18. When he went bankrupt in October 1794, he owed money to the Falkner brothers.

19. Stothert could supply Bath builders with cast-iron pipes, gates, staircases, banisters, fireplaces, ovens and grates.

20. *The New Bath Guide*, Letter VI, Bath, Cruttwell, 1776.

21. William Dyer, *A Sketch of the Life and Labour of the late Rev. William Jay, a sermon*, Bath, Gregory, 1854.

22. L.E. Elliott-Binns, *The Early Evangelicals: A Religious and Social Study*, London, Lutterworth Press, 1953, p. 339.

23. *Bath: A Glance at its Public Worship, Style of Dress, Cotillions, Masquerades, etc.*, Bath, Robbins, 1814, p. 5.

24. R.S. Neale, *Bath 1680-1850. A Social History*, London, Routledge, Kegan and Paul, 1981, p. 3.

25. Hugh Torrens, *The Evolution of a Family Firm: Stothert and Pitt of Bath*, Bath, Stothert and Pitt, 1978, p. 2.

26. *Op. cit.*, pp. 219-20.

27. In the 'K' section of the national alphabetical list of bankrupts, Francis's name is flanked by other tradesmen whose businesses failed in 1793-4: Thomas Kift, Bristol insurance broker, James Kilpatrick, London linen draper, William Kimberley, Windsor plumber, Horatio Kime, London coal merchant, and Henry King, Newbury corn dealer, etc.

28. Asa Briggs, *op. cit.*, pp. 45-6.

29. A. Ellis and B. Howard, *The Falkners, Kilverts and Stotherts*, Proceedings of the Widcombe and Lyncombe History Study Group, 1997, p. 15.

30. Later chapters show both Kilvert's father and Kilvert's aunt Sophia recording anxiety in the 1820s about these developments.

31. Ian Inkster, 'Aspects of the history of science and science culture in Britain, 1780-1850 and beyond', in Inkster and Jack Morrell (editors), *Metropolis and Province, Science in British Culture, 1780-1850*, Philadelphia, Philadelphia University Press, 1983, pp. 39-41. His italics.

32. Roger Cooter, *The Cultural Meaning of Popular Science. Phrenology and the Organisation of Consent in nineteenth-century Britain*, Cambridge, Cambridge University Press, 1984, pp. 69-71.

33. George Fox, the Quaker leader, commented on the welcome given him wherever he was in East Yorkshire by Justice Hotham, whom he described as 'a well-wisher to Friends' (*The Journal of George Fox*, edited by John L. Nicholls, Cambridge, Cambridge University Press, 1952, pp. 76, 533).

34. *The Dillwyn Collection. The Journals of Lewis Weston Dillwyn* (b.1778 d.1855), transcribed by Richard Morris, www.swansea.ac.uk/lis/historical collections.

35. Adelaide Sophia Kilvert, *Home Discipline; or Thoughts on the Origin and Exercise of Domestic Authority*, London, Joseph Masters, 1847, p. 157.

36. Lewis Weston Dillwyn's father, William (1743-1824), was born in Philadelphia, Pennsylvania. He moved to England in 1777 to start a campaign against slavery and married Sarah Weston at the Quaker Meeting House in Tottenham. His son Lewis (senior) recorded on 23 January 1825, shortly after William's death, sorting his 'Books and Tracts relating to the Slave Trade'. Lewis's sister Sarah married the Quaker banker, Alfred Janson, in Woodbridge on 7 September 1825.

37. David Nichol, physician to Swansea Infirmary and Secretary of the Royal Institution for South Wales.

38. Two weeks later (7 May) he went to a farce at the Haymarket called *Railroads for Ever*.

39. Moule devoted himself to practical inventions, e.g. the dry earth closet. He wrote pamphlets: *On the Warming of Churches, The Potato Disease: its cause and remedy*.

40. He assumed this surname on his coming-of-age.

41. Dillwyn wrote a letter on 28 October 1814 accepting Fox Talbot's 'proposed correspondence about botanical pursuits' when the latter was a Harrow schoolboy.

42. Russell Roberts, *Specimens and Marvels, William Henry Fox Talbot and the Invention of Photography*, Bradford, National Museum of Photography, Film and Television, 2000, p. 5.

43. 'Rambling Recollections', in *More Chapters from the Kilvert Saga*,

Leamington Spa, Kilvert Society, n.d., p. 115.

44. Bessie's daughter, Elizabeth Amy, became in the words of the Dillwyn *Journal* editor 'Britain's first woman industrialist when she took over her father's spelter works'.

Chapter 1
Piety, Progress and Print: Kilvert's Background

1. The SPG was founded in 1701 in order to send priests and schoolteachers to America to further the Church's ministry. A short time later the effort extended to the West Indies.

2. *Op. cit.*, pp. 101-2.

3. Note in *SPG Annual Report 1864*. I am greatly indebted to Dr Alexander Schulenburg of the St Helena Institute for this information.

4. Bodily noted disapprovingly that the inhabitants had 'not been energetic enough' to kill the ants when they first appeared.

5. Edward Millar, *Portrait of a College*, Cambridge, Cambridge University Press, 1961, p. 80.

6. Queen's College was established in 1843 initially as a centre for training medical students. Support from two wealthy Midlands clergymen resulted in the establishment of an 'Anglican university' embracing architecture, civil engineering, law, literature, theology, as well as medicine and surgery.

7. Trevor Park, *St Bees College. Pioneering higher education in 19th century Cumbria*, St Bees, St Bega Publications, 2008, p. 120.

8. See J. Toman, 'The Kilvert Quaker background: a story that could not be told', *Kilvert Society Journal*, no. 24, September 2007.

9. Preface to *The Children's Year*, London [1846], Nelson, 1892.

10. He married Ann Wood of Swansea, whose forebears had coal mines and iron forges at Wolverhampton in the early 17th century. Her great-grandfather was 'a noted iron and copper founder' (*Mary Howitt. An Autobiography* edited by her daughter Margaret, London, William Isbister, 1889, p. 13).

11. *My Own Story. Autobiography of a child*, London, William Tegg, 1844, p .7.

12. *Ibid.*, p. 7.

13. *Ibid.*, p. 94.

14. Legh Richmond visited the Lake District in 1818 and wrote letters about his tour which 'conveyed a vivid appreciation of the beauties . . . of natural scenery' ('Memoir of the Author', *Annals of the Poor*, London [1814], Nelson, 1859).

15. O. Chadwick, *The Victorian Church*, part I, London, Adam and Charles Black, 1966, p. 451. K. Hylson-Smith noted that the original readership of the *Annals* were middle-class Evangelicals (*Evangelicals in the Church of England 1734-1984*, Edinburgh, Clark, 1988, p. 101).

16. *The Young Cottager*, pp. 128, 131. The reference to an *affectionate* mind and Kilvert's use of 'touching' in relation to *The Dairyman's Daughter* are an acknowledgement of the value of *sympathy* that was crucial to both the eighteenth-century novel and Evangelicalism.

17. *The Dairyman's Daughter*, pp. 82-3.

18. *The Young Cottager*, pp. 130, 139.

19. Frederick was cousin to uncle Francis.

20. *The Falkners of Bath 1779-1818*, part I, p. 137, The Falkner Papers, D300, Dorset History Centre.

21. *DNB* entry on Sedgwick. He was an Evangelical, committed to a religion and a morality of *sympathy*, as is evident from this remark in 1815: 'I have now read the whole of *Gil Blas* twice over' (J.W. Clark and T. Hughes, *The Life and Letters of the Reverend Adam Sedgwick*, Cambridge, Cambridge University Press, 1890, vol. I, p. 136).

22. *A Discourse on the Studies of the University of Cambridge*, Cambridge, Deighton and Stevenson, 1833, p. 10 and p. 13.

23. Martin Rudwick, *Worlds before Adam. The reconstruction of geohistory in the age of reform*, Chicago, Chicago University Press, 2008, p. 423.

24. In his *Discourse* (p. 15) he rejected the idea that knowledge of God resulted only from revelation.

25. Jack Morrell and Arnold Thackray, *Gentlemen of Science. Early years of the British Association for the Advancement of Science*, Oxford, Clarendon Press, 1981, pp. 225-6.

26. Robert M. Young, *Darwin's Metaphor. Nature's place in Victorian culture*, Cambridge, Cambridge University Press, 1985, p. 10.

27. Carla Yanni, *Nature's Museums. Victorian science and the architecture of display*, Baltimore, Maryland, The Johns Hopkins University, 1999, p. 62.

28. James A. Secord, *Victorian Sensation. The extraordinary publication, reception and secret authorship of 'Vestiges of the Natural History of Creation'*, Chicago, University of Chicago Press, 2000, p. 223.

29. From Sedgwick's *Discourse*, quoted in Clark and Hughes, vol. I, p. 403.

30. Quoted in Clark and Hughes, p. 357. Sedgwick was especially pained by the fact that the ideas he found so disturbing were promulgated by one of his former students.

31. The Evangelical *Leisure Hour* magazine (24 November 1859) featured an article on him, 'Dr Mackay in America', based on his book *Life and Liberty in America*. He reported on the American Civil War for the *Times*.

32. Mackay, *Forty Years' Recollections*, London, Chapman and Hall, 1877, p. 2.

33. Secord, *op. cit.*, pp. 19-20. Thomas Huxley attacked *Vestiges* because it smacked of the approach to science of popular journals (in fact he said it read like *Chambers's Edinburgh Journal*).

34. *Vestiges of the Natural History of Creation* (1844), Leicester, Leicester University Press, 1969, p. 324.

35. Quoted in Secord, *op. cit.*, p. 13.

36. Tennyson was excited by it and bought a copy on the strength of an ecstatic review he read of it.

37. *Op. cit.*, p. 1.

38. *Ibid.*, p. 37.

39. From Francis Kilvert's *Commonplace Book*, vol. I.

40. Michael Ruse, *The Darwinian Revolution. Science red in tooth and claw*, Chicago, Chicago University Press, 1999, p. 65.

41. *Kilvert's Diary*, NLW edition, April-June 1870, 29 April.

42. Preface, pp.xi-xii, *Masterman Ready* (1841), London, Dent, 1970.

43. *Ibid.*, p. 7.

44. The quotations in this paragraph are from *Jacob Faithful* (1836), London, George Routledge, 1897, p. 16 and p. 371. When Jacob becomes an apprentice at the age of 14, he observes: 'I was no longer a little *savage* [because] I had gained *the power of knowledge*'. His schoolmaster advises him to treasure his knowledge as 'hidden wealth' (p. 41 and p. 45). Italics supplied in all the *Jacob Faithful* quotations.

45. The references to *Masterman Ready* in this paragraph can be found on pp. 53, 64, 98, 155, 161, 146, 102.

46. Anna Stott, *Hannah More. The First Victorian*, Oxford, Oxford University Press, 2003, p. xi.

47. References in this paragraph are to pp. 8, 85-7, 70, 163, 10, 196, 164-5.

48. *Kilvert's Diary*, vol. I, p. 83; vol. I, p .90; vol. II, pp. 308-9.

49. *Kilvert's Diary* is permeated by a deep sense of satisfaction and of abiding faith in the unchanging pattern of the seasons, confirmation of God's promise and benevolence.

50. *The Settlers in Canada* (1844), London, Dent, 1956, p. 154. Bone also recognised in this passage that God made the 'curious and wonderful leaf'.

51. The book's full title is: *A Geographical, Historical and Religious Account of the Parish of Aberystruth in the County of Monmouth*, Trevecca, published by the author, 1779.

52. J. Glyndwr Harris, *Edmund Jones: the old prophet*, Penygroes, Gwynedd, Argrassdy Arson, 1987, pp. 13-14 and p. 19. Jones (1702-91) was a Dissenting minister.

53. J.H. Brooks, 'The natural theology of the geologists: some theological strata', in L.J. Jordanova and Roy S. Porter, *Images of the Earth. Essays in the history of the environmental sciences*, Chalfont St Giles, The British Society for the History of Science, 1979, p. 40.

54. Ruse (*op. cit.*, p. 73) observed that the Rev. William Buckland (1784-1856), professor of geology at Oxford, argued that 'God had humans, particularly Britons, in mind when he placed coal strata and iron deposits in such convenient places'.

55. *The Victorian Amateur Astronomer. Independent Astronomical Research in Britain, 1820-1920*, London, Praxis Publishing, 1996, p. 228.

56. *Home Discipline, or Thoughts on the Origin and Exercise of Domestic Authority*, London, Joseph Masters, 1847 pp. 152, 122.

57. *Victorian Popularisers of Science. Designing Nature for New Audiences*, Chicago, Chicago University Press, 2007, p. 168.

58. In *The Stargazer of Hardwicke: the Life and Work of Thomas William Webb*, edited by Janet and Masrk Robinson, Leominster, Gracewing, 2006, Allan Chapman follows the book's editors by ignoring Kilvert's obvious interest in astronomy. Chapman asserted that the diarist had no 'particular interest

in astronomy' and warmed to Webb only as 'a genial host' (*op. cit.*, p. 107).
Several *Diary* passages confirm Kilvert's marked interest.

59. This meteor could have been the one of 24 September 1865, or the very bright one of 15 November 1867, or one of two in 1868 (5 September, 7 October).

60. *Diary of Thomas William Webb*, Hereford Cathedral Library, CF 61/52. The *Notebook* entries referred to are catalogued 6391/1/2.

61. *Mary Howitt. An Autobiography*, vol. I, pp.46-7. Her governess led her to 'the infinite richness of Nature' and a book, *The Catechism of Nature* (Dr Martinet – *sic* – 1797) figured in her youthful reading.

62. *An Autobiography*, vol. I, p. 110 and vol. II, p. 48.

63. *The Children's Year*, pp. 43-6.

64. 'The Evangelical parent, receiving Biblical order not to spare the rod, was severe' (O. Chadwick, *op. cit.*, part I, p. 445).

65 Augustus Hare's account of life at Hardenhuish school tells of the merciless use of the cane. Uncle Francis wrote a satirical poem about a recommendation that the birch be phased out of his school; he was not in favour: 'Teachers are forbid to strike; / Boys may do just what they like' (*Commonplace Book*, vol. II).

66. The first and last of these quotes are from Howitt's *The Rural Life of England* (3rd edition), London, Longman, 1844, pp. 322, 329; the other quote is from Howitt's *Homes and Haunts of the Most Eminent British Poets*, vol.II, London, Richard Bentley, 1849, p. 277 (seeing 'into the life of things' is quoted from Wordsworth's *Tintern Abbey*).

67. James Ryan, 'Images and Impressions: Printing, Reproduction and Photography', in *The Victorian Vision. Inventing New Britain*, edited by John Mackenzie, London, V and A Publications, 2001, p. 216.

68. Amice Lee, *Laurels and Rosemary. The life of William and Mary Howitt*, London, Oxford University Press, 1955, p. 167.

69. The journal was devoted to the causes of sanitary reform, temperance, peace, public education, free trade, civil liberties, and the rights of women.

70. *The Age of Atonement. The Influence of Evangelicalism on Social and Economic Thought, 1795-1865*, Oxford, Clarendon Press, 1988, p. 22.

71. Aileen Fyfe, *Science and Salvation. Evangelical popular publishing in Victorian Britain*, Chicago, Chicago University Press, 2004, pp. 272, 112, 4.

72. Richard Altick, *The English Common Reader. A social history of the mass reading public 1800-1900*, Chicago, Chicago University Press, 1957, p. 99.

73. *Kilvert's Diary*, NLW edition, April-June 1870, edited by Kathleen Hughes and Dafydd Ifans, Aberystwyth, 1982, p.78. Kilvert's ministerial manual (see *Diary* vol. III, p. 161), J.J. Blunt's *The Duties of the Parish Priest*, p. 226, recommended 'supplying the cottage with a tract or two'.

74. *Kilvert's Diary*, vol. III, pp. 439-440. The *Sunday at Home: A Family Magazine for Sabbath Reading* was launched in May 1854 because the sales of its sister periodical, *The Leisure Hour*, were so good.

75. It was generally found in Evangelical homes and advertised in such Evangelical newspapers as the *Record* (read by the Kilvert family) and the *Christian Guardian* (read by Kilvert's uncle Francis). See Fyfe, pp.171, 168.

76. The campaign culminated in the Ten Hours Act of 1847 as a result of efforts by the Evangelical Lord Shaftesbury.

77. Fyfe, *op. cit.*, p. 65.

78. *Ibid.*, p. 70. Richard D. Altick noted: '*The Leisure Hour* mingled instruction and recreation, with special emphasis on travel and natural history' (*op. cit.*, p. 361).

79. *Op. cit.*, p. 98.

80. *The Leisure Hour*, 25 September 1856.

81. *Ibid.*, 14 August 1856.

82 Teresa Williams and Frederick Grice, *The Other Francis Kilvert. Francis Kilvert of Claverton 1793-1863*, Hay-on-Wye, Kilvert Society, 1982, p. 6.

83 Emily's statements in this paragraph are from pp. 110, 113 of her *Recollections*.

84. Boyd Hilton, *op. cit.*, p. 27.

85. *Op. cit.*, p. 102.

86. *The Religion of the Heart. Anglican Evangelicalism and the Nineteenth-Century Novel*, Oxford, Clarendon Press, 1969, p. 23.

87. *The Falkners of Bath 1779-1818*, part I, p. 74.

88. Kellyanne Ure, 'The Tractarian *Penny Post*'s Early Years (1851-1852): an upper-class effort "To Triumph in the *Working-Man's Home*"', unpublished M.A. thesis, Department of English, Brigham Young University, Utah, 2009.

89. For its strong influence on Kilvert's writing and outlook, see J. Toman, *Kilvert's Diary and Landscape*, chapter two.

90. See J. Toman, *Kilvert's Diary and Landscape*, pp. 66-7, on the parallel between Keble's *New every morning is the love* hymn and Kilvert's *Honest Work* poem.

91. The Preface to the 1862 volume (no.XII) noted that its contents 'will be found similar to that of preceding volumes'.

92. Emily Wyndowe, *op. cit.*, p. 89. She added that her brother Edward still possessed them.

93. Knight, *op. cit.*, New York, Portland House, 1987.

94. *Ibid.*, vol. I, p. 3. *Kilvert's Diary*, vol. III, p. 223.

95 *Old England* contains several passages that appeared originally in these journals. The biographical note on him in *Old England* described him as 'a life-long radical [who] became a journalist in order to serve the public good'.

96. *Op. cit.*, pp. 281-3.

97. It praised the Reformation and attacked Catholic persecution of Protestants (vol.I, p.75).

98. *Op. cit.*, vol. II, p. 351 and p. 358. Kilvert's appetite for 'inventions and discovery' appears in these *Diary* entries: 'Miss Dew . . . showed the children and me some . . . ingenious Japanese sliding pictures in a kind of peep show'; 'an interesting account of his ship passing through the Suez Canal' was given to Kilvert by Arthur Dew, a midshipman in the navy (*Unpublished extracts of Kilvert's Diary relating to the Bevan and Dew families*, Hereford, Kilvert Society, *n.d.*, pp. 10, 22).

99. The quotations in this paragraph from *Old England* come from vol. II, pp. 351, 362. In his comments on machine-printing, Knight was defining what

Richard Altick called 'the democracy of print' (*op. cit.*, p.1).

100. When William trains dogs to carry letters, Ready congratulates him: 'you've established a post on the island, which is a great improvement' (*Masterman Ready*, p. 270).

101. *Masterman Ready*, p. 333.

102. The deep respect Kilvert felt for patriarchs who had devoted their lives to hard work, piety, and their families owes much to Masterman Ready (see in particular the account of the old sawyer, John Hatherell, in J. Toman, *Kilvert: The Homeless Heart*, pp.261-3).

Chapter 2
Nature's Classroom

1. In the 1858 issues there were articles, *inter alia*, on: 'The Great Comet of 1858', 'Diphtheria', 'Earthquakes', 'The Great Solar Eclipse', 'Public Health in London', 'Dr Jenner and Smallpox', 'Astronomy in Tenerife', 'Fireflies', 'The Story of Lighthouses' (three articles), 'Lightning Rods', 'Useful Knowledge of Natural History', 'Silk Worms', 'George Stephenson'.

2. An article about the miraculous escape of a young man from an Alpine crevasse combined much information on crevasses themselves, glaciers, climbing, and the work of Alpine guides, with heavy emphasis on 'the overwatching providence of God'.

3. Lynn Barber, *The Heyday of Natural History*, London, Jonathan Cape, 1980, pp. 14-15, 136, 23.

4. Lynn Merrill, *The Romance of Natural History*, Oxford, Oxford University Press, 1989, p. 30.

5. E Wyndowe, *op. cit.*, p. 121.

6. Richard Holmes, *The Age of Wonder. How the Romantic Generation Discovered the Beauty and Terror of Science*, London, Harper Press, p. 323. The earlier quotation in this paragraph is from pp. 318-19, and the italics are his.

7. R. Dawkins, *Unweaving the Rainbow: Science, Delusion and the Appetite for Wonder*, London, Allen Lane, Penguin Press, 1998, p. x.

8. *Ibid.*, p. 41.

9. Merrill, *op. cit.*, pp. 53, 88.

10. 'Curiosity in Early Modern Science', in *Word and Image*, vol. XI, no. 4, October-December 1995, London, Taylor and Francis, p. 391.

11. Collections comprised 'Pictures, Books, Rings, Animals, Plants, Fruits, Metals, and monstrous [things]' (*ibid.*, p. 396).

12. *Ibid.*, p. 403.

13. Ralph O'Connor, *The Earth on Show. Fossils and the Poetics of Popular Science, 1802-1856*, Chicago, University of Chicago Press, 2007, p. 34.

14. The last three quotations from Emily Wyndowe's *Recollections* are from pp. 121, 105, and 113. She also used 'curious' about objects and phenomena on pp. 111, 117-118.

15. *Ibid.*, p. 93. Darwin employed a children's nurse, Jessie Brodie, who had

previously been nurse to Thackeray's children. Brodie was reported to have observed that 'it was a pity Mr Darwin had not something to do like Mr Thackeray. She had seen him watching an ant-heap for a whole hour' (quoted in Randal Keynes, *Annie's Box. Charles Darwin, his daughter and human evolution*, London, Fourth Estate, 2002, p. 74).

16. They were also permitted to walk in the 'Wilderness', part of the Widcombe (Bath) estate of Thomas Clutterbuck, patron of Kilvert's father.

17. E. Wyndowe, *op. cit.*, p. 88. One of the skeins was still there in 1912 when she wrote her recollections.

18. *Ibid.*, p. 85. Mr Wyncoll was the equivalent of Mrs Parker, the teacher who shaped Mary Howitt's love of natural things.

19. One of their books was Mrs Trimmer's *History of the Robins* (*op. cit.*, p.89). Emily Kilvert pointed out that they had 'large pictures of birds and beasts . . . done in oils on canvas or linen' in their nursery.

20. Keynes, *op. cit.*, pp. 98-9.

21 William Howitt's abiding interest in the world of emigrants and colonists is seen in his books *Colonisation and Christianity* (1838), *Land, Labour and Gold; or two years in Victoria* (1855) and *The History of Discovery in Australia, Tasmania and New Zealand* (1865). A favourite book of Alfred, the Howitts' eldest son, was *The Swiss Family Robinson* (1812) by the Swiss pastor, John David Wyss. It tells the story of a family shipwrecked in the East Indies.

22. E. Wyndowe, *op. cit.*, p. 105. Dr Griffith was Charles Tapp Griffith (1789-1866), Rector and patron of Elm, Somerset from 1826; Master of Warminster Grammar School (1820-40). Herbert (born 1818) was his third son.

23. Sarah was teaching at Robert Kilvert's Hardenhuish school in 1843 as Hare recorded (*The Story of My Life*, vol. I, p. 173). She had two other English addresses before the Horsham (Sussex) one where Emily Kilvert visited in 1858 (*op. cit.*, p. 106). Emigration to Canada may have followed her marriage in 1846.

24. Her introduction to *Roughing it in the Bush, or Forest Life in Canada*, London, Richard Bentley, 1852. It was based on her 19 years (from 1832) on a farm there.

25. *Kilvert's Diary*, vol. III, p. 440. Francis Edwin Kilvert (1838-1910) was a barrister.

26. E. Wyndowe, *op. cit.*, pp. 105-6. Emily also noted that her father's nickname for her was 'E. Migrant' because there was a possibility that Grant would be added after her name in honour of some family friends called Grant.

27. Oliver Warner's introduction to *The Settlers in Canada* (1844), London, Dent, 1956, p. vii.

28. 'Memoirs, 1804-1882', p. 44.

29. *The Settlers in Canada*, pp. 8, 17.

30. When his uncle Herbert was dying of cancer (29 August 1874), he was attributing his illness to a strain 'which he remembers getting at a "logging bee" in Canada', Kilvert noted (*Diary*, vol. III, p. 73). Logging bees were occasions when workers came together to clear trees. Susanna Moodie called them 'noisy, riotous, drunken meetings' (*Roughing it in the Bush*, vol. II, chapter four).

31. *The Settlers in Canada* passages quoted in this paragraph come from pp. 21, 23-4, 50, 64, 85, 216, 16, 87, 93.

32. *The Gorilla Hunters*, London, Collins, *n.d.*, p. 166.

33. *Victorian Poetry, Drama and Miscellaneous Prose 1832-1890*, Oxford, Clarendon Press, 1990, p. 417.

34. *Ibid.*, p. 409.

35. *The Children's Year* quotations in this paragraph are from pp. 46, 44, 51-2, 61-2 (my italics).

36. *The Boy's Country Book* (1839), London, Hodder and Stoughton, *n.d.*, p. 7.

37. *Cf. Kilvert's Diary*, vol. II, pp. 62-3: 'three men at a rope walk . . . showed us all their processes and gave us a great deal of information'.

38. 'Curious' appears on pp. 28, 32, 52, 54, 58, 71, 165, 167, 192, 196, 213. 'Wonder' or 'wonderful' appears on pp. 29, 31, 34, 59, 146, 149, 186, 217, 219, 220-1.

39. *The Boy's Country Book*, pp. 20-6.

40. When at school at Tamworth, Howitt was pleased with one of his teachers who was not only 'fond of poetry' and of the countryside, but 'fond of mechanics, and of constructing all sorts of nick-nacks'. Howitt enthused about the 'glorious rambles' in the country led by this teacher (*ibid.*, pp. 212-4).

41. 'Memoirs', p. 30. Bancks's daughter, Mary, was married to Frederick Falkner.

42. *The Autobiography of John Britton, FSA*, Wiltshire Topographical Society, 1849, vol. I, p. 176.

43. *The Boy's Country Book*, p. 56.

44. R. Keynes, *op. cit.*, p. 159. Another book Darwin borrowed for Annie was William Howitt's *The Book of the Seasons* for its 'notes on the plants, insects and animal life that could be seen each month' (*ibid.*, p. 159).

45. The poem, which appears in *Remains in Verse and Prose*, edited by the Rev. W.L. Nichols, London, printed in Manchester, 1866, was dedicated to Britton and commemorated his appearance at the inauguration of the Wiltshire Archaeological Association, 12 October 1853.

46. *The Leisure Hour*, 11 June 1857. Britton had died on 1 January 1857, aged 85. His topographical work, co-author E. Brayley, was entitled *The Beauties of England and Wales: or Delineations Topographical, Historical and Descriptive of Each County*, London, various publishers, 1801-1818.

47. *Autobiography*, vol. I, p. 45.

48. Presumably, 'too quiet to interfere' is a reference to the fact that Coleman was a Quaker. It is worth noting that the Coleman fortune was built, like that of many Quakers, on trade.

49. Britton, *Autobiography*, vol. I, pp. 35, 27, 69. At the end of vol. II of his autobiography, there is a list of subscribers to his testimonial (at Richmond on 7 July 1845) which includes Knight's name, with those of Dickens, Brunel, Charles Mackay, and Richard Warner (Bath antiquarian, known to uncle Francis Kilvert).

50. *Op. cit.*, p. 18. When his grandmother died, these volumes were one of the 'indelible memories' that provoked tears as they 'passed out of view' (*ibid.*, p. 51).

51. Britton's influence is traced in J. Toman, *Kilvert's Diary and Landscape*.

52. *The Children's Year*, pp. 143-4 and 150. In the passage that touches on. moral progress, Mary Howitt tells her children that everyone 'even little boys and girls must try to do something towards improving the world still more'.

53. *Ibid.*, pp. 123-5. My italics.

54. *Op. cit.*, p. 180.

55. *Op. cit.*, pp. 31-2. The profound influence of the *Lyrical Ballads* on him is explored in detail in J. Toman, *Kilvert's Diary and Landscape*.

56. *The Prelude*, Book XII, 208 and 214-5.

57. George Levine, *Darwin Loves You. Natural selection and the re-enchantment of the world*, Princeton, New Jersey, Princeton University Press, 2008, p. 35.

58. Levine, *op. cit.*, p. 26.

59. *The Enchantment of Modern Life: attachments, crossings and ethics*, Princeton, New Jersey, Princeton University Press, 2001.

60. Levine, *op. cit.*, p. 36.

61. *Kilvert's Diary*, vol. I, p. 309. Another example is the 'delirium of joy' he experienced on a spring day (*ibid.*, vol. III, pp. 190-1), which is dealt with in chapter nine.

62. Levine, *op. cit.*, p. 36. For the importance to Kilvert of 'encounter', see J. Toman, *Kilvert's Diary and Landscape*, chapter six.

63. *Kilvert's Cornish Diary*, edited by Richard Maber and Angela Tregoning, Penzance, Alison Hodge, 1989, p. 85. My italics. Kilvert owed some of his stance and his phrasing here to Robertson, who had written of Swiss mountain scenery: 'There is a grandeur and wonder in all these things; but the *spell* is broken if human beings are near you' (Stopford Brooke, *Life and Letters of the Reverend Frederick William Robertson* [1865], London, Kegan Paul, Trench and Trübner, 1891, vol. I, p. 126. My italics).

64. *NLW* edition of *Kilvert's Diary*, April-June 1870, 7 May.

65. *Kilvert's Diary*, vol. III, p. 168. Importantly, memory played a key role in this experience: 'memory enters in and brings back the old time' – he was recalling on 13 April 1875 his first visit there on 29 May 1865.

66. *The Children's Year*, p. 141. Howitt's italics show she felt this formulation to be important.

67. Levine, *op. cit.*, p. viii and p. 40.

68. *The Fairy-Land of Science*, USA, Filiquarian Publishing LLC, 2007, p. 5.

69. Kilvert's endorsement of this Wordsworthian, sacramental vision is traced in J. Toman, *Kilvert's Diary and Landscape*, pp. 64-7, 88-9, 195-9, 289-91.

70. The foregoing quotations in this paragraph are from pp. 16, 200, 25 of *The Fairy-Land of Science*.

71. One of those references (p. 76) noted how Tyndall explained the formation of crystals by means of bar magnets. His explanation appears in his lecture 'Matter and Force' on p. 82 of his *Fragments of Science for Unscientific People*, with which Kilvert was familiar.

72. Ann Thwaite, *Emily Tennyson: The Poet's Wife*, London, Faber and Faber, 1996, p. 273.

73. The quoted portions of *Parables of Nature* (London, Bell and Daldy, 1861) in this paragraph are from pp. 50, 9.

272 Kilvert's World of Wonders

74. *Op. cit.*, p. 89. She had it re-bound and still possessed it in her old age. Presumably, it was a collection of the year's issues.

75. His photos showing the building of Brunel's *Great Eastern* (1854-6) and his *Crimean Heroes* became famous. Tennyson had his children photographed by Cundall.

76. They worked with some of the best Victorian artists including Holman Hunt, Millais, Rosetti, and Whistler and did the illustrations for Lewis Carroll's *Alice in Wonderland* and *Alice Through the Looking Glass*. Illustrations appeared in natural history books in great abundance from the 1840s chiefly because of the subject's visual appeal. Natural objects were beautiful and flowers, ferns, and seaweeds could be mounted in albums or made into pictures (Barber, *op. cit.*, p. 85).

77. 'Playmate's Address', *The Playmate*, London, printed by George Bar.clay, 1847.

78. NLW edition of *Kilvert's Diary*, June-July 1870, 9 July 1870, p. 74.

79. Gypsum: 'a mineral composed of lime and sulphuric acid, hence also called sulphate of lime' (Glossary in Lyell's *Principles of Geology*, London, Penguin Books, 1997, edited by James Secord).

80. *The Settlers at Home* (1841), London, George Routledge, *n.d.*, pp. 165-8. The children assume that the mummified body is that of an ancient Briton, fleeing from Roman invaders, who became trapped in the marsh.

81. John Russell, *Pestalozzi. Educational reformer 1746-1827* [1888], London, George Allen and Unwin, 1926, p. 1.

82. From his *How Gertrude teaches her Children* (1801), quoted in Kate Silber, *Pestalozzi. The man and his work*, London, Routledge, Kegan, Paul, 1960, p. 136.

83. Russell, *op. cit.*, p. 31.

84. *Op. cit.*, p. 122.

85. *Home Influence: a tale for mothers and daughters*, London, Groombridge, 1856, p. viii.

86. Mrs Kilvert used Aguilar's novels to this end. Kilvert was doing the. same thing when he loaned or gave stories (e.g. *Stepping Heavenward* by Elizabeth Prentiss) to children.

87. *Home Discipline*, p. 163. Her italics. Her husband was Kilvert's uncle Francis.

88. The title 'Marquis of Lansdowne' was created in 1784. The 3rd Marquis (1780-1863) promoted charitable and educational work locally. In 1813 he visited and expressed approval of the East Tytherton Moravian school attended by Kilvert's mother. He allowed the Kilvert family to use Bowood's 'lovely grounds' (Emily Wyndowe, *op. cit.*, p. 93), which it no doubt valued as an environment for the study of natural history.

89. Richard was introduced by Erasmus Darwin to the Lunar Society of Birmingham, a body intent on seeing scientific inventions applied to industry. It is intriguing to think that Richard invented a track-laying vehicle, forerunner of the tank.

90. Letter of 9 March 1792 (*The Life and Letters of Maria Edgeworth*, edited by Augustus J.C. Hare, London, Edward Arnold, 1894, vol. I, p. 20). She also took

the girls to see Mr Broderip's 'collection of natural curiosities'. Broderip (1789-1859) was born in Bristol. He trained for the law but was a keen naturalist all his life and noted particularly for his shell collection. He wrote the zoological articles in Charles Knight's *Penny Cyclopedia*.

91. She meant anaesthetics that would 'inebriate in the most delightful manner' (letter of 26 May 1799, *Life and Letters.*, vol. I, p. 65). In a letter of 10 July 1826, she praised Davy's *Discourses* for 'giving a complete view of the ... progress of science in England within the last six years' (*ibid.*, vol. II, p. 142).

92. *Ibid.*, vol. I, p. 319. The letter is dated 19 August 1820. Visitors came in great numbers to study Pestalozzi's methods from the end of the eighteenth century (Kate Silber, *op. cit.*, p. 132). The Edgeworths first met Pestalozzi in Paris in 1802.

93. *Op. cit.*, p. 1.

94. *Life and Letters of Maria Edgeworth*, vol. I, p. 41.

95. This is true for example of *The Bracelets*. The virtue of honest industry is exemplified in *The Orphans*, the proper response to poverty is the theme of *Lazy Lawrence*. *Waste not, want not* dwells on extravagance and thrift.

96. Anne Thackeray Ritchie, who wrote the book's introduction, was the daughter of the novelist Thackeray, and a writer (as 'Miss Thackeray') herself. She recorded hearing Mary Howitt say, at a tea party in March 1854, that women should become M.P.s (*Letters of Anne Thackeray Ritchie*, London, John Murray, 1924, p. 217).

97. Marilyn Butler, *Maria Edgeworth. A literary biography*, Oxford, Clarendon Press, 1972, p. 54. 'Miss Edgeworth's heroines were pleasant and easily pleased' (Miss Thackeray, *Toilers and Spinsters and Other Essays*, London, Smith and Elder, 1876, p. 124).

98. William Spiers and Christopher Pond had come together in Australia, running a restaurant in Melbourne for gold miners. Returning to London, they noticed the poor catering provided for railway passengers and established cafés for them on stations. They also built the Criterion Restaurant and Theatre in Piccadilly, which opened on 21 March 1874 (www.roll-of-honour.com, Middlesex/Ruislip Spiers and Pond, Accessed 10.10.07). When in London on 25 June 1874, Kilvert dined at the Criterion Restaurant. Mary Collett might have been a barmaid there or in one of their other theatre restaurants.

99. This is true of *Stepping Heavenward* (Elizabeth Prentiss), *Alone in London* (Hesba Stretton), *The Gorilla Hunters* (R.M. Ballantyne). All of these are strongly evangelical with much emphasis on self-improvement.

100. M. Butler, *op. cit.*, p. 172. *Practical Education*, on which she collaborated with her father, was criticised for being irreligious and radical.

101. In this too he was a man of his time: 'Race was everywhere by mid-[nineteenth] century', wrote Peter Gay, by which he meant that the concept of race was being used to explain history (*The Cultivation of Hatred. The bourgeois experience: Victoria to Freud*, London, Fontana, 1995, p. 73). The issue of Celticism was in vogue in Kilvert's day: 'Celticism was a word to juggle with in mid-Victorian Britain' (R Samuel, *Theatres of Memory*, vol. II, London, Verso, 1998, p. 59).

102. Annie Keary would have known this book, which explores the state of Ireland as an English colony (see introduction to *Castle Rackrent* [1800], London, Penguin, 1992).

103. Keary became famous first through her children's books, as did many of the writers Kilvert knew.

104. *Memoir of Annie Keary* by her sister, London, Macmillan, 1883, pp. 62, 72, 17.

105. She visited him at his Eversley (Hants) home and he gave her an autographed copy of his novel *Alton Locke*.

106. Kilvert was a member of a similar group in Clyro: 'the usual set that one meets and knows so well – Dews, Thomases, Webbs, Wyatts, Bridges, Oswalds, Trumpers' (*Diary*, vol. I, p. 175, 12 July 1870). They comprised clergy and other professions.

107. Letter of 1840 from Robertson's Oxford college (Brasenose) quoted in Stopford Brooke, *op. cit.,* vol. I, p. 30). Brooke was Irish, Evangelical and radical (an admirer of Kingsley). Robertson wrote: 'Mr Keary is a man I should much like to learn from'. Keary had 'great power of mind, intellectual tastes . . . [was] enthusiastically religious, affectionate, sensitive' (*Memoir of Annie Keary*, pp. 3-4). Robertson was articled to a solicitor for a year.

108. *Memoir of Annie Keary*, p. 76.

109. Vernon Noble, *The Man in Leather Breeches. The life and times of George Fox*, London, Edek, 1953, p. 75. See also Arthur Raistrick, *Quakers in Science and Industry*, London, Bannisdale Press, 1950, pp. 32 and 43.

110. *East Tytherton Congregation Diary 1813-1824*, East Tytherton Archive, Moravian Church Centre, Muswell Hill, London. My italics.

111. Clair Figes, *250 Years of the Moravian Settlement of East Tytherton*, privately printed, 1993, p. 17.

112. *Op. cit.*, pp. 157-8. She was writing particularly of Quaker women here, whose education was, she said, superior to that of women in other social groups.

113. *The Settlers in Canada*, pp. 316 and 117.

Chapter 3
Kilvert the Naturalist

1. 'Ordering nature: revisioning Victorian science culture' in Bernard Lightman (editor) *Victorian Science in Context*, Chicago, Chicago University Press, 1997, p. 181.

2. David Elliston Allen, *The Naturalist in Britain. A social history*, Harmondsworth, Penguin, 1978, pp. 22-3.

3. Bernard Lightman, *Victorian Popularizers of Science*, p. 40.

4. Although Henry Kirke White's book of poems that was part of Emily Kilvert's school experience was not a book of this kind, its appearance there and then perhaps indicates that it was a manifestation of this movement. Even Philip Gosse, who was a professional naturalist and a F.R.S., could write as late as 1860-1861 *The Romance of Natural History*, each chapter of which treated

different aspects of nature 'in a poetic and anecdotal manner' (from the note on p. 263 of Edmund Gosse's *Father and Son* [1907], London, Penguin, 1988).

5. D. Allen, *op. cit.*, pp. 73-6.

6. O'Connor, *op. cit.*, pp. 346-7.

7. Peter Abbs, introduction to *Father and Son*, p. 26.

8. *Ibid.*, p. 48.

9. *DNB* entry on Gosse.

10. *A Naturalist's Rambles on the Devonshire Coast*, London, John van Voorst, 1853, p. v.

11. *DNB*.

12. *The Boy's Country Book*, p. 10.

13. *Glaucus; or the Wonders of the Shore*, Cambridge, Macmillan, 1855, p. 49.

14. *Kilvert's Diary*, vol. I, p. 41.

15. *Ibid.*, vol. III, p.107. My italics.

16. Merrill, *op. cit.*, pp. 51-3, 60.

17. The Rev. George Clayton, *Three Sermons on the Great Exhibition*, preached at York Street Chapel, Walworth, London, Benjamin Green, 1851, p. 1.

18. E Wyndowe, *op. cit.*, p. 104. 'The great Kohinoor diamond, now Her Majesty's by gift of the East India Co, through right of conquest, arrived from Delhi under guard' (John W. Dodds, *The Age of Paradox. A biography of England 1841-1851*, London, Gollancz, 1953, p. 437).

19. A.N. Wilson, *The Victorians*, London, Random House, 2007, pp. 65 and 69.

20. Paxton's conservatory had been built 'to house not machinery but a very special kind of water-lily brought from South America' (Asa Briggs, *Iron Bridge to Crystal Palace. Impact and images of the Industrial Revolution*, London, Thames and Hudson, 1979, p. 168). For an account of the lily's reception in Britain, see Kate Colquhoun, *A Thing in Disguise. The visionary life of Joseph Paxton*, London, Fourth Estate, 2003, pp. 156-61.

21. Paul Greenhalgh, 'The art and industry of Mammon: international exhibitions 1851-1901' in *The Victorian Vision. Inventing new Britain*, edited by John Mackenzie, p. 266.

22. Briggs, *Iron Bridge to Crystal Palace*, p. 66.

23. From *1851, or the Adventures of Mr and Mrs Sandboys* (1851), quoted in Humphrey Jennings, *Pandaemonium 1660-1886*, edited by Mary-Lou Jennings and Charles Madge, London, Andre Deutsch, 1985, pp. 258-9.

24. E. Wyndowe, *op. cit.*, p. 104. She would have seen an engraving of the Zoological Gardens in *Old England* (engraving no.2538) and read the account of the visit there by the Howitt children in *The Children's Year* (pp. 95-9).

25. Harriet Ritvo, 'The Natural World' in Mackenzie (editor), *op. cit.*, p. 290. Kew Gardens (i.e. the Royal Botanical Gardens) had a scientific purpose yet was very popular with the Victorian public. It contained many exotic plants from all over the world.

26. E. Wyndowe, *op. cit.*, p. 104.

27. *Victorian Science in Context.*, introduction, p. 1.

28. The fact that she recalled it as a possible target for a visit shows the significance it had for the family. Her visit to London and to the hippo had

been prepared for by her reading of *Old England*, in which Knight wrote triumphantly at the very end of the volume: 'If our grandsires saw a lion or an elephant, the sight was food for wonder to the end of their days: *we* walk at leisure in zoological gardens, amid specimens of natural history from all over the globe, and may be familiar . . . with everything that crawls, runs, swims or flies' (vol. II, p. 386). His italics.

29. His father was a tax collector, one brother was a lawyer, another a merchant.

30. G.R. De Beer, *Sir Hans Sloane and the British Museum*, London, Oxford University Press, 1953, p. 116.

31. Keynes, *op. cit.*, p. 213.

32. *Ibid.*, p. 59. Maria Edgeworth visited the Darwins in the early days of their marriage.

33. *Op. cit.*, p. 105. The Kilvert children's tour of London's educational sites also included a visit to the private collection of pictures in the Ellesmere Gallery at Bridgwater House.

34. *Op. cit.* p. 38. My italics. The Kilvert children were following the example of the Howitt children in visiting the Zoological Gardens. Chapter XXIV of *The Children's Year* is devoted to 'Meggy and Herbert's (repeat) visit there.

35. Joan Richards, 'The Probable and the Possible in early Victorian England', in Lightman, *Victorian Science in Context.*, p. 52.

36. D. Allen, *op. cit.*, p. 80.

37. *The Children's Year*, pp. 120-1.

38. Jim Endersby, 'Classifying sciences: systematics and status in mid-Victorian natural history', in Martin Daunton (editor), *The Organisation of Knowledge in Victorian Britain*, Oxford, OUP, 2005, p. 61.

39. *Kilvert's Cornish Diary*, p.47. Serpentine rocks are soft and predominantly dark green, though of other colours, sometimes mottled like the skin of snakes. The rock can be polished to make decorative objects.

40. If he, like the *Cornish Diary*'s editors, had been baffled by Hockin's reference, he would have omitted it and since all that he wrote in his notebook is reproduced in the *Cornish Diary* edition, there cannot have been any comment registering confusion over it.

41. Jenny Uglow, *The Lunar Men. The friends who made the future 1730-1810*, London, Faber and Faber, 2002, p. 302. Boulton was heavily involved in supplying his steam-engines to Cornish mines to pump out water.

42. *Ibid.*, p. 145.

43. *Ibid.*, p. 47. Nereids are the sea nymphs of Green mythology.

44. *The Children's Year*, pp. 128-9.

45. So called because they met at each other's houses on Monday nights nearest the full moon so that moonlight could see them safely home in the unlit streets of the period.

46. Erasmus Darwin wrote to Boulton: 'I have got with me a mechanical friend, Mr Edgeworth – the greatest conjuror I ever saw' (quoted in Uglow, *op. cit.*, p. 126).

47. The page references for the passages concerning mines and foundries in this paragraph are: pp. 24, 28, 25, 49, 74, 90. Kilvert displayed his knowledge

of mines when he referred (p. 52) to a mine's horizontal entrance as an 'adit'. Page numbers are liable to change during typesetting.

48. W Bottrell, *Traditions and Hearthside Stories of West Cornwall* (1870), Newcastle-on-Tyne, Frank Graham, 1980.

49. *Op. cit.*, p. 129.

50. *Op. cit.*, p. 121.

51. The 16 October 1878 *Diary* entry, when Kilvert was staying in Gower, records: 'the dear girls helped me to gather some of the beautiful seaweeds among the rocks'. *Cf. The Children's Year* (pp.122-3): 'There was plenty of sea-weed to be picked up; and Herbert had not gone far before he found much finer pieces, and even two or three kinds which he had not seen before'.

52. Quotations from *Kilvert's Cornish Diary* in this paragraph are from pp.42, 44, 40, 49, 97, 67, 100, 36-7.

53. *Op. cit.*, p. 12.

54 David Elliston Allen, *The Victorian Fern Craze. A history of Pteridomania*, London, Hutchinson, 1969, p. x.

55. Peter D.A. Boyd, *The Victorian Fern Cult in South-West Britain*, in Ide, Jerry and Paul, *Fern Horticulture: past, present and future perspectives*, 35-56, 1992, Intercept, Andover, Proceedings of the British Pteridological Society, 1991 (www.peterboyd.com/ferncultsw.htm p. 2, 21.7.08).

56. It was *An Analysis of British Ferns and their Allies* by George Francis.

57. D. Allen, *The Victorian Fern Craze.*, pp. 19-20. He added that the 'passion for forming collections was . . . elevated to a virtue by Paley's *Natural Theology*' (p. 25).

58. *Glaucus; or, the Wonders of the Shore*, p. 4.

59. *A Popular History of the British Ferns*, London, Lovell Reade, 1855, p. 3.

60. London, Smith and Elder, 1865, pp. 80-81. *Cf.* Boyd: 'south-west Britain has a special place in the Victorian enthusiasm for. . . . British Ferns', though he singled out Devon as the richest source because of its mild climate and fertile soils.

61. Bellairs, *op. cit.*, pp. i, viii.

62. 'The ladies were searching for ferns among the lower rocks and found some Asplenium Marinum and Asplenium Lanceolatum' (*Kilvert's Cornish Diary*, p. 42).

63. *Extracts from some unpublished parts of Kilvert's Diary relating to the Bevan and Dew families*, Hereford, Kilvert Society publication, *n.d.*, p.7. The extracts date from 27 March 1870 to 27 March 1874.

64. *Ibid.*, p. 13. The letter he received on his birthday (3 December 1871) from his sister Emily contained two devotional photographs for his scrap book.

65. *Ibid.*, p. 17.

66. Mrs Kilvert died on 4 July 1889. The book passed by Mrs Kilvert to her daughter was published in London by Simpkin and Marshall. Maund's title was a gesture of homage to Erasmus Darwin.

67. If bought in 1825, it could have been a present for Mrs Kilvert on her seventeenth birthday (she was born in May 1808). It seems likely that she had the book from an early age.

68. John Humphreys, 'A great Bromsgrovian', paper read at the Bromsgrove Institute and published in the *Bromsgrove, Droitwich and Redditch Messenger*, 12 June 1926.

69. *DNB*.

70. William Leadbetter, 'The story of Bromsgrove', *Bromsgrove Messenger*, 1949.

71. *Op. cit.*.

72 Its full title noted that it consisted of 'Highly finished Representations of Hardy Ornamental Flowering Plants, cultivated in Great Britain, with their Classification, History, Culture and other interesting information'. It came out between 1825 and 1851. The edition used by the author was published in London by Baldwin and Cradock. Maund's *Botanic Garden* provided the good pictures that the Kilvert family always craved. Its 56 descriptions of plants were illustrated by Edwin Dalton Smith (1800-1852). Son of an engraver, Smith was an accomplished early Victorian artist. He is best known for both portrait miniatures and botanical works.

73. In this preface, Maund said that he did not intend 'to wade deep in the current of science and research' but to provide 'a nosegay to lovers of a flower garden'.

74. Its full title is *The Botanist, containing accurately coloured figures of tender and hardy Ornamental Plants; with Descriptions, scientific and popular; intended to convey both moral and intellectual Gratification*. Maund's co-author was the Rev. John Stevens Henslow, Professor of Botany at Cambridge. Son of a solicitor, Henslow (1796-1861) attended St John's College, Cambridge and in 1819 accompanied Cambridge's Professor of Geology, Adam Sedgwick, on a field trip to the Isle of Wight. Henslow's own field classes, combining geology and zoology with botany, were very popular and Charles Darwin attended them. He and Henslow were lifelong friends.

75. He is a Samuel Smiles hero: though he has been left a modest fortune by his father, he is determined to work because he is against 'being an idler in a busy world' (*The Gorilla Hunters* [1861], London, Collins, *n.d.*, p. 9).

76. The book enlarges on the relative merits of hunter and naturalist. The conclusion reached in the moral debate is that the latter needed the former in order to secure specimens.

77. Ritvo pointed out that at the time the Empire could be seen as 'Nature', in contrast to the 'civilisation' that was home (*op. cit.*, p. 283).

78. Ritvo, *op. cit.*, p. 285.

79. *Diary*, vol. I, pp. 348-9.

80. The quotations in this paragraph are from NLW *Diary* edition, June-July 1870.

81. 'Minerals were a universal passion among anyone [*sic*] with an interest in natural philosophy' (Uglow, *The Lunar Men*, p. 296). And *cf.* Allen (*The Naturalist in Britain.*, p. 32): 'By general assent fossils were "curious" and deserved to be collected'.

82. Quotations in this paragraph up to this point are from Merrill, *op. cit.*, pp. 52, 255-6.

83. *Yanni, op. cit.*, p. 2.

84. Merrill, *op. cit.*, p. 260.

Chapter 4
Steamboats, Viaducts and Railways

1. W.A. Armstrong, 'The Countryside', in *The Cambridge Social History of Britain 1750-1950*, vol. I, edited by F.M.L. Thompson, Cambridge University Press, 1993, p. 115.

2. Once Kilvert was in Dorset and searching for Holditch Court with its 'ruined tower'. He asked a boy for directions: 'It was within a stone's throw of where he lay, but out of sight behind the house. He had never heard of it' (*Kilvert's Diary*, vol. I, p. 392).

3. Nicholas Faith, *The World the Railways Made*, London, Pimlico, 1994, p. 9.

4. Quoted in John W. Dodds, *op. cit.*, p. 230.

5. 'Nature,' he said, 'doth embrace/ Her lawful offspring in Man's art' (*Steamboats, Viaducts and Railways*, 1833).

6. The railway data are from Dodds, *op. cit.*, pp. 217, 223.

7. In the early nineteenth century, the phantasmagoria, a form of theatre which used a magic lantern to project (usually) frightening images, had become very popular. It marked both a stage in film history and the public's interest in the growth of science. One development of it was the illusion called 'Pepper's Ghost', much enjoyed by Kilvert and his family.

8. A.J.C. Hare, *Memorials of a Quiet Life*, London, Strahan and Co., 1871, vol. I, p. 328.

9. 'Memoirs', p. 48.

10. *Passages of a Working Life during half a century. A Prelude of Early Reminiscences* (two vols.), London, Bradbury and Evans, 1864, vol. II, p. 81.

11. Fanny Kemble, *Records of a Girlhood* (1878), in Humphrey Jennings, *op. cit.*, pp. 172-5. After her experience, Fanny confessed she was 'most horribly in love' with Stephenson, 'master of all these marvels'.

12. Quotations in this paragraph come from Sophia Kilvert's *Home Discipline*, pp. 86-8, 131, 133.

13. *Old England*, vol. II, p. 358.

14 The Smiles quotations in this paragraph are from his *Lives of the Engineers. The Locomotive. George and Robert Stephenson*, London, John Murray, 1874, pp. 123-4, 59.

15. 'Lawyer who left his mark on a park', *The Northern Echo*, 7 April 2004.

16. He was a devoted supporter of St Cuthbert's Church in Darlington. He conducted a school for poor children in the Church.

17. L.T.C. Rolt referred to 'the shrewd Quakers who presided over the affairs of the Stockton and Darlington Railway' (*George and Robert Stephenson. The Railway Revolution* [1960], London, Penguin, 1988, p. 129).

18. *The Larchfield Diary. Extracts from the diary of the late Mr Mewburn*, 1876, p. 155, Darlington Centre for Local Studies. Larchfield was his Darlington home.

19. Jane Backhouse was the daughter of John Backhouse of Darlington and of Hannah Gurney. Hannah's sister Emma married Joseph Pease. Barclay met Pease on 29 February 1844 when he was in Darlington to discuss his forthcoming marriage with Jane's parents.

20. *Op. cit.*, pp. 180, 165.

21. *Kilvert's Diary.*, vol. II, p. 401. *Cf.* vol. III, p. 57 – excitement aroused by the '7.30 express'.

22. *Old England*, vol. II, p. 358.

23. Wolfgang Schivelbusch, *The Railway Journey. The industrialisation of time and space in the nineteenth century*, Leamington Spa, Berg, 1986, p. 52.

24. Note in *Kilvert's Cornish Diary*, p. 105.

25. The Ivy Bridge viaduct 'was the highest (114 feet) on this stretch of the South Devon Railway' (*ibid.*, p. 105, editors' note).

26. ' . . . immense beams supported by other beams upright, bolted together by threes at the bottom but spreading as they rise and reach the floor of the viaduct' (*ibid.*, p. 23).

27. It was completed in 1848. Further sections – as far as Radstock, Somerset – were finished by 1854. There were five timber viaducts on the Bradford-on-Avon/Bathampton section of this line. The line was developed by Brunel's Great Western Railway Company (Brian Lewis, *Brunel's Timber Bridges and Viaducts*, Hersham, Ian Allen Publishing, 2007, pp. 107, 110).

28. *Ibid.*, pp. 1, 115.

29. John Binding, *Brunel's Royal Albert Bridge. A Study of the Design and Construction of his 'Gateway to Cornwall' at Saltash*, Truro, Twelveheads Press, 1997, p. 6.

30. See J. Toman, *Kilvert's Diary and Landscape*, chapter three – 'The Cornish Dream'.

31. Binding, *op. cit.*, pp. 114-15.

32. *Cf.* Knight's *Old England*, vol. II, p. 358: 'the Great Western line was. planned and accomplished by Brunel, on a scale of magnificence and expense hitherto unheard of'.

33. *Op. cit.*, p. 29.

34. Dodds, *op. cit.*, p. 217.

35. Faith, *op. cit.*, p. 17.

36 The authentic detail in the entry was the result in part of the fact that it was based on an account of the accident given to Kilvert by a railway worker, William Hicks.

37. Civilian life offered little that was comparable. Kilvert typified such readers: his diary contains over 60 entries about various kinds of accidents and disasters, four of which are railway ones, thirteen are shipwrecks.

38. Terry Coleman, *The Railway Navvies. A history of the men who made the railways*, Harmondsworth, Penguin, 1986, p. 35. *Cf.* Smiles (*op. cit.*, p. 250); 'Navvies were in many respects a remarkable class ... capable of 12-16 hours' work a day'.

39. Some passengers were too nervous to brave the Tunnel so the GWR had to provide a stagecoach service from Box to Corsham in the line's early days.

40. Kilvert's awareness of continuing development of railways and of navvies' role in it is seen in the *Diary* entry for 11 March 1875: 'the inn was full of navvies who are making the new railroad to Malmesbury from Dauntesey'.

41. Francis D. Klingender, *Art and the Industrial Revolution*, London, Paladin, 1972, p. 133.

42. *Op. cit.*, p. 135.

43. 'This "making the running" was the most spectacular part of navvy work, and one of the most dangerous [parts]' (Coleman, *op. cit.*, p. 46). The phrase is now part of the English language.

44. The Tunnel, 2,400 yards long, is near Rugby, and was built by Robert Stephenson, who was chief engineer of the London-Birmingham Railway. Three years were needed to complete the Tunnel. Smiles described the building of the Tunnel in his book on the Stephensons.

45. *Drawings of the London and Birmingham Railway by John C. Bourne with an Historical and Descriptive Account by John Britton F.S.A.*, London, J.C. Bourne and Ackermann and Co., 1839, pp. 3-4, 7-8.

46. Britton summarised the history of steam navigation, culminating in an account of the rivalry between the *Sirius* and the *Great Western* on the transatlantic run.

47. His lecture, entitled 'A Lecture on Railways, particularly on the Intended Line from London to Bristol', was published in 1833.

48. The Bath firm of Stothert, Slaughter & Co. built the *Arrow* locomotive for the line.

49. London, David Bogue, 1846.

50. He was later M.P. for Oxford University. He is believed to have had close contacts with Quakers in the West of England and may have introduced uncle Francis to Sophia de Chièvre.

51. *Sir Robert Harry Inglis, Bart. The Christian – the Statesman – the Gentleman.* The poem calls him 'the universal friend' and states that 'Love ruled his heart'.

52. R.P. Cruden, *History of Gravesend and the Port of London*, London, Effingham Wilson, 1843, p. 458. Cruden also wrote a history of steamboats (1831).

53. *Gregory Watt Itinerary Letters* in the Boulton and Watt archives (Birmingham Central Library): letters MS 3147/3/52/16 (27 June 1803) and MS 3782/13/29/179 (15 December 1804).

54. There were also bowling greens, swings, a stone loggia, fountains, and a labyrinth. In 1853, the hotel became Bath Proprietary College where Kilvert's brother-in-law, William Smith, was a schoolmaster. Much of the information about the Gardens comes from Brenda Sheddon, *The Last Promenade. Sydney Gardens,* Bath, Millstream Books, 2000.

55. The quality of the canal's engineering may be seen in the fact that on 4 July 2009 the modern pump used to pump water into the docks near Crofton failed. The Boulton and Watt beam engine, installed in 1812, was used instead.

56. Andrew Swift, *The Ringing Grooves of Change. Brunel and the Coming of the Railway to Bath with the Story of the Box Tunnel,* www.akemanpress.com, Akeman Press, 2006, p. 94. J. Stothert was a son of George Stothert and the 'Mr Falkner' was Francis Henry Falkner.

57. Kilvert knew Knight's glowing account of this development, which begins: 'The spirit of enterprise, fortunately for the general weal, is never satisfied'. The plan 'to cross the Atlantic in an ocean steamer . . . [would] abridge, by at least one half, the distance between England and America' (*Old England*, vol. II, p. 355).

58. This may have been the telegram of the Brazilian Telegraph Company, which referred to the deaths of '400 emigrants and 41 crew', corresponding to Kilvert's '440 persons burnt in her'. Other telegrams (and reports) told of 476 on board.

59. She was celebrated in broadsheets, prints, articles, biographies, novels, plays, and panoramas.

60. *Visits to Remarkable Places*, pp. 356, 358.

61. 1822 saw the founding of the Newcastle-on-Tyne Literary and Philosophical Society and in 1829 of the Natural History Society of Northumberland, Durham, and Newcastle-on-Tyne.

62. Constance Smedley, *Grace Darling and her Times*, London, Blackett and Hurst, 1932, pp. 54-5.

63. *Grace had an English Heart*, London, Viking, 1988, p. 146.

64. His reference in the poem to 'winds and waves in furious conflict' and to 'shattered barks' indicates that disasters such as that of the *Forfarshire* were on his mind.

65. *The Lighthouse*, in vol. I of uncle Francis's *Commonplace Book*.

66. Described as one of the 'Seven Wonders of the Industrial World', the Bell Rock Lighthouse was built in difficult conditions by Robert Stephenson between 1807 and 1810. He modelled the design on that of Smeaton's Eddystone Lighthouse.

67. Book VII, chapter two, p. 319.

68. Knight had included a lengthy section on Steam Navigation in *Old England* (vol. II, pp. 354-5, 358). He enthused that steam ships had made the world a smaller place, bringing 'the vast empire of India within 30 days' distance of home', that steamer-lines now monopolised the Atlantic traffic. He also paid tribute to the 'invaluable invention' of the screw propeller by Mr F.P. [*sic*] Smith. One of Kilvert's memories of the Great Exhibition may have been the objects in Class V: 'Machines for direct use, including Carriages and Railway and Naval Mechanisms'.

69. By 1876 her passenger-carrying days were over. A few years later she was condemned to carrying coal from Cardiff to San Francisco.

70. Launched in July 1864, it made its maiden voyage from Liverpool to New York on 3 December 1864 – Kilvert's 24th birthday.

71. Mrs Gwatkin, Kilvert's hostess, explained that 'even five years ago there was much more trade and wealth in Liverpool'. Her husband, Theophilus Palmer Gwatkin (1814-93) was the son of General Edward Gwatkin and the grandson of the niece of Sir Joshua Reynolds, who had married Richard Lovell Gwatkin in January 1781. Theophilus Gwatkin worked in Liverpool.

72. Obituary of George Stothert in *Bath Chronicle*, 2 December 1858; obituary of Mrs Stothert in *Bath and Cheltenham Gazette*, 31 January 1855. Stothert came from Dumfriesshire Presbyterian stock.

73. Edward Hine, *The English Nation Identified with the Lost House of Israel by Twenty Seven Identifications, dedicated to the (so-called) British People, by their Kinsman, Edward Hine*, published by various publishers countrywide including Pearson of Milsom Street, Bath, 1871.

74. Hine explained that the people of Israel were initially captives of the Assyrians but, once freed, they became wanderers. The Anglo-Saxons had been

shown to have wandered in exactly the same territories as the Israelites by the English historian Sharon Turner in his book *Anglo-Saxons*. Hine cited some Biblical prophecies saying that the Israelites would be directed to the 'islands'.

75. *The English Nation*, p. 26.

76. Charles Mark Barne (1803-1891). He was another clergyman who had come (1821-1825) under Simeon's influence at Cambridge.

77. Examples were cited of the Welsh, the North American Indians, the Maoris of New Zealand, and the Kaffirs of the Cape.

78. It was actually Balboa, not Cortez, who marched his army across Mexico from its Caribbean to its Pacific coast.

79. Bourne noted in the introduction to his book on the GWR that it was only recently that 'a turning lathe' had facilitated the building of a cheap steam-engine. Kilvert was deeply impressed by what lathes could do on his visit to the Birkenhead shipbuilding yard (see next chapter).

80. *Kilvert's Diary*, vol. II, pp. 56, 53.

81. Eliza Keary, *op. cit.*, p. 51.

Chapter 5
Kilvert and Science and Technology

1. Introduction, vol. II, p. 10. Plomer, very much an aesthete, was prone to separate the two.

2. Peter Morgan Jones, 'Kilvert Days and Kilvert Ways', *Kilvert Society Journal*, No. 24, September 2007, p. 11. The phrase 'a literary shudder' is used about the writer H.J. Massingham but we are told that Kilvert possibly 'felt much the same'.

3. They noted that the 'evocative details' of his descriptions are 'as liable to be unromantic and industrial as more obviously picturesque', and this is true (Introduction, p. 6).

4. *Kilvert's Diary*, vol. I, p. 300. He followed this up with another visit to see a later model.

5. *Op. cit.*, p. 1 and p. 21.

6. B. Lightman, *Victorian Science in Context.*, p. 3.

7. J. Morrell and A. Thackray, *Gentlemen of Science. Early Years of the British Association for the Advancement of Science*, Oxford, Clarendon Press, 1981, p. 12.

8. During the 1830s and 1840s, the BAAS steadily encouraged the idea that 'science' meant, not all knowledge, but a particular form of it.

9. Holmes, *op. cit.*, p. xvi. His italics.

10. *Op. cit.*, p. ix.

11. *Op. cit.*, pp. vii, 122, 2.

12. Merrill, *op cit.*, pp. 75, 77.

13. Quotations in this paragraph are from Morrell and Thackray, *Gentlemen of Science. Early Years*, pp. 32, 227.

14. The poem appears in uncle Francis's *Commonplace Book*, vol. I. Henrietta

Fry (c.1800-1860) published *Echoes of Eternity*, a collection of religious poetry and prose (Bath, Binns and Goodwin, 1859). She acknowledged uncle Francis's help in translating some Latin pieces in it.

15. Morrell and Thackray, *Gentlemen of Science. Early Years*, pp. 149-151.

16. William Daniel Conybeare (1787-1857), geologist and lecturer at St Luke's, Brislington, Bristol. He was one of the geologists with whom Lewis Weston Dillwyn fraternised.

17. Duncan (1769-1844) promoted philanthropic schemes in Bath. He was keeper of Oxford's Ashmolean Museum. Conybeare was writing to the Rev. William Harcourt on 23 March 1833 (Morrell and Thackray, *Gentlemen of Science. Early correspondence of the British Association for the Advancement of Science*, London, Royal Historical Society of University College, London, 1984, p. 163).

18. This *Report* was published by John Murray, London, 1864. Her donation of it is recorded in the 1865 *BLSI Report* (ref. 1994. L706).

19. P.117. How privileged John Dillwyn was on 14 August 1844 to have Professor Wheatstone staying in his home and explaining the 'marvellous wires' to him.

20. Tom Standage, *The Victorian Internet*, New York, Walker and Co., 1998, p. 61.

21. Dr William Montgomerie, Indian Army surgeon, saw it used in Singapore for knife handles. It was a product of Empire, like the 'merchandise ... from all corners of the world' that Kilvert saw in Liverpool warehouses.

22. The parish was actually St Mark's, Woolwich Reach, on the north bank of the Thames. The firm of S.W. Silver began in the eighteenth century, making waterproof clothing for the army and the colonial service.

23. Telegraph wires along the Great Western Railway were insulated initially with India rubber and enclosed in gas pipe. Later, gutta percha was used. On 11 July 1874, Kilvert bought in Salisbury a pair of 'ten shilling gutta-percha soled elastic boots'.

24. *Op. cit.*, pp. 36-8.

25. *Op. cit.*, p. 217.

26. He used its treatments on patients at London's University College Hospital.

27. On the 1840 Tavistock committee was John Rundle M.P., father of Mrs Charles, whose novels Kilvert eagerly read.

28. Geoffrey Cantor, 'Friends of Science? The Role of Science in Quaker Periodicals', in Louise Henson (editor), *Culture and Science in Nineteenth-Century Media*, Aldershot, Ashgate, 2004, p. 83. Cantor noted there were *two* 'unofficial organs', the other being the Glasgow-based *British Friend*.

29. Cantor, *op. cit.*, pp. 84-5.

30. O'Connor, *op. cit.*, p. 225. The *Penny Cyclopedia* founded by Knight in 1832 (it ran till 1858) had a middle-class readership. It was the staple of the young Edmund Gosse's reading, as chapter three noted. It was probably found at some point in the Kilvert household.

31. O'Connor, *op. cit.*, pp. 227-8. Knight had communicated this viewpoint to Kilvert in his *Old England* (vol. II, chapter 3, p. 254): 'The moment science ceases to inquire or speculate it stops'. Newton didn't discover the law of gravity by 'mathematical speculations' but by imagination.

32. O'Connor, *op. cit.*, pp. 233-4.

33. Gowan Dawson, introduction to 'Science in the Nineteenth Century Periodical', www.sciper.org/ (Accessed 5.6.11), pp. 1, 3-4.

34. *A Weekend in a French Country House* (London, Smith and Elder, 1867), pp. 122, 55, 97.

35. *Op. cit.*, p. 44. Gertrude is the mother in Pestalozzi's *Leonard and Gertrude*.

36. *Ibid.*, p. 45.

37. Silber, *op. cit.*, p. 140. The quotations within the passage are from Pestalozzi's *How Gertrude Teaches her Children*.

38. Pupils at the Pestalozzian Institution at Worksop (Notts.) were being encouraged in the 1840s to catch and study butterflies and to place them and other specimens obtained from countryside walks in the school's museum.

39. Now designated a Site of Special Scientific Interest, it is near the village of Bathampton. The Bath painter, Thomas Barker (1767-1847) did a painting of it, *Hampton Rocks, Morning* which is in Bath's Victoria Art Gallery.

40. 'Added to them were many more from the circulating libraries of the city.'

41. The quoted words by Fowler about Claverton Lodge come from his *Reminiscences*, privately printed, 1921, pp. 10-12. The comments about his Oxford experiences are from his *Oxford Retrospect*, quoted in Raymond Huntingdon Coon, *William Warde Fowler: an Oxford humanist*, Oxford, Basil Blackwell, 1934, pp. 17-18.

42. The words of a Fellow of Lincoln College, quoted in Coon, *op. cit.*, p. 60. Fowler's *Year of the Birds* (1886) 'made the name of Warde Fowler a household name in many homes' (*ibid.*, p. 193).

43. He preached in many Somerset churches. He wrote *Antidote to Infidelity* (in two parts), 1702 and 1717.

44. Vailoti, Ezio and Yenter, Timothy, 'Samuel Clarke', The Stanford Encyclopedia of Philosophy (Summer 2009 Edition), Edward N. Zalta (ed.), http://plato.stanford.edu/archives/sum2009/entries/Clarke/

45. *Evidences of the Being of God*, Bath, printed by A.E. Binns, 1827, p. 4.

46. Roy M. MacLeod, 'Whigs and savants: reflections on the reform movement in the Royal Society, 1830-48', in Inkster and Morrell, *op. cit.*, p. 59.

47. Trevor Fawcett, 'Bath Scientific Societies and Institutions', in Wallis P. (editor), *Innovation and Discovery. Bath and the rise of science*, Bath, Bath Royal Literary and Scientific Institution and the William Herschel Society, 2008, pp. 155-6.

48. 'Lonsdale's advice was constantly sought both for identifying fossils and editing manuscripts and his role as mentor is exemplified by his relationship with Charles Darwin, whom he greatly assisted in the study of corals' (*DNB*).

49. When Lewis Weston Dillwyn was in Bath on 20 May 1829, he called in Gibbes to attend his ill mother-in-law.

50. *Bath and Cheltenham Gazette*, 25 January 1825, quoted by Fawcett, *op. cit.*, p. 161.

51. Its list of members, compiled by Matthews, indicates a preponderance of doctors, clergymen, and other professionals. Several of the Agricultural Society's members were also BLSI members.

52. The very words were likely to have been his, although no doubt they

represented the Committee's views. That uncle Francis had developed views on the objects of such associations is clear from the fact that he gave a lecture to the Association entitled 'On the Advantages derivable from Institutions for the Promotion of Literature, Science and the Arts' on 7 November 1862.

53. Agreed at the Committee meeting of 25 January 1826. The meeting of 23 November 1826 authorised the introduction of *two* visitors (*BLPA Minutes 1826-1834*, ref.1996 L6066).

54. The Institution's literary and general lectures also show popular appeal.

55. Such literary topics as these appeared: 'The Utility of Classical Learning', 'The Text of Shakespeare', 'Rev. Richard Graves' (by uncle Francis), Lamb, Coleridge, Cowper, Sterne, Bulwer's Novels, Chatterton. General lecture topics included: 'Somnambulism', 'Ecclesiastical Architecture of the Middle Ages' (by John Britton), 'Ralph Allen and Prior Park' (by uncle Francis).

56. Cf. Morrell and Thackray, *Gentlemen of Science. Early Years*, p. 224: 'Only if science were separated from politics and theology could members of opposing social or religious groups unite for its advancement'.

57. 1857 *Annual Report*.

58. HMS *Beagle* surveyed the coasts of South America and Captain Fitzroy wanted a young naturalist to accompany him. Darwin wrote excitedly to John Henslow from Rio de Janeiro about the new species of spiders he had collected. Darwin's *The Voyage of the Beagle* (1842) included Jenyns' account of reptiles. Jenyns edited Gilbert White's *The Natural History of Selborne* (1843) and he published his own *Observations in Natural History* (1846) and *Observations in Meteorology* (1858).

59. *Victorian Science in Context.*, p. 3.

60. T. Fawcett, *Science Lecturing in Georgian Bath*, in Willis (ed.), *op. cit.*, p. 144.

61. *Sermons Preached at Christ Church, Bath, before the National Schools*, London, John Taylor, 1827, p. 11.

62. *Op. cit.*, p. 122.

Chapter 6
Natural Law and the Mind

1. He was aware of the 1872 Congress at Leeds because he referred to it in the 10 October 1873 *Diary* entry. The Congress too focused on working men.

2. At the Bath Congress, the Bishop of Oxford and four other speakers spoke on 'The Church's Duty in Regard to Strikes and Labour'. Kilvert listened to them all. He also attended eight sections of the Congress, one of which was on 'The Church and the Masses'.

3. The cost of a ticket for the Congress was 7s 6d (very high to meet the huge costs involved) but working men's tickets were free. Kilvert said that between 6,000 and 7,000 tickets were sold.

4. *Report of 1873 Bath Church Congress*, London, Rivingtons, 1873, p. 16.

5. This quotation and those in the previous paragraph come from Brooke, *op. cit.*, vol. II, pp. 7, 38-9.

6. The novel was popular among university students but attacked in the

religious press for its outspokenness. Kingsley's significance for Kilvert is examined in J. Toman, *Kilvert: The Homeless Heart*, pp. 108-115, where it is shown that the latter shared many of the ideas of the former.

7. *DNB* entry on Buckle.

8. In 1858, Tyndall met Buckle at a dinner where Dr Livingstone was also a guest. Tyndall said Buckle was 'the literary lion of the day'.

9. Alfred Henry Huth, *The Life and Writings of Henry Thomas Buckle*, London, Sampson Low, 1880, p. 78.

10. Quotations in this paragraph are from Buckle's *History*, vol. I (London, John Parker, 1857), pp. 16, 21, 18, 36, 144, 158-9.

11. Adrian Desmond and James Moore, *Darwin*, London, Michael Joseph, 1991, pp. 463-4.

12. *History*, vol. I, p. 238. *Cf.* also Buckle's reference to 12th-century belief in 'witchcraft, in palmistry, in astrology' with Kilvert's reference to 'charms, incantations, astrology and witchcraft'. The Buckle reference occurs in *Miscellaneous and Posthumous Works of Henry Thomas Buckle*, vol. I, edited by Helen Taylor, London, Longmans Green, 1872, p. 176.

13. Quoted in *Radnorshire Legends and Superstitions* by Mrs Essex Hope, *Radnorshire Transactions*, vol. XXIV (1954), p. 5. Mrs Hope's essay, which first appeared in the *Occult Review* (1921), was based on Kilvert's manuscript. She was niece to the diarist. His ambivalent stance towards superstition – one moment highly critical of it, the next displaying a strong trait of it – is examined in J. Toman, *Kilvert's Diary and Landscape*, chapter eight.

14. *History*, vol. I, p. 239. He charged the clergy with 'discouraging all inquiry' (*ibid.*, vol. II, p. 526).

15. He was much concerned over the South Wales miners' strike in February 1873.

16. *Kilvert's Diary*, 31 January 1875. Kingsley died on 23 January and his funeral took place on 28 January.

17. The *Alton Locke* passages in the last paragraph are from pp. 367-371.

18. Martha S. Vogeler, *Frederic Harrison: the vocations of a Positivist*, Oxford, Clarendon Press, 1984, p.26. Harrison was one of Congreve's Wadham students.

19. C.H. Herford, quoted in T.R. Wright, *The Religion of Humanity: the impact of Comptean Positivism on Victorian Britain*, Cambridge, Cambridge University Press, 1985, p. 5.

20. Sutton was the pseudonym of John Frazer Corkran, a correspondent of the liberal, investigative *Morning Chronicle*, author of some novels, and husband of Charlotte Cushman (1816-1876), Eliza Cook's friend. Cushman and Corkran were close friends of Thackeray.

21. *Science and Religion*, London, Bell and Daldy, 1868, pp. 301-305.

22. Brooke, *op. cit.*, vol. II, pp. 161-2.

23. His text, Paul's *Letter to the Hebrews* (2.17-18), emphasises that Christ took to himself the ordinary sons of men and 'therefore had been made like these brothers of his in every way'.

24. Owen Chadwick, *op. cit.*, part II, p. 135. It will be recalled from chapter five

that Kilvert's uncle Francis embraced the Broad Church school personified by Adam Sedgwick and embodied in the BAAS.

25. Brooke, *op. cit.*, vol. I, pp. 254-5.

26. *Ibid.*, vol. II, p. 19. His italics. He and Ruskin were students together at Brasenose College, Oxford.

27. *Ibid.*, vol. II, pp. 42-3.

28. Secord stated that phrenology was 'a denial of man's immortal soul' (*op. cit.*, p. 86). Robert Young noted: 'Its alleged determinist, materialist and atheist implications were grasped at the outset' (*op. cit.*, p. 63).

29. Quoted in Young, *op. cit.*, p. 5.

30. *Op. cit.*, p. 2.

31. Terry M. Parsinnen, 'Mesmeric Performers', *Victorian Studies*, vol. XXI, autumn 1997, pp. 90-1.

32. Cooter, *op. cit.*, p. 146 and pp. 150-2.

33. *The Constitution of Man considered in relation to external objects* (6th edition), Edinburgh, John Anderson, 1836, pp. 18-19.

34. *Op. cit.*, p. 117.

35. *Op. cit.*, p. 91.

36. *Op. cit.*, pp. 137-8.

37. *Ibid.*, p. 121.

38. *Alton Locke*, p. 117.

39. *Ibid.*, p. 33.

40. *Op. cit.*, p. 3.

41. Quoted in Amice Lee, *op. cit.*, p. 90.

42. Cooter, *op. cit.*, p. 123.

43. *Ibid.*, p. 42.

44. *Ibid.*, pp. 72, 127.

45. Irys Herfner, 'Mesmerism', *Dublin University Magazine*, January 1844, p.

46. William Howitt, *The Boy's Country Book*, pp. 165-7, 212-20. The Electrical Society of London (founded 1837) declared that 'as a universal agent in nature and space electricity takes the first rank in the temple of knowledge' (quoted in Briggs, *Iron Bridge to Crystal Palace*, p. 145). Uglow (*The Lunar Men*, p.10) noted that it had absorbing interest to people in Erasmus Darwin's boyhood (the 1740s) and that 'electricians' gave lectures. People then speculated whether electricity was an astounding property of nature or a manifestation of divine power.

47. *Op. cit.*, vol. II, p. 242.

48. *Kilvert's Diary*, vol. III, pp. 270, 196, vol. I, p. 309.

49. D.M. Walmsley, *Anton Mesmer*, London, Robert Hale, 1967, pp. 11, 13, 103.

50. *MESMERISM by Dr Mesmer* (1779), edited by Gilbert Frankau, London, Macdonald, 1948, p. 54.

51. *Animal Magnetism or Mesmerism and its Phenomena* (1851), London, Nicholls, 1899, p. 121.

52. *Ibid*, p. 22. Gregory was one of the vice-presidents of the London Mesmeric Infirmary.

53. Frankau, *op. cit.*, p. 9.

54. Peter Ackroyd, *Dickens*, London, Minerva, 1991, p. 258.

55. Alison Winter, 'The Construction of Orthodoxies and Heterodoxies in the early Victorian Life Sciences', in *Victorian Science in Context*, edited by Bernard Lightman, p. 25.

56. Fred Kaplan, *Dickens and Mesmerism. The hidden springs of fiction*, New Jersey, Princeton University Press, 1975, pp. 34-5. The period in which mesmerism appeared was significant in Kaplan's view. It grew up in the time of the French Revolution, when 'science was transformed into magic and back into science again'. It was 'an offspring of the Enlightenment' (*ibid.*, pp. 232-3).

57. Winter, *Mesmerized. Powers of Mind in Victorian Britain'*, Chicago, University of Chicago Press, 1998, p. 4.

58. Taylor Stoehr, *Dickens: the dreamer's stance*, Ithaca, New York, Cornell University Press, 1965, pp. 272-3.

59. Winter, *Mesmerized*, p .6.

60. Peter Gay, *op. cit.*, p. 453.

61. Winter, *Mesmerized*, p. 31.

62 *Ibid.*, p. 246.

63. Parsinnen, 'Mesmeric Performers', pp. 88-9 and 98. Their importance in shaping the 'culture of science' was undeniable (*ibid.*, p. 89).

64. *Ibid.*, vol. II, pp. 24-6. His italics. Alessandro Gavazzi (1809-1889) was an Italian patriot and popular preacher. While in England, he gradually went over to the Evangelical church and became organiser of Italian Protestants in London (hence his appearance at Exeter Hall).

65. The quotations from Brooke's *Life* in this paragraph are vol. II, pp. 44, 140.

66. *Western Mercury and Somersetshire Herald*, 31 August 1872. Hume described himself as the 'World Renowned Mesmerist and Phrenologist'.

67. Cooter, *op. cit.*, p. 22.

68. *Ibid.*, pp. 120, 255.

69. The display of skulls, charts of the brain, and measuring instruments reinforced the supposed objectivity and 'scientific' basis of phrenology.

70. Cooter, *op. cit.*, p. 163.

71. The famous O'Key sisters, subjects of Dr Elliotson's experiments at University College Hospital, could name objects held up in adjacent rooms and had the unhappy knack of predicting which hospital patients were going to die.

72. This aspect of Kilvert is treated in detail in chapter eight of J. Toman, *Kilvert's Diary and Landscape*.

73. Gregory (*op. cit.*, p.17) explained that many susceptible subjects were found, especially in public exhibitions of mesmerism, among the less educated classes because such people did not exercise their intellectual powers in the same way as members of the professional classes did.

74. Winter, *Mesmerized*, p. 137.

75. Walter E. Houghton, *The Victorian Frame of Mind, 1830-1870*, New Haven, Yale University Press, 1985, p. 103.

76. Examples are: the Moccas oaks (vol. III, pp.263-4), referred to as 'strange . . . misshapen oak men'; a sick woman who told him a story of her

waking dream 'in such a strange weird way that I felt uncomfortable' (vol. I, p.283); Restormel Castle was 'a strange weird place' (*Kilvert's Cornish Diary*, p.85); a description of the eclipse of the moon: 'It was very strange and solemn' (vol. I, p. 175).

77. In this, Kilvert was typically Evangelical: 'How much do they lose who neglect to trace the leadings of God in providence' (Legh Richmond, *The Dairyman's Daughter*, p. 14); 'Evangelicals could discern a special providence in the most trivial occasions' (Lord David Cecil, *The Stricken Deer*, London, Constable, 1929, p. 81).

78. His italics. The quoted words have not been identified. The idea of 'God's messenger' is frequent in religious writings. Robertson noted that St. Paul presented himself as 'God's messenger', *Expository Lectures on St. Paul's Epistles to the Corinthians delivered at Trinity Chapel, Brighton*, London, Smith and Elder, 1864, p. 14.

79. Chapter seven of *Kilvert's Diary and Landscape* examines the Lucy Gray poems in detail.

80. The last phrase has been italicised to stress its connection with mesmerism: to sit face to face, staring into his subject's eyes, was a means by which the mesmerist induced the trance.

81. He continually emphasised 'her lovely blue eyes' (*Kilvert's Diary*, vol. II, p. 346). Kilvert's fascination with the way a person's eyes give insight into personality/ identity is seen in his meeting with the waitress at the Golden Lion, Dolgellau: 'She was a beautiful girl with blue eyes, eyes singularly lovely, the sweetest saddest most weary and most patient eyes I ever saw' (*ibid.*, vol. I, p. 352).

82. Winter, *Mesmerized*, p. 249.

83. Quoted in Capern, *op. cit.*, p. 29.

84. *Op. cit.*, p. 258.

Chapter 7
Kilvert and Tyndall

1. *Kilvert's Diary*, vol. III, p. 183. The Rev. Burns was to attend the Church of England Missionary Society's annual May Meeting at Exeter Hall, the Evangelical centre. Kilvert was not bound for this event but to stay with his brother Edward who was ill, and to tour art galleries and museums.

2. Edward Cleal, *The Story of Congregationalism in Surrey*, London, James Clarke & Co., 1908, p. 109.

3. Article on Pembroke Chapel by Mr G.H. Wicks that appeared in the *Redland Park Recorder*, November 1916 (Records of the Pembroke Congregational Church, Clifton, 1866-1922 Registers, accession no. 33778, Bristol Record Office).

4. *Congregational Yearbook*, London, Congregational Union of England and Wales, 1903, p. 170.

5. A.C. Sturney, *The Story of Kingston Congregational Church*, Kingston, published by the author, 1932, p. 34.

6. Published by Longman in 1871. Its full title was *Fragments of Science for Unscientific People: a series of detached essays, lectures, and reviews.*

7. *DNB* entry on Tyndall. His own preface stated that he wished 'to extend sympathy for science beyond the limits of the scientific public'.

8. Tyndall, *Scientific Materialism*, an address to the British Association in Norwich, 19 August 1868, *FSUP*, New York, Appleton and Co, 1871, p. 111 (Michigan Historical Reprint). This emphasis on effecting social and educational reforms connects him with Rousseau, the Edgeworths, Pestalozzi and others, often of Nonconformist stock, who fostered modern, utilitarian education.

9. He established the New Lanark mills where he introduced humanitarian working and living conditions. His workers had decent houses and a school which reflected his advanced thinking on education. Significantly, William and Mary Howitt visited New Lanark in 1821 (Amice Lee, *op.cit.*, p. 68). Frederick Robertson was reading Owen in June 1851, the year of the great Exhibition, but he rejected his vision of society because the spiritual regeneration that he (Robertson) craved could not emerge from such a materialistic outlook (Brooke, *op. cit.*, vol. II, pp. 46-8).

10. McMillan and J. Meehan, *John Tyndall. 'Xemplar of scientific and technological education*, Dublin, ETA Publications, 1980, p. 29.

11. D. Thompson, George Edmundson, *Friends Quarterly*, vol. X, 1956, p. 24. 'Ackworth was the first of a series of Quaker boarding schools which reflected in their curriculum the earlier ideas on manual education' (*ibid*, p. 25). William Howitt attended Ackworth School.

12. E. Bennett, *John Tyndall: a reminiscence*, Friends Quarterly Examiner, 1894, p. 239.

13. A.S. Eve and C.H. Creasey, *Life and Work of John Tyndall*, London, Macmillan, 1945, p. 18.

14. *Ibid.*, p. 21.

15. Frank M. Turner, 'John Tyndall and Victorian Scientific Naturalism', in W. Brock, N. McMillan, R. Mollan, *John Tyndall. Essays on a natural philosopher*, Dublin, Royal Dublin Society, 1981, p. 179.

16. Delivered to the BAAS at Liverpool, 16 September 1870. Tyndall prefaced it with these words of Sir Benjamin Brodie: 'physical investigation helps to teach us the right use of the imagination: the source of poetic genius, and the instrument of discovery in science'.

17. 'On the Scientific Use of the Imagination', in *FSUP*, p. 130.

18. To the student prize-winners in the Faculty of Arts (1868-1869 session), University College, London.

19. The quotations here are from pp. 100-1 and p.104 of the Address in *FSUP*.

20. 'Matter and Force', a lecture to the working men of Dundee, 5 September 1867, *FSUP*, p. 93.

21. *Open Fields: Science in Cultural Encounter*, Oxford, Clarendon Press, 1996, p. 248.

22. *Op.cit.*, p. 76.

23. *FSUP*, pp. 84-5. His lectures were noted for enthusiasm, warmth, informality, sense of wonder, and curiosity.

24. *Victorian Popularisers*, p. 213.

25. *Hours of Exercise in the Alps*, London, Longman Green, 1871, pp. 300-1.

26.*Ibid.*, pp. 5 and 84; the third quote is from 'The Scientific Use of the Imagination', *FSUP*, p. 159.

27. Anne Cosslett, 'Science and Value: the writings of John Tyndall', in *John Tyndall. Essays on a natural philosopher*, pp. 181-3.

28. D. Thompson, 'Contributions to Scientific Education and the Teaching of Science', in *John Tyndall. Essays on a natural philosopher*, p. 149. This blend in Kilvert's writing has been frequently underlined: Rowse (*op. cit.*, p. 237) wrote of his skill in conveying 'the direct physical impact of things'; Plomer said he presented 'the sheer physical sensation of light, air, space and atmosphere' like the Impressionists (introduction to vol. I of the *Diary*); to Massingham (*The Southern Marches*, London, Robert Hale, 1952, p. 70) Kilvert's 'physical apprehension of nature . . . is his great virtue as a writer'. Tyndall himself had a great love of poetry and was 'passionately fond of Tennyson' (Eve and Creasey, *op.cit.*, p. 257). He was also a friend of Tennyson, as Kilvert probably knew.

29. He had become Professor of Natural Philosophy at the Royal Institution in 1853 where his predecessors were Sir Humphry Davy and Faraday. Here he gave lectures on heat, sound, light and electricity.

30. In his 'Radiant Heat' lecture (*FSUP*, pp. 213-4) he posed the question 'What is sound?' and explained it was due to 'vibratory motion of the air'.

31. This is especially true of the several references to the lighthouse at Godrevy. Any description of lighthouses in the *Cornish Diary* is limited to stressing that they are white, as though their visibility was the key thing.

32. *Kilvert's Cornish Diary*, pp. 78 and 66. Concern for mariners' safety characterises Kilvert's reference to the 'solemn tolling of . . . the buoy bell moored off the Mumbles' (*Kilvert's Diary*, vol. II, p. 188).

33. *Kilvert's Diary*, vol. II, pp.103, 123, 128, 158, 162-3. For other examples of his interest in sounds' ability to carry in certain weather conditions see vol. I, pp. 286, 288, 289, vol. II, p.249, vol. III, p. 125.

34. He is remembered for the 'Tyndall effect' – the scattering of light by very small particles suspended in a medium, which enabled him to explain why the sky is blue.

35. 'On Chemical Rays and the Structure of the Light of the Sky', in *FSUP*, pp. 253 and 259.

36. *Kilvert's Diary*, vol. I, pp. 89-90 and p. 232. *Cf.* the precision of his description of the blue eyes of the girl he met at Llanthony Abbey: 'blue eyes, not the blue of the sky, but the blue of the sea' (vol. I, p. 219).

37. *Ibid.*, vol. I, p. 258. *Cf.* also vol. I, p. 231.

38. The Tyndall passage is in one of the Notes at the end of his *Hours of Exercise in the Alps* (1871) and is entitled 'Snowdon in Winter'. The papers in the book were written between 1857 and 1869 and some, including 'Snowdon in Winter', appeared in his *Mountaineering in 1861* (1862). Kilvert could therefore have seen it before he wrote his own passage on 14 March 1871. Tyndall, in company with T.H. Huxley, climbed Snowdon on 26 December 1860.

39. *Kilvert's Diary*, vol. I, pp. 308-9. *Cf. The Leisure Hour* article 'Unseasonable Passage of the Alps' (15 April 1858). The writer thought at first, like Kilvert, that he

was seeing clouds illuminated by sunlight. Then he recognised 'a long range of high serrated mountains' covered by clouds in which 'peculiar lights' were visible. 'In a few minutes I actually perceived that these lights were vast plains of snow . . . we stood wondering. . . . ' (Kilvert wrote that 'wondering . . . [I] stood rooted to the ground'). In the *Leisure Hour* article 'The enormous panorama slowly and wonderfully opened'; in the *Diary* entry, Kilvert was enchanted by 'this marvellous spectacle'. Both writers then traced the changing colours of the sunset on the snow.

40. The Kilvert quotes in this paragraph are from vol. I, pp. 308-9. The Tyndall ones are from *Hours of Exercise in the Alps*, pp. 427, 95 and 106. For another comparison with Tyndall's description of colours, see *Kilvert's Diary*, vol. II, p. 181.

41. Arnold Lunn, *Switzerland in English Prose and Poetry*, London, Eyre and Spottiswoode, 1947, p. xii.

42. Gordon T. Stewart, 'Whymper of the Matterhorn. A Victorian tragedy', *History Today*, vol. XXXIII, February 1983, p. 8.

43. *Ibid.*, p. 6.

44. Leading article, 27 July 1865.

45. Stewart, *op. cit.*, p. 6. Professor Chaix of Geneva (Corresponding Member of the Royal Geographical Society) wrote of the Hudson he knew: a man of 'perseverance, courage, stoicism, and boldness' (The *Times*, 1 August 1865). He seemed in several ways a characteristic product of St John's College.

46. Leading article, 27 July 1865. The paper implied that blame attached to the British Alpine Club for proclaiming the mountaineering 'crusade'.

47. Edward Whymper, *The Ascent of the Matterhorn*, John Murray, London, 1880, pp. 288-9. His engraving made clear that a central column, rising to the arch's summit, formed the third cross.

48. 'Weird weather' (6 January 2001) in *Trivia-Library.com* (accessed 22.11.09). Simons also described Brocken Spectres – 'huge shadowy spectres . . . created by shadows of mountaineers projected onto low clouds and reflected back by tiny water droplets in the mist'.

49. Tyndall, *Hours of Exercise in the Alps*, p. 252.

50. *Kilvert's Diary*, vol. III, p. 28. Kilvert had read about an optical illusion in *Masterman Ready*. Ready sees something in the distance and explains to Mr Seagrave: 'It is not the land which you see, but it is the trees upon the land which are refracted . . . so as to appear . . . as if they were in the air' (p. 35). It was noted in chapter five that Kilvert was intrigued by the illusion that the lights of Hay and of a train 'appeared to be travelling along in the clouds'.

51. Contributors to it included Tennyson, Matthew Arnold, Kingsley, Palgrave, and R.D. Blackmore.

52. Kilvert heard him speak at the 1873 Bath Church Congress.

53. *Kilvert's Cornish Diary*, p. 88. The house was in Trevena. Earlier, Cook had edited *The Morning Chronicle*.

54. Kilvert greatly admired George Venables's learning, noting the way he could lecture on the German Empire for 2½ hours without notes (*Diary*, vol. II, p. 94). It is another entry reflecting his respect for intellect and learning.

55. Merle Mowbray Bevington, *The Saturday Review 1855-1868. Representative Educated Opinion in Victorian England*, New York, Columbia University Press,

1941, p. 58. George Venables wrote in a *Saturday Review* piece (20 September 1856) that 'freedom depends on the political supremacy of the upper and middle classes'.

56. *The Age of Improvement.*, p. 451.

57. Kilvert referred to the 'great trouble' that Moule's father had endured over 'his poor son Horace' (vol. II, p. 440). Horace had committed suicide. He was on the staff of Marlborough College when Kilvert's brother Edward was a pupil.

58. Bevington, *op. cit.*, pp. 43, 45.

59. R.G. Cox, 'The Reviews and Magazines', in *The New Pelican Guide to English Literature 6, from Dickens to Hardy*, Harmondsworth, Penguin, 1982, p. 188.

60. It was in this way that Kilvert could have read many more novels than are mentioned in the *Diary*.

61. Handley Moule, brother of Horace, wrote a biography of Simeon; see *Charles Simeon* [1892], London, Inter-Varsity Fellowship, 1948.

62. Bearing in mind that Kilvert's aunt Sophia was brought up as a Quaker in Clapham at this time, it is worth noting that Leslie Stephen's sister Caroline was 'a Quaker much devoted to good causes' (*DNB* entry on Stephen).

63. Ralph Pite, *Thomas Hardy. The guarded life*, London, Picador, 2006, pp. 212, 104. Hardy became Evangelical under the influence of Horace and Henry Moule. Horace was a gifted teacher whose teaching inspired Hardy to learn. Hardy was a friend too of Leslie Stephen.

64. When he formally gave up his orders in March 1875, the witness was Hardy. *Far from the Madding Crowd* appeared in the *Cornhill* throughout 1874 and *The Hand of Ethelberta* from July 1875 to May 1876 (one wonders if Kilvert read them but found them too sexually explicit).

65. *DNB*. He also said that he 'wished to be sure that our Mag may lie on the table of the most refined female without calling a blush to her cheek' (*ibid.*).

66. Henry Fawcett (1833-1884) was a prominent advocate of the abolition of religious tests that barred Nonconformists from Oxbridge. He became Postmaster-General in 1880 and introduced many postal reforms. He knew Stephen from their days at Trinity Hall, Cambridge.

67. The book challenged the dogmas of popular religion.

68. He spent his honeymoon in Switzerland. His sister-in-law, Anne Thackeray (later Mrs Richmond Ritchie) wrote the preface to Mrs Sartoris's *A Week in a French Country House*.

69. F.R. Maitland, *The Life and Letters of Leslie Stephen*, London, Duckworth, 1906, p.83. Stephen complained about scientists who treated the Alps as a laboratory and when Tyndall heard of his complaint, he resigned from the Alpine Club.

70. The *Cornhill* article 'Money and Money's Worth' (January 1864) by James Fitzjames Stephen touched on the popularisation of science. An article in November 1864 covered such topics as Phrenology, Christianity, Education, Doctors, Darwinism, and Evolution.

71. T.H. Huxley and Herbert Spencer were of this group.

72. Information about *Nature* is from websites: *History of the Journal Nature* and *Lockyer's Column of Controversy in 'Nature'*, and from McMillan and Meehan, *op.cit.*, pp. 99 and 103-4.

73. Founded in Herefordshire in 1851, its aim was to study local history, archaeology, and natural history. Kilvert disliked its activities, which for him spoiled his solitary communings with nature (see *Diary*, vol. I, pp. 348-51).

74. Quoted in Maitland, *op.cit.*, p. 264. He meant during Stephen's editorship. Harrison's list of examples of its contributors reflects exactly the mixture of what we *now* see as 'major' writers and 'minor' ones found in Kilvert's reading: poems by M. Arnold, Browning and Alfred Austin, and novels (called 'romances' by Harrison) by G. Meredith, Anne Thackeray, Mrs Oliphant, Hardy, R.D. Blackmore, H. James, Mrs Lynn Linton.

75. *FSUP*, 'On Radiant Heat', pp. 232-3.

76. *Kilvert's Diary*, vol. II, p. 54.

77. Eve and Creasey, *op.cit.*, p. 216. Electric lamps were installed at this time on the Thames Embankment, Holborn Viaduct and in the Albert Hall. The sister-in-law of Leslie Stephen, Anne Thackeray, saw such modern methods of communication as the penny-post and the telegraph as means by which people were able to care for 'a greater number of people than they could have done 100 years ago' (*op.cit.*, p. 126). The same claim has been made for email.

78. Tyndall arranged for his two BAAS Addresses (Norwich 1868 and Liverpool 1870) to be published under the title *Essays on the Use and Limit of the Imagination in Science*. Included were various journal reviews of the two addresses written by supporters and critics. One was the *Record* review (dated 23 September 1870).

79. *Routledge Encyclopedia of Philosophy*, ed. Edward Craig, vol. II, London, Routledge, 1998, pp. 48-51.

80. Chadwick, *op.cit.*, part II, p. 12.

81. Lecture on 'The Scientific Use of the Imagination', in *FSUP*, pp. 156-7. Tyndall recalled being nervous of advancing the idea that the earth was millions of years old to some clergymen but they reassured him that they had long ago accepted the theory.

82. Frank M. Turner, 'Rainfall, Plagues, and the Prince of Wales: A Chapter in the Conflict of Religion and Science'. *The Journal of British Studies*, vol. XIII, No. 2, May 1974, p. 50.

83. *FSUP*, p. 40.

84. Frank M. Turner, 'Rainfall, Plagues', p. 48.

85 Frank M. Turner, 'John Tyndall', p. 177.

86. Unfortunately there is no entry for this date in the Plomer edition of the *Diary*, nor the following day. The original entries might have contained Kilvert's response to the Address.

87. Frank M. Turner, 'John Tyndall', p. 170. The Address appeared in the second volume of *FSUP*; it was also published separately by Longman in 1874.

88. 'Address delivered before the British Association at Belfast, 1874'. *The Victorian Web: literature, history and culture in the age of Victoria*. Document digitised and formatted by John van Wyke and updated by George Landow (www.victorianweb.org accessed 21.10.09).

89. *Ibid.*, p. 19.

90. Landow commented that the Address 'was popularly believed to advocate materialism as the true philosophy of science' (*ibid.*, introduction, p. 1).

However, the *Times* (20 August 1874) observed: 'There is no theological reason for recoiling from the conclusion to which Professor Tyndall would conduct us'.
91. *Ibid.*, pp. 24-5.
92. *Kilvert's Diary*, vol. III, p. 168. This *Diary* entry is examined in J. Toman, *Kilvert's Diary and Landscape*, pp.135-9, and shows Kilvert using the same phraseology and patterns of Wordsworth's poem.
93. 'Rainfall, Plagues', p. 48.
94. He was for example consistently critical of bishops, aristocrats, irresponsible, idle landowners, and inefficient generals.
95. G. Beer, *op. cit.*, p. 260.
96. He could maintain this position even though 'Cardinals, Archbishops, Bishops, the lesser clerics and laymen joined in the hue and cry in pulpit and press' over the Belfast Address (Eve and Creasey, *op.cit.*, pp. 187-8).

Chapter 8
Miracles and Wonders

1. Chadwick (*The Victorian Church*, part II, p. 31) called the Lectures 'a watershed in Christian thought' because by 1880 no theologian could argue Mozley's case as he had done.
2. This text refers to the angels that carried Lazarus to heaven after his death.
3. All Mozley quotations come from *Eight Lectures on Miracles preached before the University of Oxford* (1865), London, Rivingtons, 1883 (sixth edition).
4. 'Memoirs', pp. 70-2.
5. The *Times* review of Mozley's book appeared on 5 June 1866 and that of the *Saturday Review* on 15 September 1866.
6. *FSUP* included a highly amusing account, called 'Science and Spirits', of Tyndall's visit to a séance and his attempts to subject it to scientific scrutiny.
7. E. Chadwick, *op. cit.*, part II, p. 32.
8 *Essays and Reviews*, London, John Parker, 1860, p. 101. In his essay, Baden-Powell praised Darwin's *The Origin of the Species*, published only four months earlier.
9. *Op. cit.*, p. 20.
10. Irving and Carlyle were to become close friends later.
11. G.W.E Russell, *The Household of Faith. Portraits and Essays*, London, Hodder and Stoughton, 1903, p. 264.
12. Mrs Oliphant, *The Life of Edward Irving, Minister of the National Scotch Church, London, illustrated by his Journals and Correspondence*, London, Hurst and Blackett, 2 vols., 1862, vol. I, p. 158.
13. *Ibid.*, vol. I, p. 198.
14. It was noted in *Kilvert: The Homeless Heart* (p. 37) that in both cases of breakdown 'he had been subjected to experiences that threatened his personality and beliefs'. Quotations from Robert Kilvert's 'Memoirs' in the last two paragraphs are from pp. 57-8, 61-2, 73 and 46.
15. *The Falkners of Bath*, part II, p. 167. Mary Bancks, wife of Frederick Falkner, wrote on 10 March 1817: 'Frank Kilvert is much improved in looks, spirits and appetite' (p. 165).

16. David Newsome, *The Parting of Friends. A Study of the Wilberforces and Henry Manning*, London, John Murray, 1966, p. 10.

17. Boyd Hilton, *op. cit.*, p. 10.

18. M. Hennell, *Sons of the Prophets. Evangelical Leaders of the Victorian Church*, London, SPCK, 1979, p. 13.

19. *Memoirs of the Lives of Robert Haldane of Airthrey and of his brother James Alexander Haldane*, London, Hamilton, Adams, 1852, p. 659. Alexander Haldane was the second son of James Alexander Haldane.

20. He wrote *Refutation of the Rev. Edward Irving's Heretical Doctrine on the Person and Atonement of Christ* (1829).

21. *Sermons Preached at Christ Church, Bath, before the National Schools*, pp. 50-1. In his sermon on 'Filial Obedience', he pictured the eyes of disobedient children being plucked out by ravens.

22. Sheridan Gilley, 'The Church of England in the Nineteenth Century', in S. Gilley and W.J. Sheils, *A History of Religion in Britain. Practice and Belief from Pre-Roman Times to the Present*, Oxford, Blackwell, 1994, p. 296.

23. 'The party [Chalmers] led was identified with unbending Calvinist orthodoxy' (Bernard M.G. Reardon, *Religious Thought in the Victorian Age*, London, Longman, 1980, p. 396).

24. He had been Professor of Mathematics at the East India College. An ardent Evangelical, he was made an Honorary Governor for Life of the CMS for his sterling service.

25. 'Dr Dealtry was much esteemed for his piety . . . , his parish work, his activity at May Meetings and School Feasts'. He was a regular at Sir Robert Inglis's dinner parties (E.M. Forster, *op. cit.*, p. 146).

26. Robert Grant (1778-1838) wrote a sketch of the East India Company and sacred hymns. He was a lawyer and M.P. Charles Grant (1778-1866) was also a lawyer and a politician. He worked hard to open up India to the Gospel. Their father was Chairman of the Governors of the East India Society. Uncle Francis may have been one of the dinner guests. His literary remains show that he knew about Chalmers and that Chalmers knew about him. Chalmers wrote to the editor of Francis's *Literary Remains of Bishop Warburton* on its publication in 1841 to congratulate him upon the work, as is noted in the 'Memoir' prefacing the collection of Francis's verse and prose that appeared after his death. Furthermore, Francis referred to Chalmers in an essay on Pope in that collection.

27. Chalmers's letter is quoted in Rev. William Hanna, *Memoirs of the Life and Writings of Thomas Chalmers, D.D., LL.D.*, Sutherland and Know, Edinburgh, 1849, vol. II, pp. 349-50.

28. *Op. cit.*, p. 133.

29. *Cf. Kilvert's Diary* (vol. I, p. 282): 'William Jones was . . . of a sturdy independent character . . . and hated to be supported by the parish.'

30. *Op. cit.*, p. 105.

31. John Roxborough, 'The Legacy of Thomas Chalmers', *International Bulletin of Missionary Research*, 23(4) October 1999, p. 1.

32. Forster, *op. cit.*, pp. 133-4.

33. Letter of 1829 to Dr Chalmers, cited in Mrs Oliphant, vol. II, p. 68.

34. G.W.E. Russell, *op. cit.*, p. 250.

35. Mrs Oliphant, *op. cit.*, vol. II, p. 22.

36. Hilton (*op. cit.*, p. 8) stressed that the *Christian Guardian* (the paper taken by uncle Francis) represented 'moderate' Calvinism.

37. Lewis Weston Dillwyn went on 3 June 1847 to St Margaret's Chapel, Bath, perhaps on uncle Francis Kilvert's recommendation, to hear Marriott preach: 'a very impressive sermon,' Dillwyn recorded.

38. *Eight Sermons on 'The Signs of the Times', recently preached at St Margaret's Chapel, Bath*, Bath, Cruttwell, 1828.

39. 'Memoirs', pp. 66-8.

40 Russell, *op. cit.*, p. 273.

41. Quoted in Benjamin Worfield, *Counterfeit Miracles*, New York, Charles Scribner, 1918, pp. 137, 232-3.

42. *Op. cit.*, vol. II, pp. 130-3.

43. *Op. cit.*, pp. 147-8.

44. It is significant that the page-long *Diary* account was, according to Plomer, only part of an originally 'long account'.

45. Mozley, *op. cit.*, pp. 57-60, p. 68.

46. http://www.history.powys.org.uk/school1/builth/flood.shtml.

47 'Review of the Local and District Year', *Hereford Times*, 28 December 1872.

48. Rob Randall, 'Bath Naturalists. Apothecary to Zoologist', in Wallis, *op. cit.*, p. 78.

49. On 5 February 1873 he gave an evening lecture to the Langley Burrell faithful on 'heroism and self-sacrifice instanced by the stories of Tom Flynn of Virginia, Jim Bludso the engineer of the Mississippi steam boat, the *Birkenhead* and the drunken private of the Buffs'.

50. Kilvert's admiration for the 'manliness' of soldiers and working men is traced in *Kilvert: The Homeless Heart*, chapter seven. *Cf.* his entries about Frank Vincent: 'a noble young soldier' (14 February 1874), 'the fine handsome young dragoon in his bright scarlet uniform' (8 November 1874).

51. *Op. cit.*, p. 305.

52. *Past and Present* (1843), edited by A.M.D. Hughes, Oxford, Clarendon Press, 1927, p.110.

53. Stefan Collini, 'Character and the Victorian Mind', in Kelly Boyd and Rohan McWilliam (eds.), *The Victorian Studies Reader*, London, Routledge, 2008, p. 225.

54. *Op. cit.*, p. 184. His italics. There is a painting called *Laborare est Orare* (1862) by John Rogers, a Roman Catholic. It shows Cistercian monks harvesting in a stone-walled Leicestershire field. In the background is Mount St Bernard Abbey, the first abbey for men built in England since the Reformation.

55. *Past and Present* quotations in the last two paragraphs are from pp. 35-9, 54, 60, 63 and 104.

56. Gerald Moultrie (1829-1885) was a public school master and composer of hymns, many based on devotion to the Virgin Mary.

57. In the celestial music passage in his 'Memoirs', Robert Kilvert quoted Milton's lines (*Paradise Lost* IV, 377-78): 'Millions of spiritual creatures walk the earth/ Unseen . . . '

58. Cited in Edgar C.S. Gibson, *The Thirty Nine Articles of the Church of England*, London, Methuen, 1902, p. 641.

59. On an (inevitably) 'dark wet day' in 1872 (20 October) in Langley Burrell Church, he noted that he made 'a Declaration of Assent to the Prayer Book and the Articles', adding 'I think this proclamation rather astonished the people'. He would have been familiar with the statement in Article I that God was 'the maker of all things, both visible and invisible', an idea which Mozley made use of in his examination of miracles, which were a means of communication between the two.

60. G.W.E. Russell, *op. cit.*, p. 272.

61. Robert M. Young, *op. cit.*, p. 13.

62. Plomer noted that the picture 'is described at some length'.

Chapter 9
Kilvert and Teaching

1. W. Stewart and P. McCann, *The Educational Innovators 1750-1880*, London, Macmillan, 1967, p. 60. Owen also believed that science had to play a key role in modern education.

2. P. Elliott and S. Daniels, 'Pestalozzi, Fellenberg and British nineteenth-century geographical education', in *Journal of Historical Geography*, 32 (2006) p. 759.

3. He is the Lord Lansdowne who was a friend of Maria Edgeworth, who visited the Moravian school attended by Mrs Kilvert, and who came to Brighton to hear Robertson preach.

4. He had links with Langport in Somerset: his uncle was a banker there and it was the home of Reynolds's wife.

5. *Commonplace Book*, vol. II.

6. Emily Kilvert was convinced that 'whatever their different beliefs in religious matters, nothing could exceed the affection between the two brothers' (*op. cit.*, p. 113).

7. Brooke, *op. cit.*, vol. II, p. 16.

8. P. McCann and F. Young, *Samuel Wilderspin and the Infant School Movement*, London, Croom Helm, 1982, pp. 188, 192.

9. *Ibid.*, p. 195.

10. 'Broadly speaking, infant schools were founded by the middle class . . . for the benefit of the working classes' (*ibid.*, p. 101).

11. A. Hare, *The Story of my Life*, London, George Allen, 1900, vol. I, p. 173. Hare, gentle and sensitive, craved sympathy; instead he, and other pupils, were beaten with a cane by Robert Kilvert.

12. Wilderspin's *Infant System*, quoted in McCann and Young, *op. cit.*, p. 162.

13. *The Story of my Life*, vol. I, p. 173. Hare also recorded the keeping of small animals at the school – another Wilderspin recommendation.

14. McCann and Young, *op. cit.*, pp. 187, 197.

15. She produced these highly popular works: *Lessons on Objects* (1830), *Lessons on Shells* (1832) and *Model Lessons for Infant School Teachers* (1838). Together, the Mayos produced *Practical Remarks on Infant Education* (1837).

16. Mary Hilton, 'From Conversation to Catechism: revisiting pedagogy and ideology in Victorian elementary schools' (paper presented to Cambridge Victorian Studies Conference, July 2009), p. 3.

17. *Ibid.*, p. 5.

18. McCann and Young, p. 148. Noticeably, Kilvert highlighted this last characteristic in children, describing Katie, daughter of his sister Emily, as 'variable, changeable . . . an excitable sprite' (*Kilvert's Diary*, vol. I, p. 137). He also called her 'clever and original', in a careful, detailed, teacherly assessment of her.

19. *Lessons on Objects as given to children between the ages of six and eight, in a Pestalozzian School at Cheam, Surrey*, London, Seeley, Jackson and Halliday, 17th edition, 1861, pp. v and 3.

20. 'Memoirs', p. 23.

21. It was published in six parts between 1792 and 1796. It remained in print for 120 years. The edition used here is the London, Routledge, 1858 one, with preface by Cecil Hartley.

22. Aileen Fyfe, 'Reading Children's Books in Late-Eighteenth Century Dissenting Families', *The Historical Journal*, 43.2 (2000), p. 459.

23. *Evenings at Home*, pp. 146-7.

24. *Ibid.*, p. 113.

25. *Ibid.*, p. 73.

26. 'Reading Children's Books', p. 465.

27. 'Memoirs', p. 53. Claverton Rectory was a cultural centre for the Kilverts of the same order as Warleigh, the mansion directly opposite it across the Avon where uncle Francis Kilvert used to hasten for intellectual stimulus.

28. Marriott went to the College in 1798, uncle Francis in 1811.

29. *The Falkners of Bath, 1779-1818*, part I, pp. 74, 76.

30. 'Reading Children's Books', pp. 467-9.

31. *The Children's Year.*, pp. 13-14.

32. E. Wyndowe, *op. cit.*, p. 102.

33. Hessey's son (also James Augustus and Kilvert's cousin) was Headmaster of Merchant Taylor's School from 1845 to 1870. Charles Mayo was educated there. Hessey junior later became Archdeacon of Middlesex. His younger brother, Dr Francis Hessey, assisted Kilvert's father at Edward Kilvert's wedding in 1876.

34. They published *Endymion*, Keats' second volume of poems. Taylor had 'discovered' Clare and he and Hessey issued his first volume of poems in 1820.

35. Chris Stray, *John Taylor and Locke's Classical System*, Paradigm, No. 20, July 1996.

36. Letter from John Taylor to his brother James, 9 September 1807, quoted in Anne Falkner, *The Falkners of Bath*, part II, pp. 120-1. Anne Falkner also noted that Anna Kilvert visited Claverton Farm in spring 1811 'bringing with her that jolly little boy Robert' (i.e. Kilvert's father). This was the visit Robert Kilvert recorded ('Memoirs', pp. 22-3), which included the visit to Claverton Rectory when he read 'Transmigrations of Indur' by Mrs Barbauld.

37. *The Falkners of Bath*, part I, p. 78.

38. Coleridge's *Aids to Reflection*, which figured in Robert Kilvert's reading, was published by Taylor and Hessey.

39. *The Falkners of Bath*, part I, p. 78.

40. John Holland and James Everett, *The Life and Writings of James Montgomery, including selections from his correspondence*, London, Longman, Brown and Green, 1854, two vols., vol. I, p. v. Montgomery printed in his *Sheffield Isis* an article by his friend Aston lauding the merits of Mrs Barbauld's story 'The Transmigrations of Indur' (*ibid.*, vol. I, p. 287).

41. Marriott's interest in contemporary educational developments is seen in his *Essay on the Madras system of education, its powers, its application to classical schools* (London, 1819). Dr Andrew Bell and Joseph Lancaster had recently developed independently the 'Monitorial System', whereby abler elementary school pupils taught the less able. Bell's 'Madras System', so called because it originated in an orphan school near Madras, was adopted by the Anglican National School Society. Marriott was keen to see it applied to schools for the upper classes. Marriott's book was published by Taylor and Hessey.

42. All Mayo quotations are from his *Memoir of Pestalozzi; being the Substance of a Lecture delivered at the Royal Institution May 1826 by the Rev. C. Mayo, LL.D., Fellow of St John's College, Oxford*, London, printed for J.A. Hessey, 1828, pp. 16, 25, 24, 14, 22, 21, 28. The italics are his.

43. H. Krüsi, *Pestalozzi: his life, work and influence*, New York, Wilson and Hinkle, 1875, p. 17.

44. McCann and Young, *op. cit.*, pp. 196-8. Students worked a 56-hour week.

45. 'Teaching the younger classes the subjects of the Nativity and Crucifixion', Kilvert recorded (*Kilvert's Diary*, NLW edition, June-July 1870, 30 June, p. 54).

46. *Ibid.*, p. 57. On 8 July, Kilvert went to the school 'to give the schoolmaster the memorandum of the Scripture readings for the past week'. Josiah Evans (b.1836) was the son of the Rev. Josiah Evans, an Anglican who later became minister of the Calvinistic Methodist Chapel, Pembrey, Carmarthenshire. Josiah junior trained at the Anglican Trinity College, Carmarthen.

47. Kilvert's guide to parish work (Blunt's *Duties of the Parish Priest*) stated that the elementary school 'is intended to form the children into Bible Christians . . . of the *Reformed Church of England*. You will therefore drill them into a familiar acquaintance with the formularies of that Church'. The method recommended was 'question and answer' (pp. 189-191. His italics).

48. SPCK stands for the Society for the Promotion of Christian Knowledge.

49. H. Krüsi, *op. cit.*, pp. 209-10. Von Türk was involved in welfare work for an Evangelical Protestant church.

50. *Cf.* Kilvert's poem *Undivided*: 'At once in Nature's page we look/ And daily read the self-same book/ Of earth, and sea, and sky'.

51. Tyndall urged an audience of primary school teachers to 'get a knowledge of facts from actual observation' ('Lecture on Magnetism', in *FSUP*, p. 360).

52. Elliott and Daniels, *op.cit.*, p. 752.

53. *Ibid.*, pp. 756 and 763.

54. Wilderspin talked of 'elevating all subjects of natural science' and his object lessons focused on natural materials and where they came from.

55. *Kilvert's Diary*, vol. III, pp. 216, 228. The experience recalls closely Mary Howitt's upbringing that was described earlier.

56. Pestalozzi's diary entries for 2 and 15 February 1774, quoted in John Russell, *op.cit.*, p. 16.

57. *Kilvert's Diary*, vol. II, p. 237. Teaching about 'all parts' might seem ambiguous were it not for the influences we have traced encouraging him to specialise in geography and the fact that he bought von Türk's geography and science textbook.

58. Kilvert even went into the school before the inspection to 'examine the elder children's geography for the special subject and grant' (NLW *Diary*, 30 June, p. 54).

59. *Reports on Elementary Schools 1852-1882*, London, HMSO, 1908, pp. 141-2.

60. For example, dates of births and deaths of sovereigns and lists of principal countries, rivers and mountains (P.H. Gosden, *How They Were Taught*, Oxford, Blackwell, 1969, pp. 50, 31).

61. *Kilvert's Diary*, NLW edition, June-July 1870, pp. 57-8. Bearing in mind what has been said about Mrs Kilvert's interest in education, it is significant that she asked to be present at this inspection.

62. *Op.cit.*, p. 184. SPG tracts had such titles as 'The Church among the Heathen', 'The Church in the Colonies', 'The Monthly Record of Christian Missions'.

63. Brooke, *op.cit.*, vol. I, p. 262.

64. The *Diary* entries referred to here are: vol. I, pp. 171, 216-7. Kilvert attended a lecture by Mrs Webb on Switzerland, vol. I, p. 45.

65. Tyndall attempted the Matterhorn unsuccessfully in 1862 and made a solitary ascent of Monte Rosa in 1858. Leslie Stephen was the first to climb the Schreckhorn.

66. Bennett, *op.cit.*, p. 240. Tyndall spent years studying Switzerland's glaciers.

67. The quotations in this paragraph come from p. 2 and p. 7 of Hilton's paper. The italics are hers.

Chapter 10
Museums and Picture Galleries

1. O'Connor, *op. cit.*, p. 4.

2. 'Memoirs', p. 38.

3. E. Wyndowe, *op. cit.*, p. 99. She added that 'coloured pictures were not so nearly common then as they are now'.

4. *True Words* was first published in 1878 (i.e. after Kilvert's *Diary* entry). However, Kingsley's article, 'Picture Galleries', which contains the 'God's Beautiful World' passage, first appeared in an issue of the Christian Socialist newspaper, *Politics for the People*, in 1848, where Kilvert could have seen it. In addition, Macmillan published *True Words* as a pamphlet, which had wide distribution after the Crimean War.

5. In his *Honest work* poem, which is a pure expression of Kingsley's concept of the duty and beauty of toil, Kilvert stated that beautiful, natural things possessed 'the glory of a Sacrament'. Furthermore, Kingsley's notion of welcoming beauty in 'every fair face, every fair sky, every fair flower' epitomises Kilvert's entire aesthetic.

6. Plomer made a point of noting that the first entry of his selection was the one that began Kilvert's record.

7. Yanni, *op. cit.*, p. 25.

8. It had been known as a museum, variously called the London Museum, the Egyptian Museum, or Bullock's Museum.

9. Kilvert's reference 'Psyche is wonderful' remains obscure. Maskelyne, born in Cheltenham, exposed the Davenports at a show there in June 1865, an event no doubt known to Kilvert. Maskelyne's claim to be descended from Nevil Maskelyne, the Astronomer Royal, is disputed.

10. *Op. cit.*, pp. 107-8. Daisy Thomas also brought for Kilvert the *Graphic*, a more expensive (than its rival the *ILN*) illustrated weekly, founded in 1869 by William Luson Thomas, wood engineer, artist, and social reformer. It covered news, art, literature and science. Its contributors included George Eliot, Hardy, and Trollope. On 10 September 1870, Kilvert was admiring 'some good pictures of the [Franco-Prussian] War' in the *Graphic*.

11. *Illustrated Books and Newspapers* (1846).

12. The fishing supplement in the 1864 *ILA* issue would have been of particular interest to Robert Kilvert. All quotations in this paragraph, apart from the *Diary* one, come from Louise Henson, *Culture and Science*, pp. 105-6.

13. He was made Keeper of the new Coins and Medals Department in 1870. He had spent much of his boyhood in Egypt and his mother, Sophia Poole, was the author of *The Englishwoman in Egypt*.

14. The London visit that opens *Kilvert's Diary* included a morning (23 January) 'spent at the British Museum' (Plomer's note).

15. The Artemision had always been a place of great religious significance but was additionally a 'wonder' to Kilvert because of St Paul's activities at Ephesus.

16. He was born in Bredwardine and was Miss Newton's brother. Educated at Shrewsbury School and Christ Church, Oxford, he later became Professor of Archaeology at University College, London. He wrote about his excavations at Halicarnassus in his *History of Discoveries at Halicarnassus* (1862-1863).

17. *Kilvert's Diary*, vol. I, p. 22. The overlap of several of these natural phenomena with those covered in Bodily's St Helena lecture and in Von Türk's *Phenomena of Nature* confirms Kilvert's abiding interest in such things. The Northern Dawn (i.e. the Aurora Borealis) was popular with producers of panoramas.

18. Ethel M. Wood, *A History of the Polytechnic*, London, Macdonald, 1965, p. 13.

19. *Ibid.*, p. 17. The quoted words are from the *Times* (3 August 1838).

20. James Secord, 'Quick and Magical Shaper of Science', *Science Magazine*, vol. 297, 6 September 2002, www.sciencemag.org.

21. Altick, *The Shows of London*, Cambridge (Mass.), Harvard University Press, 1978, p. 385.

22. *Ibid.*, p. 382.

23. *Victorian Popularizers*, p. 168.

24. *Op. cit.*, p. 105.

25. Wood, *op. cit.*, p. 22.

26. David Robinson, 'Magic Lantern Shows', in *Encyclopedia of Early Cinema*, www.bookrags.com (accessed 20.11.10).

27. *The Boy's Playbook of Science*, London, Routledge, 1860, p. 218.

28. Altick, *The Shows of London*, p. 499. Edward Stanley Poole, brother of Reginald Poole of the British Museum, was chief clerk in the SKM's science and art department.

29. John Mackenzie, introduction to *The Victorian Vision*, p. 24.

30. Yanni instanced Landseer's *The Hunted Stag* among romantic paintings displayed by museums to communicate 'the violence of nature' (*op. cit.*, p. 30). Kilvert recorded studying stags 'intently for nearly an hour' in Richmond Park, adding 'I now understand Landseer's stag pictures better than I ever did before' (*Kilvert's Diary*, vol. III, p. 186).

31. The previous day he remarked that the Crystal Palace at Sydenham 'glittered upon the hill in the sunshine like an enormous diamond'.

32. There were also walks, lakes, plantations, cricket, archery and croquet grounds, gymnasia and 'novel buildings' (e.g. a Japanese house).

33. 'This fine instrument is one of five claviers. . . . The bellows are blown by two steam engines' (Black's *Guide to London and its Environs*, 8th edition, 1882).

34. *The Shows of London.*, p. 484. Blondin, the tightrope artist, was employed at the Crystal Palace in this period.

35. Robert Fox, 'The University Museum and Oxford Science, 1850-1880', in *The History of the University of Oxford*, vol.VI, 'Nineteenth Century Oxford, Part I' (edited by M.G. Brock and Mark Curthoys), Oxford, Clarendon Press, 1997, p. 641.

36. Yanni, *op. cit.*, p. 63.

37. F.H. Lawson, *The Oxford Law School 1850-1965*, Oxford, Oxford University Press, 1968, pp. 20-2.

38. Yanni, *op. cit.*, pp. 63-4. Its geological specimens came from Clarendon Hall, its anatomy specimens from Christ Church College, and its natural history specimens from the Ashmolean Museum.

Chapter 11
The Christian Geographer

1. *Old England*, vol. II, book VIII, pp. 374-5.

2. Published at this date in book form by the Religious Tract Society, the stories had first appeared in the *Christian Guardian*, the Evangelical newspaper taken by uncle Francis Kilvert.

3. Initially hostile to Evangelicalism, he changed partly as a result of reading Newton's *Cardiphonia*. Robert Kilvert was contemporary at Oriel College with one of Ryder's sons.

4. *Bath Chronicle*, 4 December 1817.

5. Michael M. Hennell, *John Venn and the Clapham Sect* (1958), Cambridge, The Lutterworth Press, 2002, p. 168.

6. *Op. cit.*, pp. 110-11.

7. Its full title was *Practical View of the Prevailing Religious System of Professing Christians in the Higher and Middle Classes*. Its message was that most of them were Christian in name only.

8. 'The Clapham Sect', in *Essays in Ecclesiastical Biography*, London (1849),

Longmans, Green, Reader and Dyer, 1867, p. 581. Sir James was the father of Sir James Fitzjames Stephen and Leslie Stephen.

9. David Spring, 'The Clapham Sect: some social and political aspects', *Victorian Studies*, September 1961, pp. 35, 39, 43-4.

10. Report of the Committee of the African Institution, 1811. A subscription of 60 guineas or more made one a Hereditary Governor of the body; 30 guineas made one a Governor for life.

11. One nephew of Sophia's stepmother, Foster Reynolds, would later marry Richenda Fry, daughter of Elizabeth Fry, while a niece, Rachel, married John Gurney Fry in 1825. The relationship through marriage of Robert Were Fox, father of Barclay Fox, with the Gurney and Reynolds families was noted in the Prologue.

12. G.W.E. Russell (*op. cit.*, p. 241) recalled that his father regularly read aloud prayers from this book, adding that 'the use of that book was a distinctive sign of true Evangelicalism'.

13. Simon Schama, *Rough Crossings. Britain, the Slaves and the American Revolution*, London, Vintage Books, 2009, p. 308. Schama's book charts SLC's story in fascinating, moving detail.

14. *Op. cit.*, in *Essays in Ecclesiastical Biography*.

15. Quoted in Stock, *op. cit.*, vol. I, p. 46. His italics.

16. The town is on the Ogun river, 64 miles north of Lagos, in modern Nigeria.

17. Stock, *op. cit.*, vol. I, p. 458.

18. He was a close friend of John Keble, Oriel College tutor of Robert Kilvert.

19. Sarah Tucker, *Sunrise within the Tropics, an Outline of the Origin and Progress of the Yoruba Mission*, New York, Robert Carter, 1859, p. 44.

20. *Op. cit.*, vol.II, p.435.

21. J.F. Ade Ajayi, *Christian Missions in Nigeria 1841-1891. The making of a new élite*, London, Longmans Green, 1965, p.71. The quotation at the start of this paragraph is from pp.38-40.

22. Stock, *op. cit.*, vol. I, p.126. There was also the *Evangelical Magazine and Missionary Chronicle*, a monthly begun in 1793. The January 1824 issue reviewed such books as *The Christian Philosopher; or the Connexion of Science with Religion* and *Tales from Switzerland*, a work of fiction that was an exception to those novels which threatened 'serious evils' to young readers.

23. *Missionary Register, containing the Principal Transactions of the Various Institutions for Propagating the Gospel*, London, Seeley, 1842.

24. Quoted in Stock, *op. cit.*, vol. I, p.124.

25. Fawn M. Brodie, *The Devil Drives. A life of Sir Richard Burton*, Harmondsworth, Penguin Books, 1967, p. 171.

26. *Kilvert's Cornish Diary*, p. 26. The statue is outside Truro. The editors noted that Kilvert 'left a large space for the name and put in "Lander" later'. It seems likely that Kilvert would have heard of Lander's exploits in connection with the important 1841 CMS expedition up the Niger, aimed to take Christianity into the heart of Africa (Tucker, *op. cit.*, p. 58 – in her chapter on the Niger).

27. His great-grandfather was a clergyman (as was one brother), his father had been an army captain, and his mother came from a wealthy merchant family.

28. Brodie, *op. cit.*, pp. 175-6.

29. He was extravagantly praised at the ceremony by Murchison, much to the chagrin of Burton, who had been too ill to accompany Speke on his journey.

30. Quoted in Stock, *op. cit.*, vol. II, p.137. The 'discovery' he referred to was that of Nyanza Victoria (known now as Lake Victoria), the source of the Nile.

31. Alexander Maitland, *Speke and the Discovery of the Source of the Nile*, London, Constable, 1971, p. 181.

32. The figures for cotton gins in Abeokuta and for Christians and school pupils in Sierra Leone are given in Stock, *op. cit.*, vol. II, pp. 110-11.

33. Tucker, *op. cit.*, pp. 160-1. The Queen had made presents of handsome Bibles; Prince Albert had sent a steel mill for grinding Indian corn.

34. *Gentleman's Magazine*, November 1863, obituary of uncle Francis.

35. He lent a copy of it to a parishioner on 29 April 1870 (*Kilvert's Diary*, NLW edition, April-June 1870).

36. *Op. cit.*, vol. I, p. 112.

37. The life of Cotton that Kilvert read, from which the 'chief friend' phrase comes, was *Memoir of George Edward Lynch Cotton D.D., Bishop of Calcutta*, London, Longmans Green, 1871, by his widow, Sophia. It had been out only a few weeks. In it (p. 7) she described her husband as 'an adherent avowedly of the Evangelical school'.

38. Similarly, the *Diary* references to Frederick Robertson and Charles Kingsley are few but the importance of these men to the diarist was huge (another aspect of the *Diary* as 'iceberg').

39. Its full title was *Missionary Travels and Researches in South Africa including a Sketch of Sixteen Years' Residence in the Interior of Africa*.

40. H.H. Johnston, *Livingstone and the Exploration of Central Africa*, London, George Philips, 1891, p. 7. Johnston was a Fellow of the Royal Geographical Society.

41. *Ibid.*, p. 181.

42. David Livingstone, *Missionary Travels and Researches in South Africa* (1857), London, Ward Lock, *n.d.*, p. 445.

43. Tim Jeal (*Livingstone*, London, Heinemann, 1973, p. 148) quoted Livingstone's description of the Falls from *Livingstone's African Journal 1853-1856* (edited I. Schapera, London, 1963) to show how 'miraculously precise and flat' it was. *Missionary Travels* was, however, for the general public.

44. Jeal, *op. cit.*, p. 163.

45. W.G. Blaikie, *The Personal Life of D. Livingstone LL.D., D.C.L.* (1880), New York, Negro Universities Press, 1969, p. 250.

46. John Arrowsmith (1790-1873) was the nephew of Aaron Arrowsmith (1750-1823), founder of the family firm of geographers. Aaron's maps were regarded as the best of the period. He was one of the founder members of the Royal Geographical Society.

47. *The Map Book*, London, Ted Smart, *n.d.*, p. 280.

48. 'Everyone will die laughing': *John Murray and the Publication of David Livingstone's Missionary Travels*, p.7 (www.livingstoneonline.ucl.ac.uk: Welcome Trust. Accessed 26 May 2011).

49. *Ibid.*, p. 1.

50. *Ibid.*, p. 2.

51. Clare Pettit, *Dr Livingstone, I Presume? Missionaries, journalists, explorers and empire*, London, Profile, 2007, p. 35.

52. George Seaver, *David Livingstone: his life and letters*, London, Lutterworth Press, 1957, p. 295.

53. Jeal, *op. cit.*, p. 165. *Cf.* Johnston (*op. cit.*, p. 233): 'the commercial spirit of the country had been attracted towards those new lands of the Zambesi . . . with support from industrial towns'.

54. *Dr Livingstone's Cambridge Lectures, edited with an introduction and life of Dr Livingstone by the Rev. William Monk, M.A., F.R.A.S., with a portrait and map*, London, Deighton and Bell, 1858, pp. 166-68. Livingstone also gave a lecture on 5 December 1857 in Cambridge Town Hall to the Mayor and Corporation.

55. *Op. cit.*, p. 102. Later the universities of Dublin and Durham were included.

56, Given this name by natives, meaning 'mother of Robert', a reference to Livingstone's wife and their son Robert.

57. *Op. cit.*, p. 248.

58. Pettit, *op. cit.*, p. 42.

59. *Ibid.*, p. 5.

60. Jeal, *op. cit.*, p. 283.

61. *Op. cit.*, p. 11.

Chapter 12
'Plunging into Ancient Chaos': Kilvert and Evolution

1. In 1849 Kingsley was involved in efforts to subdue a cholera outbreak in London.

2. *The Wonders of the Shore*, pp. 70-73.

3. Ballantyne too saw himself as a teacher. In 1864, he circularised hundreds of churchmen announcing his *Ballantyne's Miscellany*, a range of small books aimed at both adult and young poor. The books were adventure stories laced with factual information and piety.

4. Adrian Desmond, *Archetypes and Ancestors. Palaeontology in Victorian London 1850-1875*, Chicago, Chicago University Press, 1984, p. 47.

5. Richard Conniff, 'The missionary and the gorilla. A nineteenth century tale of disease, perseverance, scientific infighting, and a landmark of natural history', Yale, *Alumni Magazine*, September/October 2008, p. 1.

6. See also the *Diary* entry for 15 April 1874. Negroes appear as objects of quaintness and comedy in the 8 September 1871 entry when an upper-middle-class Clyro gentleman imitated a 'nigger minstrel', accompanying the melody "Who's that knocking at de door?"' with finger clicking and dancing with knees raised high 'in true nigger style'.

7. Livingstone, in a letter of 24 September 1869 from Africa, wrote: 'The gorilla is so hideously ugly that I can conceive no other use for him than sitting for a portrait of Satan'.

8. Jenny, supposed to be an orang-utan, arrived at the Zoological Gardens in 1837. Charles Knight soon featured her, dressed as a child, on the cover of his

Penny Magazine. His article about her compared her behaviour with that of humans. Queen Victoria saw her at the Zoological Gardens in 1842. Between 1855 and 1856 she was in Wombwell's travelling menagerie. When she died, it was discovered that she was in fact a gorilla.

9. Gowan Dawson, *Darwin, Literature and Victorian Respectability*, Cambridge, Cambridge University Press, 2007, p. 60.

10. *The Gorilla Hunters*, p. 149; *Explorations and Adventures in Equatorial Africa*, London, John Murray, 1861, p. 435.

11. *Op. cit.*, pp. 376-9.

12. The *Diary* entry for 20 February 1873 records that he attended a House of Commons debate in which 'an Irish member complained bitterly that when Irish affairs came on the English and Scotch members absented themselves from the House'.

13. Janet Browne and Sharon Messenger, 'Victorian spectacle: Julia Pastrana, the bearded and hairy female', *Endeavour*, vol.27, no. 4, December 2003, p. 159. In this paper the authors (of the Wellcome Trust Centre for the History of Medicine) tell the story of Julia Pastrana, known as the baboon-woman, who toured Britain in 1857. 'Indirectly, she participated in the evolutionary debate', and while the debate raged she was often likened to a gorilla (*ibid.*, p. 155).

14. Desmond/Moore, *op. cit.*, p. 493.

15. Robert Kilvert began on 18 October 1822; Wilberforce on 27 January 1823.

16. Accounts of the debate suggest the number of undergraduates present was small. Cyril Bibby referred to 'a small knot of pro-Darwin undergraduates' (T.H. Huxley, *Scientist, Humanist and Educator*, London, Watts, 1959, p. 69).

17. Desmond/Moore, *op. cit.*, p. 493.

18. Francis Darwin, *op. cit.*, p. 251.

19. J.R. Lucas, 'Wilberforce and Huxley: A Legendary Encounter', *Historical Journal*, 22, 2 (1979), p. 7. Huxley's retort to Wilberforce had more the form that, if forced to choose between an ape grandfather and a man of intelligence who chose to ridicule science, he would choose the ape.

20. Desmond/Moore, *op. cit.*, p. 497.

21. *Ibid.*, p. 1.

22. Keynes, *op. cit.*, p. 234.

23. Report in *The Athenaeum*, March 1861.

24. 'Note on the Resemblance and Differences in the Structure and Development of the Brain in Man and Apes', in Darwin, *The Descent of Man*, London, John Murray, 1871, pp. 309-310. Darwin's book considered natural selection in relation to sex.

25. *The Descent of Man*, pp. 930, 99.

26. *The Water-Babies* quotations in the last two paragraphs are from the 1901 Macmillan edition, pp. 26, 55, 71-2, 75-6, 148, 114, 235-6, 222, 277.

27. *Worlds before Adam*, p. 5.

28. Kate Colquhoun, *op. cit.*, p. 208.

29. He was assistant superintendent of the Great Exhibition in 1851. He was able to combine a belief in Genesis with awareness that the earth was millions of years old.

30. According to O'Connor (*op. cit.*, p .285), the display was a product of Pestalozzi's belief in visual education.

31. M. Rudwick, *The Meaning of Fossils*, p. 156.

32. 'Description of the Park Cwm Tumulus', *Archaeologica Cambrensis* (Journal of the Cambrian Archaeological Association), vol. II, fourth series, London, J. Parker, 1871. Glyn Daniel ('The Chambered Barrow in Parc le Breos, S. Wales', *Proceedings of the Prehistoric Society*, 6, 1937, p. 75) stated that he knew of no excavations prior to 1869.

33. *Pre-historic Times as illustrated by ancient remains, and the manners and customs of modern savages*, London, Williams and Norgate, 1865, p. 50. Other parallels between Kilvert's and Lubbock's descriptions are: to the former Stonehenge was 'holy ground'; to the latter it was 'a spot of great sanctity'; both then referred to it as a 'temple' and a 'cathedral'.

34. *Ibid.*, p. 55. Lubbock actually owned Silbury Hill. In 1870 he published *Origin of Civilisation* in which he speculated on man's initial mastery of the forces of nature and religious practices.

35. Evans, the Evangelical headmaster of Clyro School where Kilvert taught, was named Josiah for this Old Testament figure.

36. Local people told Glyn Daniel in 1937 that 'very big bones' had been found in the graves. He recorded that Dr Morton Douglas, who reported on the bones found in the 1869 excavation, 'described one of the skeletons as "of gigantic proportions"' (*op. cit.*, p. 71).

37. A large number of sources (articles, reports) about Cat Hole Cave have been consulted, as well as some experts, but no reference to a female outline has been found.

38. Alasdair Whittle and Michael Wysocki, 'Parc le Breos Cwm Transepted Long Cairn, Gower, West Glamorgan', *Proceedings of the Prehistoric Society*, 64, 1998, p. 141. Remains found there consisted of animal bones, flint tools, a stone hammer, a bronze axe, pottery shards, and parts of two skeletons.

39. Wood's excavation of Cat Hole Cave was never properly recorded. Dillwyn referred to the exploration of another Gower cave, Bacon Hole, by his son John on 1 April 1837.

40. Colin Speakman, *Adam Sedgwick. Geologist and Dalesman 1785-1873, A biography in twelve themes*, Heathfield, Broad Oak Press, and Geological Society (London), 1982, p. 94.

41. O'Connor, *op. cit.*, p. 22.

42. The book was published by Darton and Clark; its author was 'Rev. T. Wilson'; this name was fictitious and appeared to reassure parents that the book was theologically sound.

43. See J. Toman, 'Mrs Augustus Hare: godmother to the Kilvert Children', *Kilvert Society Journal*, no. 32, March 2011.

44. *Op. cit.*, pp. 194-5.

45. Moore and Desmond, *op. cit.*, p. 208.

46. Noah Heringman, *Romantic Rocks, Aesthetic Geology*, Ithaca, Cornell University Press, 2004, p. 1.

47. *A Syllabus of a Course of Lectures in Geology*, Cambridge, Deighton and

Stevenson, 1837, part II, chapter one. Kilvert wrote of the walls of Gwythian Church in Cornwall: 'The material is granite with a good deal of pure felspar, of which I brought away a pretty pink piece' (5 August 1870).

48. *Principles of Geology* (1830-1833), London, Penguin Books, 1997, introduction by J. Secord, p. xxvi.

49. Two significant sources of Kilvert's knowledge of basalt should be mentioned. Firstly, the museum of the BLSI contained over 70 specimens of basalt deposited by the mineralogist Frederick Page in 1826. Secondly, Sir Hans Sloane had basalt specimens in his museum, which Kilvert could have seen during his visit in 1851.

50. Dennis R. Dean, *Tennyson and Geology*, Lincoln, The Tennyson Society, Tennyson Research Centre, 1985, p. 19.

51. *The Great Chain of History. William Buckland and the English School of Geology*, Oxford, Clarendon Press, 1983, p. 10.

52. Dean, *op. cit.*, p. 13.

53. *Ibid.*, p. 87. Another (Gower) cave explored by Buckland was Goat's Hole, also called Paviland Cave, famous for the 'Red Lady' skeleton of the Palaeolithic period which he found there. He stayed at Lewis Dillwyn's home (21 January 1823) while he was excavating it. Dillwyn himself had investigated it in 1822, finding a large amount of teeth and bones.

54. Professor Stringer (Museum of Natural History) announced on 3 November 2011 that human beings were living in Kent's Cavern, Torquay, 44,000 years ago and were actually contemporary with the Neanderthals of Europe.

55. N. Rupke, 'Oxford's Scientific Awakening and the Role of Geology', *History of the University of Oxford*, part I, p. 552.

56. Kilvert recorded that he was told by 'young Cox' that it was discovered in 1838.

57. Michael Shortland, 'Darkness Visible: Underground Culture in the Golden Age of Geology', *History of Science*, 32, 1994, pp. 13-14.

58. *A Passage to India*, Harmondsworth, Penguin, 1981, pp. 159-161. Peter Burra referred to the novel's three sections, of which 'Caves' is one, as 'outward shapes of man's spiritual adventures' (his Introduction to the Everyman edition, reprinted as Appendix II of the Penguin edition).

59. *Alton Locke*, pp. 330-1.

60. *Ibid.*, pp. 336-339.

61. *Ibid.*, pp. 342-350.

62. G. Dawson, *Darwin, Literature and Victorian Respectability*, p. 27.

63. Of John Lubbock senior (a banker) Desmond/Moore wrote: 'he was less interested in money than in science' (*op. cit.*, p. 302).

64. Harry Thompson, in his brilliant fictional account (*This Thing of Darkness*, London, Headline Review, 2006) of the relationship between Fitzroy and Darwin, shows the former, sent by the Admiralty to chart the coast of Tierra del Fuego, as utterly overwhelmed by the task of bringing its 'primordial darkness under control' (p. 92). To his Evangelical mind, the primitive nature of the place and of its inhabitants elicited feelings of superstitious terror akin

to those experienced by Kilvert and Mrs Moore in similar places.

65. That this was Kilvert's view of sin is clear from the 11 March 1875 entry which records his analysis of the misfortunes suffered by Henry Ferris.

66. Lubbock, *op. cit.*, pp. 479-490. Darwin wrote to Lubbock in June 1865 congratulating him on the last chapter of his book, which contained 'an admirable and profound discussion' (Hutchinson, *op. cit.*, vol. I, p. 148).

67. Charles Tennyson, *Alfred Tennyson*, London, Macmillan, 1959, p. 267.

68. Poem CXIX.

69. The importance to Kilvert of *In Memoriam*'s statements on the power of memories to shape identity is explored in Kilvert's *Diary and Landscape*, pp. 148-9.

70. Quoted in Charles Tennyson, *op. cit.*, p. 346. Among scientific works which Tennyson was reading in 1859 was James Hinton's *Man and his Dwelling Place* (1859). He was reading *The Origin of Species* on 19 November 1859 and was 'much interested'. The poet not only read works by Mrs Gatty, but she stayed at Farringford on 20 November 1858.

71. Tennyson recommended the *Sermons* to the Queen in a May 1863 letter to Prince Albert. Robertson's son lunched at Farringford on 28 March 1864.

72. *In Memoriam*, London, Henry King, 1875 (seventh edition).

73. *Alton Locke*, pp. 379, 377.

74. For a discussion of these, see its chapter seven.

75. Dawson (*Darwin, Literature and Victorian Respectability*, p. 65) noted that the gorilla was likened to a satyr, for example by Huxley in his *Man's Place in Nature*.

Select Bibliography

Altick, R.D. (1957), *The English Common Reader: A Social History of the Mass Reading Public 1800 – 1900,* Chicago: University of Chicago Press.

Altick, R.D. (1978), *The Shows of London,* Cambridge (Mass.): Harvard University Press.

Ballantyne, R.M., (undated) *The Gorilla Hunters,* London: Collins.

Barber, L. (1980), *The Heyday of Natural History,* London: Jonathon Cape.

Bibby, C. (1959), *T. H. Huxley, Scientist, Humanist and Educator,* London: Watts.

Brooke, S.A. (1891), *Life and Letters of Frederick W. Robertson,* two vols. London: Kegan Paul, Trench, Trübner.

Buckley, A.B. (2007), *The Fairy-Land of Science,* USA: Filiquarian Publishing LLC.

Clark, J.W. and Hughes, T. (1890), *The Life and Letters of the Reverend Adam Sedgwick,* Cambridge: Cambridge University Press.

Coleman, T. (1986), *The Railway Navvies: A History of the Men Who Made the Railways,* Harmondsworth: Penguin.

Cooter, R. (1984), *The Cultural Meaning of Popular Science: Phrenology and the Organisation of Consent in Nineteenth-Century Britain,* Cambridge: Cambridge University Press.

Darwin, C. (1871), *The Descent of Man,* London: John Murray.

Dawkins, R. (1998), *Unweaving the Rainbow: Science, Delusion and the Appetite for Wonder,* London: Penguin Press.

Dawson, G. (2007), *Darwin, Literature and Victorian Respectability,* Cambridge: Cambridge University Press.

Dean, D R. (1985), *Tennyson and Geology,* Lincoln: The Tennyson Society

Desmond, A. (1984), *Archetypes and Ancestors: Palaeontology in Victorian London 1850 – 1875,* Chicago: Chicago University Press.

Dillwyn Collection, *The Journals of Lewis Weston Dillwyn,* transcribed by Richard Morris, www.swansea.ac.uk/historical collections.

Dodds, J.W. (1953), *The Age of Paradox: A Biography of England 1841 – 1851,* London: Gollancz.

Du Chaillu, P. (1861), *Explorations and Adventures in Equatorial Africa,* London: John Murray.

Eve, A.S. and Creasey, C. H. (1945), *Life and Work of John Tyndall,* London: Macmillan.

Fyfe, A. (2004), *Science and Salvation: Evangelical Popular Science Publishing in Victorian Britain,* Chicago: University of Chicago Press.

Gosse, E. (1988), *Father and Son,* London: Penguin Books.

Henson, L. (2004), *Culture and Science in Nineteenth-Century Media,* Aldershot: Ashgate.

Heringman, N. (2004), *Romantic Rocks, Aesthetic Geology,* Ithaca: Cornell University Press.

Hilton, B. (1988), *The Age of Atonement: The Influence of Evangelicalism on Social and Economic Thought, 1795 – 1865,* Oxford: Clarendon Press.

Holmes, R. (2008), *The Age of Wonder: How the Romantic Generation Discovered the Beauty and Terror of Science,* London: Harper Press.

Howitt, M. (1889), *An Autobiography,* two vols., London: William Isbister.

Howitt, M. (1892), *The Children's Year,* London: Nelson.

Jeal, T. (1973), *Livingstone,* London: Heinemann.

Jennings, H. (1985), *Pandaemonium 1660 – 1886,* London: Andre Deutsch.

Keynes, R. (2001), *Annie's Box: Charles Darwin, his Daughter and Human Evolution,* London: Fourth Estate.

Kilvert, F. (1938-40), *Kilvert's Diary,* W. Plomer (ed.) London: Jonathan Cape.

Kilvert, F. (1989), *Kilvert's Cornish Diary,* R. Maber and A. Tregoning (eds.) Penzance: Alison Hodge.

Kingsley, C. (1901), *The Water-Babies,* London: Macmillan.

Klingender, F.D. (1972), *Art and the Industrial Revolution,* London: Paladin.

Krüse, H. (1875), *Pestalozzi: His Life, Work and Influence,* New York: Wilson and Hinkle.

Levine, G. (2008), *Darwin Loves You: Natural Selection and the Re-Enchantment of the World,* Princeton (New Jersey): Princeton University Press.

Lightman, B. (2007), *Victorian Popularisers of Science: Designing Nature for New Audiences,* Chicago: University of Chicago Press.

Lightman, B. (1997), *Victorian Science in Context,* Chicago: University of Chicago Press.

Livingstone, D. (1857), *Missionary Travels and Researches in South Africa,* London: Ward Lock.

Lucas, J.R. (1979), 'Wilberforce and Huxley: A Legendary Encounter', *Historical Journal,* 22, 2.

Mackay, C. (1877), *Forty Years' Recollections,* London: Chapman and Hall.

Mackenzie, J. (ed. 2001), *The Victorian Vision. Inventing the New Britain,* London: V and A Publications.

Marryat, F. (1970), *Masterman Ready,* London: Dent.

Marryat, F. (1956), *The Settlers in Canada,* London: Dent.

Merrill, L. (1989), *The Romance of Natural History,* Oxford: Oxford University Press.

Morrell, J. and Thackray, A. (1981), *Gentlemen of Science: Early Years of the British Association for the Advancement of Science,* Oxford: Clarendon Press.

O'Connor, R. (2007), *The Earth on Show: Fossils and the Poetics of Popular Science, 1802 – 1856,* Chicago: University of Chicago Press.

Oliphant, Mrs (1862), *The Life of Edward Irving, Minister of the National Scotch Church, illustrated by his Journals and Correspondences,* two vols., London: Hurse and Blackett.

Pettit, C. (2007), *Dr. Livingstone, I Presume? Missionaries, journalists, explorers and empire,* London: Profile.

Rudwick, M. (2008), *Worlds before Adam: The Reconstruction of Geohistory in the Age of Reform,* Chicago: University of Chicago Press.

Ruse, M. (1999), *The Darwinian Revolution: Science Red in Tooth and Claw,* Chicago: University of Chicago Press.

Schama, S. (2009), *Rough Crossings: Britain, the Slaves and the American Revolution,* London: Vintage.

Schivelbusch, W. (1986), *The Railway Journey: The Industrialisation of Time and Space in the Nineteenth Century,* Leamington Spa: Berg.

Secord, J. (2000), *Victorian Sensation: The Extraordinary Publication, Reception and Secret Authorship of the Natural History of Creation,* Chicago: University of Chicago Press.

Smiles, S. (1874), *Lives of the Engineers: The Locomotive George and Robert Stephenson,* London: John Murray.

Standage, T. (1998), *The Victorian Internet,* New York: Walker and Co.

Thompson, H. (2005), *This Thing of Darkness,* London: Headline.

Toman, J. (2001), *Kilvert: The Homeless Heart,* Almeley: Logaston Press.

Toman, J. (2009), *Kilvert's Diary and Landscape,* Cambridge: Lutterworth Press.

Toman, J. (2011), *Francis Kilvert and Charles Pritchard: Clapham Connections,* The Clapham Society Local History Series 8, www.outlines.org.uk/claphamsociety/Articles/article8.html

Toman, J. (2013), *The Lost Photograph Album: A Kilvert Family Story,* Monmouth: Kilvert Society.

Uglow, J. (2002), *The Lunar Men: The Friends Who Made the Future 1730 – 1810,* London: Faber and Faber.

Wallis, P., ed. (2008), *Innovation and Discovery. Bath and the Rise of Science,* Bath: Bath Royal Literary and Scientific Institution and the William Herschel Society.

Winter, A. (1998), *Mesmerized: Powers of Mind in Victorian Britain,* Chicago: University of Chicago Press.

Wyndowe, E. (undated), 'Rambling Recollections' in *More Chapters from the Kilvert Saga,* Leamington Spa: Kilvert Society.

Index

You may be interested in

Kilvert's Diary and Landscape

By *John Toman*, 2009

www.lutterworth.com

ISBN: 9780718830953

Now available in **paperback** from The Lutterworth Press

'Why do I keep this voluminous journal?' Francis Kilvert asked himself. 'Partly because life appears to me such a curious and wonderful thing that it almost seems a pity that even such a humble and uneventful life as mine should pass all together away without some such record as this . . .'

Kilvert's Diary was an attempt to tell the story of that life as well as to depict rural society, which Victorians were prone to idealise. Kilvert's loving portraits of landscapes and country characters were often juxtaposed with the grimmest scenes of squalor and suffering.

John Toman presents here the first thorough examination of Kilvert's writing and offers a complete revaluation of the man and his work, tracing the literary and religious influences that brought him to write in the way that he did. This study takes account of Kilvert's education at his uncle's school, his reading of travel guides, his devotion to such figures as Wordsworth, William Barnes, and the Revd. Frederick Robertson, his visits to key locations, his parochial work, the role played by Romanticism and Evangelicalism in his outlook, and the significance of walking as the driving force of his writing.

For those unfamiliar with the Diary, Kilvert's Diary and Landscape is an ideal introduction; it will also take those who already know and love Kilvert back to his diary with renewed interest and deepened insight. This new study has much to offer readers interested in cultural and landscape history, literature, religion and the Victorian period.

'It is hoped that this study of Kilvert and landscape, which may be regarded as the second part of a revaluation of the diarist that began with my *Kilvert: The Homeless Heart* (2001), contributes to our appreciation of his complexity.'
(From the Author's Introduction)